Fundamentals of Data Structures in Turbo Pascal

For the IBM PC

COMPUTER SOFTWARE ENGINEERING SERIES

Fundamentals of
Data Structures in Turbo Pascal
For the IBM PC

Ellis Horowitz

University of Southern California

Sartaj Sahni

University of Minnesota

COMPUTER SCIENCE PRESS

Library of Congress Cataloging-in-Publication Data

Horowitz, Ellis.
    Fundamentals of data structures
  in Turbo Pascal: For the IBM PC/Ellis Horowitz, Sartaj Sahni.
    p. cm.—(Computer Software engineering series, ISSN
0888-2088)
    Includes bibliographies and index.
    ISBN (invalid) 0-7167-8152-2
    1. IBM Personal Computer—Programming. 2. Data structures
(Computer science) 3. Pascal (Computer program language) 4. Turbo
Pascal (Computer program)   I. Sahni, Sartaj.   II. Title.
III. Series.
QA76.8.I2594H67 1989   88-19744
005.265—dc19   CIP

Fundamentals of Data Structures in Turbo Pascal: For the IBM PC is the result of the combined efforts of the authors. Their names have been listed in alphabetical order with no implication that one is senior and the other junior.

Fundamentals of Data Structures in Turbo Pascal: For the IBM PC is another version of *Fundamentals of Data Structures* by Horowitz and Sahni. In the earlier work, all of the algorithms are written in the SPARKS language while in this work all the algorithms are written in the Turbo Pascal language.

Fundamentals of Data Structures
Copyright © 1982 Computer Science Press, Inc.

Fundamentals of Data Structures
Copyright © 1976 Computer Science Press, Inc.

Printed in the United States of America

COMPUTER SCIENCE PRESS
1803 Research Boulevard
Rockville, MD 20850
An imprint of W. H. Freeman and Company
41 Madison Avenue, New York, NY 10010
20 Beaumont Street, Oxford OX1 2NQ, England

1 2 3 4 5 6 7 8 9 0   RRD   7 6 5 4 3 2 1 0 8 9

001.6424
H816 b

235690

CONTENTS

PREFACE

This book is a special version of our popular *Fundamentals of Data Structures*. We call it special because we have designed it for people, students and instructors, who will be using the IBM PC (or equivalent) as their computer and Turbo Pascal as their programming language. This computer has become a standard in the personal computer marketplace. Most especially in colleges and universities, the IBM PC has become the dominant computer. Educational laboratories have sprung up all over campus. This spread of the PC has caused a shift in computer science instruction from the large mainframe to the personal computer. And a welcome shift it is. In the past, students were forced to suffer the frustrations of overloaded computers, especially at the end of the semester. Now for considerably under $1,000 they may purchase their own computer. Moreover, the hands-on feature of personal computers make them ideal for instruction. The student can literally get into the computer and play around.

This book is not meant for an introductory course on programming. Rather it provides a more advanced introduction to the subjects of algorithms and data structures. Therefore it is best used either in conjunction with some introductory programming language primer or as the text for a second course on programming. The book begins with an introduction to the IBM PC family: the PC, PC-XT, PC-AT and the PS/2 series. After discussing the hardware components, a primer on DOS is given. Upon completing Chapter 1, the student will be capable of operating his/her computer and invoking various application programs. Then, in Chapter 2, Turbo Pascal is introduced with an emphasis on good programming style. We include material on Turbo Pascal versions 3 and 4. Once the basic topics have been covered, the book follows the outline of a traditional course on data structures. Topics such as arrays, lists, stacks, queues, trees, and graphs are all thoroughly covered. Emphasis is on the design of good data structures and the analysis of the resulting algorithms. Only a modest mathematical background is required.

Acknowledgements

We are grateful to IBM Corporation for permitting us to reproduce Figures 1.1, 1.2, 1.4, 1.5, 1.7, and 2.16.

Ellis Horowitz
Sartaj Sahni
July 1988

CHAPTER 1

INTRODUCTION TO THE IBM PC

1.1 GETTING TO KNOW YOUR MACHINE

1.1.1 What Computer Do You Have?

Welcome to the world of computing and computer science. In this book we are going to explore the process of programming a digital computer. This process has captured the intellectual curiosity of many of the best minds of the last few decades. This has happened for two important reasons. One reason is rather obvious, namely, that computers and the programs that run them have had a great impact upon human affairs. The second reason, a bit less obvious but none the less important, is the intellectual challenge posed by the art of programming.

One of the important features of this version of *Fundamentals of Data Structures* is its emphasis on the IBM Personal Computer family. In Figure 1.1 you see a picture of the first IBM personal computer, the IBM PC. This computer was released in 1981. That was soon followed by the PC-XT, the PC-AT and the PS/2 series. The PC-RT uses the UNIX* operating system instead of DOS. So, it will not be discussed here.

The basic components of the IBM PC include the system unit, keyboard, monitor, and floppy diskette drives.

---

*UNIX is a trademark of AT&T.

1

Figure 1.1 An IBM personal computer

System Unit

The cover of the system unit is easy to remove by taking out the screws at the back. In Figure 1.2 you see a picture of the *main board* (sometimes called the *mother board*) in the PC-XT system unit. On the main board there is the microprocessor which does the actual computing and controlling of the machine, chips containing the random access memory (or RAM), the clock generator, the speaker, a DMA controller which supports a hard disk, and extra slots for circuit boards (called *expansion slots*).

The Intel 8088 microprocessor is used in the PC and PC-XT. Next to it is a space for an Intel 8087 math coprocessor. The random access memory sits at the bottom of the card with the ROM (read only memory) immediately above it. The two white switches in the middle are used to inform the machine what memory configuration is present.

The main board for the PC-AT is similar in many respects. Its two major differences are the use of the Intel 80286 microprocessor and 8 expansion slots.

The RAM comes in units of 64KB (KB means Kilobyte or 1024 bytes so 64KB = 65,536 bytes). The Intel 8088 can address up to 1,024KB, but the space that programs are permitted to use is smaller than that because of the need to store the operating system, information about the system components, and the video screen. Figure 1.3 shows where this information is stored. Thus usable memory sizes come in 64KB chunks and are either 64, 128, 192, 256, 320, 384, 448, 512, 576, or 640KB. A *byte* is 8 bits, equivalent to one character, so a computer with 640KB of RAM can hold approximately 640,000 characters in its memory at one time.

Keyboard

The keyboard, shown in Figure 1.4, has three major sections: the typewriter area in the middle, the numeric keypad on the right, and the function keys on the left. A slightly different keyboard is used with the PC-AT and the PS/2.

The typewriter area is termed the QWERTY keyboard in deference to the top row of alphabetic keys. The function keys are labeled F1 to F10. These keys differ in purpose depending upon the software you are using. The numeric keypad is used either for entering sets of numbers or for the arrow keys. A *cursor* is a highlighted area that indicates where input will appear when entered. The arrow keys are used to move the cursor around the screen.

There are several interesting features of the IBM keyboard that you should be aware of. One is the so-called *typematic* feature. This means that when you hold a key down, it is the same as if you had continued to strike the key multiple times. This is especially helpful when you want to move a cursor around the screen, as you simply continue to hold the appropriate arrow key down until the cursor is properly positioned.

Figure 1.2 The IBM PC-XT main board

memory address

1,048,575	
	ROM including BASIC+
	BIOS Extensions
786,432	
	Display Memory
655,360	
	RAM used by programs up to 640KB
	Used by DOS
0	

Figure 1.3 Memory layout for IBM-PC

Figure 1.4 The IBM PC keyboard

Another feature is the Num Lock key. When Num Lock is on, the numeric keypad will transmit only numbers and not the arrow commands. On some keyboards you cannot tell if Num Lock is on or off, leading to confusion. However, the PC-AT keyboard has as one of its features a light that indicates if Num Lock is on.

The number of keys on a keyboard will vary. In the IBM PC keyboard of Figure 1.4 there are 82 keys, while the PC-AT keyboard I am using has 83 keys. But however many keys are present, they will be capable of producing a great many more characters than just those shown on the keyboard. This is done by combining keys, that is by using two keys together to produce a signal that represents a new character. The simplest case of this is the Shift key. When it is held down no signal is sent. But when you strike an alphabetic key at the same time, you produce the uppercase form of the letter. Similarly, those keys that show two characters, one above and one below, will produce the above character when used in conjunction with the Shift key. To produce signals that are not visible on the keyboard but are recognizable by DOS you use either the keys labeled CTRL or ALT. The totality of key combinations that are recognized by DOS is referred to as the *extended IBM PC character set*. For example, CTRL-Q and CTRL-S can be used to control the way information is scrolled on the screen. CTRL-S will cause scrolling to stop and CTRL-Q will continue it again.

In Figure 1.5 you see the IBM PC family character set. These are the *printable* characters. For each character we show its decimal number, its hexadecimal equivalent, and the corresponding character as it would appear. There are many graphic characters such as the card suits ♣, ♦, ♥, and ♠, box building characters, and the Greek letters. There are 256 characters numbered 0 to 255. Thus 8 bits are required to represent one of these characters, and a byte is composed of 8 bits.

Floppy Disk Drives

The primary medium of exchange for personal computer software has become the floppy diskette, Figure 1.6. This is a 5-1/4 inch, flexible record, coated with magnetic material, that is placed into a protective cover. The cover has an oval-shaped hole so that information can be recorded and read as the diskette revolves in the drive. In the upper right-hand side is a notch. When this notch is covered over, then the disk drive will sense the cover and refuse to write anything on the disk. The disk is *write protected*.

Information is recorded on tracks, which are concentric circles. The read/write heads are movable and go from track to track as needed. There are 40 tracks numbered 0 to 39. Each track is divided into eight sectors that are 512 bytes long. A sector's information can be transferred from computer to diskette or vice versa in a single operation.

Your computer may have one or two floppy disk drives. On the PC or PC-XT, these drives take up two full spaces in the system unit. Figure 1.1 shows the PC with two floppy disk drives. More recently, these drives have been made smaller so that two can now fit into the space originally occupied by one. They are called *half-height* drives. Figure 1.7 shows the front of the system unit of a PC-AT which contains one half-height drive.

DECIMAL VALUE →		0	16	32	48	64	80	96	112	128	144	160	176	192	208	224	240
↓	HEXA-DECIMAL VALUE	0	1	2	3	4	5	6	7	8	9	A	B	C	D	E	F
0	0	BLANK (NULL)	►	BLANK (SPACE)	0	@	P	`	p	Ç	É	á	░ ¼ Dots On	└	╨	∝	≡
1	1	☺	◄	!	1	A	Q	a	q	ü	Æ	í	▒ ½ Dots On	┴	╤	β	±
2	2	☻	↕	"	2	B	R	b	r	é	FE	ó	▓ ¾ Dots On	┬	╥	γ	≥
3	3	♥	‼	#	3	C	S	c	s	â	ô	ú	│	├	╙	π	≤
4	4	♦	¶	$	4	D	T	d	t	ä	ö	ñ	┤	─	╘	Σ	⌠
5	5	♣	§	%	5	E	U	e	u	à	ò	Ñ	╡	┼	╒	σ	⌡
6	6	♠	▬	&	6	F	V	f	v	å	û	ª	╢	╞	╓	μ	÷
7	7	•	↨	'	7	G	W	g	w	ç	ù	º	╖	╟	╫	τ	≈
8	8	◘	↑	(	8	H	X	h	x	ê	ÿ	¿	╕	╚	╪	Φ	°
9	9	○	↓	)	9	I	Y	i	y	ë	Ö	⌐	╣	╔	┘	Θ	∙
10	A	◎	→	*	:	J	Z	j	x	è	Ü	¬	║	╩	┌	Ω	·
11	B	♂	←	+	;	K	[	k	{	ï	¢	½	╗	╦	█	δ	√
12	C	♀	∟	,	<	L	\	l	|	î	£	¼	╝	╠	▄	∞	η
13	D	♪	↔	-	=	M	]	m	}	ì	¥	¡	╜	═	▌	Ø	²
14	E	♫	▲	.	>	N	^	n	~	Ä	Pts	«	╛	╬	▐	∈	■
15	F	☼	▼	/	?	O	_	o	△	Å	ƒ	»	┐	╧	▀	∩	BLANK 'FF'

Figure 1.5 IBM PC family character set

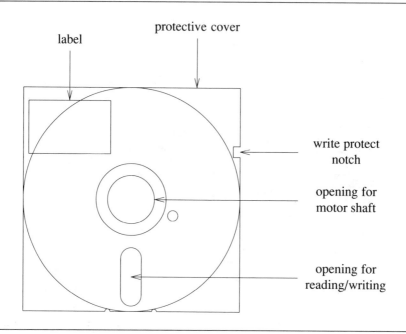

Figure 1.6 A floppy disk

A double-sided floppy disk normally holds about 320KB to 360KB of data. 320KB is about 220 pages of a book. Single-sided diskettes hold about one half of that amount or 160KB/180KB. In addition, the PC-AT may have a high capacity floppy disk drive. It stores 1200KB of data on a special 5-1/4 inch high capacity floppy diskette. A high capacity drive may be used to read a 360KB size diskette, but you should avoid using this drive to write on one as the disk may then become unusable in a conventional drive.

Hard Disk

One of the most important features of the personal computer is a hard disk. In contrast to the floppy disk, a hard disk is composed of a set of recording surfaces that are rigid, fixed in position, and revolve around a central hub. Each surface may be written upon. Read/write heads are moved over the disks. Each surface contains 306 tracks and each track has seventeen 512-byte sectors, so a disk with two records contains a total of 10,485,760 bytes. A hard disk will read/write information much faster than a floppy disk drive. Whereas a floppy disk can send 250,000 bits per second to the microprocessor, a hard disk can transfer about 5 million bits per second. In addition, it takes a floppy disk motor about 1/2 second to come up to speed, so that information can be transferred. This

Figure 1.7 Front panel of PC-AT with one half-height floppy disk

delay occurs often as the floppy drive is generally at rest. The delay for a hard disk is negligible. The IBM PC-XT introduced a hard disk to the IBM PC family. This disk is typically rated at 10 MB capacity, (MB means Megabyte or 1,048,576 bytes). On the PC-AT at least a 20MB disk is provided.

Monitor

There is a wide variety of monitors that may be attached to your PC. The first distinguishing trait is whether the monitor is monochrome or color. Color monitors are distinguished by whether they are composite video or RGB. The initials RGB stand for Red, Green, and Blue, the primary colors. Corresponding to the monitor, there is an electronic circuit that must be installed within your system unit to control the monitor. This circuit is called an Adapter Card and it fits into one of the card slots on the main board of the system unit. The IBM Monochrome monitor is controlled by the IBM Monochrome Display & Printer Adapter. The IBM Color Display is controlled by the IBM Color Graphics Monitor Adapter (referred to as the CGA). The monitor is an extremely important piece of equipment, as it is the device you stare at for so many hours. Though you may not have a monitor manufactured by IBM, we will discuss those, knowing that your monitor will likely be close.

The monochrome monitor shows text in green on a black background. Other monitors might show text in amber or white. There are two buttons on the monitor, one for controlling contrast (the top button) and the other for brightness. These should be adjusted when you first sit down at the computer. The monochrome monitor is divided into 25 lines and 80 columns. The CGA monitor can be used as a monochrome monitor showing white text on a black background. In addition to 80 column mode, it also has a 40 column mode in which text is considerably larger. This monitor also offers eight colors in two intensities.

The IBM Color monitor can be divided into lines and columns, just as the monochrome monitor. However, it can also be divided into a collection of dots, called *pixels*, short for picture elements. Each one of these pixels may take on any one of the 16 available colors. A *palette* is a combination of colors. On the CGA a palette consists of four colors. At any given time only four colors can be shown on this monitor. The CGA monitor has a resolution of 320 x 200 pixels, in the horizontal and vertical directions, respectively, for a total of 64,000 pixels. The monitor is a *bit mapped display* meaning that there is a memory in the computer that stores the image. This memory must be large enough to hold 64,000 positions and for each position to know which of the four colors it holds. Both monitors have an aspect ratio of 4:3. This is the ratio of horizontal pixel spacing to the vertical line spacing. The screen size is 13 inches along the diagonal.

The Enhanced Graphics Monitor, controlled by the enhanced graphics adapter or EGA, is designed to provide higher resolution and more colors. Just like the CGA, the EGA comes with three knobs on the front of the unit. The name plate is the only simple way to distinguish between the two monitors. The resolution is 640 x 350. Whereas the CGA monitor was capable of showing only four colors at a time, the EGA can show 16 colors.

Asynchronous Communications Adapter

This has become a standard piece of equipment with the PC-XT. This circuit board fits into one of the expansion slots found inside the system unit. Protruding out the back is an RS-232 serial port with modem controls. This board permits you to connect the PC to a modem and to communicate across the phone lines at a variety of speeds, from 300 baud to 9600 baud. Of course you still need communication software to set the speeds and coordinate the sending and receiving of information.

1.1.2 Extra Features On Your Machine

Using the Expansion Slots

Earlier we mentioned the extra expansion slots that are available on the main board of the system unit. One is taken up by your monitor adapter and another by your asynchronous communication port. The PC and PC-XT have five expansion slots and the PC-AT has eight slots. The number of open slots is important as it governs the number of extra devices that you may simultaneously attach to your PC. Examples of devices that can be added to your system by using these slots include extra printers, a modem for communication, extra memory, extra hard disk, a joystick, a digitizing tablet, plotter, etc. As there are so many extras one might like to add, but not enough space for everything, manufacturers have produced *multifunction* cards. One of the more popular ones is the AST expansion card. Included on this card are

> two serial ports
> a parallel port
> game port
> battery-pack clock/calendar
> extra memory

RAM-Disks

The maximum capacity of usable memory on the PC, PC-XT, or PC-AT is 640KB. Suppose, for example, you are creating a document in your word processor. The operating system requires around 30KB, WordStar (a popular word processor) with spelling checker and dictionary require 225KB, and your document another 50KB. That is a total of 305KB. So the question arises, can you make use of the extra 335KB of RAM? The answer is yes, namely, to treat an area of memory as if it were another hard disk attached to your system. When the operating system has to read from or write to this disk, it will take its information from RAM. The advantage of this scheme is *speed*, as all transfers are done electronically.

A software program is needed to make your RAM behave as a RAM-disk. This program divides the memory into two parts: one that holds the operating system plus the application program and a second section to emulate the drive. Instructions to the RAM-disk are trapped in the operating system and handled by the RAM-disk software. In order to determine the amount of space to allocate to your RAM-drive, you must consider the application you will use.

Math Coprocessor

If you look inside your system unit and find the Intel 8088 or 80286, next to it you may see an empty socket. This socket has been designed to take the Intel 8087 (or 80287) Math Coprocessor. This is not a general microprocessor, but a special purpose device that performs arithmetic on real numbers especially fast. Floating point arithmetic on the Intel 8088 is especially slow as the capabilities are not built-in but simulated in software. By adding this chip, you are able to write programs that work with floating point, double precision numbers up to 32 bits long. In a 32 bit double precision number, about 17 digits of accuracy are possible. This produces numbers in the range 10^{-38} to 10^{38}. If you were only using 16 bit numbers, then the smallest and largest integers you can have are -32768 to 32767. The size of floating point numbers is dependent upon the size of the exponent. The 8087 keeps 15 bits for the exponent, permitting numbers in the range 10^{-4932} to 10^{4932}. In terms of operation, the coprocessor shares both the I/O bus and the instruction stream that goes to the 8088. Thus it scans all instructions, and when it encounters one with a special code, it recognizes it as one it should execute.

Unfortunately merely adding the 8087 to your system unit will not cause your programs to run faster. These programs must have been written to make use of the coprocessor, and unfortunately most have not. For more information consult Intel's *8087 Software Support Library Reference Manual*.

Networking

A personal computer is a versatile device by itself, but if we are able to communicate with others, its usefulness multiplies greatly. We have already observed that connecting to a modem by the asynchronous communication port is one way to go beyond the boundaries of the computer. A second way is called networking. In this scheme a wire is strung from one computer to another and software and hardware are added so that files can be sent from one computer on the network to any other. Actually there are more benefits to networking than just the sending of *electronic mail*, text, or binary files. Another benefit is the ability for a group of people to share a common resource, like a laser printer or a large disk. Another is the ability to communicate over long distances by connecting the network to another network via a gateway.

The most common form of networking is based upon *Ethernet* technology. This is a packet switching access method, formally known as carrier-sense multiple access with collision detection (CSMA/CD for short). Briefly, it works this way. Firstly, every computer on the network has a unique address. When data is to be sent, it is divided into packets with each one having a copy of its destination. The sending computer first listens to the cable to see if it's busy. When it is not, the sending computer mails the packet. Each station observes that it is sent and the proper one receives it. If more than one computer sends a packet at the same time as another, then that is called a *collision*. In the Ethernet scheme, collisions are detected by the offending stations. They will then wait a random amount of time and re-send their packet. It may seem that such a scheme is doomed to failure as so much time will be wasted as computers listen and wait for a quiet cable. However, practice indicates that a cable that can transmit data at a speed of 10 million bits per second will hardly be busy, despite a high usage level, and collisions will be rare events.

In Figure 1.8 you see a picture of a typical Ethernet-PC connection. The coaxial cable is the bus along which the data is sent from one computer to another. The cable attaches to a transceiver which has a wire that goes from it to a special board in the PC. This board, an Ethernet Controller board, fits into one of the expansion slots. Note that the maximum length of the coaxial cable is limited to approximately 1500 feet, but using repeaters permits longer distances to be achieved. Similarly there is a maximum number of stations that can be handled.

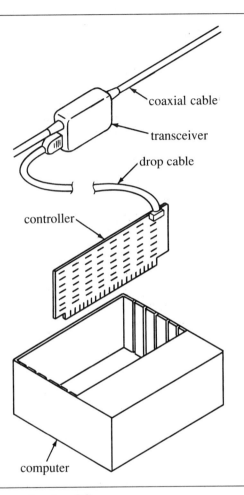

Figure 1.8 Ethernet connection to a PC

After the Ethernet hardware is installed, a software program must be used to control transmission between the logical devices of the PC and the network. The problem here is to make the operating system commands work on whatever directory one is connected to. So if you are on one computer and using another across the network, you should be able to execute all operating system commands and have them work in the same way. This transparency of operation is vital from the user's perspective.

1.1.3 Other Important Facts

The *Guide to Operations* manual contains all the installation procedures, plus a diskette called Diagnostics. When you are going to move your computer a long distance, it is CRUCIAL to run this program and execute the option:

Prepare System for Relocation

Executing this operation will cause the heads of the hard disk to be pulled back into a safe position, so if the unit is jarred, the heads will not scratch the disk.

A second word of caution has to do with saving your files. Though hard disk failures do not occur often, they need only occur once to ruin months of work. Therefore it is highly recommended that you periodically backup your important files on floppies or on some device made for backup. Recent versions of the operating system contain a BACKUP command to assist in this process.

Another interesting feature of the IBM PC family is the ability to have two monitors attached to a single system unit at the same time. One of these must be a monochrome monitor while the other may be a color monitor. Most software systems do not make use of this capability, but some do. For example, Lotus 1-2-3* will permit you to work with your spreadsheet on the monochrome monitor and show graphs on the color monitor.

1.1.4 The IBM PS/2 Family

The IBM PS/2 family of personal computers is their latest line and consists of the machines shown in Figure 1.9.

Model	Processor	Processor Speed	Bus Width	Bus	Video Board
25	8086	8 MHz	8	PC-XT	MCGA
30	8086	8 MHz	8	PC-XT	MCGA
50	80286	10 MHz	16	Micro Channel	VGA
60	80286	10 MHz	16	Micro Channel	VGA
80	80386	16/20 MHz	32	Micro Channel	VGA

Figure 1.9 Models of the new PS/2 series

---

* Lotus 1-2-3 is a trademark of Lotus Development Corp.

As you can see in Figure 1.9, this computer family is based upon the established Intel line of microprocessors, referred to as 80x86 and used in their earlier machines. One of its new contributions to hardware technology is the introduction of a new bus, called the *Micro Channel*. The bus is the hardware that connects all of the components and hence it determines the speed with which data is transferred between the various devices: cpu, memory, display, and disk. This bus is especially important for the Model 80 where the bus is different from that in the model 50 or 60 in that it offers both 16 and 32 bit slots. This means that 32-bits of addressing and 32 bits of data transmission are supported. The Model 80 is also interesting for its use of the Intel 80386 microprocessor, the most powerful in the Intel family.

Another important innovation with the PS/2 series is the abandoning of the 5 1/4 inch floppy disk in favor of the smaller 3 1/2 inch floppy disk. This follows the lead taken by others including Apple, Atari, Commodore, and Hewlett Packard.

The IBM PS/2 family introduces two new video systems, called the *video graphics array (VGA)* and the *multicolor graphics array (MCGA)*. In contrast to the PC, PC-XT and PC-AT where a separate card has to be inserted into an open slot to support the display, e.g. CGA or EGA, all the PS/2 computers come with a video subsystem already on the motherboard. Both the MCGA and the VGA can support monochrome and color displays.

The OS/2 Operating System

IBM OS/2 is the operating system for the PS/2 series. It was first shipped in December 1987. One of its most important advances is its support of multitasking, namely the ability to execute several programs simultaneously. The operating system was co-developed by IBM and Microsoft. Unfortunately this first version does not contain the windowing, graphical, interface called the *presentation manager*. This is a system that will give users popup menus, mouse support, and multiple windows in which different programs can be running.

Another important advance of OS/2 is that it is a protected-mode operating system for 80286 and 80386-based computers. There are two main modes in these microprocessors: real and protected. *Real mode* is the mode available when the power is turned on. In this mode the 80286 and 80386 processors emulate the 8086 and 8088 microprocessors. However, there are two major restrictions associated with real mode, (i) there is no memory protection, and (ii) the maximum amount of physical address space is 1 megabyte. As we shall see in the next section, PC-DOS and MS-DOS operate in real mode on the IBM PC. This operating system reduces the memory limit further, from 1Megabyte to 640K. However, in *protected mode* both of these limitations are removed, and in particular the processor checks that every memory access is legal, ensuring that one program cannot tamper with the memory of another. Additionally, in protected mode the 80286 can address 16 megabytes and the 80386 can address 4 gigabytes (1 gigabyte =

2^{30} bytes or about 1 billion bytes). All this additional hardware capability leads to enhanced functionality in the software, most noticably in OS/2 which will support multi-tasking, memory protection, and software requiring large amounts of memory.

1.2 USING DOS

1.2.1 What Version Do You Have?

DOS stands for Disk Operating System. It is the cornerstone of your PC, as it is the program that controls all of the basic functions of your computer. In particular it makes sure that your keystrokes can be read, that data can be sent to the printer, that the monitor you are using interprets the keystrokes you make, that files can be saved and read by a program, and that a program can be executed. Interestingly, DOS was not created by IBM, but by Microsoft Corporation, a company located in the state of Washington.

The first version of DOS was numbered 1.0 and appeared with the release of the PC around August 1981. Version 1.1 followed almost one year later adding among other things the ability to support double-sided diskettes. Version 2.00 in March 1983 coincided with the introduction of the PC-XT and provided support for the PC-XT's hard disk. Version 2.10 in October 1983 was followed by version 3.00 in August 1984 which supported the model PC-AT. Since then, several new versions of DOS have been released.

DOS has names for all of the devices on your PC. The monitor is called CON, short for console. A printer is called LPT or sometimes PRN. The disk drives are named using the letters A, B, C. The leftmost floppy disk drive or the topmost, if you have half-height drives, is usually configured to be the A drive. The second floppy disk drive is the B drive. The hard disk, which is located within the system unit, is the C drive. When you are in DOS you will see the name of the drive you are connected to in the left-most column of your terminal and the cursor will be just to the right, waiting for a command. For example,

A:\>

indicates that DOS is waiting for a command and the drive you are connected to is A. To change from drive A to drive C you would type C: followed by striking the Enter key. (We will usually not show striking the Enter key.)

A:\> C:

and you are connected to the C drive.

C:\>

When you turn on your computer, there is a special program that is inside of the system unit stored in ROM. This program:

- does the Power On Self Test procedure (called POST), checking components to make sure they are in working order. The time required for this can be very annoying if your computer has a full complement of RAM.

- creates the tables for processing interrupts.

- creates a list of the components currently attached and places it in low memory.

- executes a *bootstrap* program that looks for DOS.

The process followed by the bootstrap program has gotten more complicated with newer versions of DOS. It is described by the flowchart in Figure 1.10. First the A drive is examined to see if a floppy containing the file COMMAND.COM is there. If a floppy is in the drive, but it doesn't contain COMMAND.COM, an error message will appear on your screen, such as

Non-system disk or disk error
Replace the floppy and strike any key when ready

and you have to place a new floppy into the A drive and begin again. On the other hand, if there is no floppy in the A drive, then the program checks the main directory of the hard disk and the same sequence of actions will take place. Typically, the COMMAND.COM file is placed in the main directory of the hard disk and the computer is begun with no floppy diskette in either drive. The COMMAND.COM file contains the program that executes many of the DOS commands such as DIRECTORY, RENAME, ERASE, TYPE, COPY. If the command you type is not contained within COMMAND.COM, it will then search for it, a process described further on.

The bootstrap program will automatically execute a file called AUTOEXEC.BAT if it finds one on the floppy or hard disk. This file is called a *batch file* because of the suffix .BAT. It can contain a series of commands, and each of these commands will be executed in turn. For example, in Figure 1.11 you see the contents of an AUTOEXEC.BAT file.

The first two lines provide the date and time to DOS, which normally prompts for it. These two lines are not needed on a PC-AT as a clock and calendar are standard on this model and the date and time are automatically set. On the PC and PC-XT, clock and calendar cards may be added and the appropriate initializing command inserted into the AUTOEXEC.BAT file. This command would replace the DATE and TIME commands. When DOS begins, it is important to set the date and time. This is because whenever you create a file, it is stamped with the current date and time. This will be very helpful later when you try to figure out which version of a file was the latest or when a file was created. The third line makes sure that the current directory is the C drive. The last line

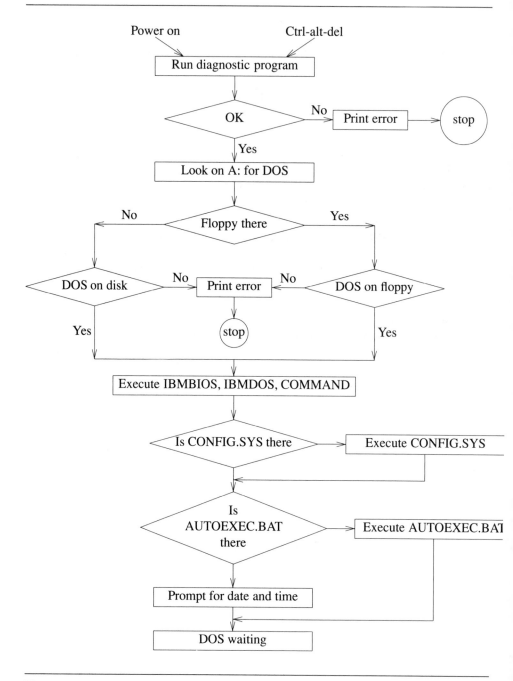

Figure 1.10 Flowchart for PC boot procedure

DATE
TIME
C:
BASICA

Figure 1.11 A sample AUTOEXEC.BAT file

actually executes a program, in this case Advanced BASIC, which is normally included with DOS.

1.2.2 Files and Naming Conventions

One of the most important features of the PC, and of computers in general, is the notion of files. A file is like a collection of papers. The papers may contain anything you wish: a list of names and addresses, a book, a program. Files can be divided into two groups. *ASCII files* are files created using the American Standard Code for Information Interchange. Basically this means that if you say TYPE and give the file name to DOS, then the contents of the file will be displayed on your monitor and it will be readable. For example, typing

A:\>TYPE AUTOEXEC.BAT

will display on your monitor the contents of the AUTOEXEC.BAT file located on the A drive just as in Figure 1.11. The alternate type of file is the *binary file*. For example, programs are binary files. If you try to type them on the screen you will generally get a funny sequence of strange looking characters. If a binary file is a program, typing its name will cause it to be executed.

There are two important issues to be concerned about when it comes to files. One is how to name a file. The other is where to store that file. Before we discuss these issues, let's review some of the basic facts about files.

A file's name is made up of two parts: its prefix and suffix. The *prefix* is one to eight characters long and may include letters of the alphabet, digits, and special characters $#@!()$-{}<>$'_`'. The *suffix* starts with a period and has one, two, or three characters. Names such as

1.X
ABC.TXT
1955.1
A$5

are all legal file names. This ability to create your own names can be a boon, but it can also be a disaster if you don't use the power wisely. A *naming convention* is a rule that one follows so that the contents of a file are more easily remembered. One common naming convention is to use the suffix to indicate what sort of file it is or where it was created. For example, a file with suffix .BAS contains a BASIC program. This is a binary file. Similarly a file with the suffix .PAS would contain a Pascal program. Data files or text files may contain a suffix that indicates how they were created. For example, a file with the suffix .WS would be a file created by the word processor called WordStar. Sometimes when you create a new version of a file, the old version will be renamed using the same prefix but substituting for the suffix the characters .BAK for backup. WordStar does this.

This seems like a good place to introduce our first DOS command. This command will list all of the files in your directory. It is invoked by typing the three letters DIR, short for DIRECTORY. Typing it either in lower or upper case is acceptable, as DOS does not distinguish between the two. If I type DIR in my current directory, I get the output of Figure 1.12.

Looking at Figure 1.12 you observe that files were created either on September 7th or September 22nd. Notice that the period separating the prefix and suffix is not shown. All of the suffixes are lined up, and unfortunately the files are not listed in alphabetical order. The file FDSPC.TEX has a size of 566 bytes and was created on Sept. 22, 1986, at 4:59 pm. As you scan the files in this directory notice the suffixes. There are many that end in .TEX. These are all files that have been written by me with the intent to use them with the TEX formatting system. When they are processed by the TEX program, a file with suffix .DVI is produced with the same prefix. Notice that at the bottom of this list is the number of files in the directory followed by a number and the phrase bytes free.'' This is a reference to the amount of space still available for use on the connected device. In this case I am connected to my hard disk and over 2 million bytes of free space remain.

Volume in drive C is ELLIS
Directory of C:\FDS

FDSPC	TEX	566	9-22-86	4:59p
TURBOP		<DIR>	9-07-86	11:10a
FDSPC	PS	37941	9-22-86	5:00p
FDSPREF	TEX	1311	9-22-86	2:38p
FDS1	TEX	18617	9-22-86	5:27p
FDS2	TEX	8473	9-22-86	4:58p
FDSPC	LOG	2250	9-22-86	4:59p
FDSPC	AUX	10	9-22-86	4:59p
FDSPC	DVI	5120	9-22-86	4:59p
FDSPREF	AUX	527	9-22-86	4:13p
FDSPC	TOC	1	9-22-86	4:59p
FDS1	AUX	2395	9-22-86	4:14p
FDS2	AUX	2353	9-22-86	4:14p

15 File(s)   2476032 bytes free

Figure 1.12 Contents of a directory

1.2.3 Files, Directories, and Subdirectories

Prior to version 2.00, DOS placed all files in the same place. A floppy diskette can hold at most around 100 different file names and has a capacity of 360K. The hard disk for the XT has a 10MB capacity. This is equivalent to 27 full floppy diskettes. If there was only one directory on the hard disk, as the number of files grew, the possibility for confusion would be enormous. Thus version 2.00 of DOS introduced the idea of *tree structured* directories. A tree structured directory refers to the fact that a directory may contain not only files, but sub-directories.

When you begin with a new computer, say one with a hard disk called C, then it has only one directory. This is called the *root* directory and it is designated as C:\. Consider Figure 1.13 which shows a possible tree structure for someone's directories. DOS has commands for creating, removing, and connecting to any directory. We will show how this structure can be created using DOS. In what follows we will always show the prompt with the complete name of the current directory. You may cause DOS to show the complete name by placing the line

PROMPT PG

in your AUTOEXEC.BAT file.

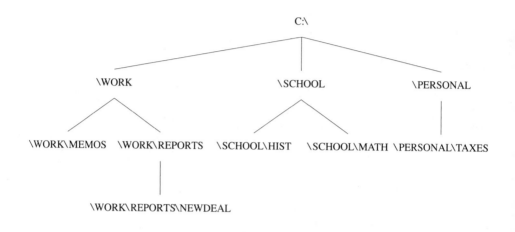

Figure 1.13 A sample tree structure

To create this hierarchy DOS offers the MAKE DIRECTORY or MKDIR command. If you are in the root directory and type

C:\> MKDIR PERSONAL

and if you do a DIR, you will see the line (with a different date and time)

PERSONAL   <DIR>   9-28-87 12:01

DOS has created a new subdirectory named PERSONAL and entered it just as it does file names, except there is no suffix, only the indicator <DIR>. To navigate through the tree of subdirectories, one uses the Change Directory command (CHDIR), abbreviated as CD. For example, if you are connected to the root directory and type

C:\> CD PERSONAL
C:\PERSONAL>

you are now in the PERSONAL directory. If you type DIR now, you will see what is shown in Figure 1.14.

Volume in drive C has no label
Directory of C:PERSONAL

```
.    <DIR>      9-28-87     12:51p
..   <DIR>      9-28-87     12:51p
```

2 File(s)   294912 bytes free

Figure 1.14 A newly created directory

The contents of a new directory is never empty but contains two files with the strange names period and double period. These files contain information about the directory structure and they are used by DOS. You may ignore them.

If you want to return to the root directory from PERSONAL, you would issue the command

C:\PERSONAL> CD \

Remember the name of the root directory is backslash. An alternate way in this case is to type

C:\PERSONAL> CD ..

as the double dots refer to the parent of the current directory, or one level higher in the tree. A subdirectory may have its own subdirectories, so referring back to the example in Figure 1.12 we could create a subdirectory of PERSONAL by saying

```
C:\> CD PERSONAL
C:\PERSONAL> MKDIR TAXES
C:\PERSONAL> CD TAXES
C:\PERSONAL\TAXES>
```

This gives us three levels of directories. If we create a file in the TAXES sub-directory, say, 1989.EST, then the full name of this file will be

C:\PERSONAL\TAXES\1989.EST

In general a file name has three components: a drive specification (C:), a path along the tree of subdirectories (\PERSONAL\TAXES), and a name (1989.EST).

All executable programs have a suffix that is either .EXE or .COM. When we execute a program we may type its full path name and prefix. It's suffix is not needed. However, typing full path names can be inconvenient and DOS offers a means by which it can locate executable programs. If no path name is given, DOS will search for the program in the current directory. If it doesn't find it, it looks at the value of a special variable, called PATH. A sample setting of the PATH variable is

PATH C:;C:\BIN;C:\EMACS;C:\LOTUS

This definition of PATH tells DOS to first examine the root directory on the C: drive, then to examine the subdirectory called \BIN, followed by the EMACS and \LOTUS subdirectories. \BIN is the name usually given to a directory that holds executable copies of various programs. EMACS is the name of an editor and \LOTUS, of course, contains the popular spreadsheet program 1-2-3.

Now let's finish creating the remaining directories from Figure 1.12. You can do this by following the sequence of commands:

```
C:\PERSONAL\TAXES> CD C:\
C:\> MKDIR WORK
C:\> CD WORK
C:\WORK> MKDIR MEMOS
C:\WORK> MKDIR REPORTS
C:\WORK> CD REPORTS
C:\WORK\REPORTS> MKDIR NEWDEAL
C:\WORK\REPORTS> CD ..
C:\WORK> CD ..
C:\> MKDIR SCHOOL
C:\> CD SCHOOL
C:\SCHOOL> MKDIR HIST
C:\SCHOOL> MKDIR MATH
C:\SCHOOL> CD \
C:\>
```

In Figure 1.15 we see an expanded view of the directory structure just defined. Each box shows the result of doing a DIR operation within the directory. For example, the root directory contains COMMAND.COM and entries for the three subdirectories: WORK, SCHOOL, and PERSONAL. The directory C:\WORK contains three files and two subdirectories.

RMDIR or RD removes a subdirectory from the specifed disk, as long as it is empty. To remove all of the files in a directory, but not any subdirectories, one may say

ERASE *.*

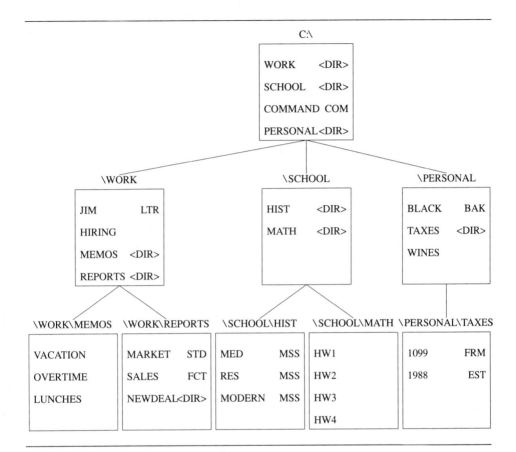

Figure 1.15 An expanded view of a directory

but this is extremely dangerous and to make sure you mean to do this, DOS will ask you

ARE YOU SURE (Y/N)?

just to give you a chance to back out. If you do this operation and then do a DIR, you should see an empty directory as shown in Figure 1.14. Now, if you go one level higher in the tree to the directory that contains the name of the directory you want to remove, you may say, for example,

C:\PERSONAL> RMDIR TAXES

and the entry for the directory and the directory itself will be gone. The use of *.* to remove all files is an example of *wild cards*. There are two wild cards in DOS, * and ?. The ? means that any character can be in that position. The * means that any character can be in that position and in the rest of the file name. A * in the suffix means that any character can be in that position and in the rest of the suffix.

1.2.4 Other Useful DOS Commands

One of the first DOS commands you will need to use is FORMAT. FORMAT marks the sectors and tracks onto a diskette. It also checks a diskette for bad spots and creates a directory that will hold information about the files that eventually will be stored on your diskette. You *must* format a diskette before storing a file on it. The DISKCOPY command automatically formats the diskette before it copies the file. If you format a diskette, *all* previous information will be lost.

CHKDSK stands for check disk. It gives you a status report on the disk and the memory. In Figure 1.16 you see the result of issuing this command on my computer.

---

volume MYDISK   Created FEB 11, 1986 12:00

21309440	bytes total disk space
40960	bytes in 4 hidden files
186368	bytes in 81 directories
17268736	bytes in 1668 user files
2664448	bytes available on disk
655360	bytes total memory
605920	bytes free

Figure 1.16 Result of CHKDSK command

Note all of the resulting information. First the time the disk was created is shown along with any name assigned. The total disk space available is approximately 21MB. There are four hidden files which include IBMBIO.COM and IBMDOS.COM. See Exercise 6 for more details. We are then given statistics about the size and number of directories and user files and the amount of free storage remaining. In this example I only have about 2.6MB left. My total memory and bytes free complete the statistics.

Of all of the DOS commands, COPY has by far the most variations. The basic idea is simple,

COPY source destination

Here are some examples. To make a second copy of MARKET.STD, connect to the directory that contains the file and type

COPY MARKET.STD MARKET.CPY

To make a copy in the C:\PERSONAL directory type

COPY MARKET.STD C:\PERSONAL\MARKET.STD

You could copy all the files in \SCHOOL\HIST to the \PERSONAL directory by saying

COPY *.MSS C:\PERSONAL

You needn't always specify the destination as DOS will assume it is the current directory. If you are attached to the A: drive, you could say

A:\> COPY C:\WORK\JIM.LST

and a copy of the file JIM.LST will be placed in the root directory on the A drive.

MODE changes the amount of information displayed on the screen. It also sets options for communication, mode switches, and modes on the color monitor. For example,

MODE MONO

will switch the active monitor to the monochrome.

MODE CO80

will switch to the color monitor in 80 character size. Similarly, MODE CO40, MODE BW40, and MODE BW80 all cause the color monitor to be active, but in different states. BW has color disabled and CO has color enabled.

RENAME lets you alter the name of a file. Its form is

RENAME source destination

For example, you could rename all the files in C:\ by typing

RENAME *.* *.TXT

1.2.5 Advanced Features: Redirection, Piping, and Filters

A program may get its input from the keyboard, or from a file, or from another program. Its output may go to the terminal or to a file. DOS lets you redirect where the input to a program is to come from and where the output may go. This process is called redirection. To do this, the characters > and < are used. For example

C:\> DIR >PRN

sends the output of DIR to the printer.

C:\> DIR >FILENAME

sends output of DIR to a file named FILENAME.

C:\> APPLICAT <INPUT.FIL

The APPLICAT program gets its input from file INPUT.FIL.

C:\> SORT <INPUT.FIL >OUTPUT.FIL

reads INPUT.FIL, sorts it, and sends it to OUTPUT.FIL.

Piping is the chaining of programs with automatic redirection of standard input and output. The names of the chained programs are separated by vertical bars. A filter is a program or command that reads data from a standard input, modifies the data, and writes the result to standard output. These topics are worth reading about but more than we can cover here.

Conclusion

This chapter has tried to give you a basic overview of DOS. If you have understood the topics discussed here, you should be able to use the application software you want and DOS will be transparent. However, if DOS proves to be a problem, you should consult your DOS Reference Manual for more details.

1.3 REFERENCES AND SELECTED READINGS

Norton, Peter, *Programmer's Guide to the IBM PC*, Microsoft Press, Bellevue, Washington, 1985.

Wolverton, Van, *Running MSDOS*, Second edition, Microsoft Press, Bellevue, Washington, 1985

IBM Technical Reference Manual, Personal Computer, IBM Corp. Boca Raton, Florida, 1984. Also for PC-XT and PC-AT.

IBM Guide to Operations, Personal Computer, IBM Corp. Boca Raton, Florida, 1982. Also for PC-XT and PC-AT.

Disk Operating System, Version 3.00, IBM Personal Computer Software, Boca Raton, Florida, May 1984. Also earlier versions including 2.00, 2.10, and 3.00.

1.4 EXERCISES

1. What computer are you using? Examine your PC and fill out the table below.

Item	Answer
Model	
Amount of RAM	
Number of floppy disk drives	
Is there a hard disk	
Hard disk capacity	
Monitor type	
Asynch port available	
Parallel port available	
Printer	
Other features	

2. Open up the system unit by removing the back screws and sliding off the front panel. For each card in an expansion slot list the function or functions it performs.

3. While your system unit is open, identify the 8259 interrupt controller, the 8237A DMA controller, the 8284A clock generator, the 8255 programmable peripheral interface, the 8253 programmable timer, the 6845 crt controller, and the PD765 diskette controller. Find an *IBM Technical Reference Manual* and determine what each of these components does.

4. Whenever one of the above devices needs the cpu, it sends a signal, called an *interrupt*. The microprocessor monitors interrupts and when it discovers one, it suspends processing to handle it. Look in the *IBM Technical Reference Manual* to find the location in low memory for each of the possible interrupts that may occur. List them.

5. A *bus* is an electronic path along which all data flows. On the Intel 8088 the data bus is only 8 bits whereas on the 80286 it is 16 bits wide. Though both microprocessors work with 16 bit numbers, the 8088 must break them into two parts whenever it moves them around. The address bus on the 8088 uses 20 bits and on the 80286 24 bits. How many addresses can the PC-AT access?

6. When the bootstrap procedure is begun, it actually looks for two hidden files before looking for COMMAND.COM. These are named IBMBIO.COM and IBMDOS.COM. The former contains additions to the I/O routines, e.g., to support new devices. The latter contains additions to DOS. Determine the full set of commands included in COMMAND.COM.

7. A quick way to create a file without using an editor is to enter the information from the terminal using the COPY command. This is done by typing

    COPY CON: A:AUTOEXEC.BAT

    Now if you type a set of commands, they will be entered into the file AUTOEXEC.BAT until you type CTRL-Z. Take the AUTOEXEC.BAT file in Figure 1.11 and create it this way.

8. Consider the contents of the directory shown in Figure 1.12. Show what would be listed by each of the following commands:

    DIR *.AUX
    DIR F?.TEX
    DIR FDS*.*

9. What is the difference between COPY and DISKCOPY?

10. Does a 5 1/4 inch floppy have a radius of 5 1/4 inches, or a diameter, or some other dimension?

11. There are times when you must look at the back of your system unit and determine what boards are present. Describe the visual characteristics of the monochrome, color graphics, and enhanced color graphics adapter cards so that they may be instantly recognized.

12. If you look at the expansion slots on the main board, you will see they are not all the same size. How many short cards does your computer have? Why were they made short?

13. The diskette that comes from IBM with DOS on it is different from Figure 1.6 in one important way. How is it different?

14. The 16 colors of the CGA are: black, blue, green, cyan, red, magenta, brown, light gray, dark gray, light blue, light green, light cyan, light red, light magenta, light yellow, and bright white. But only four colors can be shown at a single time. Determine the different colors that are included in the available palettes.

15. Determine the total number of signals that the keyboard can send to DOS.

16. As mentioned in the text, the PC-AT keyboard has one more key than the PC-XT keyboard. Which key is it, and what does it do?

17. What will happen when one tries to execute this version of the COPY command,

    COPY MYFILE.MSS

    where the destination is not explicitly provided?

18. The term *baud* is a mnemonic which refers to the number of bits that can be transferred across a line during a fixed time period. What terms does baud actually abbreviate?

19. The text mentions 4 gigabytes as the maximum memory that can be addressed in protected mode on an Intel 80386. How many bytes does it take to represent an address in a memory of this size?

20. The full IBM family of machines includes: PC, PC-XT, PCjr, PC-AT, PC-AT 3x9, XT/2, XT/286, PC-CVT, PS/2-30, PS/2-50, PS/2-60, and PS/2-80. Determine the microprocessor used in each machine, the bus, bus width, and the number of open slots.

21. TSR stands for *terminate-and-stay-resident*. This refers to a class of programs that get loaded into memory and then remain in the background until invoked by some special circumstance, such as a keystroke. They then grab the screen and keyboard, display a popup window, and await instructions. Make a list of the applications you can find that fall into this category.

CHAPTER 2

PROGRAM DEVELOPMENT

2.1 USING TURBO PASCAL

2.1.1 Getting Started With Version 3

Welcome to the world of Pascal on your IBM PC. This section will focus on version 3.0 or earlier of Turbo Pascal from Borland International. If you do not have Borland's Pascal system, but are using another Pascal compiler (such as Microsoft Pascal or UCSD Pascal), you may skip this section and go directly to Section 2.2. If you are using version 4.0 of Turbo Pascal, then you should go directly to Section 2.1.2.

First you must install the files on your diskettes. The manual has instructions and we won't bother to repeat them here. We do suggest that you create a new directory to hold these files. We assume they are placed on the hard disk labeled C: in the directory C:\TURBOP.

In Figure 2.1 you see the contents of our directory containing the Turbo Pascal system. These are the files that came with version 3.01.

Let's examine these files in groups. To begin there are the .COM files,

TURBO.COM
TURBO-87.COM
TURBOBCD.COM
TINST.COM

These are the executable programs. TURBO.COM, TURBO-87.COM, and

32

Volume in drive C is ELLIS
Directory of C:\TURBOP

.		<DIR>	9-07-86	11:10a
..		<DIR>	9-07-86	11:10a
READ	ME	9622	4-17-85	8:11p
TURBO	COM	39671	10-09-86	9:25p
TURBO	MSG	1536	3-01-85	3:33a
TURBO-87	COM	38345	4-18-85	8:24a
TURBOBCD	COM	39481	4-18-85	8:24a
GRAPH	P	3328	3-01-85	3:38a
GRAPH	BIN	5134	3-01-85	3:33a
TINST	COM	29954	3-01-85	3:38a
TINST	MSG	4224	3-05-85	2:27a
HILB	PAS	6124	3-18-85	3:28p
TEST	PAS	1447	3-18-85	3:27p
BCD	PAS	1110	3-18-85	3:26p
LISTER	PAS	5444	3-18-85	3:56p
TURTLE	PAS	7326	3-18-85	2:33p
CMDLIN	PAS	636	3-18-85	7:05p
DIRECT	PAS	2468	3-18-85	7:12p
ART	PAS	3590	3-18-85	5:15p
COLOR	PAS	4152	3-18-85	3:26p
WINDOW	PAS	3084	3-18-85	5:21p
SOUND	PAS	2451	3-18-85	5:27p
EXTERNAL	DOC	1758	1-01-80	8:14a
DOSFCALL	DOC	1309	1-01-80	7:28a
INTRPTCL	DOC	1303	1-01-80	7:33a
CALC	PAS	34469	3-18-85	3:18p
CALCDEMO	MCS	11760	3-01-85	3:35a
CALCMAIN	PAS	780	3-01-85	3:36a
CALC	HLP	4803	3-01-85	3:35a
ACCESS3	BOX	10747	3-18-85	3:34p

30 File(s)   2129920 bytes free

Figure 2.1 Turbo Pascal directory

TURBOBCD.COM are slightly different versions of the Pascal compiler, a program that translates a Pascal program into a form that can be executed by the computer's Intel microprocessor. We will be using TURBO.COM throughout. TINST.COM is a program you should have already executed, as it is the installation procedure.

The .PAS files are Pascal *source programs*, or programs written in the Pascal programming language. They can be used as input to the Pascal compiler. ART.PAS and COLOR.PAS both require a color monitor, so you won't be able to execute them unless you have one. The others can be run either on a monochrome or color monitor.

The .MSG files contain the error and help messages that appear when you run the corresponding program. There are several .DOC files and a READ.ME file. These are ASCII files containing documentation that expands on the information in the Reference Manual. All these files can be ignored for now as they describe more advanced and esoteric features of the system.

Let's run our first program. Connect to the TURBOP directory and invoke the system by typing

```
C:\> CD TURBOP
C:\TURBOP> TURBO
```

and you get Figure 2.2.

TURBO Pascal system   Version 3.01A
PC-DOS

Copyright (C) 1983,84,85   Borland Inc.

Monochrome display

Include error messages (Y/N)?

Figure 2.2 Opening screen for Turbo Pascal

This screen gives the name of the program and the version you are working with. The selected display mode is shown, in this case monochrome. There is a question being asked, namely, if you want error messages to be displayed on your screen. For the moment this is a useful option so you should type

```
Y
```

selecting error messages. Note how hitting the Enter key after Y is not necessary. The resulting screen is shown in Figure 2.3.

Logged drive: C
Active directory: \TURBO

Work file:
Main file:

Edit   Compile   Run   Save

Dir   Quit   compiler   Options

Text: 0   bytes
Free: 62024   bytes

Figure 2.3 Main menu for Turbo Pascal

This is the main command window. There are a set of 11 command names: Logged drive, Active directory, Work file, Main file, Edit, Compile, Run, Save, Dir, Quit, and compiler Options, each of which can be selected by typing the underlined letter. Either upper or lower case will work. If we type

r

for Run, we are prompted with

WORKING FILE NAME:

TURBO is expecting a Pascal source program to run. We reply SOUND followed by Enter. Note that if we do not give the entire file name, Turbo will assume a suffix of .PAS. If you have done all these steps, the speaker on your system should be playing a tune. Hit a key and a new tune is played, and hit a key again and the program terminates and you are back to the main menu. However, you may not see the main menu's command names, just the prompt

>

This indicates that the program is expecting a response. Hit Enter and the main menu will reappear.

Let's try some of the other commands on the main menu. For example, type

d

for Directory and hit the Enter key twice, and you will get a listing of all of the files in the current directory. If you forget the name of a Pascal source file, you can look for it without exiting the Turbo system. Logged drive and Active directory let you connect to other devices and other directories than the one you started at. Working file permits you to read another Pascal source program into the buffer, or work area. If you Quit, Turbo Pascal will ask if you first want to Save your work file.

2.1.2 Getting Started With Version 4.0

In this section we discuss getting started with Turbo Pascal version 4.0. This version is a major upgrade over the earlier versions. This means that getting started is more complicated, but once you master the system, you will be rewarded with ease in developing serious Pascal software. In Figure 2.4 you see the contents of our directory containing the Turbo Pascal version 4.0 system.

Let's examine these files in groups. To begin there are the *.EXE files. These are shown in Figure 2.5. Several of the executable files are used rarely, so we will only describe those used most often.

With version 4.0, you actually get *two* different Pascal compilers. One is contained in file TURBO.EXE, which includes a complete Turbo Pascal development environment. This means an *editor* with which you can create and modify your programs, a *compiler* that will check the syntax of your program and compile it if no errors are detected, and *utilities* that assist you in maintaining a large set of Pascal programs. There are other commands that are available in this environment including various DOS commands for viewing the files in your directory or changing directories. This is the program you will normally use when creating your Pascal programs.

A second executable file is TPC.EXE and this stands for Turbo Pascal Compiler. This program assumes that your source program is already created, possibly using some favorite editor, and you merely want to compile it. It lets you avoid entering the environment provided by TURBO.EXE. For example, to compile a program you would say:

C:\TURBOP> TPC MYPROG

and MYPROG.PAS will be compiled, linked possibly with other library routines, and a resulting file MYPROG.EXE is produced.

Volume in drive C is ELLIS
Directory of C:TURBO4

.		<DIR>	1-17-88	3:42a	CRT	DOC	2565	11-17-87	4:00a
..		<DIR>	1-17-88	3:42a	PRINTER	DOC	557	11-17-87	4:00a
README	COM	4066	11-17-87	4:00a	GRAPH3	DOC	2061	11-17-87	4:00a
TURBO	EXE	115272	11-17-87	4:00a	TURBO3	DOC	969	11-17-87	4:00a
TURBO	TPL	36816	11-17-87	4:00a	Q&A		20535	11-17-87	4:00a
TURBO	HLP	85344	11-17-87	4:00a	GRAPH	DOC	50323	11-17-87	4:00a
TPC	EXE	41790	11-17-87	4:00a	GRAPH	TPU	27184	11-17-87	4:00a
README		35048	11-17-87	4:00a	ATT	BGI	6029	11-17-87	4:00a
TINST	EXE	63456	11-17-87	4:00a	CGA	BGI	6029	11-17-87	4:00a
UPGRADE	EXE	42416	11-17-87	4:00a	EGAVGA	BGI	5139	11-17-87	4:00a
UPGRADE	DTA	24408	11-17-87	4:00a	HERC	BGI	5933	11-17-87	4:00a
TPMAP	EXE	10688	11-17-87	4:00a	PC3270	BGI	5837	11-17-87	4:00a
TPUMOVER	EXE	47232	11-17-87	4:00a	GOTH	CHR	8489	11-17-87	4:00a
TPCONFIG	EXE	13670	11-17-87	4:00a	LITT	CHR	2126	11-17-87	4:00a
BINOBJ	EXE	10578	11-17-87	4:00a	SANS	CHR	5452	11-17-87	4:00a
BINOBJ	DOC	4855	11-17-87	4:00a	TRIP	CHR	7213	11-17-87	4:00a
MAKE	EXE	18982	11-17-87	4:00a	GRDEMO	PAS	36317	11-17-87	4:00a
GREP	COM	5930	11-17-87	4:00a	ARTY4	PAS	9353	11-17-87	4:00a
TOUCH	COM	3992	11-17-87	4:00a	GRLINK	PAS	4491	11-17-87	4:00a
CRTDEMO	PAS	4294	11-17-87	4:00a	DRIVERS	PAS	781	11-17-87	4:00a
GR3DEMO	PAS	6771	11-17-87	4:00a	FONTS	PAS	701	11-17-87	4:00a
QSORT	PAS	1743	11-17-87	4:00a	GRLINK	MAK	902	11-17-87	4:00a
LISTER	PAS	5735	11-17-87	4:00a	MCALC	PAS	3655	11-17-87	4:00a
HILB	PAS	6227	11-17-87	4:00a	MCVARS	PAS	5045	11-17-87	4:00a
FIB8087	PAS	1148	11-17-87	4:00a	MCUTIL	PAS	9971	11-17-87	4:00a
PROCPTR	PAS	1319	11-17-87	4:00a	MCDISPLY	PAS	8037	11-17-87	4:00a
EMS	PAS	15687	11-17-87	4:00a	MCPARSER	PAS	13863	11-17-87	4:00a
AUXINOUT	PAS	2921	11-17-87	4:00a	MCLIB	PAS	12516	11-17-87	4:00a
BCD	PAS	4868	11-17-87	4:00a	MCINPUT	PAS	5576	11-17-87	4:00a
CPASDEMO	PAS	4434	11-17-87	4:00a	MCOMMAND	PAS	21352	11-17-87	4:00a
CPASDEMO	C	1681	11-17-87	4:00a	MCMVSMEM	ASM	5042	11-17-87	4:00a
CTOPAS	TC	1711	11-17-87	4:00a	MCMVSMEM	OBJ	303	11-17-87	4:00a
TURBOC	CFG	76	11-17-87	4:00a	UNPACK	COM	14710	11-17-87	4:00a
SYSTEM	DOC	1550	11-17-87	4:00a	GREXAMPL	ARC	17916	11-17-87	4:00a
DOS	DOC	3577	11-17-87	4:00a					

70 File(s) 12881920 bytes free

Figure 2.4 Turbo Pascal version 4.0 directory

TURBO.EXE	TPUMOVER.EXE	GREP.COM
TPC.EXE	TPCONFIG.EXE	TOUCH.COM
TINST.EXE	MAKE.EXE	UNPACK.COM
UPGRADE.EXE		

Figure 2.5 The executable files

TINST.EXE is the installation program. You should run this program immediately after copying the Turbo Pascal files to your hard disk. MAKE.EXE is a program that assists you in managing a large collection of programs, particularly ones that are related hierarchically. The *.PAS files contain sample Turbo Pascal source programs. The *.DOC files include documentation that is not present in the manual. For example the file GRAPH.DOC contains descriptions of the graphics routines that were available with earlier versions of Turbo Pascal, and are still supported in this version. The *.CFG files are files that contain configuration information. The file TURBO.TPL contains a library of programs that are available for you to use. TPL files, called *units* in Turbo Pascal, are binary files that can be combined with your own program.

Originally Turbo Pascal was a load-and-go system. This means that the compiler translates the source program into machine language and if there are no errors, the program is executed immediately. This feature is retained in version 4.0, but now a new possibility exists, namely to create an executable unit for later use. Units are stored in .TPU files. A compilation might start by including several .PAS files and producing a .TPU file. This file might now be combined with other .TPU files and object files, .OBJ. The latter could be assembly language routines that were transformed into object files by the assembler. These are all linked together to form an executable file, .EXE.

In Figure 2.6, you see the screen that appears when TURBO.EXE is executed. At the top there are 5 commands: **File**, **Edit**, **Run**, Compile, and **O**ptions. To invoke any of these commands either type the first letter or move the highlight via the arrow keys and then hit the Enter key. This will either invoke the command, like **R** for Run, or it will cause a menu to appear. Then you can move the highlight into the menu and select the option you wish. The File menu, in Figure 2.7, contains commands for viewing, loading, and writing files. The Edit option, in Figure 2.6, places the cursor into the main part of the window and places you in edit mode. This means you may begin to write your program, or modify an existing program. The Run command actually executes the program that is designated as your working file. The Compile command will bring up a menu (Figure 2.8), and selecting the compile option causes the compiler to start up. If an error occurs during compilation, then Turbo Pascal will stop and position the cursor at the offending place in the program. Finally, the Options menu, in Figure 2.9, allows you to define special environments and directories offered by the system.

File   Edit   **Run**   Compile   **O**ptions

LINE 1   COL 1   Insert   Indent   C:VSCALC.PAS

---Output---

F1-Help F2-Save F3-Load F5-Zoom F6-Edit F9-Make F10-Main Menu

Figure 2.6 Main screen for TURBO.EXE

File Menu	
Load	Loads a file into the editor. Masks are permitted.
Pick	Pick a file to load from the last 8 files that were used.
New	Start a new file
Save	Saves the file in the editor to the disk
Write to	Writes the file to disk using a new name
Directory	Displays the contents of a directory. Masks are permitted.
Change dir	Permits changing the current directory.
OS Shell	Exit from Turbo Pascal to DOS. To return type EXIT.
Quit	Exit from Turbo Pascal.

Figure 2.7 The file menu

The ESC key will permit you to leave a menu or go to the previous window. In Figure 2.6, you see a line marked output which about divides the screen into two windows. The top region is called the *edit window* while the bottom region is the *output window*. When a window is active, it is shown with double lines surrounding it. The

Compile Menu	
Compile	Compiles the file in the editor.
Make	Starts up MAKE.EXE which checks file for recompilation.
Build	Compiles all files described in the MAKEFILE.
Destination	Places executable code either in memory or in .EXE file.
Find error	Gives the location in memory of a runtime error.
Primary file	Tells commands MAKE or BUILD the file to compile.
Get Info	Displays data about the current file.

Figure 2.8 The compile menu

Options Menu	
Compiler	Set options for the compiler-the same as directives
Environment	Set file backup to automatic file save, save last screen, etc.
Directories	Tells Turbo what directories to examine for files.
Parameters	Supplies arguments to a program to be executed.
Load options	Loads a configuration file specifying options.
Save options	Save a configuration file specifying options.

Figure 2.9 The options menu

edit window is the region where you edit your program. The output window expands to fill the entire screen when execution takes place.

2.1.3 Mastering The Turbo Editor

In this section we will write our first Pascal program and at the same time attempt to master the Turbo Pascal editor. Our task is to create a program that will act as a very simple calculator, namely it waits for two numbers to be input and then prints their sum.

We begin by selecting the E option for Edit. When we are prompted for a work file we provide the name

VSCALC

followed by Enter. Since we have not created this file before, a blank screen appears, except for the top line which looks like

LINE	1	COL	1	Insert	Indent	C:VSCALC.PAS

This line contains status information. LINE and COL refer to the position of the cursor, which you see blinking in the upper left-hand corner. There are 24 lines, each with 80 columns. We are automatically placed in insert mode. This means whatever we type will be placed in the file. Indent means that when you hit the Enter key, the cursor will be placed at the same column that the previous line starts on. This makes it easy to produce indented programs. Though indenting styles vary (see the exercises) consistent use of a reasonable policy will enhance the readability of your program.

Try typing the line

program vscalc;

Notice how the cursor follows along as you type. Input is always placed at the cursor and the cursor moves one position to the right. The simplest way to erase is using the backspace key, shown with a left arrow on your keyboard above the Enter key. This deletes the character immediately to the left of the cursor. The key marked Del on the numeric keypad will delete the character immediately above the cursor. The cursor may be moved independently using the arrow keys on the numeric keypad. But there is an alternate method using the key marked *ctrl* and the six adjacent keys:

$$E$$
$$A \qquad S \qquad D \qquad F$$
$$X$$

The *ctrl* key by itself does not constitute a keystroke. But when it is combined with any key, it can be sensed by the Turbo Pascal editor. The cursor movement keys work in pairs. *Ctrl-d* moves the cursor one position to the right, *ctrl-s* one position to the left. *Ctrl-e* moves the cursor one line up, *ctrl-x* one line down. *Ctrl-f* moves the cursor one word forward, *ctrl-a* moves it one word back. These commands are used in the popular DOS word processing program called WordStar and hence many people already feel comfortable using them. However, if there is another set of commands that you prefer, you may substitute them when you run the installation program TINST.COM. Experiment with insertion, deletion, and moving the cursor while you type in the rest of the program shown in Program 2.1.

The general form of a Pascal program is shown in Program 2.2. Let's compare that form with program *vscalc*. There are four reserved words, printed in boldface: **program, var, begin, end**. In Program 2.2 there is no definition part, but there is a declaration part and statement part. The keyword **var** associates identifier names with types. These variables may change in value during the computation. **begin - end** enclose the

---

```
program vscalc ;
{this program takes pairs of numbers and adds them }
var i, j : real;
begin
    writeln('Welcome to the Very Simple Calculator');
    writeln('Please input 2 numbers to get their sum');
    readln(i); readln(j);
    writeln('Sum =', i + j);
end.
```

Program 2.1 Very simple calculator program

statement part which consists of two write statements, two read statements, and a final write statement. Note the two arguments of the last **writeln** statement. One is a character string and the other an expression.

```
program heading
    definition part
label
const
type
    declaration part
var
procedures and/or functions
begin
    statement part
end.
```

Program 2.2 Main form of a Pascal program

The Turbo Pascal editor contains 45 different commands. They are summarized in Figures 2.10 and 2.11. Let's try two features that are quite useful, namely, moving a block of text and searching for a string. To move a block of text, you must first mark its beginning by placing the cursor at the start and executing the command *ctrl-k ctrl-b*. Next you would move the cursor to the end of the block, using the conventional cursor movement commands, and then execute *ctrl-k ctrl-k*. To move the block you first position the cursor at the point you want to place it, and then execute *ctrl-k ctrl-v*. Similarly, to make copies of this block, execute *ctrl-k ctrl-c*. It may seem difficult to memorize these commands, but experience shows that it will not take long, and in the meantime a quick reference guide may be good to have around.

CURSOR

Character left	Ctrl-S
Alternative	Ctrl-H
Character right	Ctrl-D
Word left	Ctrl-A
Word right	Ctrl-F
Line up	Ctrl-E
Line down	Ctrl-X
Scroll up	Ctrl-W
Scroll down	Ctrl-Z
Page up	Ctrl-R
Page down	Ctrl-C
To left on line	Ctrl-Q Ctrl-S
To right on line	Ctrl-Q Ctrl-D
To top of page	Ctrl-Q Ctrl-E
To bottom of page	Ctrl-Q Ctrl-X
To top of file	Ctrl-Q Ctrl-R
To end of file	Ctrl-Q Ctrl-C
To beginning of block	Ctrl-Q Ctrl-B
To end of block	Ctrl-Q Ctrl-B
To last cursor position	Ctrl-Q Ctrl-P

INSERT and DELETE

Insert mode on/off	Ctrl-V
Insert line	Ctrl-N
Delete line	Ctrl-Y
Delete to end of line	Ctrl-Ctrl-Y
Delete right word	Ctrl-T
Delete character under cursor	Ctrl-G
Delete left character	<Del>
Alternative	Nothing

Figure 2.10 Turbo Pascal editing commands, Part I

The Find command is invoked by *ctrl-q ctrl-f*. You are prompted for a string which you terminate by hitting the Enter key. There are then several options you may specify including searching forward or backward in the file.

We are now ready to run our first program. To quit the editor, type

ctrl-k ctrl-d

BLOCK COMMAND
Mark block begin	Ctrl-K Ctrl-B
Mark block end	Ctrl-K Ctrl-K
Mark single word	Ctrl-K Ctrl-T
Hide/Display block	Ctrl-K Ctrl-W
Copy block	Ctrl-K Ctrl-C
Move block	Ctrl-K Ctrl-V
Delete block	Ctrl-K Ctrl-Y
Read block from disk	Ctrl-K Ctrl-R
Write block to disk	Ctrl-K Ctrl-W

MISCELLANEOUS
End edit	Ctrl-K Ctrl-D
Tab	Ctrl-I
Auto tab on/off	Ctrl-Q Ctrl-I
Restore line	Ctrl-Q Ctrl-L
Find	Ctrl-Q Ctrl-F
Find and replace	Ctrl-Q Ctrl-A
Repeat last find	Ctrl-L
Control character prefix	Ctrl-P

Figure 2.11 Turbo Pascal editing commands, Part II

Now to the prompt type

r

and the program should compile and go into execution showing the lines

Welcome to the Very Simple Calculator
Please input 2 numbers to get their sum

If you have made an error in the program text, a message will appear at the bottom of your screen. Hit the ESC (escape) key and you are placed in the editor with the cursor near the error. Correct the problem and run the program again. Supply a number, then hit the Enter key and follow that by a second number; their sum will be printed and the program ends. We will refine this program in the next section.

2.2 PROGRAMMING IN THE SMALL

The very simple calculator program we've built so far merely handles one addition of two real numbers. We would like to extend the simple calculator program in several important ways. First of all, there is no reason for it to end after a single operation. The program should remain active until a terminate symbol is input. We arbitrarily choose this symbol to be ^. Also, we will expand the operations to include both addition and subtraction. Moreover, we will assume that an accumulator exists which holds the current value. Thus a sample dialog between the user and program might be

```
user: 123
user: 987
user: +
Answer = 1110
user: 456
user: +
Answer = 1566
user: 896
user: −
Answer = 670
user: ^
```

The resulting program is shown in Program 2.3. Let's examine the program. There is one label declared, two variables of type *real* and one of type *char*. In Pascal, all identifiers *must* be declared before they are used. Moreover, they may only hold values of a single type throughout the execution of the program. The reserved word **begin** starts the executable portion of the program. After two write statements and one read statement, the construct **while true do** specifies an infinite loop. This is our first example of an *iteration construct*, a feature in the language that causes repeated execution of a group of statements. Observe the **case** statement testing for three possible values of *op*. This is our first example of a *selection construct*, a feature that permits different sections of code to be executed depending upon the value of an expression. The program ends when the input value for *op* is ^.

2.2.1 Good Habits Yield Good Programs

If you have had any formal training in computer programming, there are some basic rules that you most certainly have seen before. A list would include:

- *Organize your program logically.* A Pascal program is a collection of procedures and a main part. The procedures may have procedures nested within, to an arbitrary level. Therefore the problem for the programmer is not only *what* procedures to write, but *where* to place them. A procedure must be placed at a level where it is seen by the other procedures that invoke it. (More about this in the section on scope.) But it should not be placed at any outer level that is more than necessary

```
program vscalc1;
{this program takes an accumulator value, a new number,
and an operation, either + or −, and performs the operation
on these values.}
label 100;
var j, accum : real;
    op : char;
begin
  writeln('Welcome to the Very Simple Calculator');
  writeln('please enter a number');
  readln(accum);
  while true do
  begin
    writeln('please enter a number ');
    readln(j);
    writeln('please enter an operation: +, − or ^');
    readln(op);
    case op of
      '+' : accum := accum + j;
      '−' : accum := accum − j;
      '^' : goto 100;
    end;
    writeln('Answer =', accum :5:2);
  end;
  100:
end.
```

Program 2.3 Very simple calculator program, revision 1

for it to be known by its callers. As you go farther in this book, you will learn about data structures and their associated operations. A collection of procedures implementing a data structure's operations are ideally placed all at the same level. However, a routine used to help implement one or more of the data structure operations may be placed at an inner level within these operations. Above all, logically related elements should be grouped together.

- *Use meaningful names for identifiers.* There is no excuse for using $x1$, $x2$, $x3$ when *rate, time, distance* would more accurately reflect the values these identifiers hold. Choosing meaningful names for identifiers also means using names that are not too long, as on some systems only the first eight characters of an identifier are used, and besides, no one likes extra typing.

• *Document thoroughly.* Source code documentation is created by using the comment convention in Pascal. A comment may be placed anywhere a delimiter is legal. It is started by { and ended by }, though (* and *) may be used in their place. You can nest one set of comments within the other. This permits whole sections of code to be commented out, even if it already contains comments. Of course, good documentation also means avoiding trivial comments such as

$i := i + 1;$ {increase i by 1}

• *Try to make your program read from top to bottom.* One corollary of this dictum is to avoid excessive use of the *goto* statement. For example,

```
readln(month);
if month = sep then goto 100;
if month = apr then goto 100;
if month = jun then goto 100;
if month = nov then goto 100;
if month = feb then goto 200;
days := 31;
goto 300;
200: days := 28;   {ignore leap year}
goto 300;
100: days := 30;
300:
```

We don't think any of our readers would actually write a Pascal program this way. Its style is in the tradition of FORTRAN where early versions of the language provided only a stunted **IF** statement. Certainly there are clearer ways to write this program segment requiring far fewer steps.

All of the above items have one common purpose, namely, to make your programs more readable, or in effect self-documenting. Another important factor for improving program readability is the proper choice of statements. Program *vscalc1* is so straightforward that it may appear impossible to have written it in any other way. So let's look at how it might have been done, *improperly*. Consider the iteration construct. Instead of the **while** loop we might have used a **for** statement, e.g.,

```
50: for k := 1 to 1000 do
    begin
      writeln('please enter a number');
      readln(j);
      . . .
      writeln('Answer =', accum);
```

```
        end;
        goto 50;
100:
end.
```

As we don't know in advance the number of times the user is going to want to perform an operation, we choose an arbitrary, high number, like 1000, and use that as the upper limit of the **for** loop. If the **for** loop becomes exhausted, it is just started up again by the **goto** 50 statement. Why is the choice of the **for** loop improper in this program? The choice of the fixed iterate is misleading as it implies that a specific number of iterations is expected. The use of the constant 1000 only serves to confuse matters more. In Figure 2.12 you see the three main constructs for performing iterations in Pascal. The moral of this example is to *choose the iteration construct that makes the most logical sense for the problem.*

```
for vble := value1 to {or downto} value2
    do action;

while boolean value
    do action;

repeat
    action;
until boolean value;
```

Figure 2.12 Pascal iteration constructs

Let's consider another improper version of *vscalc1*. Instead of the **case** statement we might use the **if-then-else** statement. For example,

```
if op = '+' then accum := accum + j;
else if op = '−' then accum := accum − j;
            else goto 100;
writeln('Answer =', accum);
```

The **case** statement is the superior construct, as the nested **if** implies there is an order to the tests (that the test for + should precede the test for −), when actually that is arbitrary. The **case** statement accurately reflects this fact. The two forms of selection in Pascal are shown in Figure 2.13. The moral of this example is the same as for iteration: *choose the selection construct that best shows the logical intent of the computation.*

case *expression* **of**	**if** *boolean value*
value: *action*1;	**then** *action*1
value2: *action*2;	**else** *action*2; {optional}
end;	

Figure 2.13 Pascal selection constructs

Of course there are many other mistakes you can make. Textbooks often proclaim the perils of badly chosen identifier names and improper indentation. Perhaps *vscalc1* is too simple a program to point out the problem. But the point is most certainly valid, as Program 2.4 attempts to show, and we will see it more profoundly in the larger examples.

```
program vscalc2;
{this program takes an accumulator value, a new number,
and an operation, either + or −, and performs the operation
on these values.}
label 100;  var j, accum : real; op : char;
begin  writeln('Welcome to the Very Simple Calculator');
   writeln('please enter a number'); readln(accum);
   while true do begin  writeln('please enter a number ');
     readln(j); writeln('please enter an operation: +, − or ^ ');
     readln(op);
     case op of
        '+' : accum := accum + j;  '−' : accum := accum − j;
        '^' : goto 100;
     end;
     writeln('Answer =', accum);
   end;
   100:
end.
```

Program 2.4 Very simple calculator program, obfuscated

2.2.2 Antibugging

Antibugging is the process of writing programs in a way that bugs are less likely to occur. One of the tenets of this process is that you should always assume that the data is guilty until proven innocent. For example, consider program *vscalc1*. The first **readln** statement assumes a *real* and the second assumes a character, and makes no provision for faulty input. An antibugging form for this part of the program might work this way:

(1)   Read the next input as a string.

(2)   Determine if it is a number. If not, beep, ask for numeric input, and return to (1).

(3)   Read the next input as a string.

(4)   Determine if the input is either +, −, or ˆ . If not beep, ask for proper input, and return to (3).

Translating these steps into Pascal code is not too difficult. Assume functions

inputnum(**var** *arg1*: **real**): **boolean**

which returns **false** if input is not a number and **true** otherwise with the number stored in *arg1*, and

inputop(**var** *arg1*: **char**): **boolean**

which returns **false** if the input is neither +, −, or ˆ and **true** otherwise with the input assigned to *arg1*. The procedure *beep* sounds the speaker.

Then an antibugging form for *vscalc1* is given in Program 2.5.

2.2.3 Pascal Basics Reviewed

In this section we will review some of the fundamental facts about Pascal. Our review will be swift, as we assume that you either have learned Pascal before or you are using some Pascal primer along with this text. In this section you can test yourself to see how much is familiar and how much is new to you.

Types

Pascal is a *strongly typed* language. That means that the type of every identifier can be determined at compile time. This implies that the compiler can check every statement, making sure that only proper (i.e., type consistent) values are assigned to variables. However, there are some exceptions. For example, an integer may be assigned to a variable of type **real**. When this occurs, a representation conversion takes place, implying if you print the number it will be shown as a real value. One of Pascal's important contributions to programming languages was its definition of types. In Figure 2.14 we see a

---

```
var goodvalue: boolean;
  . . .
while true do
begin
    while inputnum (j) do
    begin
        beep;
        writeln('Please type a number');
    end;
    {j assigned a value}
    while inputop (op) do
    begin
        beep;
        writeln('Please type an operation: +, −, ^');
    end;
    {op assigned a value}
    case op of
        '+' : accum := accum + j;
        '−' : accum := accum − j;
        '^' : goto 100;
    end;
    writeln('Answer =', accum);
end;
100:
  . . .
```

Program 2.5 Antibugging form for very simple calculator input

hierarchy of the type system in Pascal.

One may consider these types divided into two basic categories: scalar and structured. Scalar values have in common the fact that at all times they represent a single value. This is in contrast to structured types where a value may include many scalar values. Within scalar types we distinguish between ordinal, real, and pointer types. The ordinal types: *enumeration*, **char**, **integer**, and **boolean** may be written down and listed in order, e.g., {sun, mon, tue, wed, thu, fri, sat}, {a, b, c, ..., z, A, B, C, ..., Z}, {..., −3, −2, −1, 0, 1, 2, 3, ...}, {**true, false**}. Reals are either written with decimal points {0.0, −23.4, 100.} or using scientific notation {.31415E+1, .1E−1}. Pointer values are machine addresses in RAM. They are used to point to dynamically allocated storage. Pointer values may not be printed, but one can assign them to pointer variables and compare them with other pointer variables. The structured types are essentially collections of scalar values. An array is a homogeneous collection, whereas a record is a

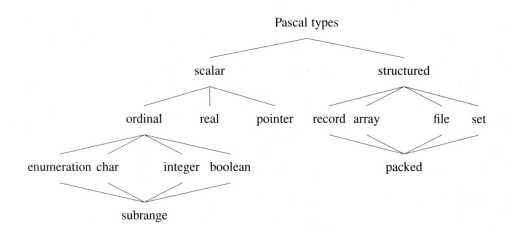

Figure 2.14 Tree of Pascal type structure

heterogeneous collection. A file is a type whose elements must be accessed in linear order. A set is a collection of like elements from a base type. In Figure 2.15 you see examples of each of the different types.

Character Set

The American Standard Code for Information Interchange has established the ASCII character set. This is a 7 bit code permitting 128 characters of which 95 are printable
!"#$%&'()*+-,./0123456789:;<=>?@A..Z[ ]^_'a..z{|}~

The first character is 'space.' On the IBM PC, a single character is stored in an 8 bit byte. Thus IBM has added an extra 128 characters. These are shown in Figure 2.16. The complete character set was given in Figure 1.5.

Expressions

The *real* operators are +, −, *, and /. The *integer* operators are +, −, *, **div** (in place of /), and **mod**. Expressions may have integer and real values mixed together, with the result

```
type
account_types = (checking, savings, commercial, moneymarket, cd);
low_interest_accts = checking..commercial;
acct_set = set of account_types;
bank_customers = record
                    name : string[20];
                    ss_num : integer;
                    mother_maiden_name : string[20];
                    class : account_types;
                    balance : real;
                 end;
customers = array [ 1..1000 ] of bank_customers;
master_file = file of bank_customers;
new_acnt_ptr = ^new_account;
new_account = record
                    name: string [20];
                    ss_num: integer;
                    next: new_acnt_ptr;
              end;
```

Figure 2.15 Example of type definitions in Pascal

always being of type *real*. Expressions with several operators work by first evaluating those operators higher in the list in Figure 2.17. When two operators at the same level occur, then the operations are done left to right. Of course, parentheses can always be used to alter the order of evaluation.

unary operators:	+, −, not
binary operators:	*, /, div, mod, and
binary operators:	+, −, or
binary operators:	=, < >, <, <=, >, >=, in

Figure 2.17 Operator precedence for Pascal

Parentheses are usually needed when writing boolean expressions. For example, we might want to express the condition

if *sum* > 100 **or** *people* <= 10 **then** . . .

DECIMAL VALUE →	128	144	160	176	192	208	224	240
↓ HEXADECIMAL VALUE	8	9	A	B	D	C	E	F
0 / 0	Ⱡ	É	á	¼ Dots On			∝	≡
1 / 1	ü	Æ	í	½ Dots On			β	±
2 / 2	é	FE	ó	¾ Dots On			γ	≥
3 / 3	â	ô	ú				π	≤
4 / 4	ä	ö	ñ				Σ	∫
5 / 5	à	ò	Ñ				σ	
6 / 6	å	û	ª				μ	÷
7 / 7	ç	ù	º				τ	≈
8 / 8	ê	ÿ	¿				Φ	°
9 / 9	ë	Ö	⌐				Θ	•
10 / A	è	Ü	¬				Ω	·
11 / B	ï	¢	½				δ	√
12 / C	î	£	¼				∞	η
13 / D	ì	¥	¡				Ø	2
14 / E	Ä	Pts	«				∈	■
15 / F	Å	ƒ	»				∩	BLANK 'FF'

Figure 2.16 Additional 128 charcters added by IBM

Looking at Figure 2.17 we see that all of the boolean operators (**not, and, or**) have higher precedence than the relational operators (=, < >, <, etc.). This means that the above expression produces a syntax error during parsing. To correctly write this expression we must write

if (*sum* > 100) **or** (*people* <= 10) **then** . . .

Assisting in our ability to create expressions is a collection of predefined functions. Some are shown in Figure 2.18. The ordering functions work on the ASCII character set and on user defined enumeration types. For example, from Figure 2.15, *pred* (*savings*) = *checking*; *succ* (*savings*) = *commercial*; *ord*('A') = 65; *chr*(65) = 'A'. The boolean functions return **true** or **false**. The arithmetic functions compute specific values given numeric inputs. We shall see other functions later on.

Constants

We have already seen **var** declarations. There is a second kind of declaration, called **const**, e.g.,
const
pi = 3.1415;
retirement = 2009;
MyLastInitial = 'H';
BirthMonth = 'February';

An identifier declared to be a constant has the property that once its value is set, it may never be changed. This implies that the identifier name cannot appear on the left-hand side of an assignment statement. Note how the definition uses the equal sign instead of the assignment operator. Note also that the type of the identifier is inferred by its right-hand side and is not explicitly declared. The last constant is a character string. The identifier *BirthMonth* cannot be used with variables of type **char** as it is longer than one character, but it may be used in **writeln**.

Scope

The *scope* of an identifier is that section of the program within which an identifier is defined with a certain set of attributes. The *scoping unit* is the area of the program or *block* in which an item can be declared. In Pascal, subprograms are used to play the role of a block. Subprograms may be nested within each other. Within a block, or subprogram, an identifier can be defined in several ways: in a **const** declaration, in a **var** declaration, as an internal procedure or function, type definition, or label. Each definition is *local* to the subprogram in which it occurs, but it may be *inherited* by any nested subprogram, so this gives rise to a potentially complex set of scopes. Identifiers declared in the main program are called *global*. They are known to all subprograms. Knowledge of an identifier is inherited by all subprograms that are contained within the

---

PREDEFINED FUNCTIONS

ARITHMETIC FUNCTIONS

sqr	square and square root
sin	trig funcs
exp	exponential and natural log
abs	absolute value
round	rounding take real to integer
trunc	truncation take real to integer
sqrt	square root
cos	trig function
ln	natural logarithm
arctan	trig function

ORDERING FUNCTIONS

succ	next ordinal value
pred	previous ordinal value
ord	position of ordinal value
chr	char value in ordinal position

BOOLEAN FUNCTIONS

odd	integer odd?
eoln	end of input line
eof	end of input file?

Figure 2.18 Predefined functions

defining subprogram. However, identifiers are not known to any containing subprogram, or to any subprogram that is not nested within the defining subprogram, or to the main program.

In Program 2.6 you see an example of a set of nested procedures. The question we wish to investigate is, when an identifier is defined in a procedure, what blocks is it known in. In Figure 2.19 you see for each procedure a summary of the names that are defined in that procedure. For example, program *nesting* contains one boolean variable, one integer, one real constant, two procedures, and one label.

```
 1 program nesting;
 2     label 300;
 3     const  pi = 3.1415;
 4     var  knobon : boolean; count : integer;
 5     procedure sort;
 6         label 100;
 7         procedure util;
 8             label 50;
 9             begin {util}
10                 50: ...
11             end; {util}
12         begin {sort}
13             100: ...
14         end; {sort}
15     procedure doinput;
16         label 250;
17         var  count : integer;
18         procedure format;
19             label 200;
20             var count: real;
21             procedure convert;
22                 label 150;
23                 begin {convert}
24                     150: ...
25                 end; {convert}
26             begin {format }
27                 200: ...
28             end; {format}
29         begin {doinput}
30             250: ...
31         end; {doinput}
32     begin {nesting}
33             300: ...
34     end. {nesting}
```

Program 2.6 Example of scope in Pascal

nesting	sort	util
knobon, boolean count, integer pi, const sort, procedure doinput, procedure 300, label	util, proc 100, label	50, label
format	*convert*	*doinput*
convert, proc 200, label count, real	150, label	format, proc count, integer 250, label

Figure 2.19 Procedures and their local names

Now we ask the question, where are the names known. To answer this question thoroughly, we treat it in several parts. In Figure 2.20 you see three sections. The top section summarizes the scope for procedures. For example, procedure *nesting* may not be called by anyone. Procedure *sort* may be called by everyone, itself, *doinput, format, convert*, and *nesting*. The scope of the **const** and **var** declarations are shown in the middle section of Figure 2.20. Note how there are three different variables all named *count*. Finally the labels and their scope are shown. The scope of a label is the block in which it is declared. It is not possible to jump into or out of procedures or functions.

2.2.4 Stepwise Refinement

When you first are faced with a problem, there is a methodology for how to proceed. It is called *top down design* and it refers to the process of breaking up a problem into subproblems whose solution imply a solution of the whole. You begin with a *specification* of the problem, and as you create smaller and smaller subproblems, you begin to introduce the algorithms and data structures that your solution will use. A related notion is termed *stepwise refinement*. This refers to a single transition from one subproblem to another, where the refinement is assumed to be closer to machine realization. Programming using top down design and stepwise refinement is most certainly an art, and in this book we will be showing you many examples. Before we present a complete Pascal program we will show you how we derived it using these techniques.

In this section we begin with a sorting problem. Given a set of n integers, create a program that will sort them into nondecreasing order. This is the specification of the problem, and as it is precise and brief it should be easy to derive a first refinement. This

procedure	can be called by
nesting	-----
sort	sort, util, doinput, format, convert, nesting
util	util, sort
doinput	doinput, format, convert, nesting
format	format, doinput, convert
convert	convert, format
variable	**known in lines**
pi	3 - 34
knobon	4 - 34
count, (nesting)	4 - 16, 32 - 34
count, (doinput)	17 - 19, 29 - 31
count, (format)	20 - 28
labels	**known in lines**
50	9 - 11
100	12 - 14
150	23 - 25
200	26 - 28
250	29 - 31
300	32 - 34

Figure 2.20 Identifiers and their scope

is now given

```
for i := 1 to n do
begin
    examine a [i] to a [n] and suppose the smallest integer
    is at a [j]; interchange a [i] and a [j];
end;
```

This is clearly not a Pascal program, but a mixture of Pascal-like statements plus English, called *pseudo-code*. On the k'th iteration, if

$a[m] \leq a[n]$ for all m, $1 \leq m \leq k - 1$ and $a[1] \leq a[2] \leq \cdots \leq a[k-1]$

and if $a[j]$ is the smallest of $a[k]$ to $a[n]$, then it follows that

$a[1] \leq a[2] \leq \cdots \leq a[k-1] \leq a[k]$

at the end of the iteration. By induction one can see that the result is a sorted set. The complete Pascal program is shown in Program 2.7.

```
procedure sort (var a : ElementList ; n : integer);
{sort the n integers a [1..n ] into nondecreasing order}
var i, j, k, t : integer;
begin
  for i := 1 to n do
  begin
    j := i;
    {find smallest integer in a [i..n]}
    for k := i +1 to n do
      if a [k ]<a [j ] then j := k;
    {interchange}
    t := a [i ]; a [i ] := a [j ]; a [j ] := t;
  end; {of for i}
end; {of sort}
```

Program 2.7 Selection sort

Sorting and searching are two operations that often go together. Once a set is sorted, searching becomes a more efficient process using the following method:

to search for x in $a [1..n]$, first examine x and $a [mid]$ where mid is the middle index, $\lfloor (n +1)/2 \rfloor$. If $x = a [mid]$ then the search is successful and the algorithm is done. If $x<a [mid]$, then the search may continue with the elements $a [1..mid - 1]$, but if $x>a [mid]$, then the search may continue with $a [mid + 1..n]$. For an unsuccessful comparison, the size of the remaining set is about one half of the original. This process may now be continued, each time reducing the remaining elements by about one half.

This method is called *binary search*. To create a Pascal program for binary search we could use a function that compares two items and determines if one is smaller, equal to, or greater than the other. Such a function is given in Program 2.8.

Using the *compare* function we can construct a binary search program as shown in Program 2.9. Part (a) of Program 2.9 shows a refinement of the earlier specification. Part (b) contains the actual Pascal program. Notice that in the procedure heading for *BinarySearch*, we have made a a **var** parameter even though it is unchanged in the procedure. In the next chapter, we shall see that this results in a more efficient inplementation.

```
function compare (x,y: element): char;
begin
    if x>y then compare := '>'
    else if x<y then compare := '<'
    else compare := '='
end;
```

Program 2.8 Comparison function

2.2.5 Recursion

One of the powerful features of Pascal's procedures is that they may be recursive. This means that the same procedure may be called several times before any of its invocations is complete. We will see recursive procedures used many times in later chapters. In this section we present our first example, solving the problem of generating all permutations of a set. If we have the set {a,b,c}, then its permutations are

{a,b,c}, {a,c,b}, {b,a,c}, {b,c,a}, {c,a,b}, {c,b,a}

To obtain these elements, you begin by placing item one, the a, in the first position. Then follow that with all permutations of the remaining elements. Next place item two, the b, in the first position and follow that with all permutations of the remaining elements. Finally place item three, the c, in the first position and follow that with all permutations of the remaining elements. This description may be enough to convince you that for a set with n elements the number of permutations will be $n*(n-1)*(n-2)* \cdots *2*1 = n!$ as there are n choices for the first element, $n-1$ for the second, etc.

It turns out that a program to generate these subsets is most naturally cast in recursive terms. In pseduo code this process would look like:

let $perm (a,k,n)$ generate all permutations of the array $a[k..n]$.
Then $perm (a, 1,n)$ will produce the answer we are after.
Let $a[1..k-1]$ be the elements of the permutation that are fixed.
if $k=n$ **then** the answer is $a[1..n]$.
otherwise **for** each element $a[i]$, i from k to n **do**
begin
    interchange $a[k]$ and $a[i]$
    call $perm (k+1,n)$
    restore $a[k]$ and $a[i]$
end

---

procedure *BinarySearch*;
{search the sorted array $a[1..n]$ for x}
initialize *lower* and *upper*
begin
 while there are more elements and x not found **do**
 begin
  let $a[mid]$ be the middle element;
  case *compare* $(x, a[mid])$ **of**
   '$>$' : set *lower* to $mid+1$;
   '$<$' : set *upper* to $mid-1$;
   '$=$' : found x;
  end; {of **case**}
 end; {of **while**}
end; {of *BinarySearch*}

(a) Pseudo Code Refinement

procedure *BinarySearch* (**var** a : *ElementList* ; x : *element*; **var** n,j : **integer**;
                  var *found* : **boolean**);
{search the sorted array $a[1..n]$ for x}
var *lower*, *upper*, *mid* : **integer**;
begin
 lower := 1; *upper* := n; *found* := **false**; j := 0;
 while (*lower* $<=$ *upper*) **and** (**not** *found*) **do**
 begin
  mid := (*lower* + *upper*) **div** 2;
  case *compare*$(x, a[mid])$ **of**
   '$>$' : *lower* := *mid* + 1; {$x > a[mid]$}
   '$<$' : *upper* := *mid* − 1; {$x < a[mid]$}
   '$=$' : **begin** j := *mid* ; *found* := **true**; **end**;
  end; {of **case**}
 end; {of **while**}
end; {of *BinarySearch*}

(b) Pascal Program

Program 2.9 Binary search

Based upon this pseudo code, the complete Pascal program is shown in Program 2.10.

```
procedure perm (a : ElementList ; k,n : integer);
{generate all the permutations of a [k..n]}
var t : element;  {type of entries in a}
    i : integer;
begin
  if k=n then
  begin  {output permutation}
    for i:=1 to n do
    write(a [i]);
    writeln;
  end
  else begin
    {a [k..n] has more than one permutation.
    Generate these recursively.}
    for i := k to n do
    begin
      {interchange a [k] and a [i]}
      t := a [k]; a [k] := a [i]; a [i] := t ;
      perm (a, k +1,n);  {all permutations of a [k +1..n]}
      t := a [k]; a [k] := a [i]; a [i] := t ;
    end;
  end;  {of else}
end;  {of perm}
```

Program 2.10 Generating permutations recursively

Program *perm* may still not be obvious, so it will be instructive to work through an example. The main items to trace are the recursive calls and the parameter values on each call. This will show the values in array *a*, *k*, and *n*. In Figure 2.21 you see a tree containing all of the recursive calls that are made for an array of size three containing the values $a[1] :=$ 'a'; $a[2] :=$ 'b'; $a[3] :=$ 'c'. The order in which the recursive calls are made is shown within parentheses just above and to the left of *perm*.

A more efficient version of *perm* results from making *a* a **var** parameter. This is examined in the exercises. Also, an alternate version that uses strings instead of an array can be found in the exercises.

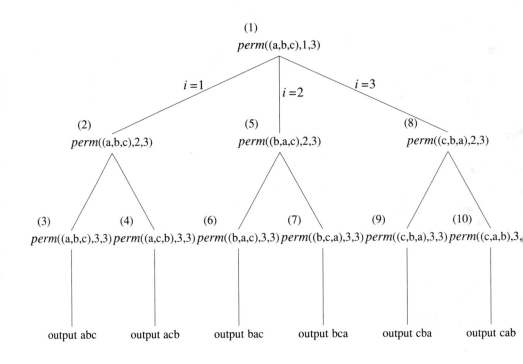

Figure 2.21 Trace of execution of PERM

2.2.6 Increasing Program Reliability

Testing is the process of detecting bugs, while *debugging* is the process of correcting bugs. According to computer scientist Edsger Dijkstra,

"Testing can show the presence of bugs but not their absence."

Since the computer is such an exacting taskmaster, the probability that a large program has one or more errors is extremely high. Thus it is important that as a professional computer scientist you take an organized approach to your own programs in terms of freeing them of bugs. The process of testing consists of four phases. In the first phase you supply only *simple inputs* to your program. This will remove all syntactic errors and possibly catch logical errors. In the second phase you would try *boundary values*. These are data values that are on the limit of acceptability. Once the program has been verified for phase one and two, you should try *invalid inputs*. This will check to see if your antibugging code was sufficient. Finally some *random inputs* would complete the circle of testing. At this point you may say that your program has been tested by yourself and appears to perform adequately. Unfortunately this is not enough. Experience shows that an independent testing organization is far superior to testing a program that you have written yourself.

We have already seen how antibugging can improve the reliability of your program. There are some other notions that have also proven useful. *Modularity* is creating subprograms whose inputs and outputs are carefully and clearly specified so that they may be easily replaced by other subprograms that purport to perform the same task. *Program verification* is that task of proving that a program is correct. *Bottom up programming* is the process of building specific modules and testing them before being sure that one can combine them into a solution for the whole.

One of the most common sources of errors is connected with the improper use of the **for** statement. For example, suppose we have two integer arrays, $a[1..n]$ and $b[1..k]$ and we wish to determine if the sequence defined by $b[]$ is also contained in $a[]$. A simple program is given in Program 2.11. Our method is the straightforward one, namely, we check the contents of $b[1..k]$ against $a[1..k]$, $a[2..k+1]$, ..., $a[n-k+1..n]$ until we find a match.

```
match := false;
for i := 1 to n−k do
begin
   for j := 1 to k do
      if b[j] <> a[i+j−1] then goto 100;
   match := true; (* a match occurred *)
   goto 200;
100: end; {of for i}
200: (* if match is false, then no match has occurred
       if match is true the string is at a[i..i+k−1] *)
```

Program 2.11 Find a matching segment of a

You may have guessed that this program has errors. Before reading on you should study the program and try to correct it.

Being *off-by-one* is a common problem with **for** loops. To see how this problem manifests itself in our example program, assume that $n = 11$ and $k = 4$. When i assumes its largest value, $i = n-k = 7$. Therefore the inner loop will compare $b[1]:a[7]$, $b[2]:a[8]$, $b[3]:a[9]$, $b[4]:a[10]$. However, $a[]$ has 11 integers and the last sequence is not tested. The proper upper limit for the outside loop is $n-k+1$. This is one example of the off-by-one error type.

Another problem with this program is that after exiting the loop, we may not know where the match was found, as i is the loop variable and the *loop variable is officially undefined upon exit*. Another problem is the *improper handling of exceptional cases*. When $k=0$ and n is positive, *match* is set to **true** as the inner loop is never entered. To correct this problem we could add a test for $k=0$ just before assigning *match* to true, but this only further complicates the inner loop and slows it down as well. Moreover, we need to also handle the exceptional case when both $n=k=0$. To handle both exceptional cases one might write

if $(k=0)$ **and** $(n<>0)$ **then** *match* := **false**
else if $(k=0)$ **and** $(n=0)$ **then** *match* := **true**
else ... place the corrected code here ...

When a Pascal program begins, *no variable has a default initial value*, but they all have some garbage value. Therefore you must be careful to assign a legitimate value to a variable before using it. The default value you should use depends upon the particular application. Pointer variables typically use the value **nil**. For integer variables the predefined constant **maxint** may be used or occasionally zero.

Another common error in Pascal programs is involved with the use of the **if** conditional statement. An example of the problem is shown here:

if $(y <> 0)$ **and** $(x/y > 1)$ **then** $z := x$
                    else $z := 0$;

Clearly we don't want to perform the second part of the boolean conditional unless we are sure that the first part is true (as we want to avoid division by zero). In some languages the order of evaluation is fixed, left to right typically, and if $y <> 0$ is false, then the rest of the conditional is aborted. This is termed *short circuit* evaluation. But in Pascal, *boolean evaluation is assumed to be complete*. Therefore we must rewrite the above as

if $(y <> 0)$ **then if** $(x/y > 1)$ **then** $z := x$
$\qquad\qquad\qquad\qquad\qquad$ **else** $z := 0$
$\qquad\quad$ **else** $z := 0$;

2.3 BUILDING A USER INTERFACE

One of the most important parts of a program is its *user interface*. This is the part of the program that is designed to communicate with the end-user of your program. With the advent of personal computers and their growing use by a population that is largely non-computer literate, the need for *user-friendly* user interfaces is more pressing than ever. In this section we will show you how to build some simple routines that use the PC monitor for communicating to the end-user and the keyboard for getting input from the end-user.

We begin with a simple program that shows you different ways that text can be displayed on the IBM PC monochrome monitor. There are four different styles, usually called modes, that control the way text is shown. The *low intensity* mode displays text using a dim style. This effect is produced using Turbo Pascal's *lowvideo* function. There is a high intensity mode, called *bright*, that is invoked using the function called *normvideo*. It is also possible to show text in *reverse video*. This is where the background is switched with the color of the text, so if normally the background is black and the characters are green, then in reversed mode the background is green and the characters are in black. Finally there is a *flashing* mode where the characters will actually turn on and off repeatedly. In Program 2.12 you see a program that exercises each of these four modes.

The *ShowText* procedure has as its inputs a monitor mode, a text string, and two integers specifying a location on the monitor. The string is displayed in the desired mode starting at the specified location. After running this program you will notice how each new line is displayed in a different mode. A mode is preserved until a new mode is established. Turbo Pascal provides functions that produce normal and bright modes directly. To get the reversed and flashing modes you must do two things: set the foreground color for characters and set the background color for the monitor. These are done by the functions *textcolor* and *textbackground*, respectively. On a monochrome monitor the numbers 0 and 7 are used to represent black and green (or white/amber), respectively. That is why 0 is a foreground parameter when *reversed* is selected and a background parameter when flashing is turned on.

Now we will construct a program that attempts to teach a viewer about the sorting algorithm described in Program 2.7. Such a program is a simple example of a *CAI* application, which is short for Computer-Assisted Instruction. The program will work in the following general way:

```
program displaymodes;
type monitormodes = (normal, bright, reversed, flashing);
     line = string[40];

procedure ShowText(i,j : integer; mode : monitormodes ; item : line );
{selects a mode for showing a line of text and displays
 it starting at position (i,j) on the monitor.}
begin
   case mode of
      normal : lowvideo;
      bright : normvideo;
      reversed : begin
                    textcolor(0);
                    textbackground (7)
                 end;
      flashing : begin
                    textcolor (−1);
                    textbackground (0)
                 end
   end;
   gotoxy (i,j);
   writeln(item );
end; {of ShowText}

begin
   writeln( 'This is a test of the modes on the IBM-PC monitor');
   writeln;  {start on line 5}
   ShowText(1, 5, normal, 'Now you should see normal');
   ShowText(1, 6, bright, 'Now you should see bright');
   ShowText(1, 7, reversed, 'Now you should see reversed');
   ShowText(1, 8, flashing, 'Now you should see flashing');
   writeln;
end.
```

Program 2.12 Program to display text in various modes

- a screen welcomes the viewer to the program;
- a message asks if the viewer wants to see a demonstration;
- one or more screens describe the sorting algorithm;
- the data is input by the viewer;
- the sorting takes place and intermediate steps are shown;
- the program asks the viewer if he or she wants to run another example.

Since we have already created the sorting routine, in this section we will focus on the other elements of the program. These are primarily concerned with communicating with the viewer, and hence they are part of the user interface. Suppose we have a director program that is going to control all of the action on the screen. Then its script (meaning program) might look like the one in Program 2.13.

---

program *director*;
1   display welcome message
2   pause for 4 seconds, then clear the screen
3   ask if the viewer wants to continue with the program
4   pause and wait for a yes/no answer
5   if no, then halt the program
6   if yes, then continue
7   place one or more screens of explanation on the monitor
8   wait for the user to press any key to go to the next screen
9   ask the viewer if he or she wants to see an example
10   if no, end the program
11   if yes, ask the viewer to input data for an example
12   run the sorting program displaying its intermediate results
13   return to step 9 and ask the viewer for another data set
14   **end**.

Program 2.13 Outline for the director

From Program 2.13 we see that there are several procedures that would be useful. These include: (1) a routine for displaying text; (2) a routine that pauses the program; (3) a routine that gets a yes/no response; (4) a routine that displays a screen full of information; (5) a routine that waits for a key to be pressed; (6) a routine that reads an integer; (7) a routine that reads an array of values; (8) a routine that runs Program 2.7 and shows the intermediate results. Some of these capabilities are directly provided in Turbo Pascal, while others must be created. All of them are now presented in their fully executable form.

- *ShowText (i, j, mode, item)* - displays the opening message *item* in the desired *mode* starting at position *i, j*. This procedure was already defined in Program 2.12.

- *delay (n)* - which pauses the program for 0.00*n* seconds. This is included with Turbo Pascal.

- *GetYorN* - returns either the character *y* or *n* corresponding to a yes or no answer. This program is complicated by the fact that we want the program to accept both lower and upper case *y* or *n* and to reject all other characters. Moreover, we do not want the key that is pressed to be echoed on the screen. The program is shown in Program 2.14. Note the **read** statement which is directed to get the input from the keyboard, *kbd*. This has been changed in version 4.0 to a function *readkey*.

```
function GetYorN:char;
{return upper case Y or N}
var reply:char;
    done:boolean;
begin
  done := false;
  repeat
    read(kbd,reply);
    if reply in ['y', 'n', 'Y', 'N']
    then  begin GetYorN := upcase (reply); done := true end
    else  writeln('Try again');
  until done;
end; {of GetYorN}
```

Program 2.14 Program *GetYorN*

- *ShowScreen (screen, i, j)* - displays a screen full of text using the contents of array *screen*, indexed from lines *i* to *j*. This procedure is shown in Program 2.15.

```
type scrdata = array[1..10] of string[80];

procedure ShowScreen (var a : scrdata ; i,j : integer);
var k : integer;
begin
  for k := i to j do
  writeln(a [k ]);
end; {of ShowScreen}
```

Program 2.15 Procedure *ShowScreen*

- *DefineText* (*screen*) - initializes the array *screen* as in Program 2.16.

---

procedure *DefineText*(**var***a* : *scrdata*);
begin
   a [1] := 'Insertion Sort works in the following way';
   a [2] := 'It first finds the smallest element of the set';
   a [3] := 'It interchanges this element with the element in';
   a [4] := 'the first position. It now repeats the process, looking ';
   a [5] := 'for the smallest element in the remaining set. Each time ';
   a [6] := 'a new smallest element is found, it is appended to the ';
   a [7] := 'already sorted set. Note that each time the algorithm must';
   a [8] := 'search through all of the elements that remain looking for the ';
   a [9] := 'next smallest. Thus its computing time will be order of n squared';
   a [10] : = 'no matter if the data is initially ordered or not. ';
end; { of *DefineText* }

Program 2.16 Procedure *DefineText*

- *keypressed* - a means of waiting until any key is pressed. This is done by using the Turbo Pascal function named *keypressed*. This function returns *true* if a key has been pressed at the console and *false* otherwise. Thus, to wait until a key is pressed, you need only write the code:

  repeat until *keypressed*;

  which uses an empty *repeat* loop that continually tests the function *keypressed*.

- *GetInt* (*answer*) - reads a single integer value from the console and stores it in *answer*, as shown in Program 2.17. Note carefully how this routine works. Using **read** or **readln** with an integer argument might appear to be the obvious way to implement this procedure. However, this routine does not work this way. The reason is because if the user does not supply an integer, then **read/readln** will fail and the program will terminate. Such behavior by the program is unacceptable. *GetInt* reads a string into *inputs* and then attemps to convert it to an integer using the *val* procedure. If this fails, then an error message is presented to the user and he or she may try again.

- *GetData* (*a,n*) - a way to input an array *a* of *n* integers as shown in Program 2.18. The input is checked for validity. At the end all values are printed out.

- *RunInsort* - a routine that executes insertion sort, but each time the array is altered it outputs the array. We use Program 2.7 but add several output lines as shown in Program 2.19.

```
procedure GetInt (var answer : integer);
{reads an integer from the console and checks that it is
within range 1 to 10 or else it asks for another value}
var inputs:string[20];
    flag : integer;
    done : boolean;
begin
  done := false;
  repeat
    readln(inputs );
    val (inputs, answer, flag);  {convert from string to integer}
    if length (inputs) = 0
    then writeln('you only hit Enter, try again')
    else if flag = 0
        then if (answer<1) or (answer>10)
            then writeln('value out of range, try again')
            else done := true
        else writeln('illegal input, try again');
  until done;
end; {of GetInt}
```

Program 2.17 Procedure *GetInt*

Now that we have built the necessary routines, we can complete program director as shown in Program 2.20.

Program *director* follows the outline given earlier. A welcome message starts the program. After four seconds the viewer is asked if he or she wants to proceed. If so, a screen full of information is displayed. After a key is hit, the program asks if the viewer wants to see an example. If so the array size and then the array elements are input. Insertion sort is run with all array values output after each iteration. The user may perform as many of these examples as he or she wishes.

```
procedure GetData (var a : ElementList ; size : integer);
{reads size integers into the integer array a}
const limit = 10;
var newnum : string[10];
    count, flag, j : integer;
    baddata : boolean;
begin
  newnum := '';
  getdata := false;
  count := 0; flag := 0;
  writeln('Please enter ', size, ' integer data items');
  writeln('each terminated with the Enter Key');
  while count<size do
  begin
    count := count+1;
    readln(newnum);
    if length (newnum)=0 then baddata := true;
    else val (newnum, a [count ], flag);
    if (flag <> 0) or baddata then
    begin
      writeln('*** bad input, try again ***');
      count:=count-1
    end;
  end; {of while}

  writeln('Data entry Complete. The data for this example is:');
  for j := 1 to count do writeln(a [j ]:6);
  ShowText (25, 20, bright, 'PRESS ANY KEY TO CONTINUE');
  repeat until keypressed;
end; {of GetData}
```

Program 2.18 Procedure *GetData*

2.4 WORKING WITH COLOR AND GRAPHICS

There are two fundamental display modes that one must be aware of when programming the IBM PC family of monitors. These are text mode and graphics mode. When you are in text mode, the screen is broken up into a series of lines, and each line into a series of columns. On the PC there are 25 lines and either 40 or 80 columns. In text mode one may either be showing just monochrome (one color for all characters and one background color), or instead you can have multiple colors for characters. All of these situations are controlled by the function in Turbo Pascal called *textmode*. In Figure 2.22 you

---

```
procedure RunInsort (var a : ElementList ; n : integer);
var i,j,k,t,col,row : integer;
begin
  clrscr;
  {pause before starting}
  ShowText(1,1, bright,'About to start Insertion Sort');
  ShowText(25, 20, bright, 'PRESS ANY KEY TO CONTINUE');
  repeat until keypressed;
    clrscr; col := 1; row := 1;
    {write out the initial array here}
    gotoxy (col,row); row := row+1;
    for j := 1 to n do write(a [j ]:6);
    ShowText(25, 20, bright, 'PRESS ANY KEY TO CONTINUE');
    repeat until keypressed;
    for i := 1 to n do
    begin
      j := i;
      for k := j +1 to n do
        if a [k ]<a [j ] then j := k;
      t := a [i ]; a [i ] := a [j ]; a [j ] := t;
      {write out the altered array here}
      gotoxy (col,row); row := row+1;
      for j := 1 to n do write(a [j ]:6);
      ShowText(25, 20, bright, 'PRESS ANY KEY TO CONTINUE');
      repeat until keypressed;
    end;
end; {of RunInsort}
```

Program 2.19 Procedure *RunInsort* with Each Step Displayed

see a table that lists the four possible text modes and the arguments to the *textmode* function that will result in those modes being set on the monitor.

Color graphics mode depends upon the graphics monitor you are using. There are two commonly used graphics monitors and associated adapters, the Color Graphics Adapter or *CGA* and the Enhanced Color Graphics Adapter or *EGA*. These were introduced earlier in section 1.1. The CGA graphics mode has two resolutions, a medium resolution of 320×200 dots, called pixels, and a high resolution of 640×200 pixels. All addressing of these pixels starts from 0. The Turbo Pascal procedure *GraphColorMode* activates medium resolution graphics on the CGA. The procedure *HiRes* activates the high resolution graphics mode.

```
program director;
type monitormodes = (normal, bright, reversed, flashing);
     line = string[40];
     scrdata = array[1..10] of string[80];
     ElementList = array[1..10] of integer;

var screendata : scrdata;
    items : ElementList;
    n : integer;

begin
    DefineText(screendata);  {sets the text array to explanation of sorting}
    clrscr;
    ShowText(10, 10, flashing,'WELCOME TO INSERTION SORT');
    delay(5000);
    clrscr;  {clears the screen}
    ShowText(10, 10, bright,'do you want to proceed?');
    ShowText(25, 20, bright, 'press y or n');
    if GetYorN = 'Y' then
    begin
      clrscr;
      ShowScreen (screendata, 1,10);
      ShowText(25, 20, bright, 'PRESS ANY KEY TO CONTINUE');
      repeat until keypressed;
      clrscr;
      ShowText(10, 10, bright, 'Do you want to see an example? y or n');
      while GetYorN <> 'N' do
      begin
        clrscr;
        ShowText(1, 1, bright, 'Please supply an array size from 1 to 10');
        GetInt (n);  {read the array size}
        GetData (items,n);  {read the array values}
        RunInsort (items,n);
        clrscr;
        ShowText(10, 10, bright, 'Do you want to see an example? y or n');
      end;  {of while}
    end;  {of if}
end.  {of director}
```

Program 2.20 Complete version of program *director*

DOS MODE arguments	Corresponding Turbo integers	Meaning
bw40	0	black and white 40 columns
c40	1	color 40 columns
bw80	2	black and white 80 columns
c80	3	color 80 columns

Figure 2.22 Arguments of function *Textmode*

color	code	color	code
Black	0	Dark Gray	8
Blue	1	Light Blue	9
Green	2	Light Green	10
Cyan	3	Light Cyan	11
Red	4	Light Red	12
Magenta	5	Light Magenta	13
Brown	6	Yellow	14
Light Gray	7	White	15

Figure 2.23 Color range for *Textmode* on the CGA

When color text mode is chosen, then on the CGA (Computer Graphics Adapter), each character may be displayed in one of 16 colors. These colors are represented by the integers 0 to 15 as shown in Figure 2.23.

A limitation of the CGA makes it impossible to produce all 16 colors on the screen at any one time. In fact a palette of only four colors is possible at any time. When you choose a background color, that determines two possible palettes that you may select. These palettes contain a background color and three foreground colors.

In order to give you some experience with using the color graphics commands of Turbo Pascal in this section we will modify the example of the previous section so that it runs on a color monitor. In addition we will make some changes to the program to improve its style as a CAI application. In the earlier version the material was ordered in a specific way: first the welcome, then the algorithm explanation, and then the examples. This is an instance of what is called *programmed instruction*. Instead, in this program we will give a menu of options to the viewer and let him or her choose the order in which the options are selected. Finally, remember that to have this color version of the program run properly, you must install Turbo Pascal on a color monitor.

Turbo Pascal comes with a set of external machine language routines that define a set of graphics commands. These can be included in your application program by including the line

{$I Graph.p}

in your program. During compilation the external routines are brought in and included with your program. Figure 2.24 shows a list of the routines that are defined in this file. We will not make use of them all, but those of particular importance are the following:

- **procedure** *GraphColorMode*;
  This program establishes medium resolution graphics mode on the CGA.

- **procedure** *Palette* (*N*:**integer**);
  This procedure chooses which of the two palettes the program wants to use, based upon the background color that has been chosen. The value of *N* is either 0 or 1.

- **procedure** *GraphBackground* (*Color* :**integer**);
  This procedure sets the background color, an integer from 0 to 3.

- **procedure** *FillPattern* (*X*1,*Y*1,*X*2,*Y*2,*Color*: **integer**);
  This procedure will fill the rectangular region that is defined by the upper left coordinate, (*X*1,*Y*1), and the lower right coordinate, (*X*2,*Y*2), with the color specified by *Color*.

Now we present the user defined procedures. Procedure *setcolormode* first establishes medium resolution graphics, then chooses a background color of 0 (black) and then chooses the first of the two available palettes. We make this a separate procedure as it is called in more than one location. Procedure *init* begins by asking if a color monitor is installed. If not it will end the program and otherwise it invokes procedure *setcolormode*. Procedure *logo* creates an opening pattern on the screen using the procedure *fillpattern*. First a large rectangle colored red appears. Then within the red rectangle a green-colored rectangle appears and within that the welcoming message is placed. Procedure *createmenu* places the four menu items at the bottom of the screen. Finally, procedure *getresponse* causes the menu to appear and then reads the keyboard for a command to be invoked. If a key other than the acceptable ones is selected, then the program prints a message to ''Try again.'' In case either D, E, or R are chosen, the actions from the earlier program *director* are invoked. The entire program *director* is shown in Program 2.21.

```
const
  North = 0;
  East  = 90;
  South = 180;
  West  = 270;
  procedure Graphics;                                          external 'GRAPH.BIN';
  procedure GraphMode;                                         external Graphics [0];
  procedure GraphColorMode;                                    external Graphics [3];
  procedure HiRes;                                             external Graphics [6];
  procedure HiResColor (Color : integer);                      external Graphics [9];
  procedure Palette (N : integer);                             external Graphics [12];
  procedure GraphBackground (Color : integer);                 external Graphics [15];
  procedure GraphWindow (X 1,Y 1,X 2,Y 2 : integer);           external Graphics [18];
  procedure Plot (X,Y,Color : integer);                        external Graphics [21];
  procedure Draw (X 1,Y 1,X 2,Y 2,Color : integer);            external Graphics [24];
  procedure ColorTable (C 1,C 2,C 3,C 4 : integer);            external Graphics [27];
  procedure Arc (X,Y,Angle,Radius,Color : integer);            external Graphics [30];
  procedure Circle (X,Y,Radius,Color : integer);               external Graphics [33];
  procedure GetPic (varBuffer;X 1,Y 1,X 2,Y 2 : integer);      external Graphics [36];
  procedure PutPic (varBuffer;X,Y : integer);                  external Graphics [39];
  function GetDotColor (X,Y : integer) : Integer;              external Graphics [42];
  procedure FillScreen (Color : integer);                      external Graphics [45];
  procedure FillShape (X,Y,FillCol,BorderCol : integer);       external Graphics [48];
  procedure FillPattern (X 1,Y 1,X 2,Y 2,Color : integer);     external Graphics [51];
  procedure Pattern (varP);                                    external Graphics [54];
  procedure Back (Dist : integer);                             external Graphics [57];
  procedure ClearScreen;                                       external Graphics [60];
  procedure Forwd (Dist : integer);                            external Graphics [63];
  function Heading : integer;                                  external Graphics [66];
  procedure HideTurtle;                                        external Graphics [69];
  procedure Home;                                              external Graphics [72];
  procedure NoWrap;                                            external Graphics [75];
  procedure PenDown;                                           external Graphics [78];
  procedure PenUp;                                             external Graphics [81];
  procedure SetHeading (Angle : integer);                      external Graphics [84];
  procedure SetPenColor (Color : integer);                     external Graphics [87];
  procedure SetPosition (X,Y : integer);                       external Graphics [90];
  procedure ShowTurtle;                                        external Graphics [93];
```

Figure 2.24 Contents of file *Graph.p* (continued on next page)

procedure *TurnLeft* (*Angle* : **integer**);	**external** *Graphics* [96];
procedure *TurnRight* (*Angle* : **integer**);	**external** *Graphics* [99];
procedure *TurtleDelay* (*Delay* : **integer**);	**external** *Graphics* [102];
procedure *TurtleWindow* (*X,Y,W,H* : **integer**);	**external** *Graphics* [105];
function *TurtleThere* : **boolean**;	**external** *Graphics* [108];
procedure *Wrap*;	**external** *Graphics* [111];
function *Xcor* : **integer**;	**external** *Graphics* [114];
function *Ycor* : **integer**;	**external** *Graphics* [117];

Figure 2.24 Contents of file *Graph.p* (continued)

2.5 TURBO PASCAL VERSUS STANDARD PASCAL

In this section we highlight all of the major differences between Standard Pascal and Turbo Pascal. Standard Pascal is not a subset of Turbo Pascal nor vice versa. For example Turbo Pascal lacks some of the standard input/output routines (*get/put*), while Turbo Pascal has added new features, such as a *string* data type. As Turbo Pascal was designed specifically for the IBM PC it has many machine specific features not defined in Standard Pascal. These include special graphics routines, the ability to interface with the DOS operating system, direct access to specific memory locations, and many more. The following sections provide an overview of the differences. Consult the appendix in the Turbo Pascal Reference Manual, either 3.0 or 4.0, for a complete list.

Program Heading

In Standard Pascal, you start a program with

program *test* (*input*, *output*);

to cause input to come from the keyboard and output to go to the terminal, or whatever the preassigned devices for *input* and *output* are. In Turbo, these values are assumed and the program (input, output) statement is optional. It is acceptable to say

program *test*;

but it is not required.

Identifiers

Turbo Pascal accepts the underscore character as legal. So in Turbo Pascal,

do_now

```
program ndirector;

{$I Graph.p}  {include graphics library}

{insert all type, variable, and procedure definitions from
program director, Program 2.20, HERE}

procedure setcolormode;
begin
  GraphColorMode;
  GraphBackground (0);  {set background}
  Palette (0);       {set palette}
end; {of setcolormode}

procedure init;
var answer:char;
begin
  clrscr;
  writeln('Do you have a color monitor? y or n');
  repeat
    read(kbd, answer);
    if upcase (answer) in ['N', #27] then
      {above checks for N, n and ESC}
      begin textmode; halt;
      end;
  until answer in ['Y', 'y'];
  setcolormode;
end; {of init}

procedure logo;
begin
  fillpattern(10, 10, 280, 180, 2);
  fillpattern(45, 30, 215, 120, 1);
  GotoXY (12, 10);
  writeln('Welcome to');
  GotoXY (11, 11);
  writeln('INSERTION SORT');
end; {of logo}
```

Program 2.21 Color CAI program (continued on next page)

```
procedure createmenu;
begin
   GotoXY (6,20);
   writeln('DefineData');
   GotoXY (22,20);
   writeln('Run');
   GotoXY (6,18);
   writeln('Quit');
   GotoXY (22,18);
   writeln('Explanation ');
   GotoXY (10,22);
   writeln('Choose D, R, E, or Q');
end; {of createmenu}

procedure getresponse;
var answer : char;
begin
   repeat
      createmenu;
      read(kbd,answer);
      case answer of
         'D' : begin
                  textmode;
                  ShowText(1, 1, bright, 'Please supply an array size from 1 to 10');
                  GetInt (n); {read the array size}
                  GetData (items,n); {read the array values}
                  setcolormode
               end;
         'R' : begin
                  textmode;
                  RunInsort (items,n);
                  setcolormode;
               end;
         'E' : begin
                  textmode;
                  ShowScreen (screendata, 1,10);
                  ShowText(25, 20, bright, 'PRESS ANY KEY TO CONTINUE');
                  repeat until keypressed;
                  setcolormode;
               end;
```

Program 2.21 Color CAI program (continued on next page)

```
        'Q' : begin  writeln('Quitting Now'); delay (2000); halt;
              end;
        else begin  writeln('Try again'); end;
      end; {of case}
    until answer = 'Q';
end; {of getresponse}
begin
  DefineText(screendata );
  init;
  logo;
  delay (6000);
  Clearscreen;
  getresponse;
  delay (6000);
end.
```

Program 2.21 Color CAI progam (continued)

is a legal identifier. As with Standard Pascal, Turbo Pascal ignores the case of characters, so

Execute, EXECUTE, execute

are all the same name.

Declarations

The Standard Pascal syntax has a strict order for declarations, namely, labels, constants, types, variables, procedures, and functions. Turbo Pascal permits each declaration section to occur as many times as desired and in any order.

Typed Constants

Typed constants are a way to provide an initialization facility in Pascal. Such a feature is found in many other languages, but not in Standard Pascal. Typed constants should be regarded as variables with a constant value. Hence they may be used any place a variable is expected, but not used where a constant is required. In addition to scalars, typed constants may also be arrays, records, and sets. Some examples are

```
const
  hours: integer = 24;
  rate: real = 9.75;
  vowels: array[0..4] of char = 'aeiou';
```

title: **string**[14] = 'FDS for IBM PC';
type
   ThreeD_image = **array**[0..2,0..2] **of integer**;
const
   spoon: *ThreeD_image* = ((10,20,30),(40,50,60),(70,80,90));

A constant name is introduced followed by its type and initial value. Even new type definitions such as *ThreeD_image* can be used in typed constants, so that *spoon* includes assigning values to the nine elements of the array, in row-wise order, namely, [0,0], [0,1], [0,2], [1,0], ... , [2,2].

Expressions

Turbo Pascal has added two operations to the normal collection. They are *shift left* (*shl*) and *shift right* (*shr*). Both are located at the same hierarchy level as the multiplying operators. Both take an integer and return an integer. *shl* will insert zeros at the low order of the word, while *shr* will insert zeros at the high order.

Numbers

There is the ability to specify hexadecimal numbers, using a preceding dollar sign, in the range $0..$FFFF.

read versus readln

The declarations

a: **integer**; *b*: **real**; *c*: **char**

and the statement

read(*a*,*b*,*c*);

will look at the input and assign the first value it finds to *a*, second to *b*, third to *c*. It will then remember where it last looked for a character so the next occurrence of a **read** statement, e.g.,

read(*a*,*c*);

will resume at precisely where the last **read** ended.

On the other hand

readln(*a*,*b*,*c*);

will assign the first three quantities it finds to a, b, c, respectively, but then it will ignore everything else on the line, so that a subsequent **read** or **readln** starts looking for input on a new line.

For interactive programs the distinction between **read** and **readln** is pertinent. If you place a question on the terminal, you want the user to be able to type and edit his or her answer, and hit the Return key when he or she is through. In Turbo Pascal, editing of a response is only permitted with **readln**. The compiler directive {$B+} causes the input for **readln** to be placed in a buffer. Keys such as Backspace are recognized, so editing of the input can be done until the Enter key is struck.

Byte Data Type

There is a built-in data type called **byte** that is defined as a subrange of the integers, namely 0..255. Variables of type **byte** may be mixed with variables of type **integer**. The only restriction is that a formal parameter of type **byte** must be matched with an actual parameter of the same type. A value of this type occupies a single byte within the memory.

There are several functions available for dealing with bytes.

Hi (*ex*) - where *ex* is an integer expression takes its high order byte and returns it as the low order byte of the result of this function. The result type is **integer**.

Lo (*ex*) - where *ex* is an integer expression takes its low order byte and returns it as the low order byte with the high order byte set to zero. The result type is **integer**.

Swap (*number*) - number is an integer. Its high and low order bytes are exchanged.

String Data Type

The basic data types in Pascal are **integer**, **real**, **boolean**, and **char**. However, Turbo Pascal also includes **string** as a built-in data type.

```
var alphabet, numbers, sentence: string[26];
    alphabet := 'abcdefghijklmnopqrstuvwxyz';
    numbers := '0123456789';
```

defines three variables that may contain any string of 26 characters or less. An empty string is legal. The maximum permitted length of a Turbo Pascal string declaration is 255, the minimum is 1. String constants can be denoted in Turbo Pascal by enclosing the desired characters within single quotes. E.g., 'abcdefghijklmnopqrstuvwxyz' is a character string constant.

Control characters may be embedded within a string by preceding its ASCII value with a #. For example, the string '#10' is the string containing a line feed (ASCII equivalent of 10). An alternate way of specifying control characters is by preceding them with a caret, so '^ c' is the character string containing a ctrl-c.

The relational operators are extended to work on strings, comparing each character's ASCII value. If two strings are identical up to the length of the smaller, than the longer string is greater than the shorter.

The characters of a string can be denoted just like array indexing, so *sentence* [3] refers to the fourth character. Whenever a **char** is expected, a string variable may be used in its place, if it is the proper length, and vice versa. Things get a little messier with arrays of type **char**. Though they may be compared with strings, and string constants may be assigned to character arrays of the same length, string variables and the results of string expressions cannot be assigned to character arrays. It is possible to define new types that are modifications of the string type, for example,

type *longstring* = **string**[255];

In Standard Pascal, if one has a record definition such as

type *person* = **record**
        Name : **packed array**[1..30] **of char**;
        Age : **integer**;
        Sex : *sextype*;
        end

the use of packed arrays of characters is the way one typically works with strings. Although Turbo Pascal recognizes the keyword *packed*, it will just ignore it. Therefore in Turbo Pascal the packed array definition should be replaced by

Name : **string**[30];

There are several built-in functions that operate on strings, e.g.,

- *concat* (*alphabet*, *numbers*) returns
  'abcdefghijklmnopqrstuvwxyz0123456789'
  An alternate to the *concat* function is to use the infix operator +. As Pascal is strongly typed, the compiler will know that the + stands for concatenation. One could say
  sentence := 'Hello ' + 'out ' + 'there.';

- *copy* (*sentence*, *start*, *amt*) returns *amt* characters from *sentence*, starting at *start* position. *start* and *amt* are integers.

- *delete* (*sentence*, *start*, *amt*) *amt* of characters are deleted from *sentence*, starting from position *start*. *start* and *amt* are integers.

- *insert* (*extrastuff*, *sentence*, *start*) in *sentence* the string *extrastuff* is inserted starting at position *start*.

- *length* (*alphabet*) returns the number of characters in the string, in this case 26.

- *pos* (*pattern*, *sentence*) looks for the string contained in *pattern* within the string *sentence*. If this string is found, then an integer is returned giving the starting position of the first occurrence of *pattern* in *sentence*, else 0 is returned.

- *str* (*number*, *strnum*) converts the numeric value of *number* into its corresponding string value and stores it in *strnum*. E.g., *str* (123, *strnum*) returns '123'.

- Consider the type definitions

  var *strnum*: **string**[5]; *eflag*: **integer**;

  num is either an integer or a real.
  val (*strnum*, *num*, *eflag*) takes the value of *strnum* and converts it to a number and assigns it to *num*. If the conversion fails, then *eflag* is assigned to the first position in *strnum* that failed to convert. A successful conversion will cause *eflag* to be set to 0.

Type Conversion

Given an enumerated type definition such as

type
days_of_the_week = (sun, mon, tue, wed, thu, fri, sat);

there is a correspondence between the elements of the data type and the natural numbers so that

ord(sun) = 0, ord(mon) = 1, ... , ord(sat) = 6

However, there is no way to take an ordinal value and return the corresponding type value. Turbo Pascal however, does provide such a mechanism, which is called the *retyping* facility. You use the type name as a function, and its argument is the ordinal value. Therefore you may say *days_of_the_week*(2) and get the result *tuesday*.

Type Equivalence

The name equivalence rule is adopted by Turbo Pascal. This rule says that two types are equivalent if and only if they are declared using the same name. Thus given these two declarations:

type *datavalues* = **array**[1..100] **of integer**;
var *collection1*: **array**[1..100] **of integer**; *collection2*: *datavalues*;

then variables *collection1* and *collection2* are of different types even though they have the same structure. If instead you had defined both variables as

var *collection1*, *collection2*: *datavalues*;

then they are the same type, or similarly as

var *collection* 1: *datavalues*; *collection* 2: *datavalues*;

Sets

A set is a list of constants, separated by commas and enclosed in square brackets, e.g. ['a', 'b', 'c', 'd'] or [0,1,2,3,4,5,6,7,8,9]. The main operator on a set is the **in** operator. You may say

if item **in** [0,1,2,3,4,5,6,7,8,9]
then *isnum* := **true else** *isnum* := **false**;

The type of *item* is restricted to be either **integer** or **char**. All of the constants in brackets must be the same type. The operator *in* is an infix operator whose result is a boolean value. A major Turbo Pascal restriction on sets is that integers must be in the range 0..255. Equality, inequality, and the subset relational operators can be used to compare two sets, just as in Standard Pascal. For example,

[0,1,2] < > [0,1,3] returns **true**
[0,1,2] <= [0,1,2,3] returns **true**

Files

A file name under DOS has three parts: a drive specification, a path name and a file name. The file name has two parts: prefix and suffix, separated by a period. So, for example,

C:\SCRIPT\TOSSIT.PAS

is a file located on the C: drive in the subdirectory of the root directory called SCRIPT, and has a name TOSSIT.PAS. See Chapter 1 for more details and examples. We begin by considering ASCII files or also known as text files. Within Turbo Pascal there is a data type, called **text**, which is used to declare file variables that contain formatted ASCII data. The file is assumed to be broken into lines, each line terminated with an end-of-line marker and the entire file terminated with ctrl-z.

If you say

var *samplefile* : **text**;

then *samplefile* is the internal name Turbo Pascal will use for such a file. To associate this variable with an actual file on disk, you use the *assign* command, e.g.,

assign (*samplefile*, *'c :\script\tossit.pas'*);

When using a file in Turbo Pascal, you must first execute an *assign* command tying it to a variable of type *text*. Before you can read/write to a file it must be opened. This is done by saying

rewrite (*samplefile*);

to open the file for writing or

reset (*samplefile*);

to open the file for reading. In the case of *rewrite*, if *samplefile* already has some data in it, then that data is lost. Now you may use the commands

write(*samplefile,data*) or **writeln**(*samplefile,data*)

to place data into the file, or correspondingly for reading, **read** and **readln** may be used. Note that the difference between

writeln(*samplefile*, 100); and **writeln**(100);

is that in the latter case the value 100 is printed on the terminal. Both **read** and **write** have many options. Other functions for operating on text files are *Eoln* (*file*), *SeekEoln* (*file*), and *SeekEof* (*file*). When all of the file operations are done, every file must be closed, by saying

close (*samplefile*);

For files other than text files, the same sequence of steps must be followed; first you open, then you read/write, and then you close the file. *reset* and *rewrite* open a file. Note that the Standard Pascal procedures called *get* and *put* are not available in Turbo Pascal. Figure 2.25 lists the file operations available in Turbo Pascal.

File Operations

Procedures	Functions
append	eof
assign	eoln
BlockRead	FilePos
BlockWrite	FileSize
chain	Seekeof
close	SeekEoln
Erase	
Execute	
Rename	
Reset	
Rewrite	
Seek	

Figure 2.25 File operations

A file is a seqence of components, all of the same type. For example,

type
```
    sextype = (male, female);
    pname = string[10];
    person = file of record
                name : pname;
                age : integer;
                sex : sextype;
            end;
```

is a Standard Pascal definition of a file of records.

Every file has the notion of a window that is positioned over one of the components. Both **read** and **write** can be used with files of any type. After each read, the window is moved one component forward and the same for write. The procedures **readln** and **writeln** only work for text files. There is a command, called *seek*, that permits moving the window to a specific component, e.g., *seek* (*samplefile*, 10);

will move the window to the tenth component. The second argument is an expression that evaluates to an integer. Components in a file are numbered starting at zero. The *seek* statement does not work for text files. Note that the predefined function *filesize* returns the number of components. Thus,

seek (*samplefile*, *filesize*(*samplefile*));

will position the window one location beyond the end of the file. This is permitted in Turbo Pascal as you may then append to the end of the file.

Each of the external devices such as the monitor, terminal, keyboard, and other auxiliary devices specified with DOS are named in Turbo Pascal as shown in Figure 2.26.

Logical Devices	
CON:	the console
TRM:	the terminal
KBD:	the keyboard
LST:	list device
AUX:	auxiliary device
USR:	user device

Figure 2.26 Logical devices

Eliminating Dynamic Data Structures

As in Standard Pascal, Turbo Pascal uses the *new* operator to allocate storage to dynamic structures and assigns a pointer to the storage to the argument supplied. Storage for these variables comes from the *heap*. This is a contiguous area of storage and should not be confused with the runtime stack. The stack contains local variables and return addresses of unfinished procedures while the heap contains storage for variables allocated via a *new* command. *MemAvail* is a function that returns an integer representing the number of 16 byte chunks that are available for the heap. You can use this function to examine how the *new* operator grabs memory. This function is important to make sure memory is available before doing any allocation.

In program *test* (Program 2.22), you see the conventional definition of a singly linked list. The procedures *mark* and *release* are used to mark a position in the heap and to release all memory in the list down to the mark. First *mark* is used. Then the **for** loop allocates storage for a set of 100 nodes. Each time through the loop we print out the amount of storage remaining. After the loop terminates, the *release* function is used to free all the storage that was used for the *nodeitems*. *Mark* and *release* are very simple to use, but you must be careful to not try and use some allocated object after giving up its storage.

```pascal
program test;
type nodeptr = ^ node;
     node = record
                 data : string[10];
                 next : nodeptr;
             end;
var nodeitem : nodeptr;
    i : integer; heap : ^ integer;
begin
  mark (heap);
  writeln;
  writeln('initial memory available = ', MemAvail);
  writeln;
  for i := 1 to 100 do
  begin
    new (nodeitem);
    writeln('After call to NEW', MemAvail:5);
  end; {of for}
  release (heap);
  writeln('final memory available =', MemAvail);
end.
```

Program 2.22

There is an alternate way to return memory to the heap. It is the *dispose* function. This function permits you to free storage for a single dynamic object that is its argument. If you use dispose, then you cannot use *mark* and *release*. When *dispose* is used, fragmentation will result, and Turbo Pascal does not provide a way to compact the heap storage. The function *MaxAvail* returns a value equal to the largest available disposed memory space. As with *MemAvail*, the result is an integer that represents the number of 16 byte chunks. The memory allocation functions available in Turbo Pascal are listed in Figure 2.27.

Memory Allocation Operations

Procedures	Functions
Dispose	MaxAvail
FreeMem	MemAvail
GetMem	Ord
Mark	Ptr
New	
Release	

Figure 2.27 Memory allocation operations

PC Graphics

Turbo Pascal has a host of features that permit you to use the Color Graphics monitor. As most of these capabilities are monitor specific, and as the capabilities are very extensive we will not fully describe them here. A later section contains some examples that use these capabilities.

Other Turbo Pascal Procedures and Functions

The following list of procedures are found in Turbo Pascal, but not generally in Standard Pascal.

clreol - clears all characters starting at the current cursor position to the end of the line. The cursor is not moved.

clrscr - clears the screen

CrtInit - sends the terminal initialization string to the terminal, that was defined during the installation procedure.

CrtExit - sends the terminal reset string to the terminal, that was defined during the installation procedure.

delay (*milliseconds*) - causes the program to pause for the specified number of milliseconds.

DelLine - deletes the line containing the cursor and scrolls all lines below the line up by one.

Exit - this is a statement that causes the current block to be exited.

FillChar (*var,amt,item*) - fills memory with item, a variable of type byte. amt of bytes are filled starting at the first byte occupied by var.

frac(*number*) - where *number* is either of type *integer /real*, it returns an integer which is the fractional part of *number*.

GotoXY (*xpos,ypos*) - moves the current cursor to positions xpos, ypos.

Halt - stops the program from further execution and returns control to DOS.

InsLine - inserts an empty line at the cursor position and scrolls all the existing lines down by one, with the bottom line disappearing.

keypressed - is a boolean valued function with no arguments, that returns true if a key was pressed and false otherwise.

move (*loc* 1,*loc* 2,*amt*) - loc1 and loc2 are variables that occupy a byte in memory. amt number of bytes are taken starting at the byte location of loc1 and moved to the byte location starting at loc2.

ParamCount - returns the number of parameters passed to the program on the command line buffer. Either a space or a tab character can be used to separate arguments.

ParamStr (*n*) - returns the *n*'th parameter from the command line as a string.

random - does not require a seed value, but requires one parameter, a positive integer, e.g., *random* (100); produces a random number between 0 and 99. Simply saying *random* ; will produce a real number in the range [0,1].

randomize - initializes the random number generator with a random value.

SizeOf (*name*) - returns the number of bytes in memory that the variable of type name occupies. The result is of type *integer*.

sound (*hertz*) - sounds a tone on the built-in speaker that corresponds to a frequency specified in hertz. The sound will continue until a command *nosound* is executed.

upcase (*char*) - takes a character and returns its corresponding upper case version of its argument.

Compiler Directives

A compiler directive is a command to the compiler that is contained within a Pascal program. Each directive has a default. They are constructed to be like Pascal comments. +/- is used to set the directive on/off. A leading dollar sign indicates that this is not just a Pascal comment statement, but an actual directive. Multiple directives can be included in a single comment, e.g.,

{$R+,B−   turn on R and turn off B}

turns the R directive on and the B directive off, and has a terminating comment. Below we list the common directives. The defaults are shown. Note that the B and C directives are global, but all others are local to the containing block.

{$B+} causes input to be buffered. This permits editing of the input during a **readln** command, but **read** will not work this way. Turning the directive off causes **readln** not to permit editing, but **read** works as in Standard Pascal. This is a global directive.

{$C+} means that during a read or readln, if a ctrl-c is entered, the program will terminate, or if ctrl-s is entered, screen output will toggle on or off. Turning off this directive loses the features.

{$I+} all I/O errors must be handled within the program. Turning the directive off permits them to be taken care of via the console.

{$I filename list} has the effect of including the specified file in the source code at the point of occurrence. It must be on a line of its own. If no suffix is given .PAS is assumed. Note than an included file may not contain an INCLUDE directive.

{$K+} when on, an initial check is made to see if space is available for local variables on the stack before the call to a subprogram is made. Without this check the program will run faster.

{$R-} array indexing operations are not checked to see if they are within defined bounds. Also, assignments to scalars and subrange types are not checked. Errors will produce unexpected results. Setting the directive on causes the checks to be performed at the expense of slowing down the system.

{$V+} actual and formal variable parameters of string types are checked for length. If they don't agree, an error occurs. If the directive is turned off, inconsistent lengths are permitted.

{$U-} means there is no way to interrupt a running program. Turning the directive on permits ctrl-c to interrupt the program, but at a loss of speed.

2.6 REFERENCES

Gries, David, *The Science of Programming*, Springer Verlag, New York, Heidelberg, 1981.

Cooper, Doug, and Michale Clancy, *Oh! Pascal! An Introduction to Programming*, W.W. Norton and Company, New York, 1982.

Turbo Pascal Version 3.00 and Version 4.00 Reference Manuals and Software, Borland International, Scotts Valley, California, 1984.

Findlay, W., and D.A. Watt, *Pascal An Introduction to Methodical Programming*, Computer Science Press, Rockville, Maryland, 1978.

2.7 EXERCISES

1. Examine the following **var** declarations and list all the errors you can find.
    var *x* ; **integer**;
        if : **boolean**;
        long name : **string**;
        real : **real**;

2. Which of the following are legal Pascal identifiers?
    averylongidentifier
    123
    1-2-3
    two_words
    ALLCAPS
    x*y
    first item
    +*id*

3. For the following **for** statements determine the number of times that the output statement is executed.
    (a) **for** *i* := 1 **to** *n* **do writeln**('loops');
    (b) **for** *i* := *n* **downto** 1 **do writeln**('loops');
    (c) **for** *i* := −10 **to** 10 **do writeln**('loops');

(d) **for** $i := -n$ **to** n **do writeln**('loops');

(e) **for** $i = j$ **to** n **do**
    for $k := i$ **to** n **do**
      writeln('loops');

Now assume that $j=3$ and n has the values 0 and 10, and recompute the number of times the **writeln** statement is printed.

4. Which of the following values are legal if they appear alone in the choice list of a case statement?
123   *ord*('a')   *chr*(65)   'a'   'abc'   **red**   **maxint**   *items* **div** *days*

5. Expressions and assignment statements can be tricky. Given the declarations

    var *initials*: **char**;
        ans, i, x, y: **integer**;
        a, b, pi, r, sum, InterestRate: **real**;

list all the errors you find below.

(a) *initials* := *eh*;

(b) *ans* := if $x > y$ **then** $10 + x$ **else** $20 + y$;

(c) *InterestRate* := 10 %;

(d) let *sum* equal *a* plus *b*;

(e) $i := r$;

(f) $r := i$;

(g) $pi := .3141592654E-01$;

6. Assume that
    var *days, nights, items*: **integer**;
        biggy, percentage: **real**;
    days := 10; *nights* := 57; *biggy* := $0.999E+10$;
    items := 15; *percentage* := 0.1;

Evaluate each of the following expressions

(a) *biggy mod days*

(b) *biggy div days*

(c) *nights mod days*

(d) *nights div days*

(e) *biggy * percentage*

(f)   *days / items*

(g)   *items / days*

(h)   *items + days * items div days*

Here are some examples using the predefined functions. See if you can evaluate
each of them.

(i)   *round*(0.5)

(j)   *round*(−0.5)

(k)   *trunc*(0.5)

(l)   *trunc*(−0.5)

(m)   *sqr*(10)

(n)   *sqrt*(99)

(o)   *sin*(3.1415)

(p)   *abs*(−0.5)

7.   What is wrong with the following procedures?
     procedure *a* (*i,j* : **integer**);
     var *time* : **integer**;
     begin
        findanswer (*time,i*);
     end; {of *a*}
     procedure *findanswer* (**var** *p,q* : **integer**);
     declarations
     begin
        statements
     end; {of *findanswer*}

8.   Consider the program below which has a procedure with formal value parameter
     named *funnyNum* and a global variable also named *funnyNum* of the same type.
     What value of *funnyNum* is printed?

     program *side _effect*;
     var *funnyNum* : **real**;
           i : **integer**;
     procedure *innerp* (*funnyNum* : **real**);
     begin
        funnyNum := *funnyNum* + *i*;
     end;
     begin
        funnyNum := 10;
        i := 2;
        innerp (*funnyNum*);

> **writeln**('The answer is ', *funnyNum*);
> **end**.

9. Explain the difference between **read** and **readln**, **write** and **writeln**.

10. List all of the Pascal reserved words used in program *vscalc1*.

11. Show how you can replace the **while** loop in Program 2.3 by a **repeat-until** clause. Is the program better or worse?

12. Extend the *vscalc1* program so it permits multiplication ($*$) and division ($/$).

13. Write a Pascal program implementing *inputnum* and *inputop* as described in Section 2.2.2.

14. The reserved words in Turbo Pascal are

absolute	external	nil	shr
and	file	not	string
array	for	of	then
begin	forward	or	to
case	function	packed	type
const	goto	procedure	until
div	if	program	var
do	in	record	while
downto	inline	repeat	with
else	label	set	xor
end	mod	shl	

The words {**absolute, external, inline, shl, shr, string**} are not part of standard Pascal. Look them up in Turbo Pascal and determine what each one of these reserved words do.

15. In your version of Pascal are the following identifiers different or the same: *BankAccount*, *bankaccount*, and *BANKACCOUNT*? What about *bank _account* and *bank _Account*?

16. When a **readln** is used, all arguments are input and the remainder of the line is lost. Given the statement **readln**(i,j,k,x) where i, j, are integers and x is real, what values will be assigned to these identifiers assuming the input looks like
    123   -9999   0
    12.0E-2   100

17. Using the input above, answer the question if the operation is **read**(i,j,k,x).

18. Is there anything wrong with the Pascal expression 4 **div** 2.0?

19. It is possible to compute the values for *tangent*, *arcsine*, and *arccosine* using the functions *sin*, *cos*, and *arctan*. This is why only these three are included in the standard Pascal set. Determine formuals for the first three functions in terms of the latter three.

20. Write expressions using the functions *chr* and *ord* that are equivalent to the *pred* and *succ* functions, respectively.

21. If you were going to design your own language, based upon Pascal, what additions, deletions, or modifications would you make? Issues to consider are: dynamic arrays, variable initializations, static variables, and more flow of control statements. For each item give a brief explanation of what it is and then discuss whether you think the facility should be added to Pascal or not and why.

22. Consider the multiple assignment statement

    $a := b := c := 100;$

    Is this legal in Pascal? How would you define the meaning of such a statement in terms of existing Pascal features?

23. Determine the number of times the strings *loop* 1, *loop* 2, and *loop* 3 are printed.

    for $i := 1$ **to** 10 **do**
      for $j := 1$ **to** 10 **do**
        writeln('loop1');

    for $i := 1$ **to** 10 **do**
      for $j := 1$ **to** i **do**
        writeln('loop2');

    for $i := 10$ **downto** 2 **do** 235690
      for $j := i$ **downto** 2 **do**
        writeln('loop3');

24. Another exception to the type consistency rule is the case of a subrange of integers. A variable of subrange type may be assigned to an integer variable. Is it possible to assign a variable of type subrange to a variable of the enumeration type?

25. In procedure *perm* one of the arguments is the array *a*. Thus, *a* will be copied for each recursive call. Write a new version of *perm* that uses only a single copy of *a* (i.e., *a* is a **var** parameter).

26. [Ramos] Program 2.23 computes all permutations on a string of $n = 3$ letters. Compare the running time of this program with that given in Program 2.10. Make a table of the run times with increasing values of *n*.

27. Write a program that takes a month as input and assigns to *days* the proper number of days in the month. Make sure to handle leap years correctly and to not use the **goto** statement.

```
program permutation;
{Find permutations using strings}
const maxletters = 3;
      charset : array[1..maxletters ] ofchar = 'abc';
type elementtype = char;
     letterset = set of char;
     word = string [maxletters ];
function EmptySet (S : letterset ) : boolean;
{Return true if the set S is empty; otherwise return false}
begin
  EmptySet := (S = [ ]);
end;
procedure perm (w : word ; n : integer; S : letterset );
{Choose the n'th letter of word w from set S}
var i : 1..maxletters; {index through characters in set S}
    x : char; {the letter chosen}
begin
  if EmptySet (S) then writeln(w )
  else
     for i := 1 to maxletters do
     begin
       x := charset [i ];
       if charset [i ] in S then
       begin
         w [n ] := x; {n'th letter for w}
         perm (w ,n +1 ,S −[x ]); {find remaining letters for w}
       end;
     end;
end;
begin
  perm (' ', 1, ['a', 'b', 'c']);
end.
```

Program 2.23 Permutations using strings

28. Is it legal to overload enumeration literals? E.g.,

```
type color = (red, green, blue);
     other_colors = (red, white, orange);
```

29. Is it legal to pass enumeration literals to a procedure? For example, using the type definitions above is *cando*(red) legal?

30. Is *succ*(**false**) = **true** or vice versa?

31. The **or** operator in Pascal returns true if one of its arguments is true. This implies that it returns true if both of its arguments are true. Write a Pascal expression that returns true if ONLY one of its arguments is true.

32. Suppose you see the assignment statement:

    n := *answer*;

    Is *answer* a function, a variable, or a literal of an enumerated type?

33. Emacs is a popular UNIX editor that uses the following cursor commands:

cursor forward	ctrl-f
cursor backward	ctrl-b
up one line	ctrl-p
down one line	ctrl-n
beginning of line	ctrl-a
end of line	ctrl-e

    Use TINST.COM and change the TURBO editor so these commands work instead of the WordStar commands. Then compare the two sets of commands in terms of ease of use.

34. One stylistic convention for Pascal indentation is matching **begin** ... **ends** are started in the same column and all statements contained therein start three columns farther to the right. **for** ... **do, case** ... **of, if** ... **then** are placed on the same line. Determine a convention for **var, const**, and **label** declarations.

35. Enhance program *RunInsort* so that it prints out each array giving a message such as Stage 1, Stage 2, Stage 3, etc.

36. Enhance program *director* so it counts the number of comparisons after each pass of the algorithm and prints the number out next to the array.

37. Enhance program *RunInsort* so that on each pass, after it locates a new minimum, it then highlights this value with the element it is going to interchange it with.

38. Enhance program *director* so that it displays a second screen full of text. Compose the screen data yourself with information that would improve a student's knowledge of the algorithm.

39. In program *ndirector* write a procedure that combines the sequence of commands *GotoXY* and **write**. This should reduce the code size of your program as this sequence arises often.

40. The user interface in program *ndirector* only permits capital letters for command invocation. Change the program so either lower case or upper case letters are permitted.

41. In program *ndirector* change the user interface so instead of the menu words at the bottom of the screen the user hits a single key and that causes a menu to pop up. This menu contains the four options. The first option is highlighted. By moving the down/up arrow the other options can be highlighted, one at a time. Hitting the Enter key causes the highlighted option to be executed.

CHAPTER 3

PERFORMANCE ANALYSIS
AND MEASUREMENT

3.1 INTRODUCTION

Once we have developed a program to solve a problem, we will be interested in knowing its performance characteristics. For our purposes, the performance of a program is determined by the amount of computer time and memory needed to run this program. There are two approaches to determining the performance characteristics of a program. One is analytical, and the other experimental. We shall consider both of these in this chapter.

Definition: The *space complexity* of a program is the amount of memory it needs to run to completion. The *time complexity* of a program is the amount of computer time it needs to run to completion. □

3.2 PERFORMANCE ANALYSIS

3.2.1 Space Complexity

Function *abc* (Program 3.1) computes the expression $a + b + b*c + (a + b - c)/(a + b) + 4.0$; function *sum* (Program 3.2) computes the sum $\sum_{i=1}^{n} a[i]$ iteratively, where the $a[i]$'s are real numbers; and function *rsum* (Program 3.3) is a recursive program that computes $\sum_{i=1}^{n} a[i]$.

```
function abc (a, b, c : real) : real;
begin
  abc := a +b +b *c +(a +b −c )/(a +b )+4.0;
end; {of abc}
```

Program 3.1

line	
	function *sum(a : ElementList ; n : integer) : real;*
1	**var** *s* : **real**; *i* : **integer**;
2	**begin**
3	*s* := 0;
4	**for** *i* := 1 **to** *n* **do**
5	*s* := *s* + *a* [*i*];
6	*sum* := *s*;
7	**end**; {of *sum*}

Program 3.2

line	
	function *rsum(a : ElementList ; n : integer) : real;*
1	**begin**
2	**if** *n*<=0 **then** *rsum* := **0**
3	**else** *rsum* := *rsum* (*a*, *n* −1) + *a* [*n*];
4	**end**; {of *rsum*}

Program 3.3

The space needed by each of these programs is seen to be the sum of the following components:

(1) A fixed part which is independent of the characteristics (e.g., number, size) of the inputs and outputs. This part typically includes the instruction space (i.e., space for the code), space for simple variables and fixed size component variables (also called *aggregate*), space for constants, etc.

(2) A variable part which consists of the space needed by component variables whose size is dependent on the particular problem instance being solved, space needed by referenced variables (to the extent that this depends on instance characteristics), and the recursion stack space (in so far as this space depends on the instance characteristics).

The space requirement $S(P)$, of any program P may therefore be written as $S(P) = c + S_P$(instance characteristics) where c is a constant.

When analyzing the space complexity of a program, we shall concentrate solely on estimating S_P (instance characteristics). For any given problem, we shall need to first determine which instance characteristics to use to measure the space requirements. This is very problem specific and we shall resort to examples to illustrate the various possibilities. Generally speaking, our choices are limited to quantities related to the number and magnitude of the inputs to and outputs from the program. At times, more complex measures of the interrelationships amongst the data items are used.

Example 3.1: For Program 3.1, the problem instance is characterized by the specific values of a, b, and c. Making the assumption that one word is adequate to store the values of each of a, b, c, and abc, we see that the space needed by function abc is independent of the instance characteristics. Consequently, S_P(instance characteristics) = 0. $\square$

Example 3.2: The problem instances for Program 3.2 are characterized by n, the number of elements to be summed. Since a and n are value formal parameters, space for these must be allocated. The space needed by the variable n is one word as it is of type **integer**. The space needed by a is the space needed by variables of type *ElementList*. This is at least n words as a must be large enough to hold the n elements to be summed. So, we obtain $S_{sum}(n) \geq n$.

Notice that if we change the formal parameter a from value to reference (or **var**), only the address of the actual parameter gets transferred to the function and the space needed by the function is independent of n. In this case, $S_{sum}(n) = 0$.

So, even though the values of the individual components of a do not get changed by *sum*, it is desirable to make a a variable parameter in order to conserve space. As a variable parameter, only enough space to store a memory address is needed. This is typically just one or two words. $\square$

Example 3.3: Let us consider the function *rsum*. As in the case of *sum*, the instances are characterized by n. The recursion stack space includes space for the formal parameters, the local variables, and the return address. Since a is a value formal parameter, the values of all its components get saved on the stack. Assume that the return address requires only one word of memory. Each call to *rsum* requires at least $(n + 3)$ words (including space for the values of n, a, and *rsum* and the return address). More space is required if *ElementList* has been declared as an array $[1..MaxSize]$ where $MaxSize > n$. In this case, each call to *rsum* takes up $(MaxSize + 3)$ space.

Since the depth of recursion is $n+1$, the recursion stack space needed is $(n+1)(MaxSize+3)$ or $(n+1)(n+3)$ depending on whether or not the size of *ElementList* is changed whenever n changes.

Now that we realize the space cost of having a a value formal parameter, we see that *rsum* will fail when n is suitably large. For example, when $n = 1000$, at least $1001 * 1003 = 1,004,003$ words of memory are needed for the recursion stack space alone.

If we make a a variable parameter, then each call to *rsum* requires only four words of space. The recursion stack space becomes $4(n+1)$ or 4004 words when $n = 1000$. We can solve much larger instances now with a given amount of memory. Of course, we can do much better by not using recursion at all and sticking with the modified version of Program 3.2 in which a is a variable formal parameter. □

3.2.2 Time Complexity

The time, $T(P)$, taken by a program P is the sum of the compile time and the run (or execution) time. The compile time does not depend on the instance characteristics. Also, we may assume that a compiled program will be run several times without recompilation. Consequently, we shall concern ourselves with just the run time of a program. This run time is denoted by t_P (instance characteristics).

Because many of the factors t_P depends on are not known at the time a program is conceived, it is reasonable to attempt to only estimate t_P. If we knew the characteristics of the compiler to be used, we could proceed to determine the number of additions, subtractions, multiplications, divisions, compares, loads, stores, etc. that would be made by the code for P. Having done this, we could present a formula for t_P. Letting n denote the instance characteristics, we might then have an expression for $t_P(n)$ of the form:

$$t_P(n) = c_a ADD(n) + c_s SUB(n) + c_m MUL(n) + c_d DIV(n) + \cdots$$

where c_a, c_s, c_m, c_d, etc., respectively, denote the time needed for an addition, subtraction, multiplication, division, etc. and *ADD*, *SUB*, *MUL*, *DIV*, etc. are functions whose value is the number of additions, subtractions, multiplications, divisions, etc. that will be performed when the code for P is used on an instance with characteristic n.

Obtaining such an exact formula is in itself an impossible task as the time needed for an addition, subtraction, multiplication, etc. often depends on the actual numbers being added, subtracted, multiplied, etc. In reality then, the true value of $t_P(n)$ for any given n can be obtained only experimentally. The program is typed, compiled, and run on a particular machine. The execution time is physically clocked and $t_P(n)$ obtained. Even with this experimental approach, one could face difficulties. In a multiuser system, the execution time will depend on system load: How many other programs are on the computer at the time program P is run? What are the characteristics of these other programs? etc.

Given the minimal utility of determining the exact number of additions, subtractions, etc. that are needed to solve a problem instance with characteristics given by n, we might as well lump all the operations together (provided that the time required by each is relatively independent of the instance characteristics) and obtain a count for the total number of operations. We can go one step further and count only the number of program steps.

A *program step* is loosely defined to be a syntactically or semantically meaningful segment of a program that has an execution time which is independent of the instance characteristics. For example, the entire statement

$abc := a + b + b * c + (a + b - c)/(a + b) + 4.0;$

of Program 3.1 could be regarded as a step as its execution time is independent of the instance characteristics (this statement isn't strictly true as the time for a multiply and divide will generally depend on the actual numbers involved in the operation).

The number of steps any program statement is to be assigned depends on the nature of that statement. The following discussion considers the various statement types that can appear in a Pascal program and states the complexity of each in terms of the number of steps:

(1) *Comments*
Comments are nonexecutable statements and have a step count of zero.

(2) *Declarative Statements*
This includes all statements of type **const, label, type,** and **var**. These count as zero steps as these are either nonexecutable or their cost may be lumped into the cost of invoking the procedure/function they are associated with.

(3) *Expressions and Assignment Statements*
Most expressions have a step count of one. The exceptions are expressions that contain function calls. In this case, we need to determine the cost of invoking the functions. This cost can be large if the functions employ many-element value parameters as the values of all actual parameters need to be assigned to the formal parameters. This is discussed further under procedure and function invocation. When the expression contains functions, the step count is the sum of the step counts assignable to each function invocation.
    The assignment statement <variable> := <expr> has a step count equal to that of <expr> unless the size of <variable> is a function of the instance characteristics. In this latter case, the step count is the size of <variable> plus the step count of <expr>. For example, the assignment $a := b$ where a and b are of type

ElementList has a step count equal to the size of *ElementList*.

(4) *Iteration Statements*

This class of statements includes the **for, while,** and **until** statements. We shall consider the step counts only for the control part of these statements. These have the form:

for i := <expr> **to** <expr1> **do**
for i := <expr> **downto** <expr1> **do**
while <expr> **do**
until <expr>;

Each execution of the control part of a **while** and **until** statement will be given a step count equal to the number of step counts assignable to <expr>. The step count for each execution of the control part of a **for** statement is one unless the counts attributable to <expr> and <expr1> are a function of the instance characteristics. In this latter case, the first execution of the control part of the **for** has a step count equal to the sum of the counts for <expr> and <expr1> (note that these expressions are computed only when the loop is started). Remaining executions of the **for** have a step count of one.

(5) *Case Statement*

This statement consists of a header followed by one or more sets of condition and statement pairs.

case <expr> **of**
   cond1: <statement1>
   cond2: <statement2>
     .
     .
     .
   else: <statement>
end

The cost of the header: **case** <expr> **of** is given a cost equal to that assignable to <expr>. The cost of each following condition - statement pair is the cost of this condition plus that of all preceding conditions plus that of this statement.

(6) *If-then-else Statement*

The if-then-else statement consists of three parts:

if <expr>
then <statements1>
else <statements2>;

Each part is assigned the number of steps corresponding to <expr>, <statements1>, and <statements2>, respectively. Note that if the **else** clause is absent, then no cost is assigned to it.

(7)   *Procedure and Function Invocation*
All invocations of procedures and functions count as one step unless the invocation involves value parameters whose size depends on the instance characteristics. In this latter case, the count is the sum of the sizes of these value parameters. In case the procedure/function being invoked is recursive, then we must also consider the local variables in the procedure or function being invoked. The sizes of local variables that are characteristic dependent need to be added into the step count.

(8)   *Begin, End, With, and Repeat Statements*
Each **with** statement counts as one step. Each **begin**, **end**, and **repeat** statement counts as zero steps.

(9)   *Procedure and Function Statements*
These count as zero steps as their cost has already been assigned to the invoking statements.

(10)   *Goto Statement*
This has a step count of 1.

With the above assignment of step counts to statements, we can proceed to determine the number of steps needed by a program to solve a particular problem instance. We can go about this in one of two ways. In the first method, we introduce a new variable, *count*, into the program. This is a global variable with initial value 0. Statements to increment *count* by the appropriate amount are introduced into the program. This is done so that each time a statement in the original program is executed, *count* is incremented by the step count of that statement.

Example 3.4: When the statements to increment *count* are introduced into Program 3.2 the result is Program 3.4. The change in the value of *count* by the time this program terminates is the number of steps executed by Program 3.2.

Since we are interested in determining only the change in the value of *count*, Program 3.4 may be simplified to Program 3.5. It should be easy to see that for every initial value of *count*, both Programs 3.4 and 3.5 compute the same final value for *count*. It is easy to see that in the **for** loop the value of *count* will increase by a total of $2n$. If *count* is zero to start with, then it will be $2n+3$ on termination. So, each invocation of *sum* (Program 3.2) executes a total of $2n+3$ steps. □

Example 3.5: When the statements to increment count are introduced into Program 3.3, Program 3.6 is obtained. In this program, we have assumed that the declared size of *ElementList* is m. Note that $m \geq n$. Let $t_{rsum}(n)$ be the increase in the value of *count* when Program 3.6 terminates. We see that $t_{rsum}(0)=2$. When $n>0$, *count* increases by $m+1$

```
function sum(a : ElementList ; n :integer) :real;
var s : real; i : integer;
begin
  s := 0;
  count := count+1; {count is global}
  for i := 1 to n do
  begin
    count := count+1; {for for}
    s := s +a [i ];
    count := count+1; {for assignment}
  end;
  count := count+1; {for last time of for}
  sum := s;
  count := count+1; {for assignment}
end; { of sum}
```

Program 3.4

```
function sum(a : ElementList ; n :integer) :real;
var s : real; i : integer;
begin
  for i := 1 to n do
    count := count+2; {end of for}
  count := count+3;
end; { of sum}
```

Program 3.5

plus whatever increase results from the invocation of *rsum* from within the **else** clause. From the definition of t_{rsum}, it follows that this additional increase is $t_{rsum}(n-1)$. So, if the value of *count* is zero initially, its value at the time of termination is $m+1+t_{rsum}(n-1)$, $n>0$.

When analyzing a recursive program for its step count, we often obtain a recursive formula for the step count (i.e., say $t_{rsum}(n) = m+1+t_{rsum}(n-1)$, $n>0$ and $t_{rsum}(0)=2$). These recursive formulas are referred to as *recurrence relations*. This recurrence may be solved by repeatedly substituting for t_{rsum} as below:

$$t_{rsum}(n) = m +1+t_{rsum}(n-1)$$
$$= m +1 + m +1 + t_{rsum}(n-2)$$

$$= 2(m+1) + t_{rsum}(n-2)$$

.

.

.

$$= n(m+1) + t_{rsum}(0)$$
$$= n(m+1)+2, \; n \geq 0.$$

So, the step count for procedure *rsum* (Program 3.3) is $n(m+1)+2$. This is significantly larger than that for the iterative version (Program 3.2). If *a* is made a variable parameter, then the step count becomes $2n+2$. □

```
function rsum(a : ElementList ; n : integer) : real;
begin
    count := count+1;  {for if conditional}
    if n<=0 then begin
                    rsum := 0;
                    count := count+1;  {for assignment}
                end
    else begin
            rsum := rsum (a, n−1) + a [n ];
            count := count+m;  {for assignment, m is the size of ElementList}
        end;
end;  {of rsum}
```

Program 3.6

Comparing the step count of Program 3.2 to that of Program 3.3 with *a* changed to a variable parameter, we see that the count for Program 3.3 is less than that for Program 3.2. From this, we cannot conclude that Program 3.2 is slower than Program 3.3. This is so because a step doesn't correspond to a definite time unit. Each step of *rsum* may take more time than every step of *sum*. So, it might well be (and we expect it) that *rsum* is slower than *sum*.

The step count is useful in that it tells us how the run time for a program changes with changes in the instance characteristics. From the step count for *sum*, we see that if *n* is doubled, the run time will also double (approximately); if *n* increases by a factor of 10, we expect the run time to increase by a factor of 10; etc. So, we expect the run time to grow *linearly* in *n*. We say that *sum* is a linear program (the time complexity is linear in the instance characteristic *n*).

Example 3.6: [Matrix addition] Program 3.7 is a program to add two $m \times n$ matrices *a* and *b* together. Introducing the *count* incrementing statements leads to Program 3.8.

Program 3.9 is a simplified version of Program 3.8 which computes the same value for *count*. Examining Program 3.9, we see that line 6 is executed n times for each value of i or a total of mn times; line 7 is executed m times; and line 9 is executed once. If *count* is zero to begin with, it will be $2mn + 2m + 1$ when Program 3.9 terminates.

From this analysis we see that if $m > n$, then it is better to interchange the two **for** statements in Program 3.7. If this is done, the step count becomes $2mn + 2n + 1$. Note that in this example the instance characteristics are given by m and n. □

```
line  procedure add (var a, b, c : matrix; m,n :integer);
1      var i, j : integer;
2      begin
3        for i := 1 to m do
4          for j := 1 to n do
5            c [i,j] := a [i,j]+b [i,j];
6      end; {of add}
```

Program 3.7 Matrix addition

```
procedure add (var a, b, c : matrix; m,n :integer);
var i, j : integer;
begin
  for i := 1 to m do
  begin
    count := count+1; {for for i}
    for j := 1 to n do
    begin
      count := count+1; {for for j}
      c [i,j] := a [i,j]+b [i,j];
      count := count+1; {for assignment}
    end;
    count := count+1; {for last time of for j}
  end;
  count := count+1; {for last time of for i}
end; {of add}
```

Program 3.8 Matrix addition with counting statements

line	**procedure** *add* (**var** *a*, *b*, *c* : *matrix*; *m,n* : **integer**);
1	**var** *i, j* : **integer**;
2	**begin**
3	**for** *i* := 1 **to** *m* **do**
4	**begin**
5	**for** *j* := 1 **to** *n* **do**
6	*count* := *count*+2;
7	*count* := *count*+2;
8	**end**;
9	*count* := *count*+1;
10	**end**; {of *add*}

Program 3.9 Simplified program with counting only

The second method to determine the step count of a program is to build a table in which we list the total number of steps contributed by each statement to *count*. This figure is often arrived at by first determining the number of steps per execution of the statement and the total number of times (i.e., frequency) each statement is executed. By combining these two quantities, the total contribution of each statement is obtained. By adding up the contributions of all statements, the step count for the entire program is obtained.

There is an important difference between the step count of a statement and its steps per execution (s/e). The step count does not necessarily reflect the complexity of the statement. For example, the statement

$$x := sum(a,m);$$

has a step count of m (assuming that a is defined to be a size m array) while the total change in *count* resulting from the execution of this statement is actually m plus the change resulting from the invocation of *sum* (i.e., $2m+3$). The steps per execution of the above statement is $m+2m+3 = 3m+3$. *The s/e of a statement is the amount by which count changes as a result of the execution of that statement.*

In Table 3.1, the number of steps per execution and the frequency of each of the statements in procedure *sum* (Program 3.2) have been listed. The total number of steps required by the program is determined to be $2n+3$. It is important to note that the frequency of line 4 is $n+1$ and not n. This is so as i has to be incremented to $n+1$ before the **for** loop can terminate.

line	s/e	frequency	total steps
1	0	0	0
2	0	0	0
3	1	1	1
4	1	$n+1$	$n+1$
5	1	n	n
6	1	1	1
7	0	1	0
		Total number of steps =	$2n+3$

Table 3.1 Step table for Program 3.2.

Table 3.2 gives the step count for procedure *rsum* (Program 3.3). Line 2(a) refers to the **if** conditional of line 2 and line 2(b) refers to the statement in the **then** clause of the **if**. Notice that under the s/e (steps per execution) column, line 3 has been given a count of $m+t_{rsum}(n-1)$. This is the total cost of line 3 each time it is executed. It includes all the steps that get executed as a result of the invocation of *rsum* from line 3. The frequency and total steps columns have been split into two parts: one for the case $n = 0$ and the other for the case $n > 0$. This is necessary as the frequency (and hence total steps) for some statements is different for each of these cases.

line	s/e	frequency		total steps	
		$n=0$	$n>0$	$n=0$	$n>0$
1	0	0	0	0	0
2(a)	1	1	1	1	1
2(b)	1	1	0	1	0
3	$m+t_{rsum}(n-1)$	0	1	0	$m+t_{rsum}(n-1)$
4	0	1	1	0	0
		Total number of steps		2	$m+1+t_{rsum}(n-1)$

Table 3.2 Step table for Program 3.3.

Table 3.3 corresponds to procedure *add* (Program 3.7). Once again, note that the frequency of line 3 is $m+1$ and not m. This is so as i needs to be incremented up to $m+1$ before the loop can terminate. Similarly, the frequency for line 4 is $m(n+1)$.

line	s/e	frequency	total steps
1	0	0	0
2	0	0	0
3	1	$m+1$	$m+1$
4	1	$m(n+1)$	$mn+m$
5	1	mn	mn
6	0	1	0
		Total	$2mn+2m+1$

Table 3.3 Step table for Program 3.7.

Summary

The time complexity of a program is given by the number of steps taken by the program to compute the function it was written for. The number of steps is itself a function of the instance characteristics. While any specific instance may have several characteristics (e.g., the number of inputs, the number of outputs, the magnitudes of the inputs and outputs, etc.), the number of steps is computed as a function of some subset of these. Usually, we choose those characteristics that are of importance to us. For example, we might wish to know how the computing (or run) time (i.e., time complexity) increases as the number of inputs increase. In this case the number of steps will be computed as a function of the number of inputs alone. For a different program, we might be interested in determining how the computing time increases as the magnitude of one of the inputs increases. In this case the number of steps will be computed as a function of the magnitude of this input alone. Thus, before the step count of a program can be determined, we need to know exactly which characteristics of the problem instance are to be used. These define the variables in the expression for the step count. In the case of *sum*, we chose to measure the time complexity as a function of the number, n, of elements being added. For procedure *add* the choice of characteristics was the number, m, of rows and the number, n, of columns in the matrices being added.

Once the relevant characteristics $(n, m, p, q, r, ...)$ have been selected, we can define what a step is. A step is any computation unit that is independent of the characteristics $(n, m, p, q, r, ...)$. Thus 10 additions can be one step; 100 multiplications can also be one step; but n additions cannot. Nor can $m/2$ additions, $p+q$ subtractions, etc. be counted as one step.

A systematic way to assign step counts was also discussed. Once this has been done, the time complexity (i.e., the total step count) of a program can be obtained using either of the two methods discussed.

The examples we have looked at so far were sufficiently simple that the time complexities were nice functions of fairly simple characteristics like the number of elements, and the number of rows and columns. For many programs, the time complexity is not dependent solely on the number of inputs or outputs or some other easily specified characteristic. Consider the procedure *BinarySearch* of Chapter 2. This procedure searches $a[1..n]$ for x. A natural parameter with respect to which you might wish to determine the step count is the number, n, of elements to be searched. I.e., we would like to know how the computing time changes as we change the number of elements n. The parameter n is, however, inadequate. For the same n, the step count varies with the position of x in a. We can extricate ourselves from the difficulties resulting from situations when the chosen parameters are not adequate to determine the step count uniquely by defining two kinds of steps counts: worst case and average.

The *worst case step count* is the maximum number of steps that can be executed for the given paramenters. The *average step count* is the average number of steps executed on instances with the given parameters.

3.2.3 Asymptotic Notation (O, Ω, Θ)

Our motivation to determine step counts is to be able to compare the time complexities of two programs that compute the same function and also to predict the growth in run time as the instance characteristics change.

Determining the exact step count (either worst case or average) of a program can prove to be an exceedingly difficult task. Expending immense effort to determine the step count exactly isn't a very worthwhile endeavor as the notion of a step is itself inexact. (Both the instructions $x := y$ and $x := y + z + (x/y) + (x*y*z-x/z)$ count as one step.) Because of the inexactness of what a step stands for, the exact step count isn't very useful for comparative purposes. An exception to this is when the difference in the step counts of two programs is very large as in $3n+3$ versus $100n+10$. We might feel quite safe in predicting that the program with step count $3n+3$ will run in less time than the one with step count $100n+10$. But even in this case, it isn't necessary to know that the exact step count is $100n+10$. Something like "it's about $80n$, or $85n$, or $75n$" is adequate to arrive at the same conclusion.

For most situations, it is adequate to be able to make a statement like $c_1 n^2 \leq t_P^{WC}(n) \leq c_2 n^2$ or $t_Q^{WC}(n,m) = c_1 n + c_2 m$ where c_1 and c_2 are nonnegative constants. This is so because if we have two programs with a complexity of $c_1 n^2 + c_2 n$ and $c_3 n$, respectively, then we know that the one with complexity $c_3 n$ will be faster than the one with complexity $c_1 n^2 + c_2 n$ for sufficiently large values of n. For small values of n, either program could be faster (depending on c_1, c_2, and c_3). If $c_1=1$, $c_2 = 2$, and $c_3=100$ then $c_1 n^2 + c_2 n \leq c_3 n$ for $n \leq 98$ and $c_1 n^2 + c_2 n > c_3 n$ for $n > 98$. If $c_1 = 1$, $c_2 = 2$, and $c_3 = 1000$, then $c_1 n^2 + c_2 n \leq c_3 n$ for $n \leq 998$.

No matter what the values of c_1, c_2, and c_3, there will be an n beyond which the program with complexity $c_3 n$ will be faster than the one with complexity $c_1 n^2 + c_2 n$. This value of n will be called the *break even point*. If the break even point is 0 then the program with complexity $c_3 n$ is always faster (or at least as fast). The exact break even point cannot be determined analytically. The programs have to be run on a computer in order to determine the break even point. To know that there is a break even point it is adequate to know that one program has complexity $c_1 n^2 + c_2 n$ and the other $c_3 n$ for some constants c_1, c_2, and c_3. There is little advantage in determining the exact values of c_1, c_2, and c_3.

With the previous discussion as motivation, we introduce some terminology that will enable us to make meaningful (but inexact) statements about the time and space complexities of a program. In the remainder of this chapter, the functions f and g are nonnegative functions.

Definition: [Big "oh"] $f(n) = O(g(n))$ (read as "f of n is big oh of g of n") iff (if and only if) there exist positive constants c and n_0 such that $f(n) \leq cg(n)$ for all $n, n \geq n_0$. $\square$

Example 3.7: $3n + 2 = O(n)$ as $3n + 2 \leq 4n$ for all $n \geq 2$. $3n + 3 = O(n)$ as $3n + 3 \leq 4n$ for all $n \geq 3$. $100n + 6 = O(n)$ as $100n + 6 \leq 101n$ for $n \geq 10$. $10n^2 + 4n + 2 = O(n^2)$ as $10n^2 + 4n + 2 \leq 11n^2$ for $n \geq 5$. $1000n^2 + 100n - 6 = O(n^2)$ as $1000n^2 + 100n - 6 \leq 1001n^2$ for $n \geq 100$. $6*2^n + n^2 = O(2^n)$ as $6*2^n + n^2 \leq 7*2^n$ for $n \geq 4$. $3n + 3 = O(n^2)$ as $3n + 3 \leq 3n^2$ for $n \geq 2$. $10n^2 + 4n + 2 = O(n^4)$ as $10n^2 + 4n + 2 \leq 10n^4$ for $n \geq 2$. $3n + 2 \neq O(1)$ as $3n + 2$ is not less than or equal to c for any constant c and all $n, n \geq n_0$. $10n^2 + 4n + 2 \neq O(n)$. $\square$

As illustrated by the previous example, the statement $f(n) = O(g(n))$ only states that $g(n)$ is an upper bound on the value of $f(n)$ for all $n, n \geq n_0$. It doesn't say anything about how good this bound is. Notice that $n = O(n^2)$, $n = O(n^{2.5})$, $n = O(n^3)$, $n = O(2^n)$, etc. In order for the statement $f(n) = O(g(n))$ to be informative, $g(n)$ should be as small a function of n as one can come up with for which $f(n) = O(g(n))$. So, while we shall often say $3n + 3 = O(n)$, we shall almost never say $3n + 3 = O(n^2)$ even though this latter statement is correct.

From the definition of O, it should be clear that $f(n) = O(g(n))$ is not the same as $O(g(n)) = f(n)$. In fact, it is meaningless to say that $O(g(n)) = f(n)$. The use of the symbol "=" is unfortunate as this symbol commonly denotes the "equals" relation. Some of the confusion that results from the use of this symbol (which is standard terminology) can be avoided by reading the symbol "=" as "is" and not as "equals."

Theorem 3.1 obtains a very useful result concerning the order of $f(n)$ (i.e., the $g(n)$ in $f(n) = O(g(n))$) when $f(n)$ is a polynomial in n.

Theorem 3.1: If $f(n) = a_m n^m + \cdots + a_1 n + a_0$, then $f(n) = O(n^m)$.

Proof: $f(n) \leq \sum_{i=0}^{m} |a_i| n^i$

$$\leq n^m \sum_{0}^{m} |a_i| n^{i-m}$$

$$\leq n^m \sum_{0}^{m} |a_i|, \text{ for } n \geq 1.$$

So, $f(n) = O(n^m)$. $\square$

Definition: [Omega] $f(n) = \Omega(g(n))$ (read as "f of n is omega of g of n") iff there exist positive constants c and n_0 such that $f(n) \geq cg(n)$ for all $n, n \geq n_0$. $\square$

Example 3.8: $3n + 2 = \Omega(n)$ as $3n + 2 \geq 3n$ for $n \geq 1$ (actually the inequality holds for $n \geq 0$ but the definition of Ω requires an $n_0 > 0$). $3n + 3 = \Omega(n)$ as $3n + 3 \geq 3n$ for $n \geq 1$. $100n + 6 = \Omega(n)$ as $100n + 6 \geq 100n$ for $n \geq 1$. $10n^2 + 4n + 2 = \Omega(n^2)$ as $10n^2 + 4n + 2 \geq n^2$ for $n \geq 1$. $6*2^n + n^2 = \Omega(2^n)$ as $6*2^n + n^2 \geq 2^n$ for $n \geq 1$. Observe also that $3n + 3 = \Omega(1)$; $10n^2 + 4n + 2 = \Omega(n)$; $10n^2 + 4n + 2 = \Omega(1)$; $6*2^n + n^2 = \Omega(n^{100})$; $6*2^n + n^2 = \Omega(n^{50.2})$; $6*2^n + n^2 = \Omega(n^2)$; $6*2^n + n^2 = \Omega(n)$; and $6*2^n + n^2 = \Omega(1)$. $\square$

As in the case of the "big oh" notation, there are several functions $g(n)$ for which $f(n) = \Omega(g(n))$. $g(n)$ is only a lower bound on $f(n)$. For the statement $f(n) = \Omega(g(n))$ to be informative, $g(n)$ should be as large a function of n as possible for which the statement $f(n) = \Omega(g(n))$ is true. So, while we shall say that $3n + 3 = \Omega(n)$ and that $6*2^n + n^2 = \Omega(2^n)$, we shall almost never say that $3n + 3 = \Omega(1)$ or that $6*2^n + n^2 = \Omega(1)$ even though both these statements are correct.

Theorem 3.2 is the analogue of Theorem 3.1 for the omega notation.

Theorem 3.2: If $f(n) = a_m n^m + \cdots + a_1 n + a_0$ and $a_m > 0$, then $f(n) = \Omega(n^m)$.

Proof: Left as an exercise. $\square$

Definition: [Theta] $f(n) = \Theta(g(n))$ (read as "f of n is theta of g of n") iff there exist positive constants c_1, c_2, and n_0 such that $c_1 g(n) \leq f(n) \leq c_2 g(n)$ for all $n, n \geq n_0$. $\square$

Example 3.9: $3n + 2 = \Theta(n)$ as $3n + 2 \geq 3n$ for all $n \geq 2$ and $3n + 2 \leq 4n$ for all $n \geq 2$, so c_1 3, $c_2 = 4$, and $n_0 = 2$. $3n + 3 = \Theta(n)$; $10n^2 + 4n + 2 = \Theta(n^2)$; $6*2^n + n^2 = \Theta(2^n)$; and $10*\log n + 4 = \Theta(\log n)$. $3n + 2 \neq \Theta(1)$; $3n + 3 \neq \Theta(n^2)$; $10n^2 + 4n + 2 \neq \Theta(n)$; $10n^2 + 4n + 2 \neq \Theta(1)$; $6*2^n + n^2 \neq \Theta(n^2)$; $6*2^n + n^2 \neq \Theta(n^{100})$; and $6*2^n + n^2 \neq \Theta(1)$. $\square$

The theta notation is more precise than both the "big oh" and omega notations. $f(n) = \Theta(g(n))$ iff $g(n)$ is both an upper and lower bound on $f(n)$.

Notice that the coefficients in all of the $g(n)$'s used in the preceding three examples has been 1. This is in accordance with practice. We shall almost never find ourselves saying that $3n + 3 = O(3n)$, or that $10 = O(100)$, or that $10n^2 + 4n + 2 = \Omega(4n^2)$, or that $6*2^n + n^2 = \Omega(6*2^n)$, or that $6*2^n + n^2 = \Theta(4*2^n)$, even though each of these statements is true.

Theorem 3.3: If $f(n) = a_m n^m + \cdots + a_1 n + a_0$ and $a_m > 0$, then $f(n) = \Theta(n^m)$.

Proof: Left as an exercise. $\square$

Let us reexamine the time complexity analyses of the previous section. For procedure *sum* (Program 3.2) we had determined that $t_{sum}(n) = 2n + 3$. So, $t_{sum}(n) = \Theta(n)$. $t_{rsum}(n) = n(m+1) + 2 = \Theta(nm)$; $t_{add}(m,n) = 2mn + 2n + 1 = \Theta(mn)$.

While we might all see that the O, Ω, and Θ notations have been used correctly in the preceding paragraphs, we are still left with the question: "Of what use are these notations if one has to first determine the step count exactly?" The answer to this question is that the asymptotic complexity (i.e., the complexity in terms of O, Ω, and Θ) can be determined quite easily without determining the exact step count. This is usually done by first determining the asymptotic complexity of each statement (or group of statements) in the program and then adding up these complexities. Tables 3.4 to 3.6 do just this for *sum*, *rsum*, and *add*.

Note that in the table for *add*, lines 4 and 5 have been lumped together even though they have different frequencies. This lumping together of these two lines is possible because their frequencies are of the same order.

line(s)	s/e	frequency	total steps
1,2	0	-	$\Theta(0)$
3	1	1	$\Theta(1)$
4	1	$n+1$	$\Theta(n)$
5	1	n	$\Theta(n)$
6	1	1	$\Theta(1)$
7	0	-	$\Theta(0)$

$$t_{sum}(n) = \Theta(\max_{0 \leq i \leq 7}\{g_i(n)\}) = \Theta(n)$$

Table 3.4 Asymptotic complexity of *sum*.

line	s/e	frequency		total steps	
		$n=0$	$n>0$	$n=0$	$n>0$
1	0	-	-	0	$\Theta(0)$
2(a)	1	1	1	1	$\Theta(1)$
2(b)	1	1	0	1	$\Theta(0)$
3	$m + t_{rsum}(n-1)$	0	1	0	$\Theta(m + t_{rsum}(n-1))$
4	0	-	-	0	$\Theta(0)$

$$t_{rsum}(n) = \begin{cases} m + t_{rsum}(n-1) & n>0 \\ 2 & n=0 \end{cases}$$

Table 3.5 Asymptotic complexity of *rsum*.

line(s)	s/e	frequency	total steps
1,2	0	0	$\Theta(0)$
3	1	$\Theta(m)$	$\Theta(m)$
4,5	1	$\Theta(mn)$	$\Theta(mn)$
6	0	-	$\Theta(0)$
		$t_{add}(m,n) =$	$\Theta(mn)$

Table 3.6 Asymptotic complexity of *add*.

While the analyses of Tables 3.4 through 3.6 are actually carried out in terms of step counts, it is correct to interpret $t_P(n) = \Theta(g(n))$, or $t_P(n) = O(g(n))$ or $t_P(n) = \Omega(g(n))$ as a statement about the computing time of program P. This is so because each step takes only $\Theta(1)$ time to execute.

After you have had some experience using the table method, you will be in a position to arrive at the asymptotic complexity of a program by taking a more global approach. We elaborate on this method in the following examples.

Example 3.11: [*perm*] Consider procedure *perm* (Program 2.11). Assume that a is of size n. When $k = n$, we see that the time taken is $\Theta(n)$. When $k < n$, the **else** clause is entered. At this time, the second **for** loop is entered $n-k+1$ times. Each iteration of this loop takes $\Theta(n + t_{perm}(k+1, n))$ time. So, $t_{perm}(k, n) = \Theta((n-k+1)(n + t_{perm}(k+1, n)))$ when $k < n$. Since, $t_{perm}(k+1, n)$, is at least n when $k+1 \leq n$, we get $t_{perm}(k, n) =$

$\Theta((n-k+1)t_{perm}(k+1, n))$ for $k < n$. Using the substitution method, we obtain $t(1,n) = \Theta(nn!), n \geq 1$. $\square$

Example 3.12: [Binary search] Let us obtain the time complexity of the binary search procedure *BinarySearch* of Chapter 2. The instance characteristic that we shall use is the number n of elements in $a[]$. Each iteration of the **while** loop takes $\Theta(1)$ time. We can show that the **while** loop is iterated at most $\lceil \log_2(n+1) \rceil$ times (see the book by S. Sahni cited in the references). Since an asymptotic analysis is being performed, we don't need such an accurate count of the worst case number of iterations. Each iteration except for the last results in a decrease in the size of the segment of a that has to be searched by a factor of about 2. So, this loop is iterated $\Theta(\log n)$ times in the worst case. As each iteration takes $\Theta(1)$ time, the overall worst case complexity of *BinarySearch* is $\Theta(\log n)$. Note that, if a were not a **var** parameter, the complexity of using *BinarySearch* would be more than this as it would take $\Omega(n)$ time just to invoke the procedure. $\square$

3.2.4 Practical Complexities

We have seen that the time complexity of a program is generally some function of the instance characteristics. This function is very useful in determining how the time requirements vary as the instance characteristics change. The complexity function may also be used to compare two programs P and Q that perform the same task. Assume that program P has complexity $\Theta(n)$ and program Q is of complexity $\Theta(n^2)$. We can assert that program P is faster than program Q for "sufficiently large" n. To see the validity of this assertion, observe that the actual computing time of P is bounded from above by cn for some constant c and for all $n, n \geq n_1$ while that of Q is bounded from below by dn^2 for some constant d and all $n, n \geq n_2$. Since $cn \leq dn^2$ for $n \geq c/d$, program P is faster than program Q whenever $n \geq \max\{n_1, n_2, c/d\}$.

You should always be cautiously aware of the presence of the phrase "sufficiently large" in the assertion of the preceding discussion. When deciding which of the two programs to use, we must know whether the n we are dealing with is, in fact, "sufficiently large." If program P actually runs in $10^6 n$ milliseconds while program Q runs in n^2 milliseconds and if we always have $n \leq 10^6$, then, other factors being equal, program Q is the one to use, other factors being equal.

To get a feel for how the various functions grow with n, you are advised to study Table 3.7 and Figure 3.1 very closely. As is evident from the table and the figure, the function 2^n grows very rapidly with n. In fact, if a program needs 2^n steps for execution, then when $n = 40$ the number of steps needed is approximately $1.1*10^{12}$. On a computer performing 1 billion steps per second, this would require about 18.3 minutes. If $n = 50$, the same program would run for about 13 days on this computer. When $n = 60$, about 310.56 years will be required to execute the program and when $n = 100$, about $4*10^{13}$

years will be needed. So, we may conclude that the utility of programs with exponential complexity is limited to small n (typically $n \leq 40$).

$\log n$	n	$n \log n$	n^2	n^3	2^n
0	1	0	1	1	2
1	2	2	4	8	4
2	4	8	16	64	16
3	8	24	64	512	256
4	16	64	256	4096	65536
5	32	160	1024	32768	4294967296

Table 3.7 Function values

Programs that have a complexity that is a polynomial of high degree are also of limited utility. For example, if a program needs n^{10} steps, then using our 1 billion steps per second computer we will need 10 seconds when $n = 10$; 3,171 years when $n = 100$; and $3.17*10^{13}$ years when $n = 1000$. If the program's complexity had been n^3 steps instead, then we would need 1 second when $n = 1000$, 110.67 minutes when $n = 10,000$; and 11.57 days when $n = 100,000$.

Table 3.8 gives the time needed by a 1 billion instructions per second computer to execute a program of complexity $f(n)$ instructions. You should note that currently only the fastest computers can execute about 1 billion instructions per second. From a practical standpoint, it is evident that for reasonably large n (say $n > 100$) only programs of small complexity (such as n, $n \log n$, n^2, n^3) are feasible. Further, this is the case even if one could build a computer capable of executing 10^{12} instructions per second. In this case, the computing times of Table 3.8 would decrease by a factor of 1000. Now, when $n = 100$ it would take 3.17 years to execute n^{10} instructions, and $4*10^{10}$ years to execute 2^n instructions.

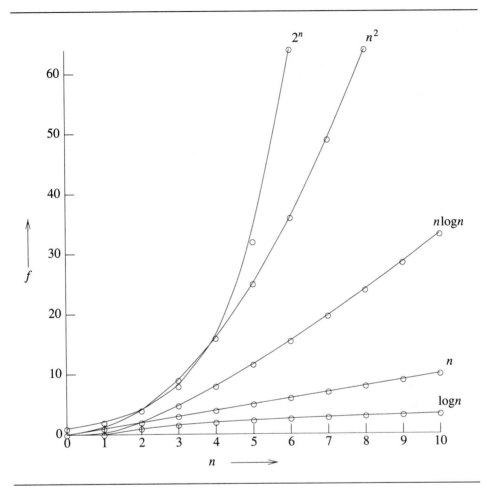

Figure 3.1 Plot of function values

Time for $f(n)$ instructions on a 10^9 instr/sec computer

n	$f(n)=n$	$f(n)=\log_2 n$	$f(n)=n^2$	$f(n)=n^3$	$f(n)=n^4$	$f(n)=n^{10}$	$f(n)=2^n$
10	.01µs	.03µs	.1µs	1µs	10µs	10sec	1µs
20	.02µs	.09µs	.4µs	8µs	160µs	2.84hr	1ms
30	.03µs	.15µs	.9µs	27µs	810µs	6.83d	1sec
40	.04µs	.21µs	1.6µs	64µs	2.56ms	121.36d	18.3min
50	.05µs	.28µs	2.5µs	125µs	6.25ms	3.1yr	13d
100	.10µs	.66µs	10µs	1ms	100ms	3171yr	$4*10^{13}$ yr
1,000	1.00µs	9.96µs	1ms	1sec	16.67min	$3.17*10^{13}$ yr	$32*10^{283}$ yr
10,000	10.00µs	130.03µs	100ms	16.67min	115.7d	$3.17*10^{23}$ yr	
100,000	100.00µs	1.66ms	10sec	11.57d	3171yr	$3.17*10^{33}$ yr	
1,000,000	1.00ms	19.92ms	16.67min	31.71yr	$3.17*10^7$ yr	$3.17*10^{43}$ yr	

µs = microsecond = 10^{-6} seconds
ms = millisecond = 10^{-3} seconds
sec = seconds
min = minutes
hr = hours
d = days
yr = years

Table 3.8 Times on a one billion instruction per second computer

3.3 PERFORMANCE MEASUREMENT

3.3.1 Introduction

Performance measurement is concerned with obtaining the actual space and time requirements of a program. These quantities are dependent on the particular compiler and options used as well as on the specific computer on which the program is run. Unless otherwise stated, all performance values provided in this book are obtained using the Turbo Pascal compiler; the default compiler options are used; and the computer used is an early model IBM-PC.

In keeping with the discussion of the preceding chapter, we shall not concern ourselves with the space and time needed for compilation. We justify this by the assumption that each program (after it has been fully debugged) will be compiled once and then executed several times. Certainly, the space and time needed for compilation are important during program testing when more time is spent on this task than in actually running the compiled code.

We shall not explicitly consider measuring the run time space requirements of a program. Rather, we shall focus on measuring the computing time of a program. In order to obtain the computing (or run) time of a program, we need a clocking procedure. Most Pascal implementations provide such a procedure. Since Turbo Pascal does not do this, we need to write our own procedure. It is possible to do this only because Turbo Pascal provides a system call procedure *MsDos*. Program 3.10 is a Pascal procedure that reads the IBM-PC clock and returns the time of day in hours, minutes, seconds, and hundredths of a second. To time a program, we need merely read the clock before the program is begun and after it has terminated. The elapsed time is the run time of our program.

Suppose we wish to measure the worst case performance of the sequential search procedure (Program 3.11). Before we can do this, we need to:

(1) Decide on the values of n for which the times are to be obtained

(2) Determine, for each of the above values of n, the data that exhibits the worst case behavior

The decision on which values of n to use is to be based on the amount of timing we wish to perform and also on what we expect to do with the times once they are obtained. Assume that for Program 3.11, our intent is to simply predict how long it will take, in the worst case, to search for x given the size n of a. An asymptotic analysis reveals that this time is $\Theta(n)$. So, we expect a plot of the times to be a straight line. Theoretically, if we know the times for any two values of n, the straight line is determined and we can obtain the time for all other values of n from this line. In practice, we need the times for more than two values of n. This is so for the following reasons:

```
procedure time (var h, m, s, f : integer);
{time of day in hours, minutes, seconds, and seconds/100}
type    twobyte = record L, H : byte; end;
        DosFunction = record {Function registers}
                        AX,BX,CX,DX,DI,SI,DS,ES,FLAG : twobyte;
                      end;
var timer: DosFunction;
begin
    timer.AX.H := 44; {IBM DOS clock read function number}
    timer.AX.L := 0;
    MsDos (timer);
    h := timer.CX.H; m := timer.CX.L;
    s := timer.DX.H; f := timer.DX.L;
end; {of time}
```

Program 3.10 Time procedure for Turbo Pascal

```
line  function seqsearch (a : ElementList ; n,x : integer): integer;
1     var i : integer;
2     begin
3       i := n; a [0] := x;
4       while a [i] <> x do
5         i := i−1;
6       seqsearch := i;
7     end; {of seqsearch}
```

Program 3.11 Sequential search

(1)   Asymptotic analysis only tells us the behavior for "sufficiently large" values of n. For smaller values of n the run time may not follow the asymptotic curve. To determine the point beyond which the asymptotic curve is followed, we need to examine the times for several values of n.

(2)   Even in the region where the asymptotic behavior is exhibited, the times may not lie exactly on the predicted curve (straight line in the case of Program 3.11) because of the effects of low order terms that are discarded in the asymptotic analysis. For instance, a program with asymptotic complexity $\Theta(n)$ can have an actual complexity that is $c_1 n + c_2 \log n + c_3$ or for that matter any other function

of n in which the highest order term is $c_1 n$ for some constant, $c_1, c_1 > 0$.

It is reasonable to expect that the asymptotic behavior of Program 3.11 will begin for some n that is smaller than 100. So, for $n > 100$ we shall obtain the run time for just a few values. A reasonable choice is $n = 200, 300, 400, \cdots, 1000$. There is nothing magical about this choice of values. We can just as well use $n = 500, 1000, 1500, \cdots,$ 10,000 or $n = 512, 1024, 2048, \cdots, 2^{15}$. It will cost us more in terms of computer time to use the latter choices and we will probably not get any better information about the run time of Program 3.11 using these choices.

For n in the range [0, 100] we shall carry out a more refined measurement as we aren't quite sure where the asymptotic behavior begins. Of course, if our measurements show that the straight line behavior doesn't begin in this range, we shall have to perform a more detailed measurement in the range [100, 200] and so on until the onset of this behavior is detected. Times in the range [0, 100] will be obtained in steps of 10 beginning at $n = 0$.

It is easy to see that Program 3.11 exhibits its worst case behavior when x is chosen such that it is not one of the $a[i]$s. For definiteness, we shall set $a[i] = i, 1 \leq i \leq n$ and $x = 0$.

At this time, we envision using a program such as the one given in Program 3.12 to obtain the worst case times.

The output obtained from this program is summarized in Figure 3.2 The times obtained are too small to be of any use to us. Most of the times are zero indicating that the precision of our clock is inadequate. The nonzero times are just noise and not representative of the actual time taken.

In order to time a short event, it is necessary to repeat it several times and divide the total time for the event by the number of repetitions.

Since our clock has an accuracy of about 1 hundredth of a second, we should not attempt to time any single event that takes less than about 1 second. With an event time of at least 1 second, we can expect our observed times to be accurate to 1 percent.

The body of Program 3.12 needs to be changed to that of Program 3.13. In this program, $r[i]$ is the number of times the search is to be repeated when the number of elements in the array is $n[i]$. Notice that rearranging the timing statements as in Programs 3.14 or 3.15 does not produce the desired results. For instance, from the data of Figure 3.2, we expect that with the structure of Program 3.14, the value output for $n = 0$ will still be 0. With the structure of Program 3.15, we expect the program to never exit the **while** loop when $n = 0$ (in reality, the loop will be exited as occasionally the measured time will turn out to be 5 or 6 hundredths of a second). Yet another alternative is to

---

```
program TimeSearch(input,output);
{Program to time Program 3.11}
type ElementList = array [0..1000] of integer;
var z : ElementList;
    i, j, k, h, m, s, f, h1, m1, s1, f1, t1 : integer;
    n : array [1..20] of integer;

{Procedure time and function seqsearch}
 .

 .

 .

begin {body of TimeSearch}
   for j := 1 to 1000 do {initialize z}
     z [j] := j;
   for j := 1 to 10 do {values of n}
   begin
     n [j] := 10*(j−1); n [j +10] := 100*j;
   end;
   writeln('n':5,' ','time');
   for j := 1 to 20 do {obtain computing times}
   begin
     time (h, m, s, f ); {get time}
     k := seqsearch (z, n [j], 0); {unsuccessful search}
     time (h1, m1, s1, f1); {get time}
     {time spent in hundredths of a second}
     t1 := (((h1−h)*60 + m1 − m)*60 + s1 − s)*100 +f1 − f;
     writeln(n [j]:5,' ',t1:5);
   end;
   writeln('Times are in hundredths of a second'};
end. {of TimeSearch}
```

Program 3.12 Program to time Program 3.11

move the first call to *time* out of the **while** loop of Program 3.15, and change the assignment to *t* within the **while** loop to

$$t := (((h1 − h)*60 + m1 − m)*60 + s1 − s)*100 +f1 − f;$$

This approach can be expected to yield satisfactory times. This approach cannot be used when the timing procedure available gives us only the time since the last invocation of *time*. Another difficulty is that the measured time includes the time needed to read the

n	Time	n	Time
0	0	100	0
10	6	200	5
20	0	300	6
30	0	400	0
40	0	500	0
50	0	600	0
60	5	700	0
70	0	800	0
80	0	900	6
90	5	1000	5

Times are in hundredths of a second

Figure 3.2 Output from Program 3.12

clock. For small n, this time may be larger than the time to run *search*. This difficulty can be overcome by determining the time taken by the timing procedure and subtracting this time later. In further discussion, we shall use the explicit repetition factor technique.

The output from the timing program, Program 3.13, is given in Figure 3.3. The times for n in the range [0, 100] are plotted in Figure 3.4. The remaining values have not been plotted as this would lead to severe compression of the range [0, 100]. The linear dependence of the worst case time on n is apparent from this graph.

The graph of Figure 3.4 can be used to predict the run time for other values of n. For example, we expect that when $n = 24$, the worst case search time will be 0.87 hundredths of a second. We can go one step further and get the equation of the straight line. The equation of this line is $t = c + mn$ where m is the slope and c the value for $n = 0$. From the graph, we see that $c = 0.78$. Using the point $n = 60$ and $t = 1.01$, we obtain $m = (t-c)/n = 0.23/60 = 0.00383$. So, the line of Figure 3.4 has the equation $t = 0.78 + 0.00383n$, where t is the time in hundredths of a second. From this, we expect that when $n = 1000$, the worst case search time will be 4.61 hsec and when $n = 500$, it will be 2.675 hsec. Comparing with the actual observed times of Figure 3.3, we see that these figures are very accurate!

An alternate approach to obtain a good straight line for the data of Figure 3.3 is to obtain the straight line that is the least squares approximation to the data. The result is $t = 0.77747 + 0.003806n$. When $n = 1000$ and 500, this equation yields $t = 4.583$ and 2.680.

```
{repetition factors}
const r: array[1..20] of integer =
        (700, 700, 600, 600, 600, 600, 500, 500, 500, 500, 500,
        400, 400, 300, 300, 200, 200, 200, 100, 100);
begin {body of TimeSearch}
   for j := 1 to 1000 do {initialize z}
     z[j] := j;
   for j := 1 to 10 do {values of n}
   begin
     n[j] := 10*(j−1); n[j+10] := 100*j;
   end;

   writeln('n':5,' ','t 1',' ','t');
   for j := 1 to 20 do {obtain computing times}
   begin
     time (h, m, s, f); {get time}
     for b := 1 to r[j] do
       k := seqsearch (z, n[j], 0); {unsuccessful search}
     time (h 1, m 1, s 1, f1); {get time}
     {time spent in hundredths of a second}
     t 1 := (((h 1−h)*60 + m 1 − m)*60 + s 1 − s)*100 + f1 − f;
     t := t 1; t := t/r[j]; {time per search}
     writeln(n[j]:5,' ',t 1:5, t:8:3);
   end;
   writeln('Times are in hundredths of a second'};
end. {of TimeSearch}
```

Program 3.13 Timing program

Now, we are probably ready to pat ourselves on the back for a job well done. This action is somewhat premature as our experiment is flawed. First, the measured time includes the time taken by the repetition **for** loop. So, the times of Figure 3.3 are excessive. This can be corrected by determining the time for each iteration of this statement. A quick test run indicates that 30,000 executions take only 65 hundredths of a second. So, subtracting the time for the **for** $b := 1$ **to** $r[j]$ **do** statement reduces the reported times by only 0.002. We can ignore this difference as the use of a higher repetition factor could well result in measured times that are lower by about 0.002 hsec per search. Our times are not accurate to a hundredth of a second and it is not very meaningful to worry about the 2 hundredths of a second spent on each repetition.

```
t := 0;
for b := 1 to r [j] do
begin
    time (h, m, s, f );
    k := seqsearch (a, n [j], 0);
    time (h 1, m 1, s 1, f1);
    t := t + (((h 1 − h)*60 + m 1 − m)*60 + s 1 − s)*100 + f1 − f;
end;
t := t/r [j ];
```

Program 3.14 Improper timing construct

```
t := 0; i := 0;
while t < DesiredTime do
begin
    time (h, m, s, f );
    k := seqsearch (a, n [j], 0);
    time (h 1, m 1, s 1, f1);
    t := t + (((h 1 − h)*60 + m 1 − m)*60 + s 1 − s)*100 + f1 − f;
    i := i +1;
end;
t := t/i;
```

Program 3.15 Another improper timing construct

The second and more serious problem is caused by the fact that *ElementList* has been defined to be an array of size 1000. Consequently, each invocation of *seqsearch* begins by copying the 1000 values of the actual parameter z into the value formal parameter a. The measured times are therefore representative of the actual time to use *seqsearch* only when *ElementList* is of this size! If the size of *ElementList* is changed to 2000 or 10000, the measured times will change. A substantial part of the time reported in this figure is the time spent copying the 1000 elements of the actual parameter into the formal parameter.

So, what constitutes a meaningful test for Program 3.11? The size of *ElementList* isn't known to us, and yet it is perhaps the most important factor. The realization that the worst case run time of Program 3.11 is a function of both n and s (the size of *ElementList*, i.e., 1001 in the case of Program 3.12) motivates us to obtain the time for the body of Program 3.11 and that for its invocation separately. The former is independent of s and the latter is independent of n. The total time to use Program 3.11 is the sum

n	$t1$	t	n	$t1$	t
0	549	0.784	100	582	1.164
10	571	0.816	200	615	1.537
20	516	0.860	300	763	1.907
30	539	0.898	400	686	2.287
40	555	0.925	500	801	2.670
50	583	0.972	600	610	3.050
60	505	1.010	700	687	3.435
70	522	1.044	800	758	3.790
80	538	1.076	900	826	4.230
90	566	1.132	1000	922	4.610

Times are in hundredths of a second

Figure 3.3 Worst case run times for Program 3.11

of these two times.

To obtain the time for the body of Program 3.11, we place the timing loop directly into function *seqsearch* as in Program 3.16. This is preferable to placing the code of *seqsearch* directly into the body of *TimeSearch*. This is because the strategy of Program 3.16 yields times that include the overhead of using parameters.

When Program 3.16 is used in place of Program 3.11, and the timing and repetition statements removed from Program 3.12, the times shown in Figure 3.5 are obtained. The repetition factors used are $r[1..20]$ = [32000, 12000, 6000, 5000, 4000, 3000, 2500, 2000, 2000, 1500, 1500, 800, 600, 500, 400, 300, 200, 200, 150, 150].

The time of 0.002 for each execution of the repetition **for** statement needs to be subtracted from the times of Figure 3.5. This subtraction has a material effect (i.e., at least 10 percent) only on the time for $n = 0$.

To time the invocation of Program 3.11 for different sizes s of *ElementList*, we delete all statements between the **begin** and **end** statements of Program 3.11 and run Program 3.12 for different values of s. The repetition factor needed varies with s. The observed times for various values of s are shown in Figure 3.6. Again, the time for the repetition **for** loop has not been subtracted. This does not materially affect the times shown.

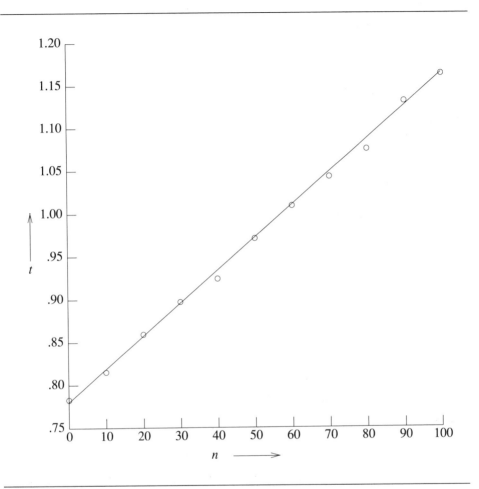

Figure 3.4 Plot of the data in Figure 3.3

The least squares straight line for the data of Figure 3.5 is $t = 0.008531 + 0.003785n$ and that for Figure 3.6 is $t = 0.018009 + 0.000756s$. Adding these two contributions, we get $t = 0.02654 + 0.000756s + 0.003785n$. We can see how good this equation is in predicting actual run times by using it with $s = 1000$. The equation becomes $t = 0.78254 + 0.003785n$. This is quite close to the least squares line for the data of Program 3.12.

Note that we can make the run time of *seqsearch* independent of s by making a a variable formal parameter.

```
function seqsearch (a : ElementList ; n,x : integer): integer;
var i, k : integer;
begin
    time (h, m, s, f ); {get time}
    for k := 1 to r [j] do {r [j] is global}
    begin
        i := n; a [0] := x;
        while a [i] <> x do
            i := i−1;
        seqsearch := i;
    end; {of repetition for}
    time (h 1, m 1, s 1, f1); {get time}
    {time spent in hundredths of a second}
    t 1 := (((h 1−h)*60 + m 1 − m)*60 + s 1 − s)*100 + f1 − f;
    t := t 1; t := t/r [j]; {time per search}
    writeln(n [j]:5,' ',t 1:5, t:8:3);
end; {of seqsearch}
```

Program 3.16 Timing the body of *seqsearch*

n	$t1$	t	n	$t1$	t
0	275	0.009	100	583	0.389
10	560	0.047	200	610	0.762
20	511	0.085	300	687	1.145
30	610	0.122	400	764	1.528
40	643	0.161	500	758	1.895
50	594	0.198	600	686	2.287
60	593	0.237	700	527	2.635
70	544	0.272	800	609	3.045
80	626	0.313	900	511	3.407
90	522	0.348	1000	571	3.807

Times in hundredths of a second

Figure 3.5 Times for body of Program 3.11 using Program 3.16

s	r	time	time/r
10	30,000	769	0.026
20	30,000	999	0.033
30	30,000	1225	0.041
40	20,000	967	0.048
50	12,000	670	0.056
60	12,000	767	0.064
70	10,000	714	0.071
80	10,000	791	0.079
90	10,000	862	0.086
100	10,000	939	0.094
200	5,000	846	0.169
500	2,000	795	0.398
1000	1,000	774	0.774
5000	200	758	3.790
10,000	100	758	7.58

Times are in hundredths of a second

Figure 3.6 Time needed to invoke Program 3.11

Summary

In order to obtain the run time of a program, we need to plan the experiment. The following issues need to be addressed during the planning stage:

(1) What is the accuracy of the clock? How accurate do our results have to be? Once the desired accuracy is known, we can determine the length of the shortest event that should be timed.

(2) For each instance size, a repetition factor needs to be determined. This is to be chosen such that the event time is at least the minimum time that can be clocked with the desired accuracy.

(3) Are we measuring worst case or average case performance? Suitable test data needs to be generated.

(4) What is the purpose of the experiment? Are the times being obtained for comparative purposes or are they to be used to predict actual run times? If the latter is the case, then contributions to the run time from such sources as the repetition loop and data generation need to be subtracted (in case they are included in the measured time). If the former is the case, then these times need not be subtracted (provided they are the same for all programs being compared).

(5) In case the times are to be used to predict actual run times, then we need to fit a curve through the points. For this, the asymptotic complexity should be known. If the asymptotic complexity is linear, then a least squares straight line can be fit; if it is quadratic, then a parabola is to be used (i.e., $t = a_0 + a_1 n + a_2 n^2$); etc. If the complexity is $\Theta(n \log n)$, then a least squares curve of the form $t = a_0 + a_1 n + a_2 n \log_2 n$ can be fit. The mathematics needed to fit a curve that is the least squares approximation to the observed data is developed in Appendix A. When obtaining the least squares approximation, one should discard data corresponding to "small" values of n as the program does not exhibit its asymptotic behavior for these n.

3.3.2 Generating Test Data

Generating a data set that results in the worst case performance of a program isn't always easy. In some cases, it is necessary to use a computer program to generate the worst case data. In other cases, even this is very difficult. In these cases, another approach to estimating worst case performance is taken. For each set of values of the instance characteristics of interest, we generate a suitably large number of random test data. The run times for each of these test data are obtained. The maximum of these times is used as an estimate of the worst case time for this set of values of the instance characteristics.

To measure average case times, it is usually not possible to average over all possible instances of a given characteristic. While it is possible to do this for sequential and binary search, it is not possible for a sort program. If we assume that all keys are distinct, then for any given n, $n!$ different permutations need to be used to obtain the average time.

Obtaining average case data is usually much harder than obtaining worst case data. So, we often adopt the strategy outlined above and simply obtain an estimate of the average time.

Whether we are estimating worst case or average time using random data, the number of instances that we can try is generally much smaller than the total number of such instances. Hence, it is desirable to analyze the algorithm being tested to determine classes of data that should be generated for the experiment. This is a very algorithm specific task and we shall not go into it here.

3.4 REFERENCES AND SELECTED READINGS

Some entertaining articles on the analysis of programs are:

Algorithms, by D. Knuth, Scientific American, April 1977.

Computer science and its relation to mathematics, by D. Knuth, Amer. Math. Monthly, April, 1974.

Our definitions of O, Ω, and Θ are due to D. Knuth and appear in:

Big omichron, big omega, and big theta, by D. Knuth, SIGACT News, ACM, April 1971.

For a more detailed discussion of performance analysis and measurement, see the text:

Software development in Pascal, by S. Sahni, Camelot Publishing Co., Minnesota, 1985.

The following books contain several programs for which asymptotic analyses are also provided:

Fundamentals of computer algorithms, by E. Horowitz and S. Sahni, Computer Science Press, Inc., Maryland, 1978.

Fundamentals of data structures in Pascal, by E. Horowitz and S. Sahni, Computer Science Press, Inc., Maryland, 1984.

The design and analysis of computer algorithms, by A. Aho, J. Hopcroft, and J. Ullman, Addison-Wesley, Massachusetts, 1974.

Combinatorial algorithms, by E. Reingold, J. Nievergelt, and N. Deo, Prentice Hall, New Jersey, 1977.

and

Concepts in discrete mathematics, 2nd edition, by S. Sahni, Camelot Publishing Co., Fridley, Minnesota, 1985.

3.5 EXERCISES

1. Obtain $S_P(n)$ for Program 2.1.

2. Obtain $S_P(n)$ for Program 2.2.

3. (a) Introduce statements to increment *count* at all appropriate points in Program 3.17.

```
procedure d (var x : list ; n : integer);
var i : integer;
begin
  i := 1;
  repeat
    x [i ] := x [i ] + 2;
    i := i + 2;
  until (i > n);
  i := 1;
  while i <= (n div 2) do
  begin
    x [i ] := x [i ] + x [i +1];
    i := i + 1;
  end;
end; {of d}
```

Program 3.17

(b) Simplify the resulting program by eliminating statements. The simplified program should compute the same value for *count* as computed by the program of (a).

(c) What is the exact value of *count* when the program terminates? You may assume that the initial value of *count* is 0.

(d) Obtain the step count for Program 3.17 using the frequency method. Clearly show the step count table.

4. Do Exercise 3 parts (a)-(c) for procedure *transpose* (Program 3.18).

5. Do Exercise 3 for Program 3.19. This program multiplies two $n \times n$ matrices a and b.

6. (a) Do Exercise 3 for Program 3.20. This program multiplies two matrices a and b where a is an $m \times n$ matrix and b is an $n \times p$ matrix.

line	**procedure** *transpose*(**var** *a* : *matrix*; *n* : **integer**);
1	**var** *i*, *j* : **integer**; *t* : *element*;
2	**begin**
3	**for** *i* := 1 **to** *n*−1 **do**
4	**for** *j* := *i*+1 **to** *n* **do**
5	**begin**
6	*t* := *a*[*i*,*j*]; *a*[*i*,*j*] := *a*[*j*,*i*]; *a*[*j*,*i*] := *t*;
7	**end**;
8	**end**; {of *transpose*}

Program 3.18

```
procedure mult (var a, b, c : matrix; n : integer);
var i, j, k : integer;
begin
  for i := 1 to n do
    for j := 1 to n do
    begin
      c [i,j] := 0;
      for k := 1 to n do
        c [i,j] := c [i,j] + a [i,k] * b [k,j];
    end;
end; {of mult}
```

Program 3.19

(b) Under what conditions will it be profitable to interchange the two outermost **for** loops?

7. Show that the following equalities are correct:

(a) $5n^2 - 6n = \Theta(n^2)$

(b) $n! = O(n^n)$

(c) $2n^2 2^n + n\log n = \Theta(n^2 2^n)$

(d) $\sum_{i=0}^{n} i^2 = \Theta(n^3)$

(e) $\sum_{i=0}^{n} i^3 = \Theta(n^4)$

(f) $n^{2^n} + 6*2^n = \Theta(2^{2^n})$

(g) $n^3 + 10^6 n^2 = \Theta(n^3)$

(h) $6n^3/(\log n + 1) = O(n^3)$

```
procedure prod (var a, b, c : matrix; m, n, p : integer);
var i, j, k : integer;
begin
   for i := 1 to m do
      for j := 1 to p do
      begin
         c [i,j] := 0;
         for k := 1 to n do
            c [i,j] := c [i,j] + a [i,k] * b [k,j];
      end;
end; {of prod}
```

Program 3.20

(i) $n^{1.001} + n\log n = \Theta(n^{1.001})$

(j) $n^{k+\varepsilon} + n^k \log n = \Theta(n^{k+\varepsilon})$ for all k and ε, $k \geq 0$, and $\varepsilon > 0$.

(k) $10n^3 + 15n^4 + 100n^2 2^n = O(100n^2 2^n)$

(l) $33n^3 + 4n^2 = \Omega(n^2)$

(m) $33n^3 + 4n^2 = \Omega(n^3)$

8. Show that the following equalities are incorrect:
   (a) $10n^2 + 9 = O(n)$
   (b) $n^2 \log n = \Theta(n^2)$
   (c) $n^2/\log n = \Theta(n^2)$
   (d) $n^3 2^n + 6n^2 3^n = O(n^3 2^n)$

9. Obtain the average run time of procedure *BinarySearch* of Chapter 2. Do this for suitable values of n in the range [0, 100]. Your report must include a plan for the experiment as well as the measured times. These times are to be provided both in a table and as a graph.

10. Obtain worst case run times for procedure *sort* (see Chapter 2, Program 2.7). Do this for suitable values of n in the range [0, 100]. Your report must include a plan for the experiment as well as the measured times. These times are to be provided both in a table and as a graph.

11. Consider procedure *add* (Program 3.7).
    (a) Obtain run times for $n = 1, 10, 20, ..., 100$.
    (b) Plot the times obtained in part (a).

12. Do the previous exercise for matrix multiplication (Program 3.20).

CHAPTER 4
ARRAYS

4.1 A SALES EXAMPLE

The array is the most elementary data structuring tool provided in programming languages. Hence, it is appropriate that we begin our study of data structures by examining several examples that are efficiently solved using arrays. In this section, we develop a program to input sales data and output a sales summary.

Problem Specification

The Widget Sales Company has sales offices in several states. Each week, corporate headquarters receives sales data from the different states. The data consists of several lines ordered by state. Each line contains a state code, an item name, and the dollar value of the item sold on each of the days of the week. The sales report to be generated by the computer can be divided into two parts. These are shown in Figures 4.1 and 4.2, respectively. The first part lists the daily sales of each item in each state together with the total sales of each item. In addition, a summary line is included for each state. This provides the dollar value of all sales in the state for each day together with the total sales for the week. The second part provides a summary of nationwide sales by day and total national sales for the week.

Program Development

We assume that the input sales data resides in the file: sdata. Our first attempt at the sales data program may result in the high level program given in Program 4.1. An analysis of this program reveals that its memory requirement is proportional to the amount of input data. If our Widget Sales Company deals in (say) ten thousand items and operates in 50 states, then we may expect 500,000 lines of input with each line

Sales Report For Week Of April 6, 1987

State = OH

item	Sun	Mon	Tu	Wed	Th	Fri	Sat	total
screws	100.50	257.80	330.95	121.98	73.89	454.88	876.21	2216.21
.	.	.	.	.	.	.	.	.
.	.	.	.	.	.	.	.	.
.	.	.	.	.	.	.	.	.

Totals for OH
| | . | . | . | . | . | . | . | . |

State = MN

item	Sun	Mon	Tu	Wed	Th	Fri	Sat	total
screws	10.50	57.80	30.95	124.98	173.89	45.88	822.21	1266.21
.	.	.	.	.	.	.	.	.
.	.	.	.	.	.	.	.	.
.	.	.	.	.	.	.	.	.

Totals for MN
| | . | . | . | . | . | . | . | . |

.
.
.

Figure 4.1 First part of sales report

Summary of Nationwide Sales for Week of April 6, 1987

Sun	Mon	Tu	Wed	Th	Fri	Sat	Total
10221.34	21324.88	8453.44	9877.54	4445.22	44562.22	98652.32	197536.96

Figure 4.2 Second part of report

having nine pieces of data (state, item, and sales for each of 7 days). While this much data will not fit onto a floppy, it will fit into a hard disk. This much data will certainly not fit into the RAM of our PC. Fortunately, there is another way to solve our problem. This new solution requires very little memory.

```
program SalesReport (input, output, sdata);
{Generate weekly nationwide sales report}
begin
    input sales data from file sdata;
    generate sales report;
    output sales report;
end.
```

Program 4.1 First attempt at sales report program

In the memory thrifty scheme to generate the sales report, the three tasks input data, generate sales report, and output sales report, are performed concurrently. Each time a line of data is input, as much of the sales report as possible is generated and output. With this strategy, we obtain the pseudo-Pascal code of Program 4.2. Program 4.3 is a refined version of Program 4.2. In this refinement, we have replaced the English statements by procedure calls. In addition, some initialization statements have been included. We now proceed to develop the procedures used in the current refinement of our program.

In order to output the state and national summaries, we need to keep two sets of data. The first gives us the total daily sales so far output for the state. The second gives us the total daily sales so far output for all states other than the current state. Additionally, we need to input the sales figures from the new data line. For these three data sets, we utilize three arrays: *StateSales*, *NationalSales*, and *NewLineSales*. These are declared as below:

```
type DaysOfWeek = (Sun, Mon, Tu, Wed, Th, Fri, Sat);
     SalesArray = array[DaysOfWeek] of real;
var StateSales, NationalSales, NewLineSales: SalesArray;
```

With these decisions made, we may refine Program 4.3 and obtain Program 4.4 The six procedures used in Program 4.4 together with other required procedures are given in Programs 4.5 through 4.12. The input and output procedures are quite straightforward. The development of more user friendly ones is left as an exercise.

```
program SalesReport (input, output, sdata);
{Generate weekly nationwide sales report}
begin
input sales week;
   while not eof (sdata) do
   begin
      input a line of data from sdata;
      if this is for a new state then
      begin
         output summary line for current state;
         begin a new state;
      end
      else continue current state;
   end;
   output summary line for current state;
   output nationwide sales summary;
end.
```

Program 4.2 Memory thrifty sales report program

4.2 ORDERED LISTS AND POLYNOMIALS

One of the simplest and most commonly found data object is the ordered or linear list. Examples are the days of the week

(MONDAY, TUESDAY, WEDNESDAY, THURSDAY, FRIDAY, SATURDAY, SUNDAY)

or the values in a card deck

(2, 3, 4, 5, 6, 7, 8, 9, 10, Jack, Queen, King, Ace)

or the floors of a building

(basement, lobby, mezzanine, first, second, third)

or the years the United States fought in World War II

(1941, 1942, 1943, 1944, 1945)

If we consider an ordered list more abstractly, we say that it is either empty, written as (),

```
program SalesReport (input, output, sdata, LPT1);
{Generate weekly nationwide sales report}
var CurrentState, state: string[2];
    SalesFile: text;
begin
   assign (SalesFile, sdata);
   reset (SalesFile);
   InputWeek;
   CurrentState := ' ';
   while not eof (SalesFile) do
   begin
      InputLine;
      if state <> CurrentState then
      begin
         OutputStateSummary;
         BeginNewState;
      end
      else ContinueCurrentState;
   end;
   OutputStateSummary;
   OutputNationalSummary;
   close (SalesFile);
end.
```

Program 4.3 Refined version of Program 4.2

or it can be written as

$$(a_1, a_2, a_3, ..., a_n)$$

where the a_i are atoms from some set S.

There are a variety of operations that are performed on these lists. These operations include:

(1)   Find the length, n, of the list

(2)   Read the list from left to right (or right to left)

(3)   Retrieve the i'th element, $1 \le i \le n$

(4)   Store a new value into the i'th position, $1 \le i \le n$

```
program SalesReport (input, output, sdata, LPT1);
{Generate weekly nationwide sales report}
const WeekSize := 20; {characters in report week}
      ItemSize := 10; {characters in item name}
      FieldSize := 9; {size of an output field}
type DaysOfWeek = (Sun, Mon, Tu, Wed, Th, Fri, Sat);
     SalesArray = array[DaysOfWeek] of real;
var StateSales, NationalSales, NewLineSales : SalesArray;
    SalesWeek : string[WeekSize ]; CurrentState, state : string[2];
    item : string[ItemSize ];
    SalesFile, OutFile : text;
    LineLength : integer; {length of an output line}
begin
  LineLength := 8*FieldSize + ItemSize;
  assign (SalesFile,'sdata');
  reset (SalesFile );
  assign (OutFile, 'LPT1'); {output to printer}
  rewrite (OutFile );
  InputWeek;
  CurrentState := ' ';
  while not eof (SalesFile ) do
  begin
    InputLine;
    if state <> CurrentState then
    begin
      OutputStateSummary;
      BeginNewState;
    end
    else ContinueCurrentState;
  end;
  OutputStateSummary;
  OutputNationalSummary;
  close (SalesFile );
  close (OutFile );
end.
```

Program 4.4 Refined version of Program 4.3

```
procedure OutputLine;
{Output a line of dashes}
var i : integer;
begin
   for i := 1 to LineLength do write(OutFile, '_');
   writeln(OutFile);
end; {of OutputLine}
```

Program 4.5 Output a line of dashes

```
procedure OutputWeekDays;
{Output a header line with days of week and total}
const WeekDays: array [DaysOfWeek] of string [FieldSize]
              = ('Sun', 'Mon', 'Tu', 'Wed', 'Th', 'Fri', 'Sat');
var i : DaysOfWeek;
begin
   for i := Sun to Sat do
      write(OutFile, WeekDays [i]: FieldSize );
   writeln(OutFile, 'total': FieldSize );
end; {of OutputWeekDays}
```

Program 4.6 Output a header line

```
procedure InputWeek;
{Input week for sales report and print report header}
begin
   writeln('Welcome to the report generator');
   writeln('Enter the report week as: Month, Day, Year');
   readln(SalesWeek);
   OutputLine;
   writeln(OutFile, 'Sales Report For Week Of ', SalesWeek);
end; {of InputWeek}
```

Program 4.7 Input sales week and print report header

```
procedure InputLine;
{Input a line of data}
var i : DaysOfWeek;
begin
   read(SalesFile, state, item);
   for i := Sun to Sat do
      read(SalesFile, NewLineSales [i ]);
   readln(SalesFile);
end; {of InputLine}
```

Program 4.8 Input a line of sales data

```
procedure OutputStateSummary;
{Print sales summary for the current state and update NationalSales}
var i : DaysOfWeek; total: real;
begin
   if CurrentState <> ' ' then
   begin
      OutputLine;
      writeln(OutFile, 'Totals for ', CurrentState);
      write(OutFile, ' ':FieldSize); {space to correct position}

      {Print daily totals, update NationalSales, and compute weekly total}
      total := 0;
      for i := Sun to Sat do
      begin
         write(OutFile, StateSales [i ]: FieldSize :2);
         total := total + StateSales [i ];
         NationalSales [i ] := NationalSales [i ] + StateSales [i ];
      end;
      writeln(OutFile, total: FieldSize :2);
   end {of then clause}
   else for i := Sun to Sat do NationalSales [i ] := 0;
end; {of OutputStateSummary}
```

Program 4.9 Print state sales summary

```
procedure BeginNewState;
{Reset variables for new state, print state header
and sales line for newly input data}
var i : DaysOfWeek; total: real;
begin
    {Print header for new state}
    writeln(OutFile);
    writeln(OutFile, 'State = ', state);
    writeln(OutFile);
    write(OutFile, 'item':ItemSize);
    OutputWeekDays;
    OutputLine;
    write(OutFile, item:ItemSize);

    {Initialize StateSales and print first sales line for new state}
    total := 0;
    for i := Sun to Sat do
    begin
        StateSales [i ] := NewLineSales [i ];
        write(OutFile, NewLineSales [i ]: FieldSize :2);
        total := total + NewLineSales [i ];
    end;
    writeln(OutFile, total: FieldSize :2);

    CurrentState := state;
end; {of BeginNewState}
```

Program 4.10 Initialize for new state

(5)   Insert a new element at the position i, $1 \leq i \leq n + 1$ causing elements numbered $i, i + 1 ..., n$ to become numbered $i + 1, i + 2, ..., n + 1$

(6)   Delete the element at position i, $1 \leq i \leq n$ causing elements numbered $i + 1, ..., n$ to become numbered $i, i + 1, ..., n - 1$

It is not always necessary to be able to perform all of these operations; many times a subset will suffice. In the study of data structures we are interested in ways of representing ordered lists so that these operations can be carried out efficiently.

Perhaps the most common way to represent an ordered list is by an array where we associate the list element a_i with the array index i. This we will refer to as *sequential mapping*, because using the conventional array representation we are storing a_i and a_{i+1}

```
procedure ContinueCurrentState;
{Another data line for the current state}
var i : DaysOfWeek; total: real;
begin
    {Print the sales line and add sales data to StateSales}
    write(OutFile, item : Itemsize);
    total := 0;
    for i := Sun to Sat do
    begin
        StateSales [i] := StateSales [i] + NewLineSales [i];
        write(OutFile, NewLineSales [i]: FieldSize :2);
        total := total + NewLineSales [i];
    end;
    writeln(OutFile, total: FieldSize :2);
end; {of ContinueCurrentSales}
```

Program 4.11 More sales for the current state

```
program OutputNationalSummary;
{Print nationwide sales figures}
var i : DaysOfWeek; total: real;
begin
    writeln(OutFile);
    OutputLine;
    writeln(OutFile, '    Summary of nationwide sales for week of ', SalesWeek);
    writeln(OutFile);
    OutputWeekDays;
    total := 0;
    for i := Sun to Sat do
    begin
        write(OutFile, NationalSales [i]: FieldSize :2);
        total := total + NationalSales [i];
    end;
    writeln(OutFile, total: FieldSize :2);
    OutputLine
end; {of OutputNationalSummary}
```

Program 4.12 Print nationwide sales summary

into consecutive locations i and $i + 1$ of the array. This gives us the ability to retrieve or modify the values of random elements in the list in a constant amount of time, essentially because a computer memory has random access to any word. We can access the list element values in either direction by changing the subscript values in a controlled way. It is only operations (5) and (6) which require real effort. Insertion and deletion using sequential allocation forces us to move some of the remaining elements so that sequential mapping is preserved in its proper form. It is precisely this overhead which leads us to consider nonsequential mappings of ordered lists in Chapter 6.

Let us jump right into a problem requiring ordered lists which we will solve by using one-dimensional arrays. This problem has become the classical example for motivating the use of list processing techniques which we will see in later chapters. Therefore, it makes sense to look at the problem and see why arrays offer only a partially adequate solution. The problem calls for building a set of subroutines which allow for the manipulation of symbolic polynomials. By "symbolic," we mean the list of coefficients and exponents which accompany a polynomial, e.g., two such polynomials are

$$A(x) = 3x^2 + 2x + 4 \text{ and } B(x) = x^4 + 10x^3 + 3x^2 + 1$$

For a start, the capabilities we would include are the four basic arithmetic operations: addition, subtraction, multiplication, and division. We will also need input and output routines and some suitable format for preparing polynomials as input. The first step is to consider how to define polynomials as a computer structure. For a mathematician a polynomial is a sum of terms where each term has a form ax^e; x is the variable, a is the coefficient, and e is the exponent. However, this is not an appropriate definition for our purposes. When defining a data object you must decide what functions will be available, what their input is, what their output is, and exactly what it is that they do.

One way to represent polynomials in Pascal is to define the data type *poly*:

```
type poly = record
            degree : 0..maxdegree;
            coef : array[0..maxdegree] of real;
        end;
```

where *maxdegree* is a constant representing the largest degree polynomial that is to be represented. Now, if a is of type *poly* and $n \leq maxdegree$, then the polynomial $A(x)$ above would be represented as

$a.degree = n$

$a.coef[i] = a_{n-i}, \ 0 \leq i \leq n$

Note that $a.coef[i]$ is the coefficient of x^{n-i} and the coefficients are stored in order of decreasing exponents. This representation leads to very simple algorithms for many of the operations you wish to perform on polynomials (addition, subtraction, evaluation, multiplication, etc.). It is, however, quite wasteful in its use of computer memory. For instance, if $a.degree \ll maxdegree$, (the double less than should be read as "is much less than"), then most of the positions in $a.coef[0..maxdegree]$ are unused. To avoid this waste, we would like to be able to define the data type *poly* using variable sized records as below:

type *poly* = **record**
        degree : 0..*maxint*;
        coef : **array**[0..*degree*] **of real**;
     end;

Such a declaration is, of course, not permitted in standard or Turbo Pascal. While such a type definition solves the problem mentioned earlier, it does not yield a desirable representation. To see this, let us consider polynomials that have many zero terms. Such polynomials are called *sparse*. For instance, the polynomial $x^{1000} + 1$ has two nonzero terms and 999 zero terms. Using variable sized records as above, 999 of the entries in *coef* will be zero.

Suppose we take the polynomial $A(x)$ above and keep only its nonzero coefficients. Then we will really have the polynomial

$$b_{m-1}x^{e_{m-1}} + b_{m-2}x^{e_{m-2}} + \cdots + b_0x^{e_0}$$

where each b_i is a nonzero coefficient of A and the exponents e_i are decreasing $e_{m-1} > e_{m-2} > \cdots > e_0 \geq 0$. If all of A's coefficients are nonzero, then $m = n + 1$, $e_i = i$, and $b_i = a_i$ for $0 \leq i \leq n$. Alternatively, only a_n may be nonzero, in which case $m = 1$, $b_0 = a_n$, and $e_0 = n$.

All our polynomials will be represented in a global array called *terms* that is defined as below:

type *term* = **record**
        coef : **real**; {coefficient}
        exp : 0..**maxint**; {exponent}
     end;
var *terms* : **array**[1..*maxterms*] **of** *term*;

where *maxterms* is a constant.

Consider the two polynomials $A(x) = 2x^{1000} + 1$ and $B(x) = x^4 + 10x^3 + 3x^2 + 1$. These could be stored in the array *terms* as shown in Figure 4.3. Note that *af* and *bf* give the location of the first term of *A* and *B*, respectively, while *al* and *bl* give the location of the last term of *A* and *B*. *free* gives the location of the next free location in the array *terms*. For our example, $af = 1$, $al = 2$, $bf = 3$, $bl = 6$, and *free* = 7.

	$\overset{af}{\downarrow}$	$\overset{al}{\downarrow}$	$\overset{bf}{\downarrow}$			$\overset{bl}{\downarrow}$	$\overset{free}{\downarrow}$
coef	2	1	1	10	3	1	
exp	1000	0	4	3	2	0	
	1	2	3	4	5	6	7

Figure 4.3 Array representation of two polynomials

This representation scheme does not impose any limit on the number of polynomials that can be stored in *terms*. Rather, the total number of nonzero terms in all the polynomials together cannot exceed *maxterms*.

Is this representation any better than the one that used records with large array size? Well, it certainly solves our problem when many zero terms are present. $A(x) = 2x^{1000} + 1$ uses only 6 units of space (one for *af*, one for *al*, two for the coefficients, and two for the exponents). However, when all terms are nonzero as in $B(x)$ above, the new scheme uses about twice as much space as the previous one that used variable sized records. Unless we know beforehand that each of our polynomials has very few zero terms in it, the representation using the array *terms* will be preferred.

When the global array *terms* is used, a polynomial $D(x) = 0$ with no nonzero terms will have *df* and *dl* such that $dl = df - 1$. In general, a polynomial E that has n nonzero terms will have *ef* and *el* such that $el = ef + n - 1$.

Let us now write a Pascal procedure to add two polynomials *A* and *B* represented as above to obtain the sum $C = A + B$. Procedure *padd* (Program 4.13) adds $A(x)$ and $B(x)$ term by term to produce $C(x)$. The terms of *C* are entered into the array *terms* starting at the position *free* (procedure *newterm*, Program 4.14). In case there isn't enough space in *terms* to accommodate *C*, an error message is printed and the program terminates.

```
1  procedure padd (af,al,bf,bl : integer; var cf,cl : integer);
2  {add A (x) and B (x) to get C (x)}
3  var p,q : integer; c : real;
4  begin
5      p := af; q := bf; cf := free;
6      while (p <= al) and (q <= bl) do
7        case compare (terms [p ].exp, terms [q ].exp) of
8          '=': begin
9              c := terms [p ].coef + terms [q ].coef;
10             if c <> 0 then newterm (c, terms [p ].exp);
11             p := p + 1; q := q + 1;
12           end;
13          '<': begin
14             newterm (terms [q ].coef, terms [q ].exp);
15             q := q + 1;
16           end;
17          '>': begin
18             newterm (terms [p ].coef, terms [p ].exp);
19             p := p + 1;
20           end;
21        end; {of case and while}
22      {add in remaining terms of A (x)}
23      while p <= al do
24      begin
25        newterm (terms [p ].coef, terms [p ].exp);
26        p := p + 1;
27      end;
28      {add in remaining terms of B (x)}
29      while q <= bl do
30      begin
31        newterm (terms [q ].coef, terms [q ].exp);
32        q := q + 1;
33      end;
34      cl := free − 1;
35  end; {of padd}
```

Program 4.13 Procedure to add two polynomials

```
procedure newterm (c : real; e :integer);
{add a new term to C (x)}
begin
  if free > maxterms
  then begin
          writeln('too many terms in polynomials');
          halt; {terminate program}
       end;
  terms [free].coef := c;
  terms [free].exp := e;
  free := free + 1;
end; {of newterm}
```

Program 4.14 Procedure to add a new term

Let us now analyze the computing time of this algorithm. It is natural to carry out this analysis in terms of the number of nonzero terms in A and B. Let m and n be the number of nonzero terms in A and B, respectively. The assignments of line 5 are made only once and hence contribute O(1) to the overall computing time. If either $n = 0$ or $m = 0$, the **while** loop of line 6 is not executed.

In case neither m nor n equals zero, the **while** loop of line 6 is entered. Each iteration of the **while** loop requires O(1) time. At each iteration, either the value of p or q or both increases by 1. Since the iteration terminates when either p or q exceeds al or bl, respectively, the number of iterations is bounded by $m+n-1$. This worst case is achieved, for instance, when $A(x) = \sum_{i=0}^{n} x^{2i}$ and $B(x) = \sum_{i=0}^{n} x^{2i+1}$. Since none of the exponents are the same in A and B, $terms[p].exp \neq terms[q].exp$. Consequently, on each iteration the value of only one of p or q increases by 1. So, the worst case for the **while** loops of lines 23 and 29 is bounded by O($n + m$), as the first cannot be iterated more than m times and the second more than n. Taking the sum of all of these steps, we obtain O($n + m$) as the asymptotic computing time of this algorithm.

As we create polynomials, *free* is continually incremented until it tries to exceed *maxterms*. When this happens must we quit? We must unless there are some polynomials which are no longer needed. There may be several such polynomials whose space can be reused. We could write a procedure which would compact the remaining polynomials, leaving a large, contiguous free space at one end. But this may require much data movement. Even worse, if we move a polynomial we must change its start and end pointers. This demands a sophisticated compacting routine coupled with a disciplined use of names for polynomials. In Chapter 6, we will see an elegant solution to these problems.

4.3 SPARSE MATRICES

A matrix is a mathematical object which arises in many physical problems. As computer scientists, we are interested in studying ways to represent matrices so that the operations to be performed on them can be carried out efficiently. A general matrix consists of m rows and n columns of numbers as in Figure 4.4.

	col 1	col 2	col 3
row 1	−27,	3,	4
row 2	6,	82,	−0.3
row 3	109,	−64,	4
row 4	.12,	8,	9
row 5	3.4,	36,	27

(a)

	col 1	col 2	col 3	col 4	col 5	col 6
	15,	0,	0,	22,	0,	−15
	0,	11,	3,	0,	0,	0
	0,	0,	0,	−6,	0,	0
	0,	0,	0,	0,	0,	0
	91,	0,	0,	0,	0,	0
row 6	0,	0,	28,	0,	0,	0

(b)

Figure 4.4 Example of two matrices

The first matrix has five rows and three columns, the second six rows and six columns. In general, we write $m \times n$ (read m by n) to designate a matrix with m rows and n columns. Such a matrix has mn elements. When m is equal to n, we call the matrix *square*.

It is very natural to store a matrix in a two-dimensional array, say $A[1..m, 1..n]$. Then we can work with any element by writing $A[i,j]$; and this element can be found very quickly, as we will see in the next section. Now if we look at the second matrix of Figure 4.4, we see that it has many zero entries. Such a matrix is called *sparse*. There is no precise definition of when a matrix is sparse and when it is not, but it is a concept which we can all recognize intuitively. Above, only eight out of 36 possible elements are nonzero and that is sparse! A sparse matrix requires us to consider an alternate form of representation. This comes about because in practice many of the matrices we want to deal with are large, e.g., 1000 × 1000, but at the same time they are sparse: say only 1000 out of 1 million possible elements are nonzero. On most computers today it would be impossible to store a full 1000 × 1000 matrix in the memory at once. Therefore, we seek an alternative representation for sparse matrices. The alternative representation should explicitly store only the nonzero elements.

Each element of a matrix is uniquely characterized by its row and column position, say i,j. We might then store a matrix as a list of 3-tuples of the form

(i,j,value).

Also it might be helpful to organize this list of 3-tuples in some way, perhaps placing them so that the row numbers are increasing. We can go one step farther and require that all the 3-tuples of any row be stored so that the column indices are increasing. Thus, we might store the second matrix of Figure 4.4 in the array $A[0..t, 1..3]$ where $t = 8$ is the number of nonzero terms (see Figure 4.5). The elements $A[0,1]$ and $A[0,2]$ contain the number of rows and columns of the matrix. $A[0,3]$ contains the number of nonzero terms.

Now what are some of the operations we might want to perform on these matrices? One operation is to compute the transpose matrix. This is where we move the elements so that the element in the i,j position gets put in the j,i position. Another way of saying this is that we are interchanging rows and columns. The elements on the diagonal will remain unchanged, since $i = j$.

The transpose of the example matrix in Figure 4.5(a) is shown in Figure 4.5(b). Since A is organized by row, our first idea for a transpose algorithm might be

for each row i **do**
    take element (i,j,val) and
    store it in (j,i,val) of the transpose;

The difficulty is in not knowing where to put the element (j,i,val) until all other elements which precede it have been processed. In our example of Figure 4.5, for instance, we have item

    $(1,1,15)$ which becomes $(1,1,15)$
    $(1,4,22)$ which becomes $(4,1,22)$
    $(1,6,-15)$ which becomes $(6,1,-15)$.

If we just place them consecutively, then we will need to insert many new triples, forcing us to move elements down very often. We can avoid this data movement by finding the elements in the order we want them, which would be as

for all elements in column j **do**
    place element (i,j,val) in position (j,i,val);

This says find all elements in column 1 and store them into row 1, find all elements in column 2 and store them in row 2, etc. Since the rows are originally in order, this means that we will locate elements in the correct column order as well.

	1]	2]	3]
A[0,	6,	6,	8
[1,	1,	1,	15
[2,	1,	4,	22
[3,	1,	6,	−15
[4,	2,	2,	11
[5,	2,	3,	3
[6,	3,	4,	−6
[7,	5,	1,	91
[8,	6,	3,	28

(a)

	1]	2]	3]
B[0,	6,	6,	8
[1,	1,	1,	15
[2,	1,	5,	91
[3,	2,	2,	11
[4,	3,	2,	3
[5,	3,	6,	28
[6,	4,	1,	22
[7,	4,	3,	−6
[8,	6,	1,	−15

(b)

Figure 4.5 Sparse matrix and its transpose stored as triples

Define the data type *sparsematrix* as below:

type *sparsematrix* = **array**[0..*maxterms*, 1..3] **of integer**;

where *maxterms* is a constant. The procedure *transpose* (Program 4.15) computes the transpose of A. A is initially stored as a sparse matrix in the array *a* and its transpose is obtained in the array *b*.

It is not too difficult to see that the procedure is correct. The variable q always gives us the position in b where the next term in the transpose is to be inserted. The terms in b are generated by rows. Since the rows of B are the columns of A, row i of B is

---

```
 1  procedure transpose (a : sparsematrix; var b : sparsematrix);
 2  {b is set to be the transpose of a}
 3  var m,n,p,q,t,col : integer;
 4  {m : number of rows in a
 5   n : number of columns in a
 6   t : number of terms in a
 7   q : position of next term in b
 8   p : current term in a}
 9  begin
10    m := a[0,1]; n := a[0,2]; t := a[0,3];
11    b[0,1] := n; b[0,2] := m; b[0,3] := t;
12    if t > 0 then {nonzero matrix}
13    begin
14      q := 1;
15      for col := 1 to n do {transpose by columns}
16        for p := 1 to t do
17          if a [p,2] = col then
18          begin
19            b [q,1] := a [p,2]; b [q,2] := a [p,1];
20            b [q,3] := a [p,3]; q := q + 1;
21          end;
22    end; {of if}
23  end; {of transpose}
```

Program 4.15 Procedure *transpose*

obtained by collecting all the nonzero terms in column i of A. This is precisely what is being done in lines 15-21. On the first iteration of the **for** loop of lines 15-21 all terms from column 1 of A are collected, then all terms from column 2 and so on until eventually, all terms from column n are collected.

How about the computing time of this algorithm? For each iteration of the loop of lines 15-21, the **if** clause of line 17 is tested t times. Since the number of iterations of the loop of lines 15-21 is n, the total time for line 17 becomes nt. The assignments in lines 19 and 20 take place exactly t times as there are only t nonzero terms in the sparse matrix being generated. Lines 10-14 take a constant amount of time. The total time for the algorithm is therefore $O(nt)$. In addition to the space needed for a and b, the algorithm requires only a fixed amount of additional space, i.e. space for the variables m, n, t, q, col and p.

We now have a matrix transpose algorithm which we believe is correct and which has a computing time of O(nt). This computing time is a little disturbing since we know that in case the matrices had been represented as two dimensional arrays, we could have obtained the transpose of an $n \times m$ matrix in time O(nm). The algorithm for this has the simple form:

```
for j := 1 to n do
  for i := 1 to m do
    B [j,i] := A [i,j];
```

The O(nt) time for procedure *transpose* becomes O(n^2m) when t is of the order of nm. This is worse than the O(nm) time using arrays. Perhaps, in an effort to conserve space, we have traded away too much time. Actually, we can do much better by using a little more storage. We can, in fact, transpose a matrix represented as a sequence of triples in time O($n + t$). This algorithm, *fasttranspose* (Program 4.16), proceeds by first determining the number of elements in each column of A. This gives us the number of elements in each row of B. From this information, the starting point in b of each of its rows is easily obtained. We can now move the elements of a one by one into their correct position in b. *maxcol* is a constant such that the number of columns in A never exceeds *maxcol*.

The correctness of procedure *fasttranspose* follows from the preceding discussion and the observation that the starting point of row i, $i > 1$ of B is $u[i - 1] + s[i - 1]$ where $s[i - 1]$ is the number of elements in row $i - 1$ of B and $u[i-1]$ is the starting point of row $i - 1$. The computation of s and t is carried out in lines 12-16. In lines 17-22 the elements of a are examined one by one starting from the first and successively moving to the t'th element. $u[j]$ is maintained so that it is always the position in b where the next element in row j is to be inserted.

There are four loops in *fasttranspose* which are executed n, t, $n-1$, and t times respectively. Each iteration of the loops takes only a constant amount of time, so the order of magnitude is O($n + t$). The computing time of O($n + t$) becomes O(nm) when t is of the order of nm. This is the same as when two dimensional arrays were in use. However, the constant factor associated with *fasttranspose* is bigger than that for the array algorithm. When t is sufficiently small compared to its maximum of nm, *fasttranspose* will be faster. Hence in this representation, we save both space and time! This was not true of *transpose* since t will almost always be greater than max$\{n,m\}$ and nt will therefore always be at least nm. The constant factor associated with *transpose* is also bigger than the one in the array algorithm. Finally, you should note that *fasttranspose* requires more space than does *transpose*. The space required by *fasttranspose* can be reduced by utilizing the same space to represent the two arrays s and t.

```
1 procedure fasttranspose (a : sparsematrix; var b : sparsematrix);
2 {The transpose of a is placed in b and is found in O(n +t) time where
3  n is the number of columns and t the number of terms in a}
4 var s,u : array[1..maxcol] of integer;
5   i,j,n,t : integer;
6 begin
7   n := a[0,2]; t := a[0,3];
8   b[0,1] := n; b[0,2] := a[0,1]; b[0,3] := t;
9   if t > 0 then {nonzero matrix}
10  begin
11    {compute s [i] = number of terms in row i of b}
12    for i := 1 to n do s [i] := 0; {initialize}
13    for i := 1 to t do s [a [i,2]] := s [a [i,2]] + 1;
14    {u [i] = starting position of row i in b}
15    u [1] := 1;
16    for i := 2 to n do u [i] := u [i−1] + s [i−1];
17    for i := 1 to t do {move from a to b}
18    begin
19      j := u [a [i,2]];
20      b [j,1] := a [i,2]; b [j,2] := a [i,1]; b [j,3] := a [i,3];
21      u [a [i,2]] := j + 1;
22    end;
23  end; {of if}
24 end; {of fasttranspose}
```

Program 4.16 Procedure *fasttranspose*

If we try the algorithm on the sparse matrix of Figure 4.5, then after execution of the third **for** loop, the values of s and t are

	[1]	[2]	[3]	[4]	[5]	[6]
$s =$	2	1	2	2	0	1
$u =$	1	3	4	6	8	8

$s [i]$ is the number of entries in row i of the transpose. $u [i]$ points to the position in the transpose where the next element of row i is to be stored.

Suppose now you are working for a machine manufacturer who is using a computer to do inventory control. Associated with each machine that the company produces, say MACH[1] to MACH[m], there is a list of parts that it is comprised of. This information could be represented in a two-dimensional table as in Figure 4.6.

	PART[1]	PART[2]	PART[3]	...	PART[n]
MACH[1]	0,	5,	2,	...,	0
MACH[2]	0,	0,	0,	...,	3
MACH[3]	1,	1,	0,	...,	8
.	.	.	.		.
.	.	.	.		.
.	.	.	.		.
MACH[m]	6,	0,	0,	...,	7
	array	MACHPT[m,n]			

Figure 4.6 Machine parts table

The table will be sparse and all entries will be nonnegative integers, MACHPT[i,j] is the number of units of PART[j] in MACH[i]. Each part is itself composed of smaller parts called microparts. This data will also be encoded in a table whose rows are PART[1] to PART[n] and whose columns are MICPT[1] to MICPT[p]. We want to determine the number of microparts that are necessary to make up each machine.

Observe that the number of MICPT[j] making up MACH[i] is

$$\text{MACHPT}[i,1] * \text{MICPT}[1,j] + \text{MACHPT}[i,2] * \text{MICPT}[2,j]$$
$$+ \cdots + \text{MACHPT}[i,n] * \text{MICPT}[n,j]$$

where the arrays are named MACHPT[m,n] and MICPT[n,p]. This sum is more conveniently written as

$$\sum_{k=1}^{n} \text{MACHPT}[i,k] * \text{MICPT}[k,j]$$

If we compute these sums for each machine and each micro part then we will have a total of mp values which we might store in a third table MACHSUM[m,p]. Regarding these tables as matrices, this application leads to the general definition of matrix product:

Given A and B where A is $m \times n$ and B is $n \times p$, the product matrix C has dimension $m \times p$. Its i,j element is defined as

$$c_{ij} = \sum_{1 \leq k \leq n} a_{ik}b_{kj}$$

for $1 \leq i \leq m$ and $1 \leq j \leq p$. The product of two sparse matrices may no longer be sparse, for instance,

$$\begin{bmatrix} 1, & 0, & 0 \\ 1, & 0, & 0 \\ 1, & 0, & 0 \end{bmatrix} \begin{bmatrix} 1, & 1, & 1 \\ 0, & 0, & 0 \\ 0, & 0 & 0 \end{bmatrix} = \begin{bmatrix} 1 & 1 & 1 \\ 1 & 1 & 1 \\ 1 & 1 & 1 \end{bmatrix}$$

Consider an algorithm which computes the product of two sparse matrices represented as an ordered list instead of an array. To compute the elements of C row-wise so we can store them in their proper place without moving previously computed elements, we must do the following: fix a row of A and find all elements in column j of B for $j = 1, 2, \cdots, p$. Normally, to find all the elements in column j of B we would have to scan all of B. To avoid this, we can first compute the transpose of B which will put all column elements consecutively. Once the elements in row i of A and column j of B have been located, we just do a merge operation similar to the polynomial addition of Section 4.2. An alternative approach is explored in the exercises.

Before we write a matrix multiplication procedure, it will be useful to define a subprocedure as in Program 4.17.

```
procedure storesum(var c : sparsematrix; var q : integer;
                   row, col: integer; var sum: integer);
{If sum ≠ 0, then it along with its row and column position
is stored as the q+1'st entry in c}
begin
  if sum <> 0 then
    if q < maxterms then begin
                    q := q + 1;
                    c [q,1] := row;
                    c [q,2] := col;
                    c [q,3] := sum;
                    sum := 0;
                  end
    else begin
         writeln('Number of terms in product exceeds maxterms');
         halt; {terminate program}
       end;
end; {of storesum}
```

Program 4.17 Storesum

The procedure *mmult* (Program 4.18) multiplies the matrices A and B to obtain the product matrix C using the strategy outlined above. A, B, and C are stored as sparse matrices in the arrays a, b, and c, respectively. Procedure *mmult* makes use of variables i, j, q, r, *col* and *rowbegin*. The variable r is the row of A that is currently being multiplied with the columns of B. *rowbegin* is the position in a of the first element of row r. *col* is the column of B that is currently being multiplied with row r of A. q is the position of c for the next element generated. i and j are used to examine successively elements of row r and column *col* of A and B, respectively. In addition to all this, line 20 of the algorithm introduces a dummy term into each of a and d. This enables us to handle end conditions (i.e., computations involving the last row of A or last column of B) in an elegant way.

```
 1 procedure mmult (a,b : sparsematrix; var c : sparsematrix);
 2 {c = a*b; a is m×n and b is n×p}
 3 var i,j,m,n,p,q,r,ta,tb,col,sum,rowbegin : integer;
 4    d : sparsematrix;
 5 begin
 6   m := a[0,1]; n := a[0,2]; ta := a[0,3];
 7   if n <> b[0,1] then begin
 8                        writeln('Incompatible matrices');
 9                        halt; {terminate program}
10                      end;
11   p := b[0,2]; tb := b[0,3];
12   if (ta >= maxterms) or (tb >= maxterms) then
13            begin
14              writeln('Too many terms in a or b');
15              halt; {terminate program}
16            end;
17   fasttranspose (b,d);
18   i := 1; q := 0; rowbegin := 1; r := a[1,1];
19   {set boundary conditions}
20   a [ta+1,1] := m + 1; d [tb+1,1] := p + 1;
21   d [tb+1,2] := 0; sum := 0;
22   while i <= ta do {generate row r of c}
23   begin
24     col := d [1,1]; j := 1;
```

Program 4.18 Procedure to multiply matrices (continued on next page)

We leave the correctness proof of this algorithm as an exercise. Let us examine its complexity. In addition to the space needed for a, b, c, and some simple variables, space is also needed for the transpose matrix d. Algorithm *fasttranspose* also needs some

```
25      while j <= tb + 1 do {multiply row r of a by column col of b}
26      begin
27        if a [i,1] <> r
28        then begin  {end of row r}
29            storesum (c,q,r,col,sum);
30            i := rowbegin;
31            {go to next column}
32            while d [j,1] = col do j := j + 1;
33            col := d [j,1];
34          end
35        else if d [j,1] <> col
36            then begin  {end of column col of b}
37                storesum (c,q,r,col,sum);
38                {set to multiply row r with next column}
39                i := rowbegin; col := d [j,1];
40              end
41            else if a [i,2] < d [j,2]
42                then i := i + 1 {advance to next term in row}
43                else if a [i,2] = d [j,2]
44                    then begin {add to sum}
45                        sum := sum + a [i,3] * d [j,3];
46                        i := i + 1;  j := j + 1;
47                      end
48                    else {advance to next term in column col}
49                        j := j + 1;
50        end; {of while j <= tb + 1}
51        while a [i,1] = r do {advance to next row}
52          i := i + 1;
53        rowbegin := i; r := a [i,1];
54      end; {end of while i <= ta}
55      c[0,1] := m; c[0,2] := p; c[0,3] := q;
56 end; {of mmult}
```

Program 4.18 Procedure *mmult* (continued from previous page)

additional space. The exercises explore a strategy for *mmult* which does not explicitly compute *d*, and the only additional space needed is the same as that required by *fast-transpose*. Turning our attention to the computing time of *mmult*, we see that lines 6-21 require only $O(p + tb)$ time. The **while** loop of lines 22-54 is executed at most *m* times (once for each row of *A*). In each iteration of the **while** loop of lines 25-50 either the value of *i* or of *j* or both increases by 1 or *i* and *col* are reset. The maximum total increment in *j* over the whole loop is *tb*. If d_r is the number of terms in row *r* of *A*, then the value of *i* can increase at most d_r times before *i* moves to the next row of *A*. When this happens, *i* is reset to *rowbegin* in line 30. At the same time *col* is advanced to the next column. Hence, this resetting can take place at most *p* times (there are only *p* columns in *B*). The total maximum increments in *i* is therefore pd_r. The maximum number of iterations of the **while** loop of lines 25-50 is therefore $p + pd_r + tb$. The time for this loop while multiplying with row *r* of *A* is $O(pd_r + tb)$. Lines 51-53 take only $O(d_r)$ time. Hence, the time for the outer **while** loop, lines 22-54, for the iteration with row *r* of *A* is $O(pd_r + tb)$. The overall time for this loop is then $O(\Sigma_r(pd_r + tb)) = O(p*ta + m*tb)$.

Once again, we may compare the computing time with the time to multiply matrices when arrays are used. The classical multiplication algorithm is

```
for i := 1 to m do
  for j := 1 to p do
  begin
    sum := 0;
    for k := 1 to n do
      sum := sum + a [i,k] * b [k,j];
    c [i,j] := sum;
  end;
```

The time for this is $O(mnp)$. Since $ta \leq nm$ and $tb \leq np$, the time for *mmult* is at most $O(mnp)$. However, its constant factor is greater than that for matrix multiplication using arrays. In the worst case when $ta = nm$ or $tb = np$, *mmult* will be slower by a constant factor. However, when *ta* and *tb* are sufficiently smaller than their maximum values, i.e., *A* and *B* are sparse, *mmult* will outperform the above multiplication algorithm for arrays.

The above analysis for *mmult* is nontrivial. It introduces some new concepts in algorithm analysis and you should make sure you understand the analysis.

This representation for sparse matrices permits one to perform operations such as addition, transpose, and multiplication efficiently. There are, however, other considerations which make this representation undesirable in certain applications. Since the number of terms in a sparse matrix is variable, we would like to represent all our sparse matrices in one array (as we did for polynomials in Section 4.2) rather than using a separate array for each matrix. This would enable us to make efficient utilization of space. However, when this is done, we run into difficulties in allocating space from this array to any individual matrix. These difficulties also arise with the polynomial representation of the previous section and will become apparent when we study a similar representation for multiple stacks and queues in Section 5.4.

4.4 REPRESENTATION OF ARRAYS

Even though multidimensional arrays are provided as a standard data object in most high level languages, it is interesting to see how they are represented in memory. Recall that memory may be regarded as one-dimensional with words numbered from 1 to m. So, we are concerned with representing n dimensional arrays in a one dimensional memory. While many representations might seem plausible, we must select one in which the location in memory of an arbitrary array element, say $A[i_1, i_2, ..., i_n]$, can be determined efficiently. This is necessary since programs using arrays may, in general, use array elements in a random order. In addition to being able to retrieve array elements easily, it is also necessary to be able to determine the amount of memory space to be reserved for a particular array. Assuming that each array element requires only one word of memory, the number of words needed is the number of elements in the array. If an array is declared $A[l_1..u_1, l_2..u_2, ..., l_n..u_n]$, then it is easy to see that the number of elements is

$$\prod_{i=1}^{n} (u_i - l_i + 1).$$

One of the common ways to represent an array is in row major order. If we have the declaration

$$A[4..5, 2..4, 1..2, 3..4]$$

then we have a total of $2*3*2*2 = 24$ elements. Using row major order, these elements will be stored as

$$A[4,2,1,3], A[4,2,1,4], A[4,2,2,3], A[4,2,2,4]$$

and continuing

$$A[4,3,1,3], A[4,3,1,4], A[4,3,2,3], A[4,3,2,4]$$

for three more sets of four until we get

$$A[5,4,1,3], A[5,4,1,4], A[5,4,2,3], A[5,4,2,4].$$

We see that the subscript at the right moves the fastest. In fact, if we view the subscripts as numbers, we see that they are, in some sense, increasing:

$$4213, 4214, \ldots, 5423, 5424.$$

A synonym for row major order is lexicographic order.

From the compiler's point of view, the problem is how to translate from the name $A[i_1, i_2, \ldots, i_n]$ to the correct location in memory. Suppose $A[4,2,1,3]$ is stored at location 100. Then $A[4,2,1,4]$ will be at 101 and $A[5,4,2,4]$ at location 123. These two addresses are easy to guess. In general, we can derive a formula for the address of any element. This formula makes use of only the starting address of the array plus the declared dimensions.

To simplify the discussion we shall assume that the lower bounds on each dimension l_i are 1. The general case when l_i can be any integer is discussed in the exercises. Before obtaining a formula for the case of an n-dimensional array, let us look at the row major representation of one-, two-, and three-dimensional arrays. To begin with, if A is declared $A[1..u_1]$, then assuming one word per element, it may be represented in sequential memory as in Figure 4.7. If α is the address of $A[1]$, then the address of an arbitrary element $A[i]$ is just $\alpha + i - 1$.

array element:	$A[1]$	$A[2]$	$A[3]$	$\cdots$	$A[i]$	$\cdots$	$A[u_1]$
address:	α	$\alpha+1$	$\alpha+2$	$\cdots$	$\alpha+i-1$	$\cdots$	$\alpha+u_1-1$

Figure 4.7 Sequential representation of $A[1..u_1]$

The two dimensional array $A[1..u_1, 1..u_2]$ may be interpreted as u_1 rows $row_1, row_2, \ldots, row_{u_1}$, each row consisting of u_2 elements. In a row major representation, these rows would be represented in memory as in Figure 4.8.

Again, if α is the address of $A[1,1]$, then the address of $A[i,1]$ is $\alpha + (i-1)u_2$, as there are $i-1$ rows each of size u_2 preceding the first element in the i'th row. Knowing the address of $A[i,1]$, we can say that the address of $A[i,j]$ is then simply $\alpha + (i-1)u_2 + (j-1)$.

Figure 4.9 shows the representation of the three-dimensional array $A[1..u_1, 1..u_2, 1..u_3]$. This array is interpreted as u_1 two-dimensional arrays of dimension $u_2 \times u_3$. To locate $A[i,j,k]$, we first obtain $\alpha + (i-1)u_2u_3$ as the address for $A[i,1,1]$ since there are $i-1$ 2 dimensional arrays of size $u_2 \times u_3$ preceding this element. From this and the formula for addressing a two-dimensional array, we obtain $\alpha + (i-1)u_2u_3 + (j-1)u_3 + (k-1)$ as the address of $A[i,j,k]$.

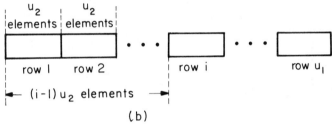

row 1
row 2
row 3
row u_1

col 1   col 2   ...   col u_2

(a)

u_2 elements | u_2 elements

row 1   row 2 ... row i ... row u_l

$(i-1)u_2$ elements

(b)

Figure 4.8 Sequential representation of $A[1..u_1, 1..u_2]$.

Generalizing on the preceding discussion, the addressing formula for any element $A[i_1,i_2,...,i_n]$ in an n-dimensional array declared as $A[1..u_1, 1..u_2,...,1..u_n]$ may be easily obtained. If α is the address for $A[1,1, ...,1]$ then $\alpha + (i_1 - 1)u_2 u_3 ... u_n$ is the address for $A[i_1,1, ...,1]$. The address for $A[i_1,i_2,1, ..., 1]$ is then $\alpha + (i_1 - 1)u_2 u_3 ... u_n + (i_2 - 1)u_3 u_4 ... u_n$.

Repeating in this way the address for $A[i_1,i_2, ...,i_n]$ is

$$
\begin{aligned}
&\alpha + (i_1 - 1)u_2 u_3 \cdots u_n \\
&+ (i_2 - 1)u_3 u_4 \cdots u_n \\
&+ (i_3 - 1)u_4 u_5 \cdots u_n \\
&\qquad\vdots \\
&+ (i_{n-1} - 1)u_n \\
&+ (i_n - 1)
\end{aligned}
$$

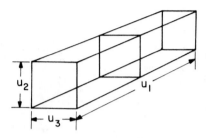

(a) 3-dimensional array $A[1..u_1,1..u_2,1..u_3]$ regarded as u_1 2-dimensional arrays.

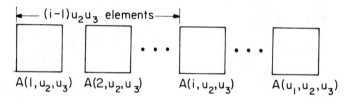

(b) Sequential row major representation of a 3-dimensional array. Each 2-dimensional array is represented as in Figure 2.5.

Figure 4.9 Sequential representation of $A[1..u_1,1..u_2,1..u_3]$

$$= \alpha + \sum_{j=1}^{n} (i_j - 1)a_j \text{ with } \begin{cases} a_j = \prod_{k=j+1}^{n} u_k & 1 \le j < n \\ a_n = 1 \end{cases}$$

Note that a_j may be computed from a_{j+1}, $1 \le j < n$ using only one multiplication as $a_j = u_{j+1}a_{j+1}$. Thus, a compiler will initially take the declared bounds $u_1, ..., u_n$ and use them to compute the constants $a_1, ..., a_{n-1}$ using $n - 2$ multiplications. The address of $A[i_1, ..., i_n]$ can then be found using the formula, requiring $n - 1$ more multiplications and n additions and n subtractions.

An alternative scheme for array representation, column major order, is considered in Exercise 19.

To review, in this chapter we have used arrays to represent ordered lists of polynomials and sparse matrices. In all cases we have been able to move values around, accessing arbitrary elements in a fixed amount of time, and this has given us efficient algorithms. However, several problems have been raised. By using a sequential mapping which associates a_i of $(a_1, ...,a_n)$ with the i'th element of the array, we are forced to move data around whenever an insert or delete operation is used. Secondly, once we adopt one ordering of the data we sacrifice the ability to have a second ordering simultaneously.

4.5 EXERCISES

1. Write a Pascal procedure which multiplies two polynomials represented using the array *terms* of Section 4.2. What is the computing time of your procedure?

2. Write a Pascal procedure which evaluates a polynomial at a value x_0 using the representation above. Try to minimize the number of operations.

3. If $A = (a_1, ...,a_n)$ and $B = (b_1, ...,b_m)$ are ordered lists, then $A < B$ if $a_i = b_i$ for $1 \le i < j$ and $a_j < b_j$ or if $a_i = b_i$ for $1 \le i \le n$ and $n < m$. Write a procedure which returns -1, 0, $+1$ depending upon whether $A < B$, $A = B$, or $A > B$. Assume you can compare atoms a_i and b_j.

4. Assume that n lists, $n > 1$, are being represented sequentially in the one-dimensional array *space* $[1..m]$. Let *front*$[i]$ be one less than the position of the first element in the i'th list and let *rear*$[i]$ point to the last element in the i'th list, $1 \le i \le n$. Further assume that *rear*$[i] \le$ *front*$[i + 1]$, $1 \le i \le n$ with *front*$[n + 1] = m$. The functions to be performed on these lists are insertion and deletion.

    (a) Obtain suitable initial and boundary conditions for *front*$[i]$ and *rear*$[i]$

    (b) Write a procedure *insert* $(i,j,item:$ **integer**$)$ to insert *item* after the $(j - 1)$'st element in list i. This procedure should fail to make an insertion only if there are already m elements in *space*.

5. Using the assumptions of (4) above write a procedure *delete* $(i,j:$ **integer; var** *item*: **integer**$)$ which sets *item* to the j'th element of the i'th list and removes it. The i'th list should be maintained as sequentially stored.

6. The polynomials $A(x) = x^{2n} + x^{2n-2} + ... + x^2 + x^0$ and $B(x) = x^{2n+1} + x^{2n-1} + ... + x^3 + x$ cause *padd* to work very hard. For these polynomials, determine the exact number of times each statement will be executed.

7. Analyze carefully the computing time and storage requirements of algorithm *fasttranspose*. What can you say about the existence of an even faster algorithm?

8. Using the idea in *fasttranspose* of m row pointers, rewrite algorithm *mmult* to multiply two sparse matrices A and B represented as in Section 4.3 without transposing B. What is the computing time of your algorithm?

9. When all the elements either above or below the main diagonal of a square matrix are zero, then the matrix is said to be triangular. Figure 4.10 shows a lower and an upper triangular matrix.

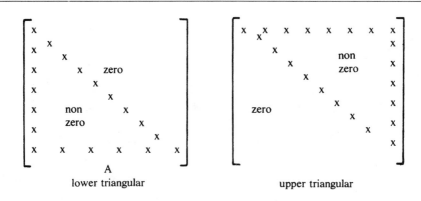

Figure 4.10 Lower and upper triangular matrices

In a lower triangular matrix, A, with n rows, the maximum number of nonzero terms in row i is i. Hence, the total number of nonzero terms is $\sum_{i=1}^{n} i = n(n+1)/2$. For large n it would be worthwhile to save the space taken by the zero entries in the upper triangle. Obtain an addressing formula for elements a_{ij} in the lower triangle if this lower triangle is stored by rows in an array $B[1 \mathinner{..} n(n+1)/2]$ with $A[1,1]$ being stored in $B[1]$. What is the relationship between i and j for elements in the zero part of A?

10. Let A and B be two lower triangular matrices, each with n rows. The total number of elements in the lower triangles is $n(n+1)$. Devise a scheme to represent both the triangles in an array $c[1 \mathinner{..} n, 1 \mathinner{..} n+1]$. [Hint: represent the triangle of A as the lower triangle of c and the transpose of B as the upper triangle of c.] Write algorithms to determine the values of $A[i,j]$, $B[i,j]$, $1 \le i$, $j \le n$ from the array c.

11. Another kind of sparse matrix that arises often in numerical analysis is the tridiagonal matrix. In this square matrix, all elements other than those on the major diagonal and on the diagonals immediately above and below this one are zero (Figure 4.11). If the elements in the band formed by these three diagonals are represented row-wise in an array, b, with $A[1,1]$ being stored in $b[1]$, obtain an algorithm to determine the value of $A[i,j]$, $1 \le i$, $j \le n$ from the array b.

12. Define a square band matrix $A_{n,a}$ to be an $n \times n$ matrix in which all the nonzero terms lie in a band centered around the main diagonal. The band includes $a - 1$ diagonals below and above the main diagonal and also the main diagonal (Figure 4.12).

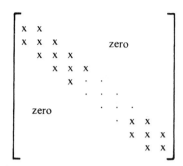

Figure 4.11 Tridiagonal matrix A

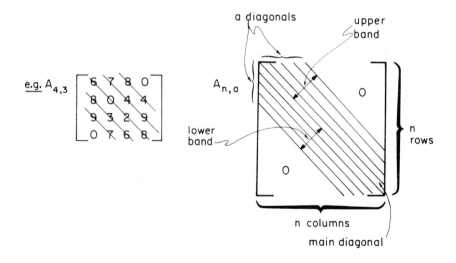

Figure 4.12 Square band matrix

(a) How many elements are there in the band of $A_{n,a}$?

(b) What is the relationship between i and j for elements a_{ij} in the band of $A_{n,a}$?

(c) Assume that the band of $A_{n,a}$ is stored sequentially in an array b by diagonals starting with the lowermost diagonal. Thus $A_{4,3}$ above would have the following representation:

b[1]	b[2]	b[3]	b[4]	b[5]	b[6]	b[7]	b[8]	b[9]	b[10]	b[11]	b[12]	b[13]	b[14]
9	7	8	3	6	6	0	2	8	7	4	9	8	4
a_{31}	a_{42}	a_{21}	a_{32}	a_{43}	a_{11}	a_{22}	a_{33}	a_{44}	a_{12}	a_{23}	a_{34}	a_{13}	a_{24}

Obtain an addressing formula for the location of an element a_{ij} in the lower band of $A_{n,a}$.

e.g., $LOC(a_{31}) = 1$, $LOC(a_{42}) = 2$ in the example above.

13. A generalized band matrix $A_{n,a,b}$ is an $n \times n$ matrix A in which all the nonzero terms lie in a band made up of $a - 1$ diagonals below the main diagonal, the main diagonal, and $b - 1$ diagonals above the main diagonal (Figure 4.13)

(a) How many elements are there in the band of $A_{n,a,b}$?

(b) What is the relationship between i and j for elements a_{ij} in the band of $A_{n,a,b}$?

(c) Obtain a sequential representation of the band of $A_{n,a,b}$ in the one-dimensional array c. For this representation write a Pascal procedure *value* (n,a,b,i,j,c) which determines the value of element a_{ij} in the matrix $A_{n,a,b}$. The band of $A_{n,a,b}$ is represented in the array c.

14. How much time does it take to locate an arbitrary element $A[i,j]$ in the representation of Section 4.3 and to change its value?

15. A variation of the scheme discussed in §4.3 for sparse matrix representation involves representing only the nonzero terms in a one-dimensional array v in the order described. In addition, a strip of $n \times m$ bits, $bits[1..n, 1..m]$ is also kept. $bits[i,j] = 0$ if $A[i,j] = 0$ and $bits[i,j] = 1$ if $A[i,j] \neq 0$. The figure below illustrates the representation for the sparse matrix of Figure 4.5.

$$\begin{bmatrix} 1 & 0 & 0 & 1 & 0 & 1 \\ 0 & 1 & 1 & 0 & 0 & 0 \\ 0 & 0 & 0 & 1 & 0 & 0 \\ 0 & 0 & 0 & 0 & 0 & 0 \\ 1 & 0 & 0 & 0 & 0 & 0 \\ 0 & 0 & 1 & 0 & 0 & 0 \end{bmatrix} \quad \begin{bmatrix} 15 \\ 22 \\ -15 \\ 11 \\ 3 \\ -6 \\ 91 \\ 28 \end{bmatrix}$$

(a) On a computer with w bits per word, how much storage is needed to represent a sparse matrix $A_{n \times m}$ with t nonzero terms?

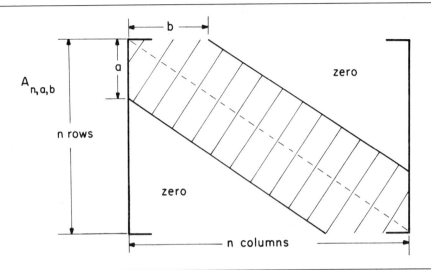

Figure 4.13 Generalized band matrix

(b) Write an algorithm to add two sparse matrices A and C represented as above to obtain $D = A + C$. How much time does your algorithm take?

(c) Discuss the merits of this representation versus the representation of Section 4.3. Consider space and time requirements for such operations as random access, add, multiply, and transpose. Note that the random access time can be improved somewhat by keeping another array ra such that $ra[i] =$ number of nonzero terms in rows 1 through $i - 1$.

16. A complex-valued matrix X is represented by a pair of matrices (A,B) where A and B contain real values. Write a program which computes the product of two complex valued matrices (A,B) and (C,D), where $(A,B) * (C,D) = (A + iB) * (C + iD) = (AC - BD) + i(AD + BC)$. Determine the number of additions and multiplications if the matrices are all $n \times n$.

17. How many values can be held by an array with dimensions $a[0..n]$, $b[-1..n, 1..m]$, $c[-n..0, 1..2]$?

18. Obtain an addressing formula for the element $A[i_1, i_2, ..., i_n]$ in an array declared as $A[l_1..u_1, l_2..u_2, ..., l_n..u_n]$. Assume a row major representation of the array with one word per element and α the address of $A[l_1, l_2, ..., l_n]$.

19. Do Exercise 18 assuming a column major representation. In this representation, a two-dimensional array is stored sequentially by columns rather than by rows.

20. An $m \times n$ matrix is said to have a *saddle point* if some entry $A[i,j]$ is the smallest value in row i and the largest value in column j. Write a Pascal program which determines the location of a saddle point if one exists. What is the computing time of your method?

21. Given an array $a[1..n]$ produce the array $z[1..n]$ such that $z[1] = a[n]$, $z[2] = a[n-1]$, ..., $z[n-1] = a[2]$, $z[n] = a[1]$. Use a minimal amount of storage.

22. There are a number of problems, known collectively as "random walk" problems, which have been of longstanding interest to the mathematical community. All but the most simple of these are extremely difficult to solve and for the most part they remain largely unsolved. One such problem may be stated as follows:

> A (drunken) cockroach is placed on a given square in the middle of a tile floor in a rectangular room of size $n \times m$ tiles. The bug wanders (possibly in search of an aspirin) randomly from tile to tile throughout the room. Assuming that he may move from his present tile to any of the eight tiles surrounding him (unless he is against a wall) *with equal probability*, how long will it take him to touch every tile on the floor at least once?

> Hard as this problem may be to solve by pure probability theory techniques, the answer is quite easy to solve using the computer. The technique for doing so is called "simulation" and is of wide-scale use in industry to predict traffic flow, inventory control, and so forth. The problem may be simulated using the following method:

> An $n \times m$ array *count* is used to represent the number of times our cockroach has reached each tile on the floor. All the cells of this array are initialized to zero. The position of the bug on the floor is represented by the coordinates $(ibug, jbug)$. The eight possible moves of the bug are represented by the tiles located at $(ibug + imove[k], jbug + jmove[k])$ where $1 \le k \le 8$ and

$$imove[1] = -1 \quad jmove[1] = 1$$
$$imove[2] = 0 \quad jmove[2] = 1$$
$$imove[3] = 1 \quad jmove[3] = 1$$
$$imove[4] = 1 \quad jmove[4] = 0$$
$$imove[5] = 1 \quad jmove[5] = -1$$
$$imove[6] = 0 \quad jmove[6] = -1$$
$$imove[7] = -1 \quad jmove[7] = -1$$
$$imove[8] = -1 \quad jmove[8] = 0$$

A *random* walk to one of the eight given squares is simulated by generating a random value for k lying between 1 and 8. Of course the bug cannot move outside the room, so that coordinates which lead up a wall must be ignored and a new random combination formed. Each time a square is entered, the count for that square is incremented so that a nonzero entry shows the number of times the bug has landed on that square so far. When every square has been entered at least once, the experiment is complete.

Write a program to perform the specified simulation experiment. Your program *MUST*:

(a) Handle all values of n and m, $2 < n \leq 40$, $2 \leq m \leq 20$.

(b) Perform the experiment for

   (1) $n = 15$, $m = 15$ starting point: $(20,10)$

   (2) $n = 39$, $m = 19$ starting point: $(1,1)$

(c) Have an iteration limit, that is, a maximum number of squares the bug may enter during the experiment. This assures that your program does not get "hung" in an "infinite" loop. A maximum of 50,000 is appropriate for this exercise.

(d) For each experiment, print: (1) the total number of legal moves which the cockroach makes; (2) the final *count* array. This will show the "density" of the walk, that is, the number of times each tile on the floor was touched during the experiment. (Have an aspirin.) This exercise was contributed by Olson.

23. Chess provides the setting for many fascinating diversions which are quite independent of the game itself. Many of these are based on the strange "L-shaped" move of the knight. A classical example is the problem of the knight's tour, which has captured the attention of mathematicians and puzzle enthusiasts since the beginning of the eighteenth century. Briefly stated, the problem is to move the knight, beginning from any given square on the chessboard, in such a manner that it travels successively to all 64 squares, touching each square once

and only once. It is convenient to represent a solution by placing the numbers 1, 2, ..., 64 in the squares of the chessboard indicating the order in which the squares are reached. Note that it is not required that the knight be able to reach the initial position by one more move; if this is possible the knight's tour is called re-entrant. One of the more ingenious methods for solving the problem of the knight's tour was that given by J. C. Warnsdorff in 1823. His rule was that the knight must always be moved to one of the squares from which there are the fewest exits to squares not already traversed.

The goal of this exercise is to write a computer program to implement Warnsdorff's rule. The ensuing discussion will be much easier to follow, however, if you first try to construct a particular solution to the problem by hand before reading any further.

The most important decisions to be made in solving a problem of this type are those concerning how the data is to be represented in the computer. Perhaps the most natural way to represent the chessboard is by an 8×8 array *board* as shown in the figure below. The eight possible moves of a knight on square (5,3) are also shown in Figure 4.14.

Figure 4.14 Legal moves for a knight

In general a knight at (i,j) may move to one of the squares $(i-2,j+1)$, $(i-1,j+2)$, $(i+1,j+2)$, $(i+2,j+1)$, $(i+2,j-1)$, $(i+1,j-2)$, $(i-1,j-2)$, $(i-2,j-1)$. Notice, however, that if (i,j) is located near one of the edges of the board, some of these possibilities could move the knight off the board, and of course this is not permitted. The eight possible knight moves may conveniently be represented by two arrays *ktmov1* and *ktmov2* as shown below.

ktmov1	ktmov2
−2	1
−1	2
1	2
2	1
2	−1
1	−2
−1	−2
−2	−1

Then a knight at (i,j) may move to $(i+ktmov1[k],j+ktmove2[k])$, where k is some value between 1 and 8, provided that the new square lies on the chessboard.

Below is a description of an algorithm for solving the knight's tour problem using Warnsdoff's rule. The data representation discussed in the previous section is assumed.

(a) [Initialize chessboard] For $1 \leq i,j \leq 8$ set $board[i,j]$ to 0.

(b) [Set starting position] Read and print i,j and then set $board[i,j]$ to 1.

(c) [Loop] For $2 \leq m \leq 64$, do steps (d) through (g).

(d) [Form set of possible next squares] Test each of the eight squares one knight's move away from (i,j) and form a list of the possibilities for the next square $(nexti[l],nextj[l])$. Let $npos$ be the number of possibilities. (That is, after performing this step we will have $nexti[l] = i+ktmov1[k]$ and $nextj[l] = j+ktmov2[k]$, for certain values of k between 1 and 8. Some of the squares $(i+ktmov1[k], j+ktmov2[k])$ may be impossible for the next move either because they lie off the chessboard or because they have been previously occupied by the knight -- i.e., they contain a nonzero number. In every case we will have $0 \leq npos \leq 8$.)

(e) [Test special cases] If $npos = 0$ the knight's tour has come to a premature end; report failure and then go to step (h). If $npos = 1$ there is only one possibility for the next move; set $min = 1$ and go right to step (g).

(f) [Find next square with minimum number of exits] For $1 \leq l \leq npos$ set $exits[l]$ to the number of exits from square $(nexti[l],nextj[l])$. That is, for each of the values of l examine each of the next squares $(nexti[l]+ktmov1[k], nextj[l]+ktmov2[k])$ to see if it is an exit from $(nexti[l],nextj[l])$, and count the number of such exits in $exits[l]$. (Recall that a square is an exit if it lies on the chessboard and has not been previously occupied by the knight.) Finally, set min to the location of the minimum value of $exits$. (There may be more than one occurrence of the minimum value of $exits$. If this happens, it is convenient to let min denote the first such occurrence, although it is important to realize that by so doing we are not actually guaranteed of find a solution. Nevertheless, the chances of finding a complete knight's tour in this way are remarkably good, and that is sufficient for the purposes of this exercise.)

(g) [Move knight] Set $i = nexti\,[min\,]$, $j = nextj\,[min\,]$ and $board[i,j] = m$. (Thus, (i,j) denotes the new position of the knight, and board[i,j] records the move in proper sequence.)

(h) [Print] Print out *board* showing the solution to the knight's tour, and then terminate the algorithm.

The problem is to write a Pascal program which corresponds to this algorithm. This exercise was contributed by Legenhausen and Rebman.

CHAPTER 5

STACKS AND QUEUES

5.1 FUNDAMENTALS

Two of the more common data objects found in computer algorithms are stacks and queues. They arise so often that we will discuss them separately before moving on to more complex objects. Both these data objects are special cases of the more general data object, ordered list, which we considered in the previous chapter. Recall that $A = (a_1, a_2, ..., a_n)$ is an ordered list of $N \geq 0$ elements. The a_i are referred to as atoms or elements which are taken from some set. The null or empty list has $n = 0$ elements.

A *stack* is an ordered list in which all insertions and deletions are at one end, called the *top*. A *queue* is an ordered list in which all insertions take place at one end, the *rear*, while all deletions take place at the other end, the *front*. See Figure 5.1 for an example of both. Given a stack $S = (a_1, ..., a_n)$, we say that a_1 is the *bottommost* element and element a_i is on *top* of element a_{i-1}, $1 < i \leq n$. When viewed as a queue with a_n as the rear element, we say that a_{i+1} is behind a_i, $1 \leq i < n$.

The restrictions on a stack imply that if the elements A,B,C,D,E are added to the stack, in that order, then the first element to be removed/deleted must be E. Equivalently we say that the last element to be inserted into the stack will be the first to be removed. For this reason stacks are sometimes referred to as *Last In First Out* (LIFO) lists. The restrictions on a queue require that the first element which is inserted into the queue will be the first one to be removed. Thus A is the first letter to be removed, and queues are known as *First In First Out* (FIFO) lists. Note that the data object queue defined here need not necessarily correspond to the mathematical concept of queue in which the insert/delete rules may be different.

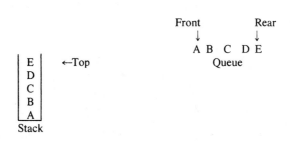

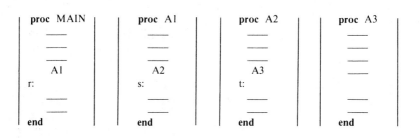

Figure 5.1 Example stack and queue

One natural example of stacks which arises in computer programming is the processing of procedure calls and their terminations. Suppose we have four procedures as shown in Figure 5.2.

Figure 5.2 Sequence of subroutine calls

The MAIN procedure invokes procedure $A1$. On completion of $A1$ execution of MAIN will resume at location r. The address r is passed to $A1$ which saves it in some location for later processing. $A1$ then invokes $A2$ which in turn invokes $A3$. In each case the invoking procedure passes the return address to the invoked procedure. If we examine the memory while $A3$ is computing there will be an implicit stack which looks like

$$(q,r,s,t).$$

The first entry, q, is the address to which MAIN returns control. This list operates as a stack since the returns will be made in the reverse order of the invocations. Thus t is removed before s, s before r and, r before q. Equivalently, this means that $A3$ must finish processing before $A2$, $A2$ before $A1$, and $A1$ before MAIN. This list of return addresses need not be maintained in consecutive locations. For each procedure there is usually a single location associated with the machine code which is used to retain the return address. This can be severely limiting in the case of recursive and reentrant procedures, since every time we invoke a procedure the new return address wipes out the old one. For example, if we inserted a call to $A1$ within procedure $A3$, expecting the return to be at location u, then at execution time the stack would become (q,u,s,t) and the return address r would be lost. When recursion is allowed, it is no longer adequate to reserve one location for the return address of each procedure. Since returns are made in the reverse order of calls, an elegant and natural solution to this procedure return problem is afforded through the explicit use of a stack of return addresses. Whenever a return is made, it is to the top address in the stack.

Associated with the object stack there are several operations that are necessary:

CREATE(S)	which creates S as an empty stack
ADD(i,S)	which inserts the element i onto the stack S and returns the new stack
DELETE(S)	which removes the top element of stack S and returns the new stack
TOP(S)	which returns the top element of stack S
ISEMTS(S)	which returns true if S is empty, else false

These five functions constitute a working definition of a stack. However we choose to represent a stack, it must be possible to build these operations.

The simplest way to represent a stack is by using a one-dimensional array, say $stack[1..n]$, where n is the maximum number of allowable entries. The first or bottom element in the stack will be stored at $stack[1]$, the second at $stack[2]$ and the i'th at $stack[i]$. Associated with the array will be a variable, top, which points to the top element in the stack. With this decision made, the following implementations result:

```
CREATE (stack) ::= var stack : array[1..n] of items ; top : 0..n ;
                       top := 0;
ISEMTS (stack) ::= if top = 0 then true
                              else false;
TOP (stack) ::= if top = 0 then error
                           else stack [top ];
```

The implementations of these three operations using an array are so short that we needn't make them separate procedures but can just use them directly whenever we need to. The ADD and DELETE operations are only a bit more complex. The corresponding procedures (Programs 5.1 and 5.2) have been written assuming that *stack*, *top*, and *n* are global.

---

procedure *add* (*item* : *items*);
{add *item* to the global stack *stack*;
top is the current top of *stack*
and *n* is its maximum size}
begin
 if *top* = *n* **then** *stackfull*
   else begin
       top := *top* + 1;
       stack [*top*] := *item*;
     end;
end; {of *add*}

Program 5.1 Add to a stack

---

procedure *delete*(**var** *item* : *items*);
{remove top element from the stack *stack* and put it in *item*}
begin
 if *top* = 0 **then** *stackempty*
   else begin
       item := *stack* [*top*];
       top := *top* − 1;
     end;
end; {of *delete*}

Program 5.2 Delete from a stack

Programs 5.1 and 5.2 are so simple that they perhaps need no more explanation. Procedure *delete* actually combines the functions TOP and DELETE. *Stackfull* and *stackempty* are procedures which we leave unspecified since they will depend upon the particular application. Often when a stack becomes full, the *stackfull* procedure will signal that more storage needs to be allocated and the program rerun. *Stackempty* is often a meaningful condition. In Section 5.3 we will see a very important computer application of stacks where *stackempty* signals the end of processing.

Queues, like stacks, also arise quite naturally in the computer solution of many problems. Perhaps the most common occurrence of a queue in computer applications is for the scheduling of jobs. In batch processing the jobs are ''queued-up'' as they are read-in and executed, one after another in the order they were received. This ignores the possible existence of priorities, in which case there will be one queue for each priority.

As mentioned earlier, when we talk of queues we talk about two distinct ends: the front and the rear. Additions to the queue take place at the rear. Deletions are made from the front. So, if a job is submitted for execution, it joins at the rear of the job queue. The job at the front of the queue is the next one to be executed. A minimal set of useful operations on a queue includes the following:

CREATEQ(Q)   which creates Q as an empty queue
ADDQ(i,Q)   which adds the element i to the rear of a queue
                and returns the new queue
DELETEQ(Q)   which removes the front element from the queue Q
                and returns the resulting queue
FRONT(Q)   which returns the front element of Q
ISEMTQ(Q)   which returns true if Q is empty else false

The representation of a finite queue in sequential locations is somewhat more difficult than a stack. In addition to a one-dimensional array $q[1..n]$, we need two variables, *front* and *rear*. The conventions we shall adopt for these two variables are that *front* is always one less than the actual front of the queue and *rear* always points to the last element in the queue. Thus, *front* = *rear* if and only if there are no elements in the queue. The initial condition then is *front* = *rear* = 0. With these conventions, let us try an example by inserting and deleting jobs, J_i, from a job queue.

front	rear	Q[1]	[2]	[3]	[4]	[5]	[6]	[7]	...	Remarks
0	0		queue		empty					Initial
0	1	J1								Job 1 joins Q
0	2	J1	J2							Job 2 joins Q
0	3	J1	J2	J3						Job 3 joins Q
1	3		J2	J3						Job 1 leaves queue
1	4		J2	J3	J4					Job 4 joins Q
2	4			J3	J4					Job 2 leaves Q

With this scheme, the following implementation of the CREATEQ, ISEMTQ, and FRONT operations is desired for a queue with capacity n:

$CREATEQ(q) ::= $ **var** q : **array** $[1..n]$ **of** $items$; $front, rear$: $0..n$:
$\qquad\qquad\qquad front := 0; rear := 0;$
$ISEMTQ(q) \quad := $ **if** $front = rear$ **then true**
$\qquad\qquad\qquad\qquad\qquad$ **else false;**
$FRONT(q) \quad ::= $ **if** $ISEMTQ(q)$ **then error**
$\qquad\qquad\qquad\qquad\qquad$ **else** $q\,[front + 1];$

The procedures for ADDQ and DELETEQ are given as Programs 5.3 and 5.4.

---

procedure $addq$ $(item : items);$
$\{$ add $item$ to the queue $q\}$
$\{q, rear,$ and n are global variables$\}$
begin
$\quad$ **if** $rear = n$ **then** $queuefull$
$\qquad\qquad$ **else begin**
$\qquad\qquad\qquad rear := rear + 1;$
$\qquad\qquad\qquad q\,[rear] := item;$
$\qquad\qquad$ **end;**
end; $\{$ of $addq\}$

Program 5.3 Add to a queue

---

procedure $deleteq$(**var** $item : items);$
$\{$ delete from the front of q and put into $item\}$
begin
if $front = rear$ **then** $queueempty$
$\qquad\qquad$ **else begin**
$\qquad\qquad\qquad front := front + 1;$
$\qquad\qquad\qquad item := q\,[front];$
$\qquad\qquad$ **end;**
end; $\{$ of $deleteq\}$

Program 5.4 Delete from a queue

The correctness of this implementation may be established in a manner akin to that used for stacks. With this set up, notice that unless the front regularly catches up with the rear and both pointers are reset to zero, then the *queuefull* signal does not necessarily imply that there are *n* elements in the queue. That is, the queue will gradually move to the right. One obvious thing to do when *queuefull* is signaled is to move the entire queue to the left so that the first element is again at $q[1]$ and *front* = 0. This is time consuming, especially when there are many elements in the queue at the time of the *queuefull* signal.

Let us look at an example (Figure 5.3) which shows what could happen, in the worst case, if each time a queue of size n becomes full we choose to move the entire queue left so that it starts at $q[1]$. To begin, assume there are n elements $J_1, ..., J_n$ in the queue and we next receive alternate requests to delete and add elements. Each time a new element is added, the entire queue of $n-1$ elements is moved left.

front	rear	$q[1]$	[2]	[3]	.....	[n]	next operation
0	n	J_1	J_2	J_3	.....	J_n	initial state
1	n		J_2	J_3	.....	J_n	delete J_1
0	n	J_2	J_3	J_4	.....	J_{n+1}	add J_{n+1} (jobs J_2 through J_n are moved)
1	n		J_3	J_4	.....	J_{n+1}	delete J_2
0	n	J_3	J_4	J_5	.....	J_{n+2}	add J_{n+2}

Figure 5.3 Queue example

A more efficient queue representation is obtained by regarding the array $q[1..n]$ as circular. It now becomes more convenient to declare the array as $q[0..n-1]$. When *rear* = $n-1$, the next element is entered at $q[0]$ in case that spot is free. Using the same conventions as before, *front* will always point one position counterclockwise from the first element in the queue. Again, *front* = *rear* if and only if the queue is empty. Initially we have *front* = *rear* = 1. Figure 5.4 illustrates some of the possible configurations for a circular queue containing the four elements J1-J4 with $n > 4$. The assumption of circularity changes the *addq* and *deleteq* procedures slightly. In order to add an element, it will be necessary to move *rear* one position clockwise, i.e.,

if *rear* = $n - 1$ **then** *rear* := 0
        else *rear* := *rear* + 1.

Using the modulo operator which computes remainders, this is just *rear* := (*rear* + 1) **mod** n. Similarly, it will be necessary to move *front* one position clockwise each time a deletion is made. Again, using the modulo operator, this can be accomplished by *front* := (*front* + 1)**mod** n. An examination of the algorithms (Programs 5.5 and 5.6) indicates that addition and deletion can now be carried out in a fixed amount of time or O(1).

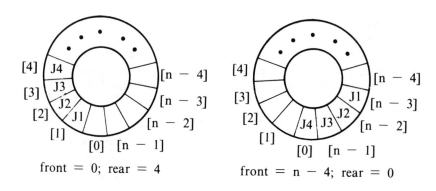

Figure 5.4 Circular queue of *n* elements and four jobs *J* 1, *J* 2, *J* 3, *J* 4

---

procedure *addq* (*item* : *items*);
{insert *item* into the circular queue stored in *q*[0..*n*−1]}
begin
    rear := (*rear* + 1)**mod** *n*; {advance *rear* clockwise}
    if *front* = *rear* **then** *queuefull*
                    else *q* [*rear*] := *item*; {insert}
end; {of *addq*}

Program 5.5 Add to a circular queue

One surprising point in the two algorithms is that the test for queue full in *addq* and the test for queue empty in *deleteq* are the same. In the case of *addq*, however, when *front* = *rear* is evaluated and found to be true, there is actually one space free, i.e., *q* [*rear*], since the first element in the queue is not at *q* [*front*] but is one position clockwise from this point. However, if we insert an item here, then we will not be able to distinguish between the cases full and empty, since this insertion would leave *front* = *rear*. To avoid this, we signal *queuefull*, thus permitting a maximum of *n*−1 rather than *n* elements to be in the queue at any time. One way to use all *n* positions would be to use another variable, *tag*, to distinguish between the two situations, i.e., *tag* = 0 if and only if the queue is empty. This would, however, slow down the two procedures. Since the *addq* and *deleteq* procedures will be used many times in any problem involving queues, the loss of one queue position will be more than made up for by the reduction in computing time.

```
procedure deleteq(var item : items);
{remove front element from q and put into item}
begin
  if front = rear then queueempty
              else begin
                    front := (front + 1) mod n; {advance front clockwise}
                    item := q [front];
                  end;
end; {of deleteq}
```

Program 5.6 Delete from a circular queue

The procedures *queuefull* and *queueempty* have been used without explanation, but they are similar to *stackfull* and *stackempty*. Their function will depend on the particular application. Note however that when *queuefull* is invoked the rear pointer has already been moved. This should be taken into account by this procedure.

5.2 A MAZING PROBLEM

The rat-in-a-maze experiment is a classical one from experimental psychology. A rat (or mouse) is placed through the door of a large box without a top. Walls are set up so that movements in most directions are obstructed. The rat is carefully observed by several scientists as it makes its way through the maze until it eventually reaches the exit. There is only one way out, but at the end is a nice hunk of cheese. The idea is to run the experiment repeatedly until the rat will zip through the maze without taking a single false path. The trials yield its learning curve.

We can write a computer program for getting through a maze and it will probably not be any smarter than the rat on its first try through. It may take many false paths before finding the right one. But the computer can remember the correct path far better than the rat. On its second try it should be able to go right to the end with no false paths taken, so there is no sense rerunning the program. Why don't you sit down and try to write this program yourself before you read on and look at our solution. Keep track of how many times you have to go back and correct something. This may give you an idea of your own learning curve as we rerun the experiment throughout the book.

Let us represent the maze by a two-dimensional array, $maze[1..m, 1..p]$, where a value of 1 implies a blocked path, while a 0 means one can walk right on through. We assume that the rat starts at $maze[1,1]$ and the exit is at $maze[m,p]$.

entrance →

0	1	0	0	0	1	1	0	0	0	1	1	1	1	1
1	0	0	0	1	1	0	1	1	1	0	0	1	1	1
0	1	1	0	0	0	0	1	1	1	1	0	0	1	1
1	1	0	1	1	1	1	0	1	1	0	1	1	0	0
1	1	0	1	0	0	1	0	1	1	1	1	1	1	1
0	0	1	1	0	1	1	1	0	1	0	0	1	0	1
0	1	1	1	1	0	0	1	1	1	1	1	1	1	1
0	0	1	1	0	1	1	0	1	1	1	1	1	0	1
1	1	0	0	0	1	1	0	1	1	0	0	0	0	0
0	0	1	1	1	1	1	0	0	0	1	1	1	1	0
0	1	0	0	1	1	1	1	1	0	1	1	1	1	0

→ exit

Figure 5.5

With the maze represented as a two-dimensional array, the location of the rat in the maze can at any time be described by the row, i, and the column, j, of its position. Now let us consider the possible moves the rat can make at some point $[i,j]$ in the maze. Figure 5.6 shows the possible moves from any point $[i,j]$. The position $[i,j]$ is marked by an X. If all the surrounding squares have a 0 then the rat can choose any of these eight squares as its next position. We call these eight directions by the names of the points on a compass: north, northeast, east, southeast, south, southwest, west, and northwest, or N, NE, E, SE, S, SW, W, NW.

We must be careful here because not every position has eight neighbors. If $[i,j]$ is on a border where either $i = 1$ or m, or $j = 1$ or p, then less than eight and possibly only three neighbors exist. To avoid checking for these border conditions we can surround the maze by a border of ones. The array will therefore be declared as $maze[0..m+1,0..p+1]$.

Another device that will simplify the problem is to predefine the possible directions to move in a table, *move*, as below

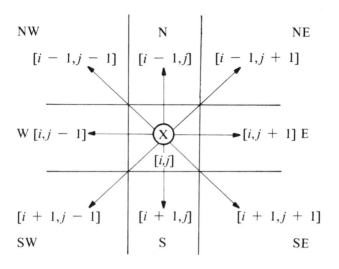

Figure 5.6

```
type offsets = record
            a : -1..1;
            b : -1..1;
        end;
    directions = (N, NE, E, SE, S, SW, W, NW);
var move : array[directions] of offsets;
```

q	move [q].a	move [q].b
N	-1	0
NE	-1	1
E	0	1
SE	1	1
S	1	0
SW	1	-1
W	0	-1
NW	-1	-1

If we are at position $[i,j]$ in the maze and we wish to find the position $[g,h]$ that is southwest of us, then we set

$g := i + move[SW].a;\ h := j + move[SW].b;$

For example, if we are at position [3,4], then position [3 + 1 = 4,4 + (−1) = 3] is southwest.

As we move through the maze we may have the chance to go in several directions. Not knowing which one to choose, we pick one but save our current position and the direction of the last move in a list. This way if we have taken a false path we can return and try another direction. With each new location we will examine the possibilities, starting from the north and looking clockwise. Finally, in order to prevent us from going down the same path twice we use another array $mark[0:m+1,0:p+1]$ which is initially zero. $mark[i,j]$ is set to 1 once we arrive at that position. We assume $maze[m,p] = 0$ as otherwise there is no path to the exit. Program 5.7 is a first pass at an algorithm.

```
initialize list to the maze entrance coordinates and direction north;
while list is not empty do
begin
  (i,j,mov) := coordinates and direction from front of list;
  while there are more moves do
  begin
    (g,h) := coordinates of next move;
    if (g = m) and (h = p) then success;
    if maze [g,h] = 0 {legal move}
      and (mark [g,h] = 0) {haven't been here before}
    then begin
         mark [g,h] := 1;
         add (i,j,mov) to front of list;
         i := g; j := h; mov := 0;
       end;
  end;
end;
writeln('no path found');
```

Program 5.7 First pass at maze algorithm

This is not a Pascal program and yet it describes the essential processing without too much detail. The use of indentation for delineating important blocks of code plus the use of Pascal reserved words make the looping and conditional tests transparent.

What remains to be pinned down? Using the three arrays *maze*, *mark*, and *move* we need only specify how to represent the list of new triples. Since the algorithm calls for removing first the most recently entered triple, this list should be a stack. We can use the sequential representation we saw before. All we need to know now is a reasonable bound on the size of this stack. Since each position in the maze is visited at most once, at most mp elements can be placed into the stack. Thus mp locations is a safe but somewhat conservative bound. In the following maze the only path has at most $\lceil m/2 \rceil (p+1)$ positions.

$$\begin{bmatrix} 0 & 0 & 0 & 0 & 0 & 0 \\ 1 & 1 & 1 & 1 & 1 & 0 \\ 0 & 0 & 0 & 0 & 0 & 0 \\ 0 & 1 & 1 & 1 & 1 & 1 \\ 0 & 0 & 0 & 0 & 0 & 0 \\ 1 & 1 & 1 & 1 & 1 & 0 \\ 0 & 0 & 0 & 0 & 0 & 0 \\ 0 & 1 & 1 & 1 & 1 & 1 \\ 0 & 0 & 0 & 0 & 0 & 0 \end{bmatrix}$$

Thus mp is not too crude a bound. We are now ready to give a precise maze algorithm (Program 5.8).

While using nonnumeric indices for *move* keeps the correspondence with direction transparent, it makes the resulting Pascal program somewhat cumbersome. This is so because the predecessor of N and the successor of NW are not defined. For this reason, in writing procedure *path* (Program 5.8), we assume that *move* is actually declared as:

var *move*: **array**[1..8] **of** *offsets;*

The correspondence is *move*[1] = *move*[N], ..., *move*[8] = *move*[NW].

The arrays *maze, mark, move*, and *stack* along with the variables or constants *top, m, p,* and *n* are assumed global to *path*. Further, it is assumed that *stack* [1..n] is an array of *items* where the type *items* is defined as:

type *items* = **record**
         $x : 1..m;$
         $y : 1..p;$
         $dir : 1..9;$
      end;

If n is at least mp, then the *stackfull* condition will never occur.

Now, what can we say about the computing time of this procedure? It is interesting that even though the problem is easy to grasp, it is difficult to make any but the most trivial statement about the computing time. The reason for this is because the number of

---

```
procedure path
{output a path (if any) in the maze. maze[0,i] = maze [m +1,i] =
maze [j,0] = maze [j,p +1] = 1, 0≤i≤p +1, 0≤j≤m+1}
label 99;
var position : items; d,g,h,i,j,q : integer;
begin
 {start at (1,1)}
 mark[1,1] := 1; top := 1;
 with stack[1] do begin x := 1; y := 1; dir := 2; end;
 while top > 0 do {stack not empty}
 begin
  delete (position); {unstack}
  with position do begin i := x; j := y; d := dir; end;
  while d <= 8 do {move forward}
  begin
  g := i + move [d].a; h := j + move [d].b;
  if (g = m) and (h = p) then {reached exit}
  begin {output path}
    for q := 1 to top do
      writeln(stack [q]);
    writeln(i, j);  writeln(m,p);
    goto 99; {end of procedure}
  end; {of if}
  if (maze [g,h] = 0) and mark [g,h] = 0)
  then begin {new position}
          mark [g,h] := 1;
          with position do x := i; y := j; dir := d+1; end;
          add (position); {stack it}
          i := g; j := h; d := 1; {move to (g,h)}
      end
      else d := d+1; {try next direction}
  end; {of while d <= 8}
 end; {of top > 0}
 writeln('no path in maze');
99: end; {of path}
```

Program 5.8 Procedure *path*

iterations of the main **while** loop is entirely dependent upon the given maze. What we can say is that each new position [i,j] that is visited gets marked, so paths are never taken twice. There are at most eight iterations of the inner **while** loop for each marked position. Each iteration of the inner **while** loop takes a fixed amount of time, O(1), and if the number of zeros in *maze* is z then at most z positions can get marked. Since z is bounded above by mp, the computing time is O(mp). (In actual experiments, however, the rat may be inspired by the watching psychologists and the invigorating odor from the cheese at the exit. It might reach its goal by examining far fewer paths than those examined by algorithm *path*. This may happen despite that fact that the rat has no pencil and only a very limited mental stack. It is difficult to incorporate the effect of the cheese odor and the cheering of the psychologists into a computer algorithm.) The array *mark* can be eliminated altogether and *maze*[g,h] changed to 1 instead of setting *mark*[g,h] to 1, but this will destroy the original maze.

5.3 EVALUATION OF EXPRESSIONS

When pioneering computer scientists conceived the idea of higher level programming languages, they were faced with many technical hurdles. One of the biggest was the question of how to generate machine language instructions which would properly evaluate any arithmetic expression. A complex assignment statement such as

$$X := A/B - C + D * E - A * C \tag{5.1}$$

might have several meanings, and even if it were uniquely defined, say by a full use of parentheses, it still seemed a formidable task to generate a correct and reasonable instruction sequence. Fortunately the solution we have today is both elegant and simple. Moreover, it is so simple that this aspect of compiler writing is really one of the more minor issues.

An expression is made up of operands, operators and delimiters. The expression above has five operands: $A,B,C,D,$ and E. Though these are all one letter variables, operands can be any legal variable name or constant in our programming language. In any expression the values that variables take must be consistent with the operations performed on them. These operations are described by the operators. In most programming languages there are several kinds of operators which correspond to the different kinds of data a variable can hold. First, there are the basic arithmetic operators: plus, minus, times, and divide (+, −, *, /). Other arithmetic operators include unary minus, **mod**, and **div**. The latter two may sometimes be library subroutines rather than predefined operators. A second class is the relational operators: <, <=, =, < >,>=, >. These are usually defined to work for arithmetic operands, but they can just as easily work for character string data. ('CAT' is less than 'DOG' since it precedes 'DOG' in alphabetical order.) The result of an expression which contains relational operators is one of the two constants: **true** or **false**. Such an expression is called boolean, named after the mathematician George Boole, the father of symbolic logic. There also may be logical operators such as **and**, **or**, and **not**.

The first problem with understanding the meaning of an expression is to decide in what order the operations are carried out. This means that every language must uniquely define such an order. For instance, if $A = 4$, $B = C = 2$, $D = E = 3$, then in Eq.5.1 we might want X to be assigned the value

$$((4/2) - 2) + (3 * 3) - (4 * 2)$$
$$= 0 + 9 - 8$$
$$= 1$$

However, the true intention of the programmer might have been to assign X the value

$$(4/(2 - 2 + 3)) * (3 - 4) * 2$$
$$= (4/3) * (-1) * 2$$
$$= -0.6666666$$

Of course, he could specify the latter order of evaluation by using parentheses:

$$X := ((A/(B - C + D)) * (E - A) * C$$

To fix the order of evaluation, we assign to each operator a priority. Then within any pair of parentheses we understand that operators with the highest priority will be evaluated first. A set of sample priorities from Turbo Pascal is given in Figure 5.7. The highest priority is 1. **shl** and **shr** stand for shift left and shift right. For example, 2 **shl** 5 = 64 and 64 **shl** 5 = 2.

priority	operator
1	unary minus
2	**not**
3	*, /, **div, mod, and, shl, shr**
4	+, −, **or, xor**
5	<, <=, =, <>, >=, >, **in**

Figure 5.7 Priority of operators in Turbo Pascal, version 3.0

Notice that all of the relational operators have the same priority. Unary minus has top priority followed by boolean negation. When we have an expression where two adjacent operators have the same priority, we need a rule to tell us which one to perform first. For example, do we want the value of $-A+B$ to be understood as $(-A) + B$ or $-(A + B)$? Convince yourself that there will be a difference by trying $A = -1$ and $B = 2$. The Pascal rule is that for all priorities, evaluation of operators of the same priority will proceed left to right. Remember that by using parentheses we can override these rules, as expressions are always evaluated with the innermost parenthesized expression first.

Now that we have specified priorities and rules for breaking ties we know how $X:=A/B-C+D*E-A*C$ will be evaluated, namely, as

$$X:=(((A/B)-C)+(D*E))-(A*C)$$

How can a compiler accept such an expression and produce correct code? The answer is given by reworking the expression into a form we call postfix notation. If e is an expression with operators and operands, the conventional way of writing e is called *infix*, because the operators come *in*-between the operands. (Unary operators precede their operand.) The *postfix* form of an expression calls for each operator to appear *after* its operands. For example,

$$\text{infix: } A*B/C \text{ has postfix: } AB*C/.$$

If we study the postfix form of $A*B/C$ we see that the multiplication comes immediately after its two operands A and B. Now imagine that $A*B$ is computed and stored in T. Then we have the division operator, $/$, coming immediately after its two operands T and C.

Let us look at our previous example

$$\text{infix: } A/B-C+D*E-A*C$$

$$\text{postfix: } AB/C-DE*+AC*-$$

and trace out the meaning of the postfix.

Every time we compute a value let us store it in the temporary location T_i, $i \geq 1$. Reading left to right, the first operation is division.

Operation	Postfix
$T_1 := A/B$	$T_1C-DE*+AC*-$
$T_2 := T_1-C$	$T_2DE*+AC*-$
$T_3 := D*E$	T_2T_3+AC*-
$T_4 := T_2+T_3$	T_4AC*-
$T_5 := A*C$	T_4T_5-
$T_6 := T_4-T_5$	T_6

So T_6 will contain the result. Notice that if we had parenthesized the expression, this would change the postfix only if the order of normal evaluation were altered. Thus,

$(A/B)-C+(D*E)-A*C$ will have the same postfix form as the previous expression without parentheses. But $(A/B)-(C+D)*(E-A)*C$ will have the postfix form $AB/CD+EA-*C*-$.

Before attempting an algorithm to translate expressions from infix to postfix notation, let us make some observations regarding the virtues of postfix notation that enable easy evaluation of expressions. To begin with, the need for parentheses is eliminated. Secondly, the priority of the operators is no longer relevant. The expression may be evaluated by making a left to right scan, stacking operands, and evaluating operators using as operands the correct number from the stack and finally placing the result onto the stack (see Program 5.9). This evaluation process is much simpler than attempting direct evaluation from infix notation.

```
procedure eval (e : expression);
{evaluate the postfix expression e. It is assumed that the last
token (a token is either an operator, operand, or '#')
in e is '#.' A procedure nexttoken is used to extract from e
the next token. A one-dimensional array
stack[1..n] is used as a stack.}
var x : token;
begin
  top := 0; {initialize stack}
  x := nexttoken (e);
  while x <> '#' do
  begin
    if x is an operand
    then add (x) {add to stack}
    else begin {operator}
         remove the correct number of operands for operator
         x from stack; perform the operation x and store the
         result (if any) onto the stack;
      end;
    x := nexttoken (e);
  end; {of while}
end; {of eval}
```

Program 5.9 Algorithm to evaluate postfix expressions

To see how to devise an algorithm for translating from infix to postfix, note that the order of the operands in both forms is the same. In fact, it is simple to describe an algorithm for producing postfix from infix:

(1)   Fully parenthesize the expression

(2)   Move all operators so that they replace their corresponding right parentheses

(3)   Delete all parentheses

For example, $A/B-C+D*E-A*C$ when fully parenthesized yields

$$((((A / B) - C) + (D * E)) - A * C))$$

The arcs join an operator and its corresponding right parenthesis. Performing steps 2 and 3 gives

$$AB/C-DE*+AC*-$$

The problem with this as an algorithm is that it requires two passes: the first one reads the expression and parenthesizes it while the second actually moves the operators.

As we have already observed, the order of the operands is the same in infix and postfix. So as we scan an expression for the first time, we can form the postfix by immediately passing any operands to the output. Then it is just a matter of handling the operators. The solution is to store them in a stack until just the right moment and then to unstack and pass them to the output.

For example, since we want $A+B*C$ to yield $ABC*+$ our algorithm should perform the following sequence of stacking (these stacks will grow to the right):

Next Token	Stack	Output
none	empty	none
A	empty	A
+	+	A
B	+	AB

At this point the algorithm must determine if $*$ gets placed on top of the stack or if the $+$ gets taken off. Since $*$ has higher priority we should stack $*$ producing

$*$	$+*$	AB
C	$+*$	ABC

Now the input expression is exhausted, so we output all remaining operators in the stack to get

ABC*+

For another example, $A*(B+C)*D$ has the postfix form $ABC+*D*$, and so the algorithm should behave as

Next Token	Stack	Output
none	empty	none
A	empty	A
$*$	$*$	A
(	$*($	A
B	$*($	AB
$+$	$*(+$	AB
C	$*(+$	ABC

At this point we want to unstack down to the corresponding left parenthesis, and then delete the left and right parentheses; this gives us:

)	$*$	ABC+
$*$	$*$	ABC+*
D	$*$	ABC+*D
done	empty	ABC+*D*

These examples motivate a priority based scheme for stacking and unstacking operators. The left parenthesis complicates things as when it is not in the stack, it behaves as an operator with high priority while once it gets in it behaves as one with low priority (no operator other than the matching right parenthesis should cause it to get unstacked). We establish two priorities for operators: *isp* (in-stack priority) and *icp* (in-coming priority). The *isp* and *icp* of all operators in Figure 5.7 is the priority given in this figure. In addition, we define $isp['('] = 5$, $icp['('] = 0$, and $isp['\#'] = 5$. These priorities result in the following rule: *operators are taken out of the stack as long as their in-stack priority is numerically less than or equal to the in-coming priority of the new operator.* Our algorithm to transform from infix to postfix is given in Program 5.10.

```
procedure postfix(e : expression);
{output the postfix form of the infix expression e.
nexttoken and stack are as in procedure eval. It is
assumed that the last token in e is '#.' Also, '#' is used
at the bottom of the stack.}
var x,y : token;
begin
  stack[1] := '#'; top := 1; {initialize stack}
  x := nexttoken (e);
  while x <> '#' do
  begin
    if x is an operand
    then write(x)
    else if x = ')'
        then begin {unstack until '('}
                while stack [top] <> '(' do
                begin delete (y); write(y); end;
                delete (y); {delete '('}
             end
        else begin
                while isp [stack [top]] <= icp [x] do
                begin delete (y); write(y); end;
                add (x);
             end;
    x := nexttoken (e);
  end; {of while}
  {end of expression; empty stack}
  while top > 1 do
  begin delete (y); write(y); end;
  writeln('#');
end; {of postfix}
```

Program 5.10 Convert from infix to postfix form

As for the computing time, the algorithm makes only one pass across the input. If the expression has n symbols, then the number of operations is proportional to some constant times n.

5.4 MULTIPLE STACKS AND QUEUES

Up to now we have been concerned only with the representations of a single stack or a single queue in the memory of a computer. For these two cases we have seen efficient sequential data representations. What happens when a data representation is needed for several stacks and queues? Let us once again limit ourselves to sequential mappings of these data objects into an array $v[1..m]$. If we have only two stacks to represent, then the solution is simple. We can use $v[1]$ for the bottommost element in stack 1 and $v[m]$ for the corresponding element in stack 2. Stack 1 can grow towards $v[m]$ and stack 2 towards $v[1]$. It is therefore possible to utilize efficiently all the available space. Can we do the same when more than two stacks are to be represented? The answer is no, because a one-dimensional array has only two fixed points, $v[1]$ and $v[m]$, and each stack requires a fixed point for its bottom most element. When more than two stacks, say n, are to be represented sequentially, we can initially divide out the available memory $v[1..m]$ into n segments and allocate one of these segments to each of the n stacks. This initial division of $v[1..m]$ into segments may be done in proportion to expected sizes of the various stacks if these are known. In the absence of such information, $v[1..m]$ may be divided into equal segments. For each stack i we shall use $b[i]$ to represent a position one less than the position in v for the bottommost element of that stack. $t[i]$, $1 \le i \le n$ will point to the topmost element of stack i. We shall use the boundary condition $b[i] = t[i]$ iff the i'th stack is empty. If we grow the i'th stack in lower memory indices than the $(i+1)$'th, then with roughly equal initial segments we have

$$b[i] = t[i] = \lfloor m/n \rfloor (i - 1), \ 1 \le i \le n$$

as the initial values of $b[i]$ and $t[i]$ (see Figure 5.8). Stack i, $1 \le i \le n$ can grow from $b[i] + 1$ up to $b[i+1]$ before it catches up with the $(i+1)$'th stack. It is convenient both for the discussion and the algorithms to define $b[n+1] = m$. Using this scheme, the add and delete algorithms of Programs 5.11 and 5.12 result.

The algorithms to add and delete appear to be as simple as in the case of only one or two stacks. This really is not the case since the *stackfull* condition in algorithm *add* does not imply that all m locations of v are in use. In fact, there may be a lot of unused space between stacks j and $j + 1$ for $1 \le j \le n$ and $j \ne i$ (Figure 5.9). The procedure *stackfull(i)* should therefore determine whether there is any free space in v and shift stacks around so as to make some of this free space available to the i'th stack.

Several strategies are possible for the design of algorithm *stackfull*. We shall discuss one strategy in the text and look at some others in the exercises. The primary objective of algorithm *stackfull* is to permit the adding of elements to stacks so long as there is some free space in v. One way to guarantee this is to design *stackfull* along the following lines:

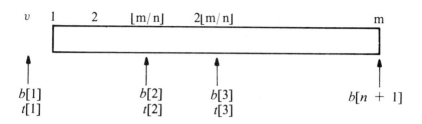

Figure 5.8 Initial configuration for n stacks in $v[1..m]$. All stacks are empty and memory is divided into roughly equal segments.

procedure *add* (i : **integer**; x : *items*);
{add x to the i'th *stack*}
begin
  if $t[i] = b[i+1]$ **then** *stackfull* (i)
                  else begin
                       $t[i] := t[i] + 1$;
                       $v[t[i]] := x$; {add to i'th stack}
                  end;
end; {of *add*}

Program 5.11 Add to i'th stack

(1)   Determine the least, j, $i < j \le n$ such that there is free space between stacks j and $j + 1$, i.e., $t[j] < b[j+1]$. If there is such a j, then move stacks $i + 1, i + 2, ..., j$ one position to the right (treating $v[1]$ as leftmost and $v[m]$ as rightmost), thereby creating a space between stacks i and $i + 1$.

(2)   If there is no j as in (1), then look to the left of stack i. Find the largest j such that $1 \le j < i$ and there is space between stacks j and $j + 1$, i.e., $t[j] < b[j + 1]$. If there is such a j, then move stacks $j + 1, j + 2, ..., i$ one space left creating a free space between stacks i and $i + 1$.

(3)   If there is no j satisfying either the conditions of (1) or (2), then all m spaces of v are utilized and there is no free space.

procedure *delete* (*i* : **integer**; **var** *x* : *items*);
{*delete* topmost item of stack *i*}
begin
  if $t[i] = b[i]$ **then** *stackempty* (*i*)
         else begin
            $x := v[t[i]]$;
            $t[i] := t[i] - 1$;
         end;
end; {of *delete*}

Program 5.12 Delete from *i*'th stack

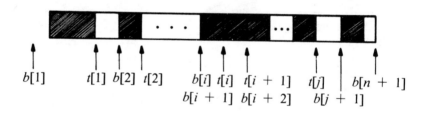

Figure 5.9 Configuration when stack *i* meets with stack *i* + 1 but there is still free space elsewhere in *v*

    The writing of algorithm *stackfull* using the above strategy is left as an exercise. It should be clear that the worst case performance of this representation for the *n* stacks together with the above strategy for *stackfull* would be rather poor. In fact, in the worst case O(*m*) time may be needed for each insertion (see exercises). In the next chapter we shall see that if we do not limit ourselves to sequential mappings of data objects into arrays, then we can obtain a data representation for *m* stacks that has a much better worst case performance than the representation described here. Sequential representations for *n* queues and other generalizations are discussed in the exercises.

5.5 EXERCISES

1. Consider the railroad switching network given below:

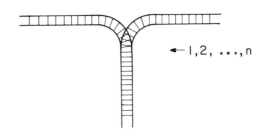

⟵ 1, 2, ..., n

   Railroad cars numbered 1, 2, 3 ..., n are at the right. Each car is brought into the stack and removed at any time. For instance, if $n = 3$, we could move 1 in, move 2 in, move 3 in, and then take the cars out producing the new order 3, 2, 1. For $n = 3$ and 4 what are the possible permutations of the cars that can be obtained? Are any permutations not possible?

2. Using a boolean variable to distinguish between a circular queue being empty or full, write insert and delete procedures.

3. Complete the correctness proof for the stack implementation of section 5.1.

4. A double-ended queue (deque) is a linear list in which additions and deletions may be made at either end. Obtain a data representation mapping a deque into a one-dimensional array. Write algorithms to add and delete elements from either end of the deque.

5. A linear list is being maintained circularly in an array $c[0..n-1]$ with *front* and *rear* set up as for circular queues.

   (a) Obtain a formula in terms of *front*, *rear*, and n for the number of elements in the list.

   (b) Write an algorithm to delete the k'th element in the list.

   (c) Write an algorithm to insert an element y immediately after the k'th element. What is the time complexity of your algorithms for (b) and (c)?

6. Let $L = (a_1, a_2, ..., a_n)$ be a linear list represented in the array $v[1..n]$ using the mapping: the i'th element of L is stored in $v[i]$. Write an algorithm to make an in-place reversal of the order of elements in v. I.e., the algorithm should transform v such that $v[i]$ contains the $(n - i + 1)$'th element of L. The only additional space available to your algorithm is that for simple variables. The input to the algorithm is v and n. How much time does your algorithm take to accomplish the reversal?

7. (a) Find a path through the maze of Figure 5.5.

    (b) Trace out the action of procedure *path* on the maze of Figure 5.5. Compare this to your own attempt in (a).

8. What is the maximum path length from start to finish for any maze of dimensions $n \times m$?

9. Write the postfix form of the following expressions:

    (a) $A * B * C$

    (b) $-A + B - C + D$

    (c) $A * -B + C$

    (d) $(A + B) * D + E / (F + A * D) + C$

    (e) A **and** B **or** C **or** **not** $(E > F)$ (assuming Pascal precedence)

    (f) **not** $(A$ **and** **not** $((B < C)$ **or** $(C > D)))$ **or** $(C < E)$

10. Use the priorities of Figure 5.7 together with those for '(' and '#' to answer the following:

    (a) In algorithm *postfix* what is the maximum number of elements that can be on the stack at any time if the input expression e has n operators and delimiters?

    (b) What is the answer to (a) if e has n operators, and the depth of nesting of parentheses is at most 6?

11. Another expression form that is easy to evaluate and is parenthesis free is known as *prefix*. In this way of writing expressions, the operators precede their operands. For example:

infix	prefix
$A * B / C$	$/ * ABC$
$A / B - C + D * E - A * C$	$- + - / ABC * DE * AC$
$A * (B + C) / D - G$	$- / * A + BCDG$

    Notice that the order of operands is not changed in going from infix to prefix.

    (a) What is the prefix form of the expressions in Exercise 9?

    (b) Write an algorithm to evaluate a prefix expression, e. (Hint: Scan e right to left and assume that the leftmost token of e is '#.')

    (c) Write an algorithm to transform an infix expression e into its prefix equivalent. Assume that the input expression e begins with a '#' and that the prefix expression should begin with a '#.'

    What is the time complexity of your algorithms for (b) and (c)? How much space is needed by each of these algorithms?

12. Write an algorithm to transform from prefix to postfix. Carefully state any assumptions you make regarding the input. How much time and space does your algorithm take?

13. Do the preceding exercise but this time for a transformation from postfix to prefix.

14. Write an algorithm to generate fully parenthesized infix expressions from their postfix form. What is the complexity (time and space) of your algorithm?

15. Do the preceding exercise starting from prefix form.

16. Two stacks are to be represented in an array $v[1..m]$ as described in Section 5.4. Write algorithms $add(i,x)$ and $delete(i)$ to add x and delete an element from stack i, $1 \leq i \leq 2$. Your algorithms should be able to add elements to the stacks so long as there are fewer than m elements in both stacks together.

17. Obtain a data representation mapping a stack s and a queue q into a single array $v[1..n]$. Write algorithms to add and delete elements from these two data objects. What can you say about the suitability of your data representation?

18. Write a Pascal procedure implementing the strategy for $stackfull(i)$ outlined in Section 5.4.

19. For the add and $delete$ algorithms of Section 5.4 and the $stackfull(i)$ algorithm of the preceding exercise produce a sequence of adds and deletes that will require $O(m)$ time for each add. Use $n = 2$ and start from a configuration representing a full utilization of $v[1..m]$.

20. Another strategy for the $stackfull(i)$ condition of Section 5.4 is to redistribute all the free space in proportion to the rate of growth of individual stacks since the last call to $stackfull$. This would require the use of another array $lt[1..n]$ where $lt[j]$ is the value of $t[j]$ at the last call to $stackfull$. Then the amount by which each stack has grown since the last call is $t[j] - lt[j]$. The amount for stack i is actually $t[i] - lt[i] + 1$, since we are not attempting to add another element to i.

    Write algorithm $stackfull(i)$ to redistribute all the stacks so that the free space between stacks j and $j + 1$ is in proportion to the growth of stack j since the last call to $stackfull$. $Stackfull(i)$ should assign at least one free location to stack i.

21. Design a data representation sequentially mapping n queues into an array $v[1..m]$. Represent each queue as a circular queue within v. Write procedures $addq$, $deleteq$, and $queuefull$ for this representation.

22. Design a data representation, sequentially mapping n data objects into an array $v[1..m]$. n_1 of these data objects are stacks and the remaining $n_2 = n - n_1$ are queues. Write algorithms to add and delete elements from these objects. Use the same $spacefull$ algorithm for both types of data objects. This algorithm should provide space for the i'th data object if there is some space not currently being used. Note that a circular queue with space for r elements can hold only $r - 1$.

23. [Landweber]
    People have spent so much time playing card games of solitaire that the gambling casinos are now capitalizing on this human weakness. A form of solitaire is described below. Your assignment is to write a computer program to play the game thus freeing hours of time for people to return to more useful endeavors.

    To begin the game, 28 cards are dealt into seven piles. The leftmost pile has one card, the next two cards, and so forth up to seven cards in the rightmost pile. Only the uppermost card of each of the seven piles is turned face-up. The cards are dealt left to right, one card to each pile, dealing to one less pile each time, and turning the first card in each round face-up. On the topmost face-up card of each pile you may build in descending sequences red on black or black on red. For example, on the 9 of spades you may place either the 8 of diamonds or the 8 of hearts. All face up cards on a pile are moved as a unit and may be placed on another pile according to the bottommost face up card. For example, the 7 of clubs on the 8 of hearts may be moved as a unit onto the 9 of clubs or the 9 of spades.

    Whenever a face down-card is uncovered, it is turned face-up. If one pile is removed completely, a face-up King may be moved from a pile (together with all cards above it) or the top of the waste pile (see below) into the vacated space. There are four output piles, one for each suit, and the object of the game is to get as many cards as possible into the output piles. Each time an Ace appears at the top of a pile or the top of the stack it is moved into the appropriate output pile. Cards are added to the output piles in sequence, the suit for each pile being determined by the Ace on the bottom.

    From the rest of the deck, called the stock, cards are turned up one by one and placed face up on a waste pile. You may always play cards off the top of the waste pile, but only one at a time. Begin by moving a card from the stock to the top of the waste pile. If there is ever more than one possible play to be made, the following order must be observed:

    (a) Move a card from the top of a playing pile or from the top of the waste pile to an output pile. If the waste pile becomes empty, move a card from the stock to the waste pile.

    (b) Move a card from the top of the waste pile to the leftmost playing pile to which it can be moved. If the waste pile becomes empty move a card from the stock to the waste pile.

    (c) Find the leftmost playing pile which can be moved and place it on top of the leftmost playing pile to which it can be moved.

(d)   Try (a), (b) and (c) in sequence, restarting with (a) whenever a move is made.

(e)   If no move is made via (a) - (d) move a card from the stock to the waste pile and retry (a).

Only the topmost card of the playing piles or the waste pile may be played to an output pile. Once played on an output pile, a card may not be withdrawn to help elsewhere. The game is over when either

- all the cards have been played to the output or

- the stock pile has been exhausted and no more cards can be moved.

When played for money, the player pays the house $52 at the beginning, and wins $5 for every card played to the output piles. Write your program so that it will play several games and determine your net winnings. Use a random number generator to shuffle the deck. Output a complete record of two games in easily understood form. Include as output the number of games played and the net winnings (+ or −).

CHAPTER 6
LINKED LISTS

6.1 SINGLY LINKED LISTS

In the previous chapters, we studied the representation of simple data structures using an array and a sequential mapping. These representations had the property that successive nodes of the data object were stored a fixed distance apart. Thus, (1) if the element a_{ij} of a table was stored at location L_{ij}, then $a_{i,j+1}$ was at the location $L_{ij} + c$ for some constant c; (2) if the i'th node in a queue was at location L_i, then the $(i + 1)$'th node was at location $L_i + c$ mod n for the circular representation; (3) if the topmost node of a stack was at location L_T, then the node beneath it was at location $L_T - c$, etc. These sequential storage schemes proved adequate given the functions you wish to perform (access to an arbitrary node in a table, insertion or deletion of nodes within a stack or queue). However, when a sequential mapping is used for ordered lists, operations such as insertion and deletion of arbitrary elements become expensive. For example, consider the following list of three letter English words ending in AT:

(BAT, CAT, EAT, FAT, HAT, JAT, LAT, MAT,

OAT, PAT, RAT, SAT, TAT, VAT, WAT)

To make this list complete we naturally want to add the word GAT, which means gun or revolver. If we are using an array to keep this list, then the insertion of GAT will require us to move elements already in the list either one location higher or lower. We must either move HAT, JAT, LAT, ..., WAT or else move BAT, CAT, EAT, and FAT. If we have to do many such insertions into the middle, then neither alternative is attractive because of the amount of data movement. On the other hand, suppose we decide to remove the word LAT which refers to the Latvian monetary unit. Then again, we have to move many elements so as to maintain the sequential representation of the list.

When our problem called for several ordered lists of varying sizes, sequential representation again proved to be inadequate. By storing each list in a different array of maximum size, storage may be wasted. By maintaining the lists in a single array a potentially large amount of data movement is needed. This was explicitly observed when we represented several stacks, queues, polynomials, and matrices. All these data objects are examples of ordered lists. Polynomials are ordered by exponent while matrices are ordered by rows and columns. In this chapter we shall present an alternate representation for ordered lists which will reduce the time needed for arbitrary insertion and deletion.

An elegant solution to this problem of data movement in *sequential* representations is achieved by using *linked* representations. Unlike a sequential representation where successive items of a list are located a fixed distance apart, in a linked representation these items may be placed anywhere in memory. Another way of saying this is that in a sequential representation the order of elements is the same as in the ordered list, while in a linked representation these two sequences need not be the same. To access elements in the list in the correct order, with each element we store the address or location of the next element in that list. Thus, associated with each data item in a linked representation is a pointer to the next item. This pointer is often referred to as a link. In general, a *node* is a collection of data, *data*1, ..., *datan* and links *link*1, ..., *linkm*. Each item in a node is called a *field*. A field contains either a data item or a link.

Figure 6.1 shows how some of the nodes of the list we considered before may be represented in memory by using pointers. The elements of the list are stored in a one-dimensional array called *data*. But the elements no longer occur in sequential order, BAT before CAT before EAT, etc. Instead we relax this restriction and allow them to appear anywhere in the array and in any order. To remind us of the real order, a second array, *link*, is added. The values in this array are pointers to elements in the *data* array. Since the list starts at *data*[8] = BAT, let us set a variable $f = 8$. *link*[8] has the value 3, which means it points to *data*[3] which contains CAT. The third element of the list is pointed at by *link*[3] which is EAT. By continuing in this way we can list all the words in the proper order. We recognize that we have come to the end when *link* has a value of zero.

Some of the values of *data* and *link* and undefined such as *data*[2], *link*[2], *data*[5], *link*[5], etc. We shall ignore this for the moment.

It is customary to draw linked lists as an ordered sequence of nodes with links being represented by arrows as in Figure 6.2. We shall use the name of the pointer variable that points to the list as the name of the entire list.

Thus the list of Figure 6.2 is the list *f*. Notice that we do not explicitly put in the values of the pointers but simply draw arrows to indicate they are there. This is so that we reinforce in our own mind the facts that (1) the nodes do not actually reside in sequential

	data	*link*
1	HAT	15
2		
3	CAT	4
4	EAT	9
5		
6		
7	WAT	0
8	BAT	3
9	FAT	1
10		
11	VAT	7
	.	.
	.	.
	.	.

Figure 6.1 Nonsequential list representation

locations, and (2) the locations of nodes may change on different runs. Therefore, when we write a program which works with lists, we almost never look for a specific address except when we test for zero.

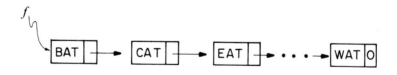

Figure 6.2 Usual way to draw a linked list

Let us now see why it is easier to make arbitrary insertions and deletions using a linked list rather than a sequential list. To insert the data item GAT between FAT and HAT the following steps are adequate:

(1)   Get a node which is currently unused; let its address be x

(2)   Set the *data* field of this node to GAT

(3)   Set the *link* field to x to point to the node after FAT which contains HAT

(4)   Set the *link* field of the node containing FAT to x

Figure 6.3(a) shows how the arrays *data* and *link* will be changed after we insert GAT.

	data	link
1	HAT	15
2		
3	CAT	4
4	EAT	9
5	GAT	1
6		
7	WAT	0
8	BAT	3
9	FAT	5
10		
11	VAT	7

Figure 6.3(a) Insert GAT into *data*[5]

Figure 6.3(b) shows how we can draw the insertion using our arrow notation. The new arrows are dashed. The important thing to notice is that when we insert GAT we do not have to move any elements which are already in the list. We have overcome the need to move data at the expense of the storage needed for the second field, *link*. But we will see that this is not too severe a penalty.

Now suppose we want to delete GAT from the list. All we need to do is find the element which immediately precedes GAT, which is FAT, and set *link*[9] to the position of HAT which is 1. Again, there is no need to move the data around. Even though the *link* field of GAT still contains a pointer to HAT, GAT is no longer in the list (see Figure 6.4).

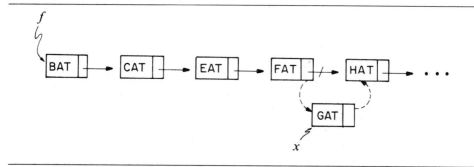

Figure 6.3(b) Insert node GAT into list

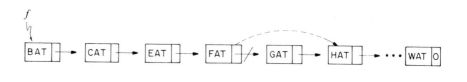

Figure 6.4 Delete GAT from list

From our brief discussion of linked lists, we see that the following capabilities are needed to make linked representations possible:

(1)   A mechanism to define the structure of a node (i.e., the fields that it is composed of)

(2)   A means to create nodes as needed

(3)   A way to free nodes that are no longer in use

These capabilities are provided in the programming language Pascal. To define a node structure, we need to know the **type** of each of its fields. The data field in the above example is simply an array of characters while the *link* field is a pointer to another node. In Pascal, pointer types are defined as:

type *pointertype* = ↑*nodetype*;

where *nodetype* refers to the type of nodes that the pointer may point to. *The symbol* ↑ *denotes the indirection operator* ^. *When keying in a Pascal program, you must use the* ^

key where ever the symbol ↑ appears in this text. In texts, it is customary to use ↑ rather than ^ to denote a pointer.

If the type of the nodes in our earlier example is denoted by *threeletternode* then *ptr*, defined below, gives the type of the *link* field of the nodes.

type *ptr* = ↑*threeletternode*;

The data type *threeletternode* may itself be defined as a record as below;

type *threeletternode* = **record**
                data : **array**[1..3] **of char**;
                link : *ptr*;
           end;

Note that the variable *f* in the *threeletternode* example is also a pointer and its type is to be declared as:

var *f* : *ptr*;

The fields of the node pointed to by *f* may be referenced in the following way:

f↑.*data*, *f*↑.*link*

and the components of the data field are referenced as:

f↑.*data* [1], *f*↑.*data* [2], *f*↑.*data* [3]

This is shown diagrammatically in Figure 6.5.

Example 6.1: If a linked list is to consist of nodes that have a *data* field of type integer and a *link* field, the following type definition can be used:

type *pointer* = ↑*listnode*;
      listnode = **record**
                data : **integer**;
                link : *pointer*;
            end;

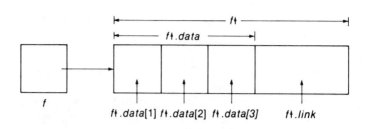

Figure 6.5 Referencing the fields of a node

The type definition

type *ptra* = ↑*nodea*;
    ptrb = ↑*nodeb*;
    nodea = **record**
           data 1 : **integer**;
           data 2 : **char**;
           data 3 : **real**;
           linka : *ptra*;
           linkb : *ptrb*;
        end;
    nodeb = **record**
           data : **integer**;
           link : *ptrb*;
        end;

defines the type *nodea* to consist of three data fields and two link fields while nodes of type *nodeb* will consist of one data field and one link field. Note that the *linkb* field of nodes of type *nodea* must point to nodes of type *nodeb*. □

Nodes of a predefined type may be created using the procedure *new*. If *f* is of type *ptr* then following the call *new* (*f*),*f*↑ denotes the node (or variable) of type *threeletter-node* that is created. Similarly, if *x, y,* and *z* are, respectively, of type *pointer, ptra,* and *ptrb* (cf. Example 6.1), then following the sequence of calls

new(*x*); *new*(*y*); *new*(*z*);

x↑, *y*↑, and *z*↑ will, respectively, denote the nodes of type *listnode, nodea,* and *nodeb* that are created. These nodes may be disposed in the following way:

dispose(f); dispose(x); dispose(y); dispose(z);

Note that some implementations of Pascal do not provide a *dispose* function.

Pascal also provides a special constant **nil** that may be assigned to any pointer variable, regardless of type. This is generally used to denote a pointer field that points to no node (for example, the link field in the last node of Figure 6.3(b)) or an empty list (as in $f =$ **nil**).

Arithmetic on pointer variables is not permitted. However, two pointer variables of the same type may be compared to see if both point to the same node. Thus if x and y are pointer variables of the same type then the expressions

$x = y, x < > y, x =$ **nil**, and $x < >$ **nil**

are valid while the expressions

$x + 1$ and $y * 2$

are invalid.

The effect of the assignments:

$x := y$ and $x\uparrow := y\uparrow$

on the initial configuration of Figure 6.6(a) is given in Figure 6.6(b) and (c). Note also that pointer values may neither be input nor output. In many applications, these restrictions on the use of pointers create no difficulties.

In fact, in most applications, it does not even make sense to perform arithmetic on pointers. However, there are applications where we will want to perform arithmetic and/or input/output on pointers. We shall see applications where arithmetic on pointers is required in Sections 6.7 and 6.9. Applications requiring input/output of pointer values will be seen in Chapters 8 and 10. When arithmetic and/or input/output on pointers is to be performed, we can implement our own pointer type by using integers. This is discussed in Section 6.7.

Example 6.2: Procedure *create2* creates a linked list with two nodes of type *listnode* (cf. Example 6.1). The *data* field of the first node is set to 10 and that of the second to 20. *first* is a pointer to the first node. The resulting list structure is:

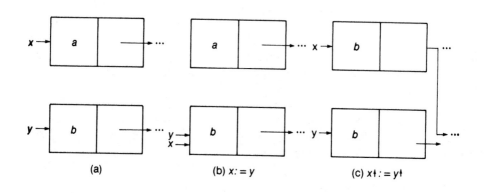

Figure 6.6 Effect of pointer assignments

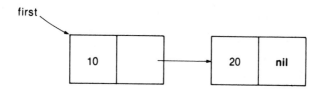

```
procedure create 2(var first : pointer);
var second : pointer;
begin
  new (first);
  new (second);
  first ↑. link := second;  {link first node to second}
  second ↑. link := nil;  {last node}
  first ↑. data := 10;  {set data of first node}
  second ↑. data := 20;  {set data of second node}
end; {of create2}
```

Program 6.1 Create2

Example 6.3: Let *first* be a pointer to a linked list as in Example 6.2. *first* = **nil** if the list is empty (i.e., there are no nodes on the list). Let *x* be a pointer to some arbitrary node in the list. Program 6.2 inserts a node with data field 50 following the node pointed at by *x*. The resulting list structures for the two cases *first* = **nil** and *first* ≠ **nil** are:

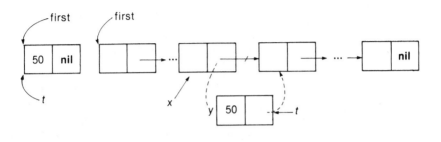

procedure *insert* (**var** *first* : *pointer* ; *x* : *pointer*);
var *t* : *pointer* ;
begin
  new (*t*); {get a new node}
  t↑. *data* := 50; {set its data field}
  if *first* = **nil then begin** {insert into empty list}
               first := *t*;
               t↑. *link* := **nil**;
          end
  else begin {insert after *x*}
      t↑. *link* := *x*↑. *link*;
      x↑. *link* := *t*;
    end;
end; {of insert}

Program 6.2 Insert

Example 6.4: Let *first* and *x* be as in Example 6.3. Let *y* point to the node (if any) that precedes *x* and let *y* = **nil** if *x* = *first*. Procedure *delete* (Program 6.3) deletes node *x* from the list. □

---

procedure *delete* (*x*,*y* : *pointer* ; **var** *first* : *pointer*);
begin
 if *y* = **nil then** *first* := *first*↑. *link*
      else *y* ↑. *link* := *x* ↑. *link*;
 dispose (*x*); {return the node}
end; {of delete}

Program 6.3 Delete

6.2 LINKED STACKS AND QUEUES

We have already seen how to represent stacks and queues sequentially. Such a representation proved efficient if we had only one stack or one queue. However, when several stacks and queues coexist, there was no efficient way to represent them sequentially. In this section we present a good solution to this problem using linked lists. Figure 6.7 shows a linked stack and a linked queue.

Notice that the direction of links for both the stack and queue are such as to facilitate easy insertion and deletion of nodes. In the case of Figure 6.7(a), you can easily add a node at the top or delete one from the top. In Figure 6.7(b), you can easily add a node at the rear and both addition and deletion can be performed at the front, though for a queue we normally would not wish to add nodes at the front. If we wish to represent n stacks and m queues simultaneously, then the set of algorithms (Programs 6.4-6.7) and initial conditions given below will serve our purpose.

The following global arrays of type *pointer* are used:

$top[i]$ = node at top of i'th stack, $1 \le i \le n$
$front[i]$ = node at front of i'th queue, $1 \le i \le m$
$rear[i]$ = last node in i'th queue, $1 \le i \le m$

The initial conditions are

$top[i]$ = **nil**, $1 \le i \le n$
$front[i]$ = **nil**, $1 \le i \le m$

and the boundary conditions are

$top[i]$ = **nil** iff the i'th stack is empty
$front[i]$ = **nil** iff the i'th queue is empty

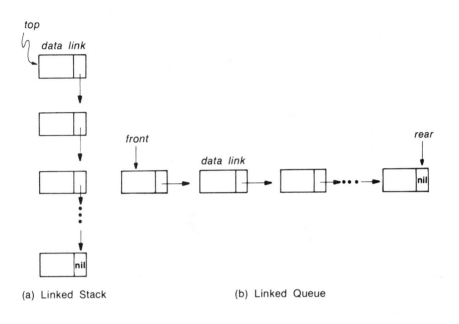

(a) Linked Stack   **(b)** Linked Queue

Figure 6.7 Linked stack and queue

```
type pointer = ↑node ;
     node = record
                 data : integer;
                 link : pointer;
            end;
```

The solution presented above to the *n*-stack, *m*-queue problem is seen to be both computationally and conceptually simple. There is no need to shift stacks or queues around to make space. Computation can proceed so long as there are free nodes. Though additional space is needed for the link field, the cost is no more than a factor of 2. Sometimes the *data* field does not use the whole word and it is possible to pack the *link* and *data* fields into the same word. In such a case the storage requirements for sequential and linked representations would be the same. For the use of linked lists to make sense, the overhead incurred by the storage for links must be overridden by (1) the virtue of

---

```
procedure addstack (i,y : integer);
{add y to the i'th stack, 1 ≤ i ≤ n}
var x : pointer;
begin
  new (x); {get a node}
  x↑.data := y; {set its data field}
  x↑.link := top [i]; {attach to top of i'th stack}
  top [i] := x; {update stack pointer}
end; {of addstack}
```

Program 6.4 Add to a linked stack

```
procedure deletestack (i : integer; var y : integer);
{delete top node from stack i and set y
to be its data field, 1 ≤ i ≤ n}
var x : pointer;
begin
  if top [i] = nil then stackempty;
  x := top [i];
  y := x↑.data; {data field of top node}
  top [i] := x↑.link; {remove top node}
  dispose (x); {free the node}
end; {of deletestack}
```

Program 6.5 Delete from a linked stack

---

being able to represent complex lists in a simple way, and (2) the computing time for manipulating the lists is less than for a sequential representation.

6.3 POLYNOMIAL ADDITION

Let us tackle a reasonable size problem using linked lists. This problem, the manipulation of symbolic polynomials, has become a classical example of the use of list process. As in Chapter 2, we wish to be able to represent any number of different polynomials as long as their combined size does not exceed our block of memory. In general, we want to represent the polynomial

$$A (x) = a_m x^{e_m} + \cdots + a_1 x^{e_1}$$

---

procedure *addqueue* (*i*,*y* : **integer**);
{add *y* to queue *i*, 1≤*i* ≤*m*}
var *x* : *pointer*;
begin
  new (*x*);
  x ↑. *data* := *y*; *x* ↑. *link* := **nil**;
  if *front*[*i*] = **nil**
  then *front*[*i*] := *x* {empty queue}
  else *rear* [*i*]↑. *link* := *x*;
  rear [*i*] := *x*;
end; {of *addqueue*}

Program 6.6 Add to a linked queue

---

procedure *deletequeue* (*i* : **integer**; **var** *y* : **integer**);
{delete the first node in queue *i* and set *y*
to its data field, 1≤*i* ≤*m*}
var *x* : *pointer*;
begin
  if *front*[*i*] = **nil then** queueempty;
  x := *front*[*i*];
  front[*i*] := *x* ↑. *link*; {delete first node}
  y := *x* ↑. *data*;
  dispose (*x*); {free the node}
end; {of *deletequeue*}

Program 6.7 Delete from a linked queue

where the a_i are nonzero coefficients with exponents e_i such that $e_m > e_{m-1} > \cdots > e_2 > e_1 \geq 0$. Each term will be represented by a node. A node will be of fixed size having three fields which represent the coefficient and exponent of a term plus a pointer to the next term.

Assuming that all coefficients are integer, the required type declarations are

type *polypointer* = ↑*polynode*;
    polynode = **record**
                  coef : **integer**; {coefficient}
                  exp : **integer**; {exponent}
                  link : *polypointer*;
        end;

Polynodes will be drawn as:

coef	exp	link

For instance, the polynomial $a = 3x^{14} + 2x^8 + 1$ would be stored as

while $b = 8x^{14} - 3x^{10} + 10x^6$ would look like

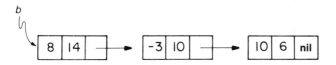

    In order to add two polynomials together we examine their terms starting at the nodes pointed to by a and b. Two pointers p and q are used to move along the terms of a and b. If the exponents of two terms are equal, then the coefficients are added and a new term created for the result. If the exponent of the current term in a is less than the exponent of the current term of b, then a duplicate of the term of b is created and attached to c. The pointer q is advanced to the next term. Similar action is taken on a if $p↑.exp > q↑.exp$. Figure 6.8 illustrates this addition process on the polynomials a and b above.

    Each time a new node is generated its *coef* and *exp* fields are set and it is appended to the end of the list c. In order to avoid having to search for the last node in c each time a new node is added, we keep a pointer d which points to the current last node in c. The complete addition algorithm is specified by the procedure *padd* (Program 6.9). *padd*

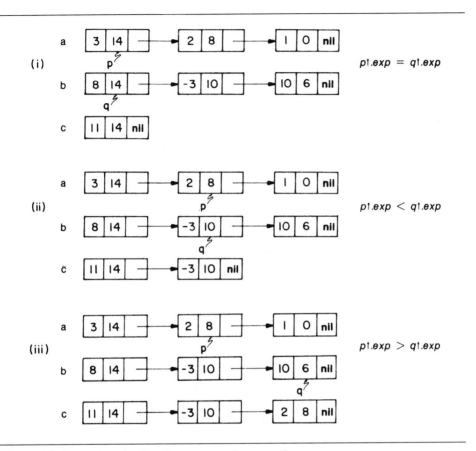

Figure 6.8 Generating the first three terms of $c = a + b$

makes use of a procedure *attach* (Program 6.8), which creates a new node and appends it to the end of c. To make things work out neatly, c is initially given a single node with no values which is deleted at the end of the algorithm. Though this is somewhat inelegant, it avoids more computation. As long as its purpose is clearly documented, such a tactic is permissible.

This is our first really complete example of the use of list processing, so it should be carefully studied. The basic algorithm is straightforward, using a merging process which streams along the two polynomials either copying terms or adding them to the result. Thus, the main **while** loop of lines 8-23 has three cases depending upon whether the next pair of exponents are =, <, or >. Notice that there are five places where a new term is created, justifying our use of the procedure *attach*.

---

procedure *attach*(*c*, *e* : **integer**; **var** *d* : *polypointer*);
{create a new node with *coef*=*c*, and *exp*=*e* and attach it to the
node pointed at by *d*. *d* is updated to point to this new node.}
var *x* : *polypointer*;
begin
 new (*x*);
 with *x*↑ **do begin** *coef* := *c*; *exp* := *e*; **end**;
 d↑. *link* := *x*;
 d := *x*; {*d* points to new last node}
end; {of *attach*}

Program 6.8 Attach a node to the end of a list

Finally, some comments about the computing time of this algorithm. In order to carry out a computing time analysis it is first necessary to determine which operations contribute to the cost. For this algorithm there are several cost measures:

(1) Coefficient additions

(2) Coefficient comparisons

(3) Additions/deletions to available space

(4) Creation of new nodes for *c*

Let us assume that each of these four operations, if done once, takes a single unit of time. The total time taken by algorithm *padd* is then determined by the number of times these operations are performed. This number clearly depends on how many terms are present in the polynomials *a* and *b*. Assume that *a* and *b* have *m* and *n* terms, respectively.

$$a(x) = a_m x^{e_m} + \cdots + a_1 x^{e_1}, \; b(x) = b_n x^{f_n} + \cdots + b_1 x^{f_1}$$

where

$$a_i, b_i \neq 0 \text{ and } e_m > \cdots > e_1 \geq 0, f_n > ... > f_1 \geq 0.$$

Then clearly the number of coefficient additions can vary as

$$0 \leq \text{coefficient additions} \leq \min\{m, n\}.$$

The lower bound is achieved when none of the exponents are equal, while the upper bound is achieved when the exponents of one polynomial are a subset of the exponents of the other.

```
 1  procedure padd (a,b : polypointer; var c : polypointer);
 2  {polynomials a and b represented as singly linked lists
 3   are summed to form the new list named c}
 4  var p,q,d : polypointer ; x : integer;
 5  begin
 6   p := a ; q :=b; {p,q point to next term of a and b}
 7   new (c); d := c; {initial node for c, returned later}
 8   while (p <> nil) and (q <> nil) do
 9     case compare (p ↑ .^exp, q ↑ . exp) of
10       '=':begin
11           x := p↑. coef + q↑. coef;
12           if x <> 0 then attach (x,p↑. exp,d);
13           p := p↑. link ; q :=q↑. link; {advance to next term}
14         end;
15       '<': begin
16           attach (q ↑. coef, q↑. exp, d);
17           q := q↑. link; {next term of b}
18         end;
19       '>': begin
20           attach (p ↑. coef, p↑. exp, d);
21           p := p↑. link; {next term of a}
22         end;
23     end; {of case and while}
24   while p <> nil do {copy rest of a}
25   begin
26     attach (p ↑. coef, p↑. exp, d);
27     p := p↑. link;
28   end;
29   while q <> nil do {copy rest of b}
30   begin
31     attach (q ↑. coef, q↑. exp, d);
32     q := q↑. link;
33   end;
34   d↑. link := nil; {last node}
35   {delete extra initial node}
36   p := c ; c := c↑. link ; dispose (p);
37  end; {of padd}
```

Program 6.9 Procedure to add two polynomials

As for exponent comparisons, one comparison is made on each iteration of the **while** loop of lines 8-23. On each iteration either p or q or both move to the next term in their respective polynomials. Since the total number of terms is $m+n$, the number of iterations and hence the number of exponent comparisons is bounded by $m + n$. You can easily construct a case when $m + n - 1$ comparisons will be necessary: e.g., $m = n$ and

$$e_m > f_n > e_{m-1} > f_{n-1} > \cdots > f_2 > e_{n-m+2} > \cdots > e_1 > f_1.$$

The maximum number of terms in c is $m + n$, and so no more than $m + n$ new nodes are created (this excludes the additional node which is attached to the front of c and later returned). In summary then, the maximum number of executions of any of the statements in *padd* is bounded above by $m + n$. Therefore, the computing time is $O(m + n)$. This means that if the algorithm is implemented and run on a computer, the time taken will be $c_1 m + c_2 n + c_3$ where c_1, c_2, c_3 are constants. Since any algorithm that adds two polynomials must look at each nonzero term at least once, algorithm *padd* is optimal to within a constant factor.

The use of linked lists is well suited to polynomial operations. We can easily imagine writing a collection of procedures for input, output, addition, subtraction, and multiplication of polynomials using linked lists as the means of representation. A hypothetical user wishing to read in polynomials $a(x)$, $b(x)$, and $c(x)$ and then compute $d(x) = a(x) * b(x) + c(x)$ would write in his or her main program

read (a);
read (b);
read (c);
$t := pmul(a,b)$;
$d := padd(t,c)$;
print (d);

Now our user may wish to continue computing more polynomials. At this point it would be useful to reclaim the nodes which are being used to represent $t(x)$. This polynomial was created only as a partial result towards the answer $d(x)$. By returning the nodes of $t(x)$, they may be used to hold other polynomials.

Procedure *erase* (Program 6.10) frees up the nodes in t one by one. It is possible to free all the nodes in t in a more efficient way by modifying the list structure in such a way that the *link* field of the last node points to the first node in t (see Figure 6.9). A list in which the last node points back to the *first* is called a *circular* list. A singly linked list in which the last node has a **nil** link is called a *chain*.

The reason we dispose of nodes that are no longer in use is so that these nodes may be reused later. This objective, together with an efficient erase algorithm for circular lists, may be met by maintaining our own list (as a chain) of nodes that have been

```
procedure erase(var t : pointer);
{free all the nodes in the chain t}
var x : polypointer;
begin
    while t <> nil do
    begin
        x := t↑. link;
        dispose (t);
        t := x;
    end;
end; {of erase}
```

Program 6.10 Erasing a chain.

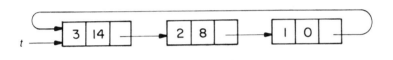

Figure 6.9 Circular list representation of $t = 3x^{14} + 2x^8 + 1$

"disposed." When a new node is needed, we may examine this list. If this list is not empty, then one of the nodes on it may be made available for use. Only when this list is empty do we need to use procedure *new* to create a new node.

Let *av* be a variable of type *polypointer* that points to the first node in our list of nodes that have been "disposed." This list will henceforth be called the *available space list* or *av list*. Initially, *av* = **nil**. Instead of using the procedures *new* and *dispose*, we shall now use the procedures *getnode* (Program 6.11) and *retnode* (Program 6.12).

A circular list may now be erased in a fixed amount of time independent of the number of nodes on the list. Procedure *cerase* (Program 6.13) does this.

Figure 6.10 is a schematic showing the link changes involved in erasing a circular list.

```
procedure getnode(var x : polypointer);
{provide a node for use}
begin
   if av = nil
   then new (x)
   else begin x := av ; av := av↑. link; end;
end; {of getnode}
```

Program 6.11 Getnode

```
procedure retnode (x : polypointer);
{free the node pointed to by x}
begin
   x↑. link := av;
   av := x;
end; {of retnode}
```

Program 6.12 Return a node

```
procedure cerase ( var t : polypointer);
{erase the circular list t}
var second : polypointer;
begin
   if t <> nil
   then begin
         second := t↑. link; {second node}
         t↑. link := av; {first node linked to av}
         av := second; {second node of t becomes front of av list}
         t := nil;
      end;
end; {of cerase}
```

Program 6.13 Erasing a circular list

A direct changeover to the structure of Figure 6.9, however, causes some problems during addition, etc., as the zero polynomial has to be handled as a special case. To avoid such special cases you may introduce a head node into each polynomial; i.e., each polynomial, zero or nonzero, will contain one additional node. The *exp* and *coef* fields

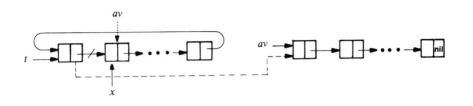

Figure 6.10 Dashes indicate changes involved in erasing a circular list

of this node will not be relevant. Thus, the zero polynomial will have the representation

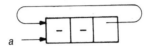

while $a = 3x^{14} + 2x^8 + 1$ will have the representation:

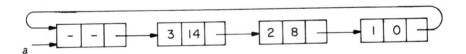

For this circular list with head node representation the test for $t = $ **nil** may be removed from *cerase*. The only changes to be made to algorithm *padd* are:

(1)   Change line 6 to: $p := a\uparrow.link\,; q := b\uparrow.link\,;$
(2)   Change line 8 to: **while** $(p <> a)$ **and** $(q <> b)$ **do**
(3)   Change line 24 to: **while** $p <> a$ **do**
(4)   Change line 29 to: **while** $q <> b$ **do**
(5)   Change line 36 to: $d\uparrow.link := c:$

Thus the algorithm stays essentially the same. Zero polynomials are now handled in the same way as nonzero polynomials.

A further simplification in the addition algorithm is possible if the *exp* field of the head node is set to −1. Now when all nodes of *a* have been examined $p = a$ and $exp(p) = -1$. Since $-1 \le exp(q)$ the remaining terms of *b* can be copied by further executions of the case statement. The same is true if all nodes of *b* are examined before those of *a*. This implies that there is no need for additional code to copy the remaining terms as in *padd*. The final algorithm (*cpadd*) takes the simple form given in Program 6.14.

```
procedure cpadd (a,b : polypointer; var c : polypointer);
{polynomials a and b are represented as circular lists with head
nodes so that a↑.exp = b↑.exp = −1. Their sum, c, is returned
as a circular list.}
var p,q,d : polypointer ; x : integer; done : boolean;
begin
  p := a↑.link ; q := b↑.link;
  getnode (c); c↑.exp := −1; {head node for c}
  d := c; {last node in c}; done := false
  repeat
    case compare (p↑.exp, q↑.exp) of
    '=': if p = a then done := true
        else begin
              x := p↑.coef + q↑.coef;
              if x <> 0 then attach (x, p↑.exp, d);
              p := p↑.link ; q := q↑.link;
            end;
    '<': begin
            attach (q↑.coef, q↑.exp, d);
            q := q↑.link;
         end;
    '>': begin
            attach (p↑.coef, p↑.exp, d);
            p := p↑.link;
         end;
    end; {of case}
  until done;
  d↑.link := c; {link last node to first}
end; {of cpadd}
```

Program 6.14 Adding circularly represented polynomials

Let us review what we have done so far. We have introduced the notions of a singly linked list, a chain, and a singly linked circular list. Each node on one of these lists consists of exactly one link field and some number of other fields. In all of our examples, all nodes on any given list had the same fields. The concept of a singly linked list does not require this and in subsequent sections, we shall see lists that violate this property.

In dealing with polynomials, we found it convenient to use circular lists. This required us to introduce the notion of an available space list. Such a list consists of all nodes that have been used at least once and are currently not in use. By using the available space list and the procedures *getnode*, *retnode*, and *cerase*, it became possible to erase circular lists in constant time and also to reuse all nodes currently not in use. As we continue, we shall see more problems that call for variations in node structure and list representation because of the operations we wish to perform.

6.4 MORE ON LINKED LISTS

It is often necessary and desirable to build a variety of routines for manipulating singly linked lists. Some that we have already seen are (1) *getnode* and (2) *retnode* which get and return nodes to *av*. Another useful operation is one which inverts a chain (Program 6.15). This routine is especially interesting because it can be done "in place" if we make use of three pointers.

```
procedure invert(var x : pointer);
{a chain pointed at by x is inverted so that if x=(a₁, ..., aₙ)
then after execution x = (aₙ, ..., a₁)}
var p,q,r : pointer;
begin
  p := x; q := nil; {q trails p}
  while p <> nil do
  begin
    r := q; q := p; {r trails q}
    p := p↑.link; {p moves to next node}
    q↑.link := r; {link q to preceding node}
  end;
  x := q;
end; {of invert}
```

Program 6.15 Invert a list

You should try this algorithm out on at least three examples the empty list and lists of length 1 and 2, to convince yourself that you understand the mechanism. For a list of $m \geq 1$ nodes, the **while** loop is executed m times and so the computing time is linear or $O(m)$.

Another useful procedure is one which concatenates two chains x and y (Program 6.16). The complexity of this algorithm is also linear in the length of the list x.

```
procedure concatenate (x,y : pointer; var z : pointer);
{x = (a₁, ..., aₘ) and y=(b₁, ..., bₘ), m, n≥0
produces the new chain z = (a₁, ..., aₘ,b₁, ..., bₙ)}
var p : pointer;
begin
  if x = nil
  then z := y
  else begin
          z := x;
          if y <> nil
          then begin {find last node in x}
                  p := x;
                  while p↑.link <> nil do p := p↑.link;
                  p↑.link := y; {link last of x to first of y}
               end;
       end;
end; {of concatenate}
```

Program 6.16 Concatenate

Now let us take another look at circular lists like the one that follows:

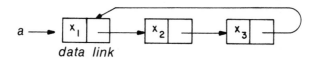

$a = (x_1, x_2, x_3)$. Suppose we want to insert a new node at the front of this list. We have to change the *link* field of the node containing x_3. This requires that we move down the entire length of a until we find the last node. It is more convenient if the name of a circular list points to the last node rather than the first, for example:

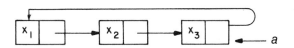

Now we can write procedures which insert a node at the front (Program 6.17) or at the rear of a circular list and take a fixed amount of time. To insert x at the rear, one only needs to add the additional statement $a := x$ to the **else** clause of *insertfront*.

---

procedure *insertfront*(**var** a : *pointer* ; x : *pointer*);
{insert the node pointed at by x at the "front" of the circular
list a, where a points to the last node in the list}
begin
  if a = **nil**
  then begin {empty list}
      $a := x$;
      $x\uparrow.link := x$;
    end
  else begin
      $x\uparrow.link := a\uparrow.link$;
      $a\uparrow.link := x$;
    end;
end; {of *insertfront*}

Program 6.17 Insert at the front

As a last example of a simple procedure for circular lists, we write a function (Program 6.18) which determines the length of a such a list.

6.5 EQUIVALENCE RELATIONS

Let us put together some of these ideas on linked and sequential representations to solve a problem which arises in the design and manufacture of very large scale integrated (VLSI) circuits. One of the steps in the manufacture of a VLSI circuit involves exposing a silicon wafer using a series of masks. Each mask consists of several polygons. Polygons that overlap are electrically equivalent. Electrical equivalence specifies a relationship among mask polygons. This relation has several properties which it shares with

---

```
function length (a : pointer): integer;
{find the length of the circular list a}
var x : pointer;
begin
    length := 0;
    if a <> nil
    then begin
            x := a;
            repeat
                length := length + 1;
                x := x↑. link;
            until x = a;
        end;
end; {of length}
```

Program 6.18 Length

other relations such as the conventional mathematical equals. Suppose we denote an arbitrary relation by the symbol $\equiv$ and suppose that:

(1)   For any polygon x, $x \equiv x$, e.g., x is electrically equivalent to itself. Thus $\equiv$ is *reflexive*.

(2)   For any two polygons x and y, if $x \equiv y$ then $y \equiv x$. Thus, the relation $\equiv$ is *symmetric*.

(3)   For any three polygons x, y, and z, if $x \equiv y$ and $y \equiv z$ then $x \equiv z$, e.g., if x and y are electrically equivalent and y and z are also, then so also are x and z. The relation $\equiv$ is *transitive*.

Definition: A relation, $\equiv$, over a set S, is said to be an *equivalence relation* over S iff it is symmetric, reflexive, and transitive over S.

Examples of equivalence relations are numerous. For example, the "equal to" ($=$) relationship is an equivalence relation since (1) $x = x$, (2) $x = y$ implies $y = x$, and (3) $x = y$ and $y = z$ implies $x = z$. One effect of an equivalence relation is to partition the set S into equivalence classes such that two members x and y of S are in the same equivalence class iff $x \equiv y$. For example, if we have 12 polygons numbered 1 through 12 and the following overlap pairs are defined:

$1 \equiv 5$, $4 \equiv 2$, $7 \equiv 11$, $9 \equiv 10$, $8 \equiv 5$, $7 \equiv 9$, $4 \equiv 6$, $3 \equiv 12$, and $12 \equiv 1$

then, as a result of the reflexivity, symmetry, and transitivity of the relation $\equiv$, we get the following partitioning of the 12 polygons into three equivalence classes:

$\{1, 3, 5, 8, 12\}; \{2, 4, 6\}; \{7, 9, 10, 11\}.$

These equivalence classes are important as each such class defines a *signal net*. The signal nets can be used to verify the correctness of the masks.

The algorithm to determine equivalence classes works in essentially two phases. In the first phase the equivalence pairs (i, j) are read in and stored somewhere. In phase two we begin at 1 and find all pairs of the form $(1, j)$. The values 1 and j are in the same class. By transitivity, all pairs of the form (j, k) imply k is in the same class as 1. We continue in this way until the entire equivalence class containing 1 has been found, marked, and printed. Then we continue on.

```
procedure equivalence;
begin
    initialize;
    while more pairs do
    begin
        read the next pair (i, j);
        process this pair;
    end;
    initialize for output;
    repeat
        output a new equivalence class;
    until done;
end; {of equivalence}
```

Program 6.19 First pass at equivalence algorithm

The first design for this algorithm might go as in Program 6.19. Let m and n represent the number of related pairs and the number of objects, respectively. Now we need to determine which data structure should be used to hold these pairs. To determine this we examine the operations that are required. The pair (i, j) is essentially two random integers in the range 1 to n. Easy random access would dictate an array, say *pairs*[$1..n$, $1..m$]. The i'th row would contain the elements j which are paired directly to i in the input. However, this would potentially be very wasteful of space since very few of the array elements would be used. It might also require considerable time to insert a new pair, (i, k), into row i since we would have to scan the row for the next free location or use more storage.

These considerations lead us to consider a linked list to represent each row. Each node on the list requires only a *data* and a *link* field. However, we still need random access to the i'th row so a one-dimensional array, *seq*[$1..n$] can be used as the head nodes of the *n* lists. Looking at the second phase of the algorithm we need a mechanism which tells us whether or not object *i* has yet to be printed. A boolean array, *out*[1..*n*] can be used for this. The next refinement of the algorithm is Program 6.20. This refinement assumes that *n* is a global constant.

---

procedure *equivalence*;
declare *seq*, *out*, and other local variables;
begin
    initialize *seq* to **nil** and *out* to **true**;
    while more pairs **do** {input pairs}
    begin
        read the next pair (*i*,*j*);
        put *j* on the *seq* [*i*] list;
        put *i* on the *seq* [*j*] list;
    end;
    for *i* := 1 **to** *n* **do** {output equivalence classes}
        if *out* [*i*] **then begin**
                out [*i*] := **false**;
                output this equivalence class;
            end;
end; {of *equivalence*}

Program 6.20 A more detailed version of equivalence algorithm

Let us simulate the algorithm as we have it so far, on the previous data set. After the **while** loop is completed the lists will look like this:

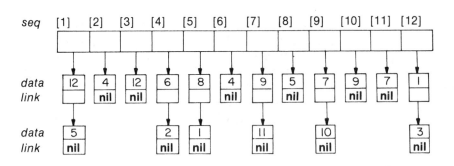

For each relation *i* ≡ *j*, two nodes are used. *seq* [*i*] points to a list of nodes which contains every number which is directly equivalenced to *i* by an input relation.

In phase two we can scan the *seq* array and start with the first, i, $1 \le i \le n$ such that *out* [i] = **true**. Each element in the list *seq* [i] is printed. In order to process the remaining lists which, by transitivity, belong in the same class as i, a stack of their nodes is created. This is accomplished by changing the *link* fields so they point in the reverse direction. The complete procedure is given in Program 6.21.

```
procedure equivalence;
{input the equivalence pairs and output the equivalence classes}
type pointer = ↑node;
      node = record
                  data : 1..n;
                  link : pointer;
              end;
var  seq : array [1..n] of pointer;
      out : array [1..n] of boolean;
      i,j : integer;
      x,y,top : pointer;
      done : boolean;
begin
   {initialize seq and out}
   for i := 1 to n do begin seq [i] := nil; out [i] := true; end;
   {Phase 1: input equivalence pairs}
   while not eof (input) do
   begin
      readln(i,j);
      new (x); {add j to list seq [i]}
      x↑.data := j; x↑.link := seq [i]; seq [i] :=x;
      new (x); {add i to list seq [j]}
      x↑.data :=i; x↑.link := seq [j]; seq [j]:=x;
   end;
   {Phase 2: output the equivalence classes}
   for i := 1 to n do
   if out [i] {needs to be output}
   then begin
           writeln('A new class:', i);
           out [i] := false;
           x := seq [i]; top := nil; {init stack} done := false;
           repeat {find rest of class}
              while x <> nil do {process the list}
              begin
                 j := x↑.data;
                 if out [j]
                 then begin
                         writeln(j); out [j] := false;
```

$$y := x\uparrow.link; x\uparrow.link := top;$$
$$top := x; x := y;$$
end
    else $x := x\uparrow.link;$
end; {of **while** $x <>$ **nil**}
if $top =$ **nil then** $done :=$ **true**
else begin
    $x := seq\,[top\uparrow.data\,];$
    $top := top\uparrow.link;$ {unstack}
    end;
  until $done$;
end; {of **if**}
end; {of $equivalence$}

Program 6.21 Algorithm to find equivalence classes

Analysis of Procedure EQUIVALENCE

The initialization of seq and out takes O(n) time. The processing of each input pair in phase 1 takes a constant amount of time. Hence, the total time for this phase is O(m) where m is the number of input pairs. In phase 2 each node is put onto the linked stack at most once. Since there are only $2m$ nodes and the **for** loop is executed n times, the time for this phase is O($m + n$). Hence, the overall computing time is O($m + n$). Any algorithm which processes equivalence relations must look at all m equivalence pairs and also at all the n polygons at least once. Thus, there can be no algorithm with a computing time less than O($m + n$). This means that procedure $equivalence$ is optimal to within a constant factor. Unfortunately, the space required by the algorithm is also O($m + n$). In Chapter 7 we shall see an alternate solution to this problem which requires only O(n) space.

6.6 SPARSE MATRICES

In Chapter 4, we saw that when matrices were sparse (i.e., many of the entries were zero), then much space and computing time could be saved if only the nonzero terms were retained explicitly. In the case where these nonzero terms did not form any "nice" pattern such as a triangle or a band, we devised a sequential scheme in which each nonzero term was represented by a node with three fields: row, column, and value. These nodes were sequentially organized. However, as matrix operations such as addition, subtraction, and multiplication are performed, the number of nonzero terms in matrices will vary. Matrices representing partial computations (as in the case of polynomials) will be created and will have to be destroyed later on to make space for further matrices. Thus, sequential schemes for representing sparse matrices suffer from the same inadequacies as similar schemes for polynomials. In this section we shall study a very general linked list scheme for sparse matrix representation. As we have already seen, linked schemes facilitate efficient representation of varying size structures and here, too, our scheme will overcome the aforementioned shortcomings of the sequential representation studied in Chapter 4.

In the data representation we shall use, each column of a sparse matrix will be represented by a circularly linked list with a head node. In addition, each row will also be a circularly linked list with a head node.

Each node will have a field called *head*. This field will be used to distinguish between head nodes and nodes representing nonzero matrix elements. Each head node has three additional fields: *down*, *right*, and *next*. The total number of head nodes is max {number of rows, number of columns}. The head node for row i is also the head node for column i. The *down* field of a head node is used to link into a column list while the *right* field is used to link into a row list. The *next* field links the head nodes together.

Every other node has five additional fields: *row*, *col*, *down*, *right*, and *value* (Figure 6.11). The *down* field is used to link to the next nonzero term in the same column and the *right* field links to the next nonzero term in the same row. Thus if $a_{ij} \neq 0$, then there is a node with *head* = **false**, *value* = a_{ij}, *row* = i, and *col* = j. This node is linked into the circular linked lists for row i and column j. Hence, it is simultaneously in two different lists.

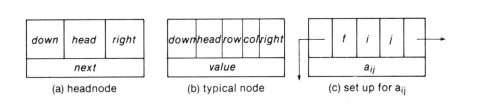

(a) headnode   (b) typical node   (c) set up for a_{ij}

Figure 6.11 Node structure for sparse matrices

As remarked earlier, each head node is in three lists: a row list, a column list, and a list of head nodes. The list of head nodes itself has a head node which is identical to the six field nodes used to represent nonzero elements. The *row* and *col* fields of this node are used to store the matrix dimensions.

Figure 6.13 shows the linked structure obtained for the 6×7 matrix, A, of Figure 6.12.

$$\begin{bmatrix} 0, & 0, & 11, & 0, & 0, & 13, & 0 \\ 12, & 0, & 0, & 0, & 0, & 0, & 14 \\ 0, & -4, & 0, & 0, & 0, & -8 & 0 \\ 0, & 0, & 0, & 0, & 0, & 0, & 0 \\ 0, & 0, & 0, & 0, & 0, & 0, & 0 \\ 0, & -9, & 0, & 0, & 0, & 0, & 0 \end{bmatrix}$$

Figure 6.12 6×7 sparse matrix A

While Figure 6.13 does not show the value of the *head* fields, these values are readily determined from the node structure shown. For each nonzero term of A, we have one six field node which is in exactly one column list and one row list. The head nodes are marked H1-H7. As can be seen from the figure, the *right* field of the head node list header is used to link into the list of head nodes. Notice that the whole matrix may be referenced through the head node, *a*, of the list of head nodes.

If we wish to represent an $n \times m$ sparse matrix with r nonzero terms, then the number of nodes needed is $\max\{n,m\} + r + 1$. While each node may require several words of memory, the total storage needed will be less than nm for sufficiently small r.

Having arrived at this representation for sparse matrices, let us see how to manipulate it to perform efficiently some of the common operations on matrices. But first, let us see how the required node structure may be defined in Pascal. This time, we need to use variant records.

```
type matrixpointer = ↑matrixnode
     matrixnode = record
                     down : matrixpointer;
                     right : matrixpointer;
                     case head : boolean of
                        true: (next : matrixpointer);
                        false: (value : integer;
                                row : integer;
                                col : integer);
                  end;
```

The first operation we shall consider is that of reading in a sparse matrix and obtaining its linked representation. We shall assume that the first input line consists of *n* (the number of rows), *m* (the number of columns), and *r* (the number of nonzero terms).

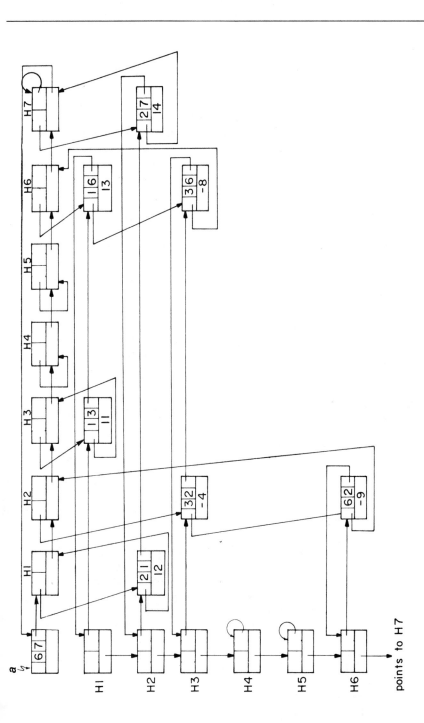

Figure 6.13 Linked Representation of the sparse matrix A. The *head* field of a node is not shown. Its value for each node should be clear from the node structure.

The line is followed by r lines of input; each of these is a triple of the form (i,j,a_{ij}). These triples consist of the *row*, *col*, and *value* of the nonzero terms of the matrix. It is further assumed that these triples are ordered by rows and within rows by columns.

For example, the input for the 6×7 sparse matrix of Figure 6.11, which has seven nonzero terms, would take the form: 6,7,7; 1,3,11; 1,6,13; 2,1,12; 2,7,14; 3,2,-4; 3,6,-8; 6,2,-9. We shall not concern ourselves here with the actual format of this input on the input media (tapes, disk, terminal, etc.) but shall just assume we have some mechanism to get the next triple (see the exercises for one possible input format). The procedure *mread* will also make use of an auxiliary array *headnode*, which will be assumed to be at least as large as the largest dimensioned matrix to be input. *headnode* [i] will be a pointer to the head node for column i and hence also for row i. This will permit us to efficiently access columns at random while setting up the input matrix. Procedure *mread* (Program 6.22) proceeds by first setting up all the head nodes and then setting up each row list, simultaneously building the column lists. The *next* field of head node i is initially used to keep track of the last node in column i. Eventually, in line 39, the head nodes are linked together through this field.

```
1  procedure mread (var a : matrixpointer);
2  {read in a matrix and set up its linked representation.
3   An auxilliary global array hdnode is used}
4  var i,m,n,p,r,rrow,ccol,val,currentrow : integer;
5      x,last : matrixpointer;

6  begin
7    readln(n,m,r); {matrix dimensions}
8    if m > n then p := m else p := n;

9    {set up head node for list of head nodes}
10   new (a); a↑. head := false ; a↑. row := n ; a↑. col := m;

11   if p = 0 then a↑. right := x;
12   else begin {at least one nonzero term}

13   for i := 1 to p do {initialize head nodes}
14   begin
15     new (x); hdnode [i ] := x;
16     with x↑ do begin head := true; right := x ; next := x; end;
17   end;
18   currentrow := 1; last := hdnode [1]; {last node in current row}

19   for i := 1 to r do {input triples}
20   begin
21     readln(rrow,ccol,val);
```

```
22      if rrow > currentrow
23      then begin {close current row}
24              last↑.right := hdnode [currentrow ];
25              currentrow := rrow; last := hdnode [rrow ];
26          end;
27      new (x); {node for new triple}
28      with x↑ do begin head := false; row := rrow; col := ccol;
29                       value := val; end;
30      last↑.right := x; last := x; {link into row list}
31      {link into column list}
32      hdnode [ccol ]↑.next↑.down := x; hdnode [ccol ]↑.next := x;
33      end; {of input triples}

34      {close last row}
35      if r > 0 then last↑.right := hdnode [currentrow ];

36      for i := 1 to m do {close all column lists}
37          hdnode [i ]↑.next↑.down := hdnode [i ];

38      {link the head nodes together}
39      for i := 1 to p − 1 do hdnode [i ]↑.next := hdnode [i + 1];
40      hdnode [p ]↑.next := a;
41      a↑.right := hdnode [1];
42      end; {of if p = 0}
43 end; {of mread}
```

Program 6.22 Read in a sparse matrix

Analysis of Algorithm MREAD

Since *new* works in a constant amount of time, all the head nodes may be set up in $O(\max\{n,m\})$ time, where n is the number of rows and m the number of columns in the matrix being input. Each nonzero term can be set up in a constant amount of time because of the use of the variable *last* and a random access scheme for the bottommost node in each column list. Hence, the **for** loop of lines 15-28 can be carried out in $O(r)$ time. The rest of the algorithm takes $O(\max\{n,m\})$ time. The total time is therefore $O(\max\{n,m\}+r) = O(n+m+r))$. Note that this is asymptotically better than the input time of $O(nm)$ for an $n \times m$ matrix using a two-dimensional array, but slightly worse than the sequential sparse method of Section 2.3.

Before closing this section, let us take a look at an algorithm to return all nodes of a sparse matrix. These nodes may be returned one at a time using *dispose*. A faster way to return the nodes is to set up an available space list as was done in Section 6.3 for polynomials. Assume that *av* points to the front of this list and that this list is linked through the field *right*. Procedure *merase* (Program 6.23) solves our problem in an efficient way.

```
procedure merase(var a : matrixpointer);
{Return all nodes of a to the av list. This list is a chain linked
via the right field. av points to its first node.}
var x,y : matrixpointer;
begin
   x := a↑.right; a↑.right := av; av := a; {return a}
   while x < > a do {erase by rows}
   begin
      y := x↑.right;
      x↑.right := av;
      av := y;
      x := x↑.next; {next row}
   end;
   a := nil;
end; {of merase}
```

Program 6.23 Erasing a sparse matrix

Analysis of Procedure MERASE

Since each node is in exactly one row list, it is sufficient to just return all the row lists of the matrix *a*. Each row list is circularly linked through the field *right*. Thus, nodes need not be returned one by one as a circular list can be erased in a constant amount of time. The computing time for the algorithm is readily seen to be $O(n+m)$. Note that even if the available space list had been linked through the field *down*, then erasing could still have been carried out in $O(n+m)$ time. The subject of manipulating these matrix structures is studied further in the exercises. The representation studied here is rather general. For most applications this generality is not needed. A simpler representation resulting in simpler algorithms is discussed in the exercises.

6.7 DOUBLY LINKED LISTS

So far we have been working chiefly with singly linked linear lists. For some problems these would be too restrictive. One difficulty with these lists is that if we are pointing to a specific node, say p, then we can easily move only in the direction of the links. The only way to find the node which precedes p is to start back at the beginning of the list. The same problem arises when one wishes to delete an arbitrary node from a singly linked list. As can be seen from Example 6.4, in order to easily delete an arbitrary node you must know the preceding node. If we have a problem where moving in either direction is often necessary, then it is useful to have doubly linked lists. Each node now has two link fields, one linking in the forward direction and one in the backward direction.

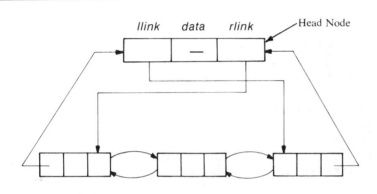

Figure 6.14 Doubly linked circular list with head node

A node in a doubly linked list has at least three fields, say *data, llink* (left link) and *rlink* (right link). A doubly linked list may or may not be circular. A sample doubly linked circular list with three nodes is given in Figure 6.14. Besides these three nodes a special node has been added called a head node. As was true in the earlier sections, head nodes are again convenient for the algorithms. The *data* field of the head node will usually contain no information. Now suppose that p points to any node in a doubly linked list. Then it is the case that

$$p = p\uparrow.llink\uparrow.rlink = p\uparrow.rlink\uparrow.llink$$

This formula reflects the essential virtue of this structure, namely, that one can go back and forth with equal ease. An empty list is not really empty since it will always have its head node and it will look like:

Now to work with these lists we must be able to insert and delete nodes. Procedure *ddelete* (Program 6.24) deletes node *x* from list *l*. *x* now points to a node which is no longer part of the list *l*. Figure 6.15 shows how the method works on a doubly linked list with only a single node. Even though the *rlink* and *llink* fields of node *x* still point to the head node, this node has effectively been removed as there is no way to access *x* through *l*.

```
procedure ddelete (x,l : dpointer);
begin
    if x = l then nomorenodes; {empty list}
    x↑.llink↑.rlink := x↑.rlink;
    x↑.rlink↑.llink := x↑.llink;
    dispose (x);
end; {of ddelete}
```

Program 6.24 Deleting from a doubly linked circular list

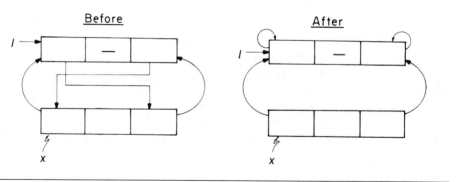

Figure 6.15 Deletion from a doubly linked circular list

Insertion is only slightly more complex (Program 6.25).

---

procedure *dinsert* (*p*, *x* : *dpointer*);
{insert node *p* to the right of node *x*}
begin
  p↑. *llink* := *x*; *p*↑. *rlink* := *x*↑. *rlink*;
  x↑. *rlink*↑. *llink* := *p*; *x*↑. *rlink* := *p*;
end; {of *dinsert*}

Program 6.25 Insertion into a doubly linked circular list

6.8 GENERALIZED LISTS

In Chapter 4, a linear list was defined to be a finite sequence of $n \geq 0$ elements, $\alpha_1, ..., \alpha_n$, which we write as $A = (\alpha_1, ..., \alpha_n)$. The elements of a linear list are restricted to be atoms and thus the only structural property a linear list has is the one of position, i.e., α_i precedes α_{i+1}, $1 \leq i < n$. It is sometimes useful to relax this restriction on the elements of a list, permitting them to have a structure of their own. This leads to the notion of a generalized list in which the elements α_i, $1 \leq i \leq n$ may be either atoms or lists.

Definition: A *generalized list, A,* is a finite sequence of $n \geq 0$ elements, $\alpha_1, ..., \alpha_n$ where the α_i are either atoms or lists. The elements α_i, $1 \leq i \leq n$ which are not atoms are said to be the *sublists* of *A*.

The list *A* itself is written as $A = (\alpha_1, ..., \alpha_n)$. *A* is the *name* of the list $(\alpha_1, ..., \alpha_n)$ and *n* its *length*. By convention, all list names will be represented by capital letters. Lower case letters will be used to represent atoms. If $n \geq 1$, then α_1 is the *head* of *A* while $(\alpha_2, ..., \alpha_n)$ is the *tail* of *A*.

The above definition is our first example of a recursive definition so one should study it carefully. The definition is recursive because within our description of what a list is, we use the notion of a list. This may appear to be circular, but it is not. It is a compact way of describing a potentially large and varied structure. We will see more such definitions later on. Some examples of generalized lists are:

(1) $D = ()$ the null or empty list; its length is zero.
(2) $A = (a,(b,c))$ a list of length two; its first element

is the atom 'a' and its second element is the linear list (b,c).

(3) $B = (A,A, ())$ a list of length three whose first two elements are the list A, the third element the null list.

(4) $C = (a,C)$ a recursive list of length two. C corresponds to the infinite list $C = (a,(a,(a, ...))$.

Example (1) is the empty list and is easily seen to agree with the definition. For list A, we have

$$head(A) = \text{`}a\text{'}, tail(A) = ((b,c)).$$

The *tail* (A) also has a head and tail which are (b,c) and ( ), respectively. Looking at list B, we see that

$$head(B) = A, tail(B) = (A, ())$$

Continuing, we have

$$head\,(tail\,(B)) = A, \quad tail\,(tail\,(B)) = (())$$

both of which are lists.

Two important consequences of our definition for a list are (1) lists may be shared by other lists as in example (3), where list A makes up two of the sublists of B; and (2) lists may be recursive as in example (4). The implications of these two consequences for the data structures needed to represent lists will become evident as we go along.

First, let us restrict ourselves to the situation where the lists being represented are neither shared nor recursive. To see where this notion of a list may be useful, consider how to represent polynomials in several variables. Suppose we need to devise a data representation for them and consider one typical example, the polynomial

$$P(x,y,z) = x^{10}y^3z^2 + 2x^8y^3z^2 + 3x^8y^2z^2 + x^4y^4z + 6x^3y^4z + 2yz$$

You can easily think of a sequential representation for P, say using nodes with four fields: *coef, expx, expy,* and *expz.* But this would mean that polynomials in a different number of variables would need a different number of fields, adding another conceptual inelegance to other difficulties we have already seen with the sequential representation of polynomials. If we used linear lists, we might conceive of a node of the form

coef	expx	expy
expz	link	

These nodes would have to vary in size depending on the number of variables, causing difficulties in storage management. The idea of using a general list structure with fixed size nodes arises naturally if we consider rewriting $P(x,y,z)$ as

$$((x^{10} + 2x^8)y^3 + 3x^8y^2)z^2 + ((x^4 + 6x^3)y^4 + 2y)z$$

Every polynomial can be written in this fashion, factoring out a main variable z, followed by a second variable y, etc. Looking carefully now at $P(x,y,z)$ we see that there are two terms in the variable z, $Cz^2 + Dz$, where C and D are polynomials themselves but in the variables x and y. Looking closer at $C(x,y)$, we see that it is of the form $Ey^3 + Fy^2$, where E and F are polynomials in x. Continuing in this way we see that every polynomial consists of a variable plus coefficient exponent pairs. Each coefficient is itself a polynomial (in one less variable) if we regard a single numerical coefficient as a polynomial in zero variables.

From the preceding discussion, we see that every polynomial, regardless of the number of variables in it, can be represented using nodes of the type *polynode* defined below:

```
type triple = (variable, ptr, no);
     polypointer = ↑polynode;
     polynode = record
                   link : polypointer;
                   exp : integer;
                   case trio : triple of
                      variable : (vble : char);
                      ptr : (dlink : polypointer);
                      no : (coef : integer);
                end;
```

Note that the type of the field *vble* can be changed to **integer** in case all variables are kept in a table and *vble* just gives the corresponding table index.

The polynomial $P = 3x^2y$ now takes the representation given in Figure 6.16 while $P(x,y,z)$ defined before has the list representation shown in Figure 6.17. For simplicity, the *trio* field is omitted from Figure 6.17. The value of this field for each node is self evident.

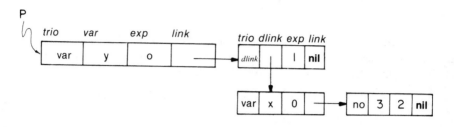

Figure 6.16 Representation of $3x^2y$

It is a little surprising that every generalized list can be represented using the node structure:

| tag = true/false | data/dlink | link |

This structure may be defined in Pascal as below:

type *listpointer* = ↑*listnode*;
    listnode = **record**
            link : *listpointer*;
           case *tag* : **boolean of**
           false : (*data* : **char**);
           true : (*dlink* : *listpointer*);
      end;

where the type of the *data* field will change from one application to the next. You should convince yourself that this node structure is adequate for the representation of any list A. The *link* field may be used as a pointer to the tail of the list while the *data/dlink* field can hold an atom in case *head*(*A*) is an atom or be a pointer to the list representation of *head*(*A*) in case it is a list. Using this node structure, the example lists (1)-(4) have the representation shown in Figure 6.18. In these examples, the data field is of type **char**.

Recursive Algorithms for Lists

Now that we have seen a particular example where generalized lists are useful, let us return to their definition again. Whenever a data object is defined recursively, it is often easy to describe algorithms which work on these objects recursively. To see how recursion is useful, let us write a procedure (Program 6.25) which produces an exact copy of a nonrecursive list p in which no sublists are shared. We will assume the nodes

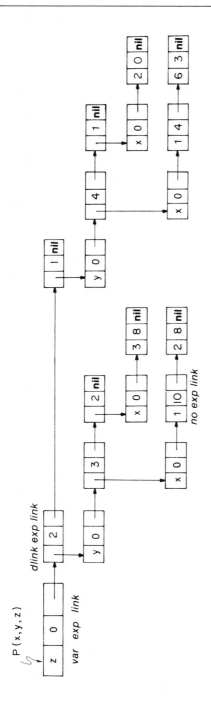

Figure 6.17 Representation of $P(x, y, z)$ using three fields per node. The *trio* field has not been shown.

of *p* are of type *listnode* as defined earlier.

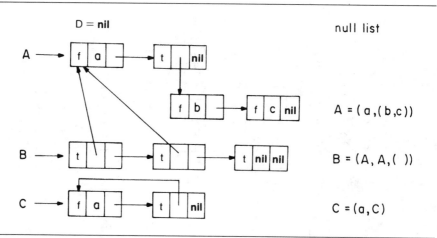

Figure 6.18 Representation of lists (1)-(4). An *f* in the *tag* field represents the value false while a *t* represents the value true.

```
function copy (p: listpointer): listpointer;
{copy the nonrecursive list with no shared sublists
 pointed at by p}
var q: listpointer;
begin
  q := nil;
  if p <> nil
  then begin
          new (q); q↑.tag := p↑.tag;
          if not p↑.tag then q↑.data := p↑.data
                      else q↑.dlink := copy (p↑.dlink);
          q↑.link := copy (p↑.link);
        end;
  copy := q;
end; {of copy}
```

Program 6.25 Copy a list

Program 6.25 reflects exactly the definition of a list. We immediately see that *copy* works correctly for an empty list. A simple proof using induction will verify the correctness of the entire procedure.

Now let us consider the computing time of this algorithm. The null list takes a constant amount of time. For the list

$$A = ((a,b),((c,d),e))$$

which has the representation of Figure 6.19, p takes on the values given in Figure 6.20. The sequence of values should be read down the columns b, r, s, t, u, v, w, x are the addresses of the eight nodes of the list. From this particular example one should be able to see that nodes with $tag =$ **false** will be visited twice, while nodes with $tag =$ **true** will be visited three times. Thus, if a list has a total of m nodes, no more than $3m$ executions of any statement will occur. Hence, the algorithm is O(m) or linear which is the best we could hope to achieve. Another factor of interest is the maximum depth of recursion or, equivalently, how many locations one will need for the recursion stack. Again, by carefully following the algorithm on the previous example we see that the maximum depth is a combination of the lengths and depths of all sublists. However, a simple upper bound to use is m, the total number of nodes. Though this bound will be extremely large in many cases, it is achievable, for instance, if

$$A = (((((a))))).$$

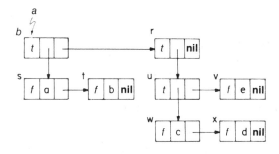

Figure 6.19 Linked representation for A

Another procedure which is often useful is one which determines whether two lists are identical. This means they must have the same structure and the same data in corresponding fields. Again, using the recursive definition of a list we can write a short recursive procedure (Program 6.26) which accomplishes this task.

Procedure *equal* is a function which returns either the value **true** or **false**. Its computing time is clearly no more than linear when no sublists are shared since it looks at each node of s and t no more than three times. For unequal lists the procedure terminates as soon as it discovers that the lists are not identical.

Levels of recursion	Value of p	Continuing Levels	p	Continuing Levels	p
1	b	2	r	3	u
2	s	3	u	4	v
3	t	4	w	5	o
4	o	5	x	4	v
3	t	6	o	3	u
2	s	5	x	2	r
1	b	4	w	3	o
				2	r
				1	b

Figure 6.20 Values of parameter in execution of *copy(A)*

function *equal* (*s,t* : *listpointer*): **boolean**;
{*s* and *t* are nonrecursive lists. This function has value
true iff the two lists are identical}
var *x* : **boolean**;
begin
  equal := **false**;
  if (*s* = **nil**) **and** (*t* = **nil**)
  then *equal* := **true**
  else if (*s* <> **nil**) **and** (*t* <> **nil**)
      then if *s* ↑. *tag* = *t* ↑. *tag*
          then begin
              if not *s* ↑. *tag*
              then if *s* ↑. *data* = *t* ↑. *data* **then** *x* := **true**
                                  else *x* := **false**
              else *x* := *equal* (*s* ↑. *dlink,t* ↑. *dlink*);
              if *x* **then** *equal* := *equal* (*s* ↑. *link,t* ↑. *link*)
          end;
end; {of *equal*}

Program 6.26 Function *equal*

Another handy operation on nonrecursive lists is the function which computes the depth of a list. The depth of the empty list is defined to be zero and in general

$$depth(s) = \begin{cases} 0, \text{ if } s \text{ is an atom} \\ 1 + \max \{depth(x_1), ..., depth(x_n)\}, \text{ if } s \text{ is the list} \\ \qquad\qquad\qquad\qquad\qquad (x_1, ..., x_n), n \geq 1. \end{cases}$$

Procedure *depth* (Program 6.27) is a very close transformation of the definition which is itself recursive. By now you have seen several programs of this type and you should be feeling more comfortable both reading and writing recursive algorithms. To convince yourself that you understand the way these work, try Exercises 23, 24, and 25.

```
function depth (s : listpointer): integer;
{compute the depth of the nonrecursive list s}
var p : listpointer; m,n : integer;
begin
 if s <> nil
 then begin
        p := s; m := 0;
        while p <> nil do
        begin
          if p ↑. tag
          then begin
                 n := depth (p ↑. dlink);
                 if m < n then m := n;
               end;
          p := p ↑. link;
        end;
        depth := m + 1;
      end
 else depth := 0;
end; {of depth}
```

Program 6.27 Function *depth*

Reference Counts, Shared and Recursive Lists

In this section we shall consider some of the problems that arise when lists are allowed to be shared by other lists and when recursive lists are permitted. Sharing of sublists can in some situations result in great savings in storage used, as identical sublists occupy the same space. In order to facilitate ease in specifying shared sublists, we extend the definition of a list to allow for naming of sublists. A sublist appearing within a list definition may be named through the use of a list name preceding it. For example, in the list $A = (a, (b,c))$, the sublist (b,c) could be assigned the name Z by writing $A = (a,Z(b,c))$. In fact, to be consistent we would then write $A(a,Z(b,c))$ which would define the list A as above.

Lists that are shared by other lists, such as list A of Figure 6.18, create problems when you wish to add or delete a node at the front. If the first node of A is deleted, it is necessary to change the pointers from the list B to point to the second node. In case a new node is added then pointers from B have to be changed to point to the new first node. However, we normally do not know all the points from which a particular list is being referenced. (Even if you did have this information, addition and deletion of nodes could require a large amount of time.) This problem is easily solved through the use of head nodes. In case you expect to perform many add/deletes from the front of lists, then the use of a head node with each list or named sublist will eliminate the need to retain a list of all pointers to any specific list. If each list is to have a head node, then lists (1)-(4) are represented as in Figure 6.21. Even in situations where you do not wish to add or delete nodes from lists dynamically, as in the case of multivariate polynomials, head nodes prove useful in determining when the nodes of a particular structure may be returned to the storage pool. For example, let t and u be program variables pointing to the two polynomials $(3x^4 + 5x^3 + 7x)y^3$ and $(3x^4 + 5x^3 + 7x)y^6 + (6x)y$ of Figure 6.22. If $perase$ is to erase a polynomial, then the invocation $perase(t)$ should not return the nodes corresponding to the coefficient $3x^4 + 5x^3 + 7x$ since this sublist is also part of u.

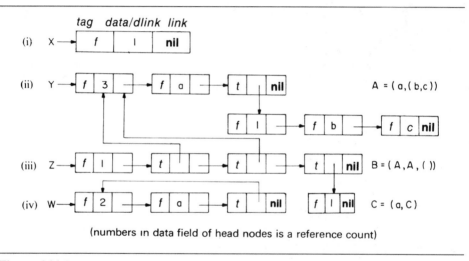

Figure 6.21 Structure with head nodes for lists (1)-(4)

Thus, whenever lists are being shared by other lists, we need a mechanism to help determine whether or not the list nodes may be physically returned to the available space list. This mechanism is generally provided through the use of a reference count maintained in the head node of each list. Since the *data* field of the head nodes is free, the reference count is maintained in this field. (Alternatively a third variant may be introduced with *tag* having three possible values 0, 1, 2.) This reference count of a list is the number of pointers (either program variables or pointers from other lists) to that list. If the lists (1)-(4) of Figure 6.21 are accessible via the program variables x, y, z, and w, then the reference counts for the lists are:

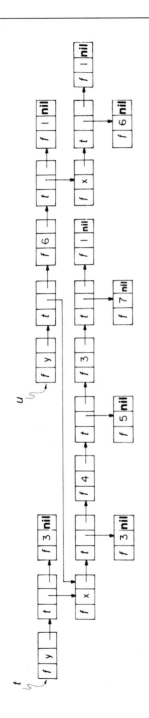

Figure 6.22 $T = (3x^4 + 5x^3 + 7x)y^3$, $U = (3x^4 + 5x^3 + 7x)y^6 + 6xy$

(1) $ref(x) = 1$ accessible only via x
(2) $ref(y) = 3$ pointed to by y and two pointers from z
(3) $ref(z) = 1$ accessible only via z
(4) $ref(w) = 2$ two pointers to list c

Now a call to *lerase(t)* (list erase) should result only in a decrementing by 1 of the reference counter of *t*. Only if the reference count becomes zero are the nodes of *t* to be physically returned to the available space list. The same is to be done to the sublists of *t*.

Assume that the data type *listpointer* is defined as

type *listpointer* = ↑*listnode*;
    three = 0..2;
    listnode = **record**
            link : *listpointer*;
            case *tag* : *three* **of**
            0 : (*data* : **integer**);
            1 : (*dlink* : *listpointer*);
            2 : (*ref* : **integer**);
        end;

An algorithm to erase a list x could proceed by examining the top level nodes of a list whose reference count has become zero. Any such sublists encountered are erased and finally, the top level nodes are linked into the available space list. The list erase algorithm is given in Program 6.28.

A call to *lerase(y)* will now only have the effect of decreasing the reference count of y to 2. Such a call followed by a call to *lerase(z)* will result in

(1)   Reference count of z becomes zero;

(2)   Next node is processed and y↑.*ref* reduces to 1;

(3) y↑.*ref* becomes zero and the five nodes of list A (a, (b,c)) are returned to the available space list;

(4)   The top level nodes of z are linked into the available space list.

The use of head nodes with reference counts solves the problem of determining when nodes are to be physically freed in the case of shared sublists. However, for recursive lists, the reference count never becomes zero. *lerase(w)* just results in w↑.*ref* becoming one. The reference count does not become zero even though this list is no longer accessible either through program variables or through other structures. The same is true in the case of indirect recursion (Figure 6.23). After calls to *lerase(r)* and *lerase(s)*, r↑.*ref*= 1 and s↑.*ref*= 2 but the structure consisting of r and s is no longer being used and so it should have been returned to the available space list.

procedure *lerase* (**var** *x* : *listpointer*);
{recursively erase a nonrecursive list. Each
head node has a reference count.}
var *y* : *listpointer*;
begin
  x ↑. *ref* := *x* ↑. *ref*−1; {decrement reference count}
  if *x* ↑. *ref* = 0
then begin
       y := *x*; {*y* traverses top level of *x*}
       while *y* ↑. *link* < > **nil do**
       begin
         y := *y* ↑. *link*;
         if *y* ↑. *tag* **then** *lerase* (*y* ↑. *dlink*);
       end;
       y ↑. *link* := *av*; {attach top level nodes to *av* list}
       av := *x*; *x* := **nil**;
     end;
end; {of *lerase*}

Program 6.28 Procedure *lerase*

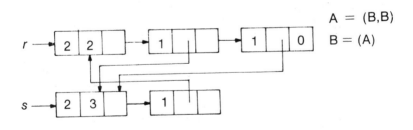

A = (B,B)

B = (A)

Figure 6.23 Indirect recursion of lists *A* and *B* pointed to by program variables *r* and *s*

     Unfortunately, there is no simple way to supplement the list structure of Figure 6.23 so as to be able to determine when recursive lists may be physically erased. It is no longer possible to return all free nodes to the available space list when they become free. So when recursive lists are being used, it is possible to run out of available space even though not all nodes are in use. When this happens, it is possible to collect unused nodes (i.e., garbage nodes) through a process known as garbage collection. This will be described in the next section.

6.9 GARBAGE COLLECTION AND COMPACTION

As remarked at the close of the last section, garbage collection is the process of collecting all unused nodes and returning them to available space. This process is carried out in essentially two phases. In the first phase, known as the marking phase, all nodes in use are marked. In the second phase all unmarked nodes are returned to the available space list. This second phase is trivial when all nodes are of the same size. In this case, the second phase requires only the examination of each node to see whether or not it has been marked. If there are a total of n nodes, then the second phase of garbage collection can be carried out in $O(n)$ steps. In this situation it is only the first or marking phase that is of any interest in designing an algorithm. When variable size nodes are in use, it is desirable to compact memory so that all free nodes form a contiguous block of memory. In this case the second phase is referred to as memory compaction. Compaction of disk space to reduce average retrieval time is desirable even for fixed size nodes. In this section we shall study two marking algorithms and one compaction algorithm.

Marking

In order to be able to carry out the marking, we need a mark field in each node. It will be assumed that this mark field can be changed at any time by the marking algorithm. Marking algorithms mark all directly accessible nodes (i.e., nodes accessible through program variables referred to as pointer variables) and also all indirectly accessible nodes (i.e., nodes accessible through link fields of nodes in accessible lists). It is assumed that a certain set of variables has been specified as pointer variables and that these variables at all times are either **nil** (i.e., point to nothing) or are valid pointers to lists. It is also assumed that the link fields of nodes always contain valid link information.

Knowing which variables are pointer variables, it is easy to mark all directly accessible nodes. The indirectly accessible nodes are marked by systematically examining all nodes reachable from these directly accessible nodes. Before examining the marking algorithms let us review the node structure in use. Each node regardless of its usage will have two boolean fields: *mark* and *tag*. If *tag* = **false**, then the node contains only atomic information in a field called *data*. If *tag* = **true**, then the node has two link fields: *dlink* and *rlink*. Atomic information can be stored only in nodes that have *tag* = **false**. Such nodes are called *atomic* nodes. All other nodes are list nodes. This node structure is slightly different from the one used in the previous section where a node with *tag* = **false** contained atomic information as well as a *link*. With this new node structure, the list $(a, (b))$ is represented as in Figure 6.24. The type definition for the new nodes is given below:

```
type  listpointer = ↑listnode;
      listnode = record
                   mark : boolean;
                   case tag : boolean of
                      true : (dlink : listpointer;
                              rlink : listpointer);
                      false : (data : char)
                 end;
```

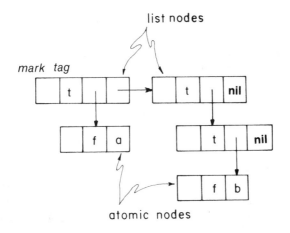

Figure 6.24 List $(a, (b))$

Both of the marking algorithms we shall discuss will require that all nodes be initially unmarked (i.e., $x↑.mark = $ **false** for every node $x↑$). Procedure *driver* (Program 6.29) will repeatedly call a marking algorithm to mark all nodes accessible from each of the pointer variables being used. In line 6, procedure *mark*1 is invoked. If we wish to use the second marking algorithm, then we need merely invoke *mark*2 instead of *mark*1. Both the marking algorithms have been written to work on arbitrary list structures (not just generalized lists as described here).

The first marking algorithm *mark*1 (Program 6.30) will start from the list node x and mark all nodes that can be reached from x via a sequence of *rlink*'s and *dlink*'s; examining all such paths will result in the examination of all reachable nodes. While examining any node of type list we will have a choice as to whether to move to the *dlink* or

---

```
1 procedure driver
2 begin
3   for each pointer variable x that points to an unmarked node do
4   begin
5     x↑.mark := true;
6     if x↑.tag then mark1(x);  {x is a list node}
7   end;
8 end; {of driver}
```

Program 6.29 Procedure *driver*

to the *rlink*. *mark*1 will move to the *dlink* but will at the same time place the *rlink* on a stack in case the *rlink* is a list node not yet marked. The use of this stack will enable us to return at a later point to the *rlink* and examine all paths from there. This strategy is similar to the one used in the previous section for *lerase*.

Analysis of *mark*1

In lines 12-14 of *mark*1 we check to see if $q = p↑.rlink$ can lead to other unmarked accessible nodes. If so q is stacked. The examination of nodes continues with the node at $p↑.dlink$. When we have moved downwards as far as possible, we exit from the loop of lines 10-23. At this point we try out one of the alternative moves from the stack, line 9. You may verify that *mark*1 does indeed mark all previously unmarked nodes which are accessible from x.

In analyzing the computing time of this algorithm we observe that on each iteration (except for the last) of the loop of lines 10-23, at least one previously unmarked node gets marked (line 21). Thus, if the **while** loop, lines 7-25, is iterated r times and the total number of iterations of the **repeat** loop, lines 10-23, is u then at least $w = u - r$ previously unmarked nodes get marked by the algorithm. Let m be the number of new nodes marked. Then $m \geq w = u - r$. Also, the number of iterations of the loop of lines 7-25 is one plus the number of nodes that get stacked. The only nodes that can be stacked are those previously unmarked (line 14). Once a node is stacked it gets marked (line 15). Hence $r \leq m + 1$. From this and the knowledge that $m \geq u - r$, we conclude that $u \leq 2m + 1$. The computing time of the algorithm is $O(u + r)$. Substituting for u and r we obtain $O(m)$ as the computing time. The time is linear in the number of new nodes marked! Since any algorithm to mark nodes must spend at least one unit of time on each new node marked, it follows that there is no algorithm with a time less than $O(m)$. Hence *mark*1 is optimal to within a constant factor (recall that $2m = O(m)$ and $10m = O(m)$).

```
 1  procedure mark1(x : listpointer);
 2  {mark all nodes accessible from the list node x. add and delete
 3   are the standard stack procedures. top points to the stack top.}
 4  var p,q : listpointer; done : boolean;
 5  begin
 6      top := 0; add (x); {put x on the stack}
 7      while top > 0 do {stack not empty}
 8      begin
 9        delete (p); {unstack}; done := false;
10        repeat {move down stacking rlinks as needed}
11          q := p↑.rlink;
12          if q <> nil
13          then begin
14              if q↑.tag and not q↑.mark then add (q); {unmarked list node}
15              q↑.mark := true; {mark q}
16            end;
17          p := p↑.dlink;
18          if p <> nil then
19            {a marked or atomic node cannot lead to new nodes}
20            if p↑.mark or not p↑.tag then done := true
21                                 else p↑.mark := true;
22                  else done := true;
23        until done;
24        if p <> nil then p↑.mark := true;
25      end; {of while}
26  end; {of mark1}
```

Program 6.30 First marking algorithm

Having observed that *mark*1 is optimal to within a constant factor you may be tempted to sit back in your arm chair and relish a moment of smugness. There is, unfortunately, a serious flaw with *mark*1. This flaw is sufficiently serious as to make the algorithm of little use in many garbage collection applications. Garbage collectors are invoked only when we have run out of space. This means that at the time *mark*1 is to operate, we do not have an unlimited amount of space available in which to maintain the stack. In some applications each node might have a free field which can be used to maintain a linked stack. In fact, if variable size nodes are in use and storage compaction is to be carried out then such a field will be available (see the compaction algorithm *compact*). When fixed size nodes are in use, compaction can be efficiently carried out without this additional field and so we will not be able to maintain a linked stack (see exercises for another special case permitting the growth of a linked stack). Realizing this deficiency in *mark*1, let us proceed to another marking algorithm *mark*2. *mark*2 will not require any additional space in which to maintain a stack. Its computing time is also $O(m)$ but the constant factor here is larger than that for mark1.

Unlike *mark1* which does not alter any of the links in the list x, the algorithm *mark2* will modify some of these links. However, by the time it finishes its task the list structure will be restored to its original form. Starting from a list node x, *mark2* traces all possible paths made up of *dlink*'s and *rlink*'s. Whenever a choice is to be made the *dlink* direction is explored first. Instead of maintaining a stack of alternative choices (as was done by *mark1*) we now maintain the path taken from x to the node p that is currently being examined. This path is maintained by changing some of the links along the path from x to p.

Consider the example list of Figure 6.25(a). Initially, all nodes except node A are unmarked and only node E is atomic. From node A we can either move down to node B or right to node I. *mark2* will always move down when faced with such a choice. We shall use p to point to the node currently being examined and t to point to the node preceding p in the path from x to p. The path t to x will be maintained as a chain comprised of the nodes on this $t - x$ path (read as "t to x"). If we advance from node p to node q then either $q = p\uparrow.rlink$ or $q = p\uparrow.dlink$ and q will become the node currently being examined. The node preceding q on the $x - q$ path is p and so the path list must be updated to represent the path from p to x. This is simply done by adding node p to the $t - x$ path already constructed. Nodes will be linked onto this path either through their *dlink* or *rlink* field. Only list nodes will be placed onto this path chain. When node p is being added to the path chain, p is linked to t via its *dlink* field if $q = p\uparrow.dlink$. When $q = p\uparrow.rlink$, p is linked to t via its *rlink* field. In order to be able to determine whether a node on the $t - x$ path list is linked through its *dlink* or *rlink* field we make use of the *tag* field. Notice that since the $t - x$ path list will contain only list nodes, the tag on all these nodes will be **true**. When the *dlink* field is used for linking, this tag will be changed to **false**. Thus, for nodes on the $t - x$ path we have

$$tag = \begin{cases} \textbf{false} \text{ if the node is linked via its } dlink \text{ field} \\ \textbf{true} \text{ if the node is linked via its } rlink \text{ field} \end{cases}$$

The tag will be reset to true when the node gets off the $t - x$ path list. (While this use of the *tag* field represents a slight abuse of the language, it is preferable to introducing an additional field.)

Figure 6.25(b) shows the $t - x$ path list when node p is being examined. Nodes A, B, and C have a tag of zero (for false) indicating that linking on these nodes is via the *dlink* field. This also implies that in the original list structure, $B = A\uparrow.dlink$, $C = B\uparrow.dlink$ and $D = p = C\uparrow.dlink$. Thus, the link information destroyed while creating the $t - x$ path list is present in the path list. Nodes B, C, and D have already been marked by the algorithm. In exploring p we first attempt to move down to

$q = p\uparrow.dlink = E$. E is an atomic node so it gets marked and we then attempt to move right from p. Now, $q = p\uparrow.rlink = F$. This is an unmarked list node. So, we add p to the path list and proceed to explore q. Since p is linked to q by its *rlink* field, the linking of p onto the $t - x$ path is made through its *rlink* field. Figure 6.25(c) shows the list structure at the time node G is being examined. Node G is a dead end. We cannot move further either down or right. At this time we move backwards on the $x - t$ path resetting links and tags until we reach a node whose *rlink* has not yet been examined. The marking continues from this node. Because nodes are removed from the $t - x$ path list in the reverse order in which they were added to it, this list behaves as a stack. The remaining details of *mark*2 are spelled out in Program 6.31. The same driver as for *mark*1 is assumed.

The procedure *mark*2 given in Program 6.31(a) makes use of three other procedures which are given in Programs 6.31(b)-(d). These latter are to be physically placed between the **var** and first **begin** statement of *mark*2. Procedure *mark*2 first attempts to move p one node down. If it cannot, then an attempt is made to move p one node to the right. If this cannot be done, then we attempt to backup on the $t - x$ list and move p to a node from which a downward move may be possible. When even this backup is not possible, *mark*2 terminates. The correctness of the procedures of Programs 6.31(a)-(d) is easily established.

Analysis of *mark*2

Figure 6.25(e) shows the path taken by p on the list of Figure 6.25(a). It should be clear that a list node previously unmarked gets visited at most three times. Except for node x, each time a node already marked is reached at least one previously unmarked node is also examined (i.e., the one that led to this marked node). Hence the computing time of *mark*2 is $O(m)$ where m is the number of newly marked nodes. The constant factor associated with m is, however, larger than that for *mark*1 but *mark*2 does not require the stack space needed by *mark*1. A faster marking algorithm can be obtained by judiciously combining the strategies of *mark*1 and *mark*2 (see the exercises).

When the node structure of Section 6.8 is in use, an additional boolean field in each node is needed to implement the strategy of *mark*2. This field is used to distinguish between the case when a *dlink* is used to link into the path list and when an *rlink* is used. The existing tag field cannot be used as some of the nodes on the $t - x$ path list will originally have *tag* = **true** while others will have *tag* = **false** and so it will not be possible to reset tag values correctly when nodes are removed from the $t - x$ list.

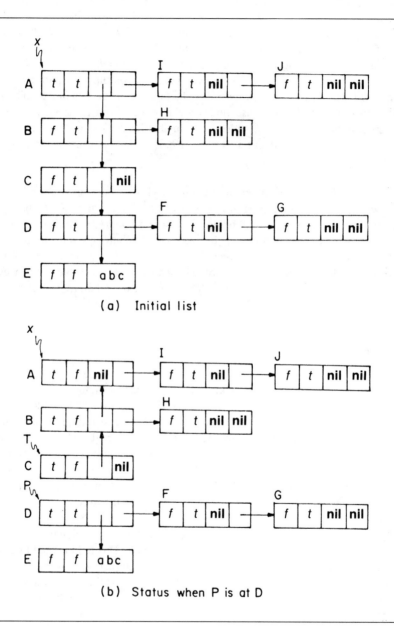

(a)   Initial list

(b)   Status when P is at D

Figure 6.25 Example list for *mark2*

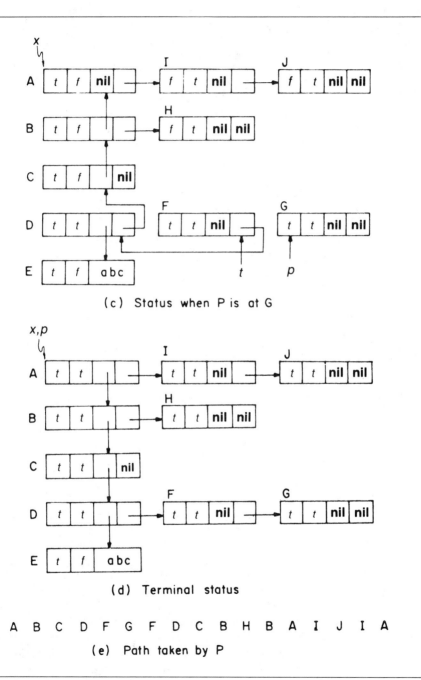

(c) Status when P is at G

(d) Terminal status

A B C D F G F D C B H B A I J I A

(e) Path taken by P

Figure 6.25 Example list for *mark*2 (contd.).

```
 1 procedure mark2(x : listpointer);
 2 {same function as mark1 }
 3 var p, q, t : listpointer; failure : boolean;
 4 begin
 5    p := x; t := nil; {initialize t−x path list}
 6    repeat
 7       movedown ;
 8       if failure then begin
 9                       moveright;
10                       if failure then backup;
11                    end;
12    until failure;
13 end; {of mark2}
```

Program 6.31 (a) Second marking algorithm

```
 1 procedure movedown;
 2 {Attempt to move p one node down}
 3 begin
 4    q := p↑.dlink; {go down list}; failure := true;
 5    if q <> nil
 6    then if not q↑.mark and q↑.tag
 7       then begin {unmarked list node}
 8             q↑.mark := true; p↑.tag := false;
 9             p↑.dlink := t; t := p; {add p to t−x path list}
10             p := q; failure := false;
11          end
12       else q↑.mark := true;
13 end; {of movedown}
```

Program 6.31(b) Procedure to move down one node

Storage Compaction

When all requests for storage are of a fixed size, it is enough to just link all unmarked (i.e. free) nodes together into an available space list. However, when storage requests may be for blocks of varying sizes, it is desirable to compact storage so that all the free space forms one contiguous block. Consider the memory configuration of Figure 6.26. Nodes in use have a *mark* field = t (for true) while free nodes have their *mark* field = f (for false). The nodes are labeled 1 through 8, with n_i, $1 \le i \le 8$ being the size

```
 1 procedure moveright;
 2 {Attempt to move p one node right}
 3 begin
 4     q := p↑.rlink; {move right}; failure := true;
 5     if q <> nil
 6     then if not q↑.mark and q↑.tag
 7          then begin {unmarked list node}
 8                   q↑.mark := true; p↑.rlink := t;
 9                   t := p; p := q; failure := false;
10               end
11          else q↑.mark := true;
12 end; {of moveright}
```

Program 6.31(c) Procedure to move right one node

```
 1 procedure backup;
 2 {Attempt to backup on t−x list}
 3 begin
 4     failure := true;
 5     while (t <> nil) and failure do
 6     begin
 7         q := t;
 8         if not q↑.tag
 9         then begin {linked via dlink}
10                 t := q↑.dlink; q↑.dlink := p;
11                 q↑.tag := true; p := q;
12                 moveright;
13              end
14         else begin {linked via rlink}
15                 {p is to right of q}
16                 t := q↑.rlink; q↑.rlink := p;
17                 p := q;
18              end;
19     end; {of while}
20 end; {of backup}
```

Program 6.31(d) Procedure to back up on the t−x list

of the i'th node.

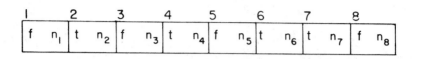

Figure 6.26 Memory configuraton after marking. Free nodes have mark field = f

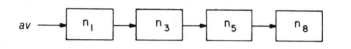

Figure 6.27 Available space list corresponding to Figure 6.26

The free nodes could be linked together to obtain the available space list of Figure 6.27. While the total amount of memory available is $n_1 + n_3 + n_5 + n_8$, a request for this much memory cannot be met since the memory is fragmented into four nonadjacent nodes. Further, with more and more use of these nodes, the size of free nodes will get smaller and smaller. Ultimately, it will be impossible to meet requests for all but the smallest of nodes. In order to overcome this, it is necessary to reallocate the storage of the nodes in use so that the used part of memory (and hence also the free portion) forms a contiguous block at one end as in Figure 6.28. This reallocation of storage resulting in a partitioning of memory into two contiguous blocks (one used, the other free) is referred to as storage compaction. Since there will, in general, be links from one node to another, storage compaction must update these links to point to the relocated address of the respective node. If node n_i starts at location l_i before compaction and at l_i' after compaction, then all link references to l_i must also be changed to l_i' in order not to disrupt the linked list structures existing in the system. Figure 6.29(a) shows a possible link configuration at the time the garbage collection process is invoked. Links are shown only for those nodes that were marked during the marking phase. It is assumed that there are only two links per node. Figure 6.29(b) shows the configuration following compaction. Note that the list structure is unchanged even though the actual addresses represented by the links have been changed.

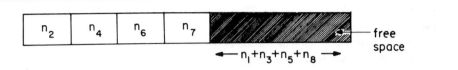

Figure 6.28 Memory configuraton after reallocating storage to nodes in use

With storage compaction we may identify three tasks: (1) determine new addresses for nodes in use; (2) update all links in nodes in use; and (3) relocate nodes to new addresses. Our storage compaction algorithm, *compact* (Program 6.32), is fairly straightforward, implementing each of these three tasks in a separate scan of memory. The algorithm assumes that each node, free or in use, has a *size* field giving the length of the node and an additional field, *newaddr*, which may be used to store the relocated address of the node. Further, it is assumed that each node has two link fields *link1* and *link2*. The extension of the algorithm to the most general situation in which nodes have a variable number of links is simple and requires only a modification of phase II. As in the case of the dynamic storage management algorithms of Section 6.7, the link fields contain integer values that give us the index of the first word in the node pointed at. 0 denotes a **nil** link. The fields in a node may be set and extracted using appropriate procedures and functions, respectively. In addition, we assume that the memory to be compacted is the array *memory* [1..*m*].

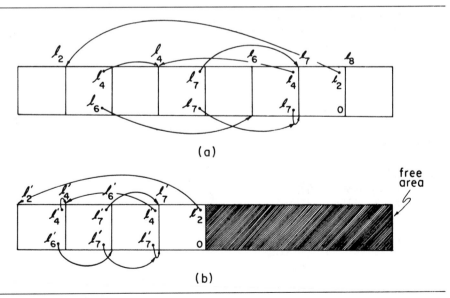

Figure 6.29 Configurations before and after compaction

---

procedure *compact*;
{compact the array *memory* [1..*m*]. Every node that is in
use has *mark* = **true**; a *newaddr* field, and two link fields.
size (*i*) = number of words in the node.}
var *i,j,k* : **integer**;
begin
  {phase I: Scan memory left to right assigning new
  addresses to nodes in use. *av* = next available word.}
  av := 1; *i* := 1;
  while *i* <= *m* **do**
  begin
   if *mark*(*i*)
   then begin {assign new address}
       setnewaddr (*i*) := *av*;
       av := *av* + *size* (*i*);
     end;
   i := *i* +*size* (*i*); {next node}
  end;
  {phase II: Update all links. Assume that *newaddr* (0) = 0}
  i := 1;
  while *i* <= *m* **do**
  begin
   if *mark*(*i*)
   then begin
       setlink 1(*i*, *newaddr* (*link* 1(*i*)));
       setlink 2(*i*, *newaddr* (*link* 2(*i*)));
     end;
   i := *i* + *size* (*i*);
  end;
  {phase III: relocate nodes}
  i := 1;
  while *i* <= *m* **do**
   if *mark*(*i*)
   then begin
       k := *i* −*newaddr* (*i*); *l* := *newaddr* (*i*);
       for *j* := *i* **to** *i* +*size* (*i*)−1 **do**
        memory [*j*−*k*] := *memory* [*j*];
       i := *i* +*size* (*l*);

end
    else $i := i + size\,(i)$;
end; {of *compact*}

Program 6.32 Memory compaction

In analyzing this algorithm, we see that if the number of nodes in memory is n, then phases I and II each require n iterations of their respective **while** loops. Since each iteration of these loops takes a fixed amount of time, the time for these two phases is $O(n)$. Phase III, however, will in general be more expensive. Though the **while** loop of this phase is also executed only n times, the time per iteration depends on the size of the node being relocated. If s is the amount of memory in use, then the time for this phase is $O(n + s)$. The overall computing time is, therefore, $O(n + s)$. The value of av at the end of phase I marks the beginning of the free space. At the termination of the algorithm the space *memory*[av] to *memory*[m] is free space. Finally, the physical relocation of nodes in phase III can be carried out using a long shift in case your computer has this facility.

In conclusion, we remark that both marking and storage compaction are slow processes. The time for the former is O(number of nodes) while the time for the latter is O(number of nodes + Σ(size of nodes relocated)). In the case of generalized lists, garbage collection is necessitated by the absence of any other efficient means to free storage when needed. Garbage collection has found use in some programming languages where it is desirable to free the user from the task of returning storage. In both situations, a disciplined use of pointer variables and link fields is required. Clever coding tricks involving illegal use of link fields could result in chaos during marking and compaction.

While compaction has been presented here primarily for use with generalized list systems using nodes of variable size, compaction can also be used in other environments such as the dynamic storage allocation environment of Section 6.7. Even though coalescing of adjacent free blocks takes place in algorithm *free* of Section 6.7, it is still possible to have several small nonadjacent blocks of memory free. The total size of these blocks may be large enough to meet a request and it may then be desirable to compact storage. The compaction algorithm in this case is simpler than the one described here. Since all addresses used within a block will be relative to the starting address rather than the absolute address, no updating of links within a block is required. Phases I and III can, therefore, be combined into one phase and phase II eliminated altogether. Since compaction is very slow, one would like to minimize the number of times it is carried out. With the introduction of compaction, several alternative schemes for dynamic storage management become viable. The exercises explore some of these alternatives.

6.10 REFERENCES AND SELECTED READINGS

A general reference for the topics discussed here is *Fundamentals of Data Structures in Pascal* by E. Horowitz and S. Sahni, Computer Science Press, 1986.

More list copying and marking algorithms may be found in:

"Copying list structures using bounded workspace," by G. Lindstrom, *CACM*, vol. 17, no. 4, April 1974, pp. 198-202.

"A nonrecursive list moving algorithm," by E. Reingold, *CACM*, vol. 16, no. 5, May 1973, pp. 305-307.

"Bounded workspace garbage collection in an address-order preserving list processing environment," by D. Fisher, *Information Processing Letters*, vol. 3, no. 1, July 1974, pp. 29-32.

6.11 EXERCISES

Exercises 1-6 assume that each node has two fields: *data* and *link*.

1. Write an algorithm *length* to count the number of nodes in a singly linked list p, where p points to the first node in the list. The last node has link field **nil**.

2. Let p be a pointer to the first node in a singly linked list and x a pointer to an arbitrary node in this list. Write an algorithm to delete this node from the list. If $x=p$, then p should be reset to point to the new first node in the list.

3. Let $x = (x_1,x_2, ..., x_n)$ and $y = (y_1,y_2, ..., y_m)$ be two linked lists. Write an algorithm to merge the two lists together to obtain the linked list $z = (x_1,y_1,x_2,y_2, ..., x_m,y_m,x_{m+1}, ..., x_n)$ if $m \le n$ and $z = (x_1,y_1, x_2,y_2, ..., x_n,y_n,y_{n+1}, ..., y_m)$ if $m > n$. No additional nodes may be used.

4. Do Exercise 1 for the case of circularly linked lists.

5. Do Exercise 2 for the case of circularly linked lists.

6. Do Exercise 3 for the case of circularly linked lists.

7. Devise a representation for a list where insertions and deletions can be made at either end. Such a structure is called a deque. Write a procedure for inserting at either end.

8. Consider the hypothetical data object $X2$. $X2$ is a linear list with the restriction that while additions to the list may be made at either end, deletions can be made from one end only. Design a linked list representation for $X2$. Write addition and deletion algorithms for $X2$. Specify initial and boundary conditions for your representation.

9. Give an algorithm for a singly linked circular list which reverses the direction of the links.

10. Let p be a pointer to a circularly linked list. Show how this list may be used as a queue. I.e., write algorithms to add and delete elements. Specify the value for p when the queue is empty.

11. It is possible to traverse a singly linked list in both directions (i.e., left to right and a restricted right-to-left traversal) by reversing the links during the left-to-right traversal. A possible configuration for a list p under this scheme would be:

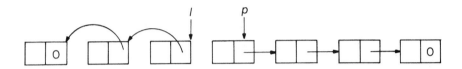

   p points to the node currently being examined and l to the node on its left. Note that all nodes to the left of p have their links reversed.

   (a) Write an algorithm to move p, n nodes to the right from a given position (l,p).

   (b) Write an algorithm to move p, n nodes left from any given position (l,p).

12. Write an algorithm $pread(x)$ to read in n pairs of coefficients and exponents, (c_i,e_i) $1 \le i \le n$ of a univariate polynomial, x, and to convert the polynomial into the circular linked list structure of Section 6.3. Assume $e_i > e_{i+1}$, $1 \le i < n$, and that $c_i \ne 0$, $1 \le i \le n$. Your algorithm should leave x pointing to the head node. Show that this operation can be performed in time O(n).

13. Let a and b be pointers to the head nodes of two polynomials represented as in Exercise 12. Write an algorithm to compute the product polynomial $c = a*b$. Your algorithm should leave a and b unaltered and create c as a new list. Show that if n and m are the number of terms in a and b, respectively, then this multiplication can be carried out in time O(nm^2) or O(mn^2). If a, b are dense show that the multiplication takes O(mn).

14. Let a be a pointer to the head node of a univariate polynomial as in Section 6.3. Write an algorithm, $peval\ (a,x)$ to evaluate the polynomial a at the point x, where x is some real number.

In Exercises 15-19, the sparse matrices are represented as in Section 6.6.

15. Let a and b be two sparse matrices represented as in Section 6.6. Write an algorithm, $madd(a,b,c)$ to create the matrix $c = a + b$. Your algorithm should leave the matrices a and b unchanged and set up c as a new matrix in accordance with this data representation. Show that if a and b are $n \times m$ matrices with r_A and r_B

nonzero terms, then this addition can be carried out in $O(n + m + r_A + r_B)$ time.

16. Let a and b be two sparse matrices. Write an algorithm $mmul\,(a,b,c)$ to set up the structure for $c = a*b$. Show that if a is an $n \times m$ matrix with r_A nonzero terms and if b is an $m \times p$ matrix with r_B nonzero terms, then c can be computed in time $O(pr_A + nr_B)$. Can you think of a way to compute c in $O(\min\{pr_A, nr_B\})$?

17. Write an algorithm to write out the terms of a sparse matrix a as triples (i, j, a_{ij}). The terms are to be output by rows and within rows by columns. Show that this operation can be performed in time $O(n + r_A)$ if there are r_A nonzero terms in a and a is an $n \times m$ matrix.

18. Write an algorithm $mtrp\,(a,b)$ to compute the matrix $b = a^T$, the transpose of the sparse matrix a. What is the computing time of your algorithm?

19. Design an algorithm to copy a sparse matrix. What is the computing time of your algorithm?

20. A simpler and more efficient representation for sparse matrices can be obtained when one is restricted to the operations of addition, subtraction, and multiplication. In this representaton, nodes have the fields *down*, *right*, *row*, *col*, and *value*. Each nonzero term is represented by a node. These nodes are linked together to form two circular lists. The first list, the row list, is made up by linking nodes by rows and within rows by columns. This is done via the *right* field. The second list, the column list, is made up by linking nodes via the *down* field. In this list, nodes are linked by columns and within columns by rows. These two lists share a common head node. In addition, a node is added to contain the dimensions of the matrix. The matrix a of Figure 6.12 has the representation shown in Figure 6.30.

Using the same assumptions as for algorithm *mread* of Section 6.6 write an algorithm to read in a matrix and set up its internal representation as above. How much time does your algorithm take? How much additional space is needed?

21. For the representation of Exercise 20 write algorithms to
    (a) Erase a matrix
    (b) Add two matrices
    (c) Multiply two matrices
    (d) Print out a matrix

For each of the above obtain computing times. How do these times compare with the corresponding times for the representation of Section 6.6?

22. Compare the sparse representations of Exercise 20 and Section 6.6 with respect to some other operations. For example, how much time is needed to output the entries in an arbitrary row or column?

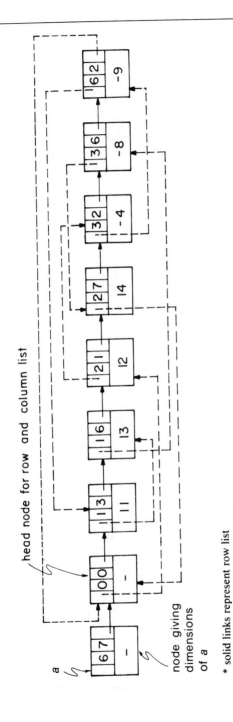

Figure 6.30 Representation of matrix *A* of Figure 6.12 using the scheme of Exercise 20.

23. Write a nonrecursive version of algorithm *lerase* (*x*) of Section 6.8.

24. Write a nonrecursive version of algorithm *equal* (*s,t*) of Section 6.8.

25. Write a nonrecursive version of algorithm *depth* (*s*) of Section 6.8.

26. Write a procedure which takes an arbitrary nonrecursive list *l* with no shared sub-lists and inverts it and all of its sublists. For example, if *l* = (*a*, (*b,c*)), then inverse (*l*) = ((*c,b*),*a*).

27. Devise a procedure that produces the list representation of an arbitrary list given its linear form as a string of atoms, commas, blanks, and parentheses. For example, for the input *l* = (*a*, (*b,c*)), your procedure should produce the structure

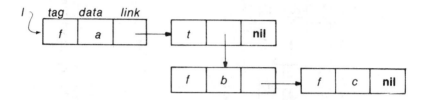

28. One way to represent generalized lists is through the use of two field nodes and a symbol table which contains all atoms and list names together with pointers to these lists. Let the two fields of each node be named *alink* and *blink*. Then *blink* either points to the next node on the same level, if there is one, or is **nil**. The *alink* field either points to a node at a lower level or, in the case of an atom or list name, to the appropriate entry in the symbol table. For example, the list *B* (*A*, (*D,E*),( ),*B*) would have the representation:

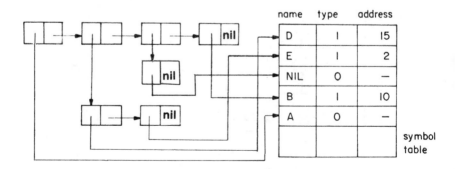

(The list names *D* and *E* were already in the table at the time the list *B* was input. *A* was not in the table and is assumed to be an atom.)

The symbol table retains a type bit for each entry. Type = 1 if the entry is a list name and type = 0 for atoms. The NIL atom may either be in the table or *alink* can be set to **nil** to represent the NIL atom. Write an algorithm to read in a list in parentheses notation and to set up its linked representation as above with x set to point to the first node in the list. Note that no head nodes are in use. The following subalgorithms may be used by *lread*.

(a) *get(a,p)* ... searches the symbol table for the name a. p is set to 0 if a is not found in the table; otherwise, p is set to the position of a in the table.

(b) *put(a,t,p)* ... enters a into the table. p is the position at which a was entered. If a is already in the table, then the type and address fields of the old entry are changed. $t =$ **nil** to enter an atom or $t <>$ **nil** to enter a list with first node t. (*Note*: this permits definition of lists using indirect recursion.) The diagram is for the case when the addresses t are integers.

(c) *nexttoken* ... gets next token in input list. (A token may be a list name, atom, '(','(' or ','. A '#' is returned if there are no more tokens.)

(d) *new(x)* ... gets a node for use.
You may assume that the input list is syntactically correct. In case a sublist is labeled as in the list $C(D,E(F,G))$ the structure should be set up as in the case $C(D,(F,G))$ and E should be entered into the symbol table as a list with the appropriate starting address.

29. Rewrite algorithm *mark*1 of Section 6.9 using the conventions of Section 6.8 for a tag field.

30. Rewrite algorithm *mark*1 of Section 6.9 for the case when each list and sublist has a head node. Assume that the *dlink* field of each head node is free and so may be used to maintain a linked stack without using any additional space. Show that the computing time is still O(m).

31. When the *dlink* field of a node is used to retain atomic information as in Section 6.8, implementing the marking strategy of *mark*2 requires an additional bit in each node. In this exercise we shall explore a marking strategy which does not require this additional bit. Its worst case computing time will however be O(mn) where m is the number of nodes marked and n the total number of nodes in the system. Write a marking algorithm using the node structure and conventions of Section 6.8. Each node has the fields: *mark, tag, dlink* and *rlink*. Your marking algorithm will use variable p to point to the node currently being examined and *next* to point to the next node to be examined. If l is the address of the as yet unexplored list node with least address and p the address of the node currently being examined then the value of *next* will be min $\{l, p + 1\}$. Show that the computing time of your algorithm is O(mn).

32. Prove that *mark* 2(x) marks all unmarked nodes accessible from x.

33. Write a composite marking algorithm using *mark1*, *mark2*, and a fixed amount *m* of stack space. Stack nodes as in *mark1* until the stack is full. When the stack becomes full, revert to the strategy of *mark2*. On completion of *mark2*, pick up a node from the stack and explore it using the composite algorithm. In case the stack never overflows, the composite algorithm will be as fast as *mark1*. When *m* = 0, the algorithm essentially becomes *mark2*. The computing time will in general be somewhere in between that of *mark1* and *mark2*.

34. Write a storage compaction algorithm to be used following the marking phase of garbage collection. Assume that all nodes are of a fixed size and can be addressed as *node* [*i*], $1 \le i \le m$. Show that this can be done in two phases, where in the first phase a left-to-right scan for free nodes and a right to left scan for nodes in use is carried out. During this phase, used nodes from the right end of memory are moved to free positions at the left end. The relocated address of such nodes is noted in one of the fields of the old address. At the end of this phase all nodes in use occupy a contiguous chunk of memory at the left end. In the second phase, links to relocated nodes are updated.

35. [Programming Project]
Design a linked allocation system to represent and manipulate univariate polynomials with integer coefficients (use circular linked lists with head nodes). Each term of the polynomial will be represented as a node. Thus, a node in this system will have three fields as below:

Exponent	Link
Coefficient	

In order to erase polynomials efficiently, we shall need to use an available space list and associated procedures as described in Section 6.3. The external (i.e., for input or output) representation of a univariate polynomial will be assumed to be a sequence of integers of the form: $n, e_1, c_1, e_2, c_2, e_3, c_3 \dots, e_n, c_n$, where the e_i represent the exponents and the c_i the coefficients. n gives the number of terms in the polynomial. The exponents are in decreasing order, i.e., $e_1 > e_2 > \dots > e_n$.

Write and test the following procedures:

(a) *pread(x)* ... read in an input polynomial and convert it to its circular list representation using a head node. *x* is set to point to the head node of this polynomial.

(b) *pwrite(x)* ... convert the polynomial *x* from its linked list representation to its external representation and output it.

(c) *padd(x, y, z)* ... $z = x + y$

(d) $psub(x,y,z) \dots z = x - y$

(e) $pmul(x,y,z) \dots z = x * y$

(f) $peval(x,a,v) \dots a$ is a real constant and the polynomial x is evaluated at the point a. v is set to this value.

Note: Procedures (c)-(f) should leave the input polynomials unaltered after completion of their respective tasks.

(g) $perase(x) \dots$ return the circular list x to the available space list.

36. [Programming Project]
In this project, we shall implement a complete linked list system to perform arithmetic on sparse matrices using the representation of Section 6.6. First, design a convenient node structure assuming *value* is an integer.

Since we shall need to erase circular lists, we shall utilize the space list concept introduced in Section 6.3. So, we may begin by writing and testing the procedures associated with this list. Next, write and test the following procedures for matrix operations:

(a)   *mread* $(a) \dots$ read matrix a and set up according to the representation of Section 6.6. The input has the following format:

line 1: $n\ m\ r$ n = # or rows
                            m = # or columns
                            r = # of nonzero terms

line 2
 .   triples of (row, column, value)
 .
 .

These triples are in increasing order by rows. Within rows, the triples are in increasing order of columns. The data is to be read in one line at a time and converted to internal representation. The variable a is set to point to the head node of the circular list of head nodes (as in the text).

(b)   *mwrite*$(a) \dots$ print out the terms of a. To do this, you will have to design a suitable output format. In any case, the output should be ordered by rows and within rows by columns.

(c)   *merase*$(a) \dots$ return all nodes of the sparse matrix a to the available space list.

(d)   *madd*$(a,b,c) \dots$ create the sparse matrix $c = a + b$. a and b are to be left unaltered.

(e)   *msub(a,b,c)* ... *c* = *a* − *b*. *a* and *b* are to be left unaltered.

(f)   *mmult(a,b,c)* ... create the sparse matrix *c* = *a* ∗ *b*. *a* and *b* are to be left unaltered.

(g)   *mtrp(a,b)* ... create the sparse matrix *b* = a^t. *a* is to be left unaltered.

37. [Programming Project]
     Do the project of Exercise 36 using the matrix representation of Exercise 20.

38. [Landweber]
     This problem is to simulate an airport landing and takeoff pattern. The airport has three runways, runway 1, runway 2, and runway 3. There are four landing holding patterns, two for each of the first two runways. Arriving planes will enter one of the holding pattern queues, where the queues are to be as close in size as possible. When a plane enters a holding queue, it is assigned an integer *id* number and an integer giving the number of time units the plane can remain in the queue before it must land (because of low fuel level). There is also a queue for takeoffs for each of the three runways. Planes arriving in a takeoff queue are also assigned an integer *id*. The takeoff queues should be kept approximately the same size.

     At each time up to three planes may arrive at the landing queues and up tp three planes may arrive at the takeoff queues. Each runway can handle one takeoff or landing at each time slot. Runway 3 is to be used for takeoffs except when a plane is low on fuel. At each time unit, planes in either landing queue whose air time has reached zero must be given priority over other landings and takeoffs. If only one plane is in this category, runway 3 is to be used. If more than one, then the other runways are also used (at each time at most three planes can be serviced in this way).

     Use successive even (odd) integers for *id*'s of planes arriving at takeoff (landing) queues. At each time unit assume that arriving planes are entered into queues before takeoffs or landings occur. Try to design your algorithm so that neither landing nor takeoff queues grow excessively. However, arriving planes must be placed at the ends of queues. Queues cannot be reordered.

     The output should clearly indicate what occurs at each time unit. Periodically output (a) the contents of each queue; (b) the average takeoff waiting time; (c) the average landing waiting time; (d) the average flying time remaining on landing; and (e) the number of planes landing with no fuel reserve. (b) and (c) are for planes that have taken off or landed, respectively. The output should be self explanatory and easy to understand (and uncluttered).

     The input can be from cards, a terminal, a file, or it can be generated by a random number generator. For each time unit the input is of the form:

col1:	0-3	indicating the number of planes arriving at takeoff queues
col2:	0-3	indicating # of planes arriving at landing queues
col4-5	1-20	
col6-7	1-20	units of flying time for planes arriving in landing queues
col8-9	1-20	(from col2)

CHAPTER 7

TREES

7.1 BASIC TERMINOLOGY

In this chapter we shall study a very important data object, trees. Intuitively, a tree structure means that the data are organized so that items of information are related by branches. One very common place where such a structure arises is in the investigation of genealogies. There are two types of genealogical charts which are used to present such data: the *pedigree* and the *lineal* chart. Figure 7.1 gives an example of each.

The pedigree chart shows someone's ancestors, in this case those of Dusty, whose two parents are Honey Bear and Brandy. Brandy's parents are Nuggett and Coyote, who are Dusty's grandparents on her father's side. The chart continues one more generation farther back to the great-grandparents. By the nature of things, we know that the pedigree chart is normally two-way branching, though this does not allow for inbreeding. When that occurs we no longer have a tree structure unless we insist that each occurrence of breeding is separately listed. Inbreeding may occur frequently when describing family histories of flowers or animals.

The lineal chart of Figure 7.1(b), though it has nothing to do with people, is still a genealogy. It describes, in somewhat abbreviated form, the ancestry of the modern European languages. Thus, this is a chart of descendants rather than ancestors and each item can produce several others. Latin, for instance, is the forebear of Spanish, French, Italian, and Rumanian. Proto Indo-European is a prehistoric language presumed to have existed in the fifth millenium B.C. This tree does not have the regular structure of the pedigree chart, but it is a tree structure nevertheless.

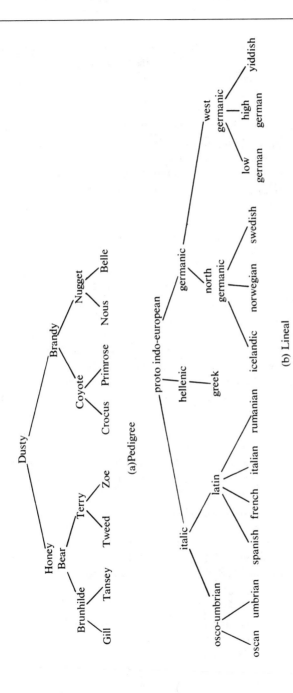

Figure 7.1 Two types of geneological charts

With these two examples as motivation let us define formally what we mean by a tree.

Definition: A *tree* is a finite set of one or more nodes such that (1) there is a specially designated node called the *root*; (2) the remaining nodes are partitioned into $n \geq 0$ disjoint sets T_1, ..., T_n where each of these sets is a tree. T_1, ..., T_n are called the *subtrees* of the root.

Again we have an instance of a recursive definition (compare this with the definition of a generalized list in Section 6.8). If we return to Figure 7.1 we see that the roots of the trees are Dusty and Proto Indo-European. Tree (a) has two subtrees whose roots are Honey Bear and Brandy while tree (b) has three subtrees with roots Italic, Hellenic, and Germanic. The condition that T_1, ..., T_n be disjoint sets prohibits subtrees from ever connecting together (no cross breeding). It follows that every item in a tree is the root of some subtree of the whole. For instance, West Germanic is the root of a subtree of Germanic which itself has three subtrees with roots: Low German, High German, and Yiddish. Yiddish is a root of a tree with no subtrees.

There are many terms which are often used when referring to trees. A *node* stands for the item of information plus the branches to other nodes. Consider the tree in Figure 7.2. This tree has 13 nodes, each item of data being a single letter for convenience. The root is A and we will normally draw trees with the root at the top. The number of subtrees of a node is called its *degree*. The degree of A is 3, of C is 1, and of F is zero. Nodes that have degree zero are called *leaf* or *terminal* nodes. $\{K,L,F,G,M,I,J\}$ is the set of leaf nodes. Consequently, the other nodes are referred to as *nonterminals*. The roots of the subtrees of a node, X, are the *children* of X. X is the *parent* of its children. Thus, the children of D are H, I, J; the parent of D is A.

Children of the same parent are said to be *siblings*. H, I, and J are siblings. We can extend this terminology if we need to so that we can ask for the grandparent of M which is D, etc. The *degree of a tree* is the maximum degree of the nodes in a tree. The tree of Figure 7.2 has degree 3. The *ancestors* of a node are all the nodes along the path from the root to that node. The ancestors of M are A, D, and H.

The *level* of a node is defined by initially letting the root be at level one. If a node is at level l, then its children are at level $l + 1$. Figure 7.2 shows the levels of all nodes in that tree. The *height* or *depth* of a tree is defined to be the maximum level of any node in the tree.

A *forest* is a set of $n \geq 0$ disjoint trees. The notion of a forest is very close to that of a tree because if we remove the root of a tree we get a forest. For example, in Figure 7.2 if we remove A we get a forest with three trees.

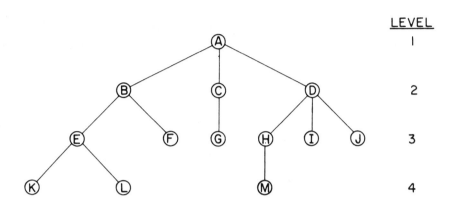

Figure 7.2 A sample tree

There are other ways to draw a tree. One useful way is as a list. The tree of Figure 7.2 could be written as the list

$$(A (B (E (K,L),F),C (G),D (H (M),I,J)))$$

The information in the root node comes first followed by a list of the subtrees of that node.

Now, how do we represent a tree in memory? If we wish to use linked lists, then a node must have a varying number of fields depending upon the number of branches.

DATA	LINK 1	LINK 2	⋯	LINK n

However, it is often simpler to write algorithms for a data representation when the node size is fixed. Using data and pointer fields we can represent a tree using the fixed node size list structure we devised in Chapter 6. The list representation for the tree of Figure 7.2 is on page 290. We can now make use of many of the general procedures that we originally wrote for handling lists. Thus, the data object tree is a special instance of the data object list and we can specialize the list representation scheme to them. In a later section we will see that another data object which can be used to represent a tree is the data object binary tree.

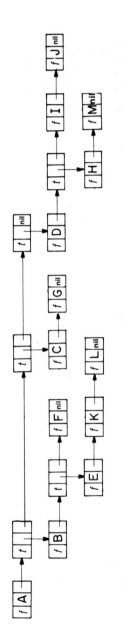

List representation of the tree of Figure 7.2

7.2 BINARY TREES

A binary tree is an important type of tree structure which occurs very often. It is charac-terized by the fact that any node can have at most two branches, i.e., there is no node with degree greater than two. For binary trees we distinguish between the subtree on the left and on the right, whereas for trees the order of the subtrees was irrelevant. Also a binary tree may have zero nodes. Thus a binary tree is really a different object than a tree.

Definition: A *binary tree* is a finite set of nodes which is either empty or consists of a root and two disjoint binary trees called the *left subtree* and the *right subtree*.

The distinctions between a binary tree and a tree should be analyzed. First of all there is no tree having zero nodes, but there is an empty binary tree. The two binary trees below

are different. The first one has an empty right subtree while the second has an empty left subtree. If the above are regarded as trees, then they are the same despite the fact that they are drawn slightly differently.

Figure 7.3 shows two sample binary trees. These two trees are special kinds of binary trees. The first is a *skewed* tree, skewed to the left, and there is a corresponding one which skews to the right. Tree 7.3(b) is called a *complete* binary tree. This kind of binary tree will be defined formally later on. Notice that all terminal nodes are on adja-cent levels. The terms that we introduced for trees such as degree, level, height, leaf, parent, and child all apply to binary trees in the natural way. Before examining data representations for binary trees, let us first make some relevant observations regarding such trees. First, what is the maximum number of nodes in a binary tree of depth k?

Lemma 7.1 (1) The maximum number of nodes on level i of a binary tree is $2^{i-1}, i \geq 1$ and
(2) The maximum number of nodes in a binary tree of depth k is $2^k - 1, k \geq 1$.

Proof: (1) The proof is by induction on i.
Induction Base: The root is the only node on level $i = 1$. Hence the maximum number

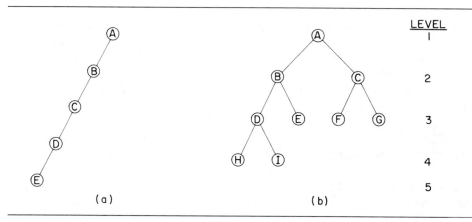

Figure 7.3 Two sample binary trees

of nodes on level $i = 1$ is $2^0 = 2^{i-1}$.

Induction Hypothesis: For all j, $1 \leq j < i$, the maximum number of nodes on level j is 2^{j-1}.

Induction Step: The maximum number of nodes on level $i-1$ is 2^{i-2}, by the induction hypothesis. Since each node in a binary tree has maximum degree 2, the maximum number of nodes on level i is 2 times the maximum number on level $i-1$ or 2^{i-1}.

(2) the maximum number of nodes in a binary tree of depth k is

$$\sum_{i=1}^{k} (\text{maximum number of nodes on level } i) = \sum_{i=1}^{k} 2^{i-1} = 2^k - 1. \quad \square$$

Next, let us examine the relationship between the number of terminal nodes and the number of nodes of degree 2 in a binary tree.

Lemma 7.2: For any nonempty binary tree, T, if n_0 is the number of terminal nodes and n_2 the number of nodes of degree 2, then $n_0 = n_2 + 1$.

Proof: Let n_1 be the number of nodes of degree 1 and n the total number of nodes. Since all nodes in T are of degree ≤ 2 we have

$$n = n_0 + n_1 + n_2 \tag{7.1}$$

If we count the number of branches in a binary tree, we see that every node except for the root has a branch leading into it. If B is the number of branches, then $n = B + 1$. All branches emanate either from a node of degree 1 or from a node of degree 2. Thus, $B = n_1 + 2n_2$. Hence, we obtain

$$n = 1 + n_1 + 2n_2 \tag{7.2}$$

Subtracting (7.2) from (7.1) and rearranging terms we get

$$n_0 = n_2 + 1 \quad \square$$

In Figure 7.3(a) $n_0 = 1$ and $n_2 = 0$ while in Figure 7.3(b) $n_0 = 5$ and $n_2 = 4$.

As we continue our discussion of binary trees, we shall derive some other interesting properties.

7.3 BINARY TREE REPRESENTATIONS

A *full* binary tree of depth k is a binary tree of depth k having $2^k - 1$ nodes. By Lemma 7.1, this is the maximum number of nodes such a binary tree can have. Figure 7.4 shows a full binary tree of depth 4. A very elegant sequential representation for such binary trees results from sequentially numbering the nodes, starting with nodes on level 1, then those on level 2 and so on. Nodes on any level are numbered from left to right (see Figure 7.4). This numbering scheme gives us the definition of a complete binary tree. A binary tree with n nodes and a depth k is *complete* iff its nodes correspond to the nodes which are numbered 1 to n in the full binary tree of depth k. The nodes may now be stored in a one dimensional array *tree*, with the node numbered i being stored in *tree*[i]. Lemma 7.3 enables us to determine easily the locations of the parent, left child, and right child of any node i in the binary tree.

Lemma 7.3: If a complete binary tree with n nodes (i.e., depth $= \lfloor \log_2 n \rfloor + 1$) is represented sequentially as above then for any node with index, i, $1 \le i \le n$ we have

(1) *parent*(i) is at $\lfloor i/2 \rfloor$ if $i \ne 1$. When $i = 1$, i is the root and has no parent.

(2) *lchild*(i) is at $2i$ if $2i \le n$. If $2i > n$, then i has no left child.

(3) *rchild*(i) is at $2i + 1$ if $2i + 1 \le n$. If $2i + 1 > n$, then i has no right child.

Proof: We prove (2). (3) is an immediate consequence of (2) and the numbering of nodes on the same level from left to right. (1) follows from (2) and (3). We prove (2) by induction on i. For $i = 1$, clearly the left child is at 2 unless $2 > n$ in which case 1 has no left child. Now assume that for all j, $1 \le j \le i$, *lchild*(j) is at $2j$. Then, the two nodes immediately preceding *lchild*($i + 1$) in the representation are the right child of i and the left child of i. The left child of i is at $2i$. Hence, the left child of $i + 1$ is at $2i + 2 = 2(i + 1)$ unless $2(i + 1) > n$ in which case $i + 1$ has no left child. $\square$

This representation can clearly be used for all binary trees though in most cases there will be a lot of unutilized space. For complete binary trees the representation is ideal as no space is wasted. For the skewed tree of Figure 7.3(a) however, less than half

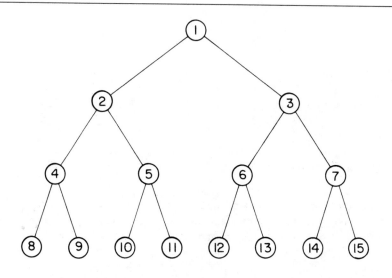

Figure 7.4 Full binary tree of depth 4 with sequential node numbers.

the array is utilized. In the worst case a skewed tree of depth k will require 2^k-1 spaces. Of these only k will be occupied.

While the above representation appears to be good for complete binary trees it is wasteful for many other binary trees. In addition, the representation suffers from the general inadequacies of sequential representations. Insertion or deletion of nodes from the middle of a tree requires the movement of potentially many nodes to reflect the change in level number of these nodes. These problems can be easily overcome through the use of a linked representation. Each node will have three fields, *leftchild*, *data*, and *rightchild* and is defined in Pascal as

```
type treepointer = ↑treerecord ;
     treerecord = record
                     leftchild : treepointer ;
                     data : char;
                     rightchild : treepointer ;
                  end;
```

We shall draw such a node using either of the representations:

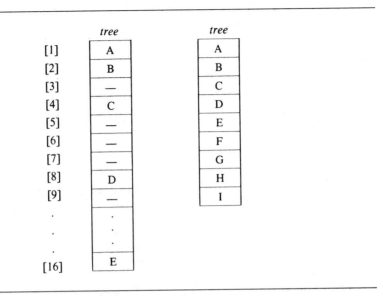

Figure 7.5 Array representation of the binary trees of Figure 7.3

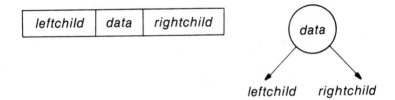

While this node structure will make it difficult to determine the parent of a node, we shall see that for most applications, it is adequate. In case it is necessary to be able to determine the parent of random nodes, then a fourth field *parent* may be included. The representation of the binary tree of Figure 7.3 using this node structure is given in Figure 7.6. A tree is referred to by the variable that points to its root.

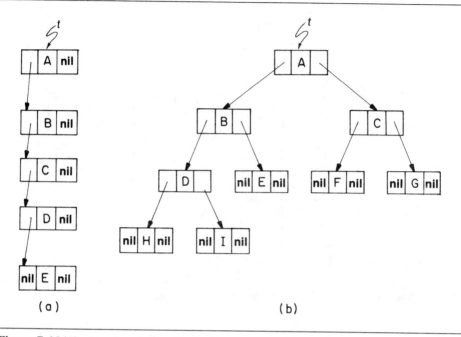

Figure 7.6 Linked representation for the binary trees of Figure 7.3

7.4 BINARY TREE TRAVERSAL

There are many operations that we often want to perform on trees. One notion that arises frequently is the idea of traversing a tree or visiting each node in the tree exactly once. A full traversal produces a linear order for the information in a tree. This linear order may be familiar and useful. When traversing a binary tree we want to treat each node and its subtrees in the same fashion. If we let L, D, R stand for moving left, printing the data, and moving right when at a node then there are six possible combinations of traversal: *LDR, LRD, DLR, DRL, RDL,* and *RLD.* If we adopt the convention that we traverse left before right then only three traversals remain: *LDR, LRD,* and *DLR.* To these we assign the names inorder, postorder, and preorder because there is a natural correspondence between these traversals and producing the infix, postfix, and prefix forms of an expression. Consider the binary tree of Figure 7.7. This tree contains an arithmetic expression with binary operators: add(+), multiply (∗), divide(/), and variables $A, B, C,$ $D,$ and $E.$ We will not worry for now how this binary tree was formed but assume that it is available. We will define three types of traversals and show the results for this tree.

Inorder Traversal: informally this calls for moving down the tree towards the left until

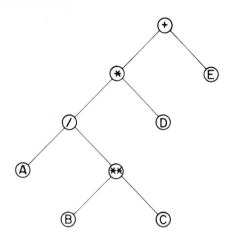

Figure 7.7 Binary tree with arithmetic expression

you can go no farther. Then you ''visit'' the node, move one node to the right and continue again. If you cannot move to the right, go back one more node. A precise way of describing this traversal is to write it as a recursive procedure (Program 7.1).

```
 1 procedure inorder (currentnode : treepointer);
 2 {currentnode is a pointer to a node in a binary tree. For full
 3   tree traversal, pass inorder the pointer to the top of the tree}
 4 begin {inorder}
 5   if currentnode < > nil
 6   then
 7   begin
 8     inorder (currentnode↑. leftchild);
 9     write(currentnode↑. data );
10     inorder (currentnode↑. rightchild);
11   end
12 end; {of inorder}
```

Program 7.1 Algorithm *inorder*

Recursion is an elegant device for describing this traversal. Figure 7.8 is a trace of how **procedure** *inorder* (Program 7.1) works on the tree of Figure 7.7. You should first read down the left column and then the right one. Including the initial (MAIN) invocation, the procedure is invoked a total of 19 times.

Call of *inorder*	Value in root	Action	Call of *inorder*	Value in root	
MAIN	+		10	C	
1	*		11	**nil**	
2	*		10	C	write('C')
3	/		12	**nil**	
4	A		1	*	write('*')
5	**nil**		13	D	
4	A	write('A')	14	**nil**	
6	**nil**		13	D	write('D')
3	/	write('/')	15	**nil**	
7	B		MAIN	+	write('+')
8	**nil**		16	E	
7	B	write ('B')	17	**nil**	
9	**nil**		16	E	write('E')
2	*	write('*')	18	**nil**	

Figure 7.8 Trace of Program 7.1

The elements get output in the order

$$A / B * C * D + E$$

which is the *in*fix form of the expression.

A second form of traversal is *preorder*. Program 7.2 is the Pascal code for this. In words we would say "visit a node, traverse left, and continue again. When you cannot continue, move right and begin again or move back until you can move right and resume."

The nodes of Figure 7.7 would be output in *pre*order as

$$+ * * / A B C D E$$

which we recognize as the *pre*fix form of the expression.

```
 1 procedure preorder (currentnode : treepointer);
 2 {currentnode is a pointer to a node in a binary tree. For full
 3   tree traversal, pass preorder the pointer to the top of the tree}
 4 begin {preorder}
 5   if currentnode < > nil
 6   then
 7   begin
 8     write(currentnode ↑. data);
 9     preorder (currentnode ↑. leftchild);
10     preorder (currentnode ↑. rightchild);
11   end {of if}
12 end; {of preorder}
```

Program 7.2 Algorithm *preorder*

At this point it should be easy to guess the next traversal method which is called *postorder*. The output produced by **procedure** *postorder* (Program 7.3) is

$$A \ B \ / \ C \ * \ D \ * \ E \ +$$

which is the *post*fix of our expression.

```
 1 procedure postorder (currentnode : treepointer);
 2 {currentnode is a pointer to a node in a binary tree. For full
 3   tree traversal, pass postorder the pointer to the top of the tree}
 4 begin {postorder}
 5   if currentnode < > nil
 6   then
 7   begin
 8     postorder (currentnode ↑. leftchild);
 9     postorder (currentnode ↑. rightchild);
10     write(currentnode ↑. data);
11   end {of if}
12 end; {of postorder}
```

Program 7.3 Algorithm *postorder*

Though we have written these three algorithms using recursion, it is very easy to produce equivalent nonrecursive versions. We leave this as an exercise. The run time of each of the traversal algorithms is readily seen to be $O(n)$, where n is the number of nodes in the tree. The space required for the recursion stack is proportional to the depth of the tree. This depth is at most n.

7.5 MORE ON BINARY TREES

Using the definition of a binary tree and the recursive version of the traversals, we can easily write other routines for working with binary trees. For instance, if we want to produce an exact copy of a given binary tree we can modify the postorder traversal algorithm only slightly to get Program 7.4.

```
 1 function copy (originaltree : treepointer) : treeponter ;
 2 {This function returns a pointer to an exact
 3   copy of the binary tree originaltree}
 4 var temptree : treepointer ;
 5 begin
 6   if originaltree < > nil
 7   then
 8   begin
 9     new(temptree);
10     temptree↑.leftchild := copy (originaltree↑.leftchild);
11     temptree↑.rightchild := copy(originaltree↑.rightchild);
12     temptree↑.data := temptree ;
13     copy := temptree ;
14   end
15   else copy := nil;
16 end {of copy}
```

Program 7.4 Algorithm *copy*

Another problem that is especially easy to solve using recursion is determining the equivalence of two binary trees. Binary trees are equivalent if they have the same topology and the information in corresponding nodes is identical. By the same topology we mean that every branch in one tree corresponds to a branch in the second in the same order and vice versa. Algorithm *equal*, Program 7.5, traverses the binary trees in preorder, though any order could be used.

As an example of the usefulness of binary trees, consider the set of formulas we can construct by taking variables $x_1, x_2, x_3, \ldots$ and the operators $\wedge$ (**and**), $\vee$ (**or**), and $\neg$ (**not**). These variables can only hold one of two possible values, true or false. The set of expressions which can be formed using these variables and operators is defined by the

```
 1 function equal (firsttree, secondtree : treepointer ) : boolean;
 2 {this procedure returns false if the binary trees firsttree and
 3 secondtree are not equivalent. Otherwise, it will return true}
 4 begin
 5   equal := false; {initialize answer}
 6   if ((firsttree = nil) and (secondtree = nil))
 7   then equal := true
 8   else
 9    if ((firsttree < > nil) and (second < > nil))
10    then
11      if firsttree↑. data = secondtree↑. data
12      then
13        if equal (firsttree↑. leftchild, secondtree↑. leftchild)
14        then
15          equal := equal (firsttree↑. rightchild, secondtree↑. rightchild);
16 end; {of equal}
```

Program 7.5 Algorithm *eval*

rules: (1) a variable is an expression; (2) if x and y are expressions then $x \wedge y$, $x \vee y$, $\neg x$ are expressions. Parentheses can be used to alter the normal order of evaluation which is **not** before **and** before **or**. This comprises the formulas in the *propositional calculus* (other operations such as implication can be expressed using $\wedge$, $\vee$, $\neg$). The expression

$$x_1 \vee (x_2 \wedge \neg x_3)$$

is a formula (read "x_1 or x_2 and not x_3"). If x_1 and x_3 are false and x_2 is true, then the value of this expression is

$$false \vee (true \wedge \neg false)$$

$$= false \vee true$$

$$= true$$

The *satisfiability problem* for formulas of the propositional calculus asks if there is an assignment of values to the variables which causes the value of the expression to be true. This problem is of great historical interest in computer science. It was originally used by Newell, Shaw, and Simon in the late 1950s to show the viability of heuristic programming (the Logic Theorist).

Again, let us assume that our formula is already in a binary tree, say

$$(x_1 \wedge \neg x_2) \vee (\neg x_1 \wedge x_3) \vee \neg x_3$$

in the tree of Figure 7.9. The inorder of this tree is

$$x_1 \wedge \neg x_2 \vee \neg x_1 \wedge x_3 \vee \neg x_3$$

which is the infix form of the expression. The most obvious algorithm to determine satisfiability is to let (x_1, x_2, x_3) take on all possible combinations of truth and a falsity and to check the formula for each combination. For n variables there are 2^n possible combinations of true $= t$ and false $= f$, e.g., for $n = 3$, the eight combinations are: (t,t,t), (t,t,f), (t,f,t), (t,f,f), (f,t,t), (f,t,f), (f,f,t), (f,f,f). The algorithm will take at least $O(g\,2^n)$ or exponential time where g is the time to substitute values for x_1, x_2, x_3 and evaluate the expression.

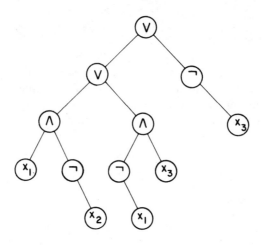

Figure 7.9 Propositional formula in a binary tree

To evaluate an expression one method would traverse the tree in postorder, evaluating subtrees until the entire expression is reduced to a single value. This corresponds to the postfix evaluation of an arithmetic expression that we saw earlier. Viewing this from the perspective of the tree representation, for every node we reach, the values of its arguments (or children) have already been computed. So when we reach the $\vee$ node on level 2, the values of $x_1 \wedge \neg x_2$ and $\neg x_1 \wedge x_3$ will already be available to us and we can apply the rule for **or**. Notice that a node containing $\neg$ has only a single right branch since **not** is a unary operator.

For the purposes of this algorithm we assume each node has four fields:

leftchild	data	value	rightchild

where *leftchild, data, rightchild* are as before and *value* is of type boolean. This node structure may be defined in Pascal as below:

```
type typesofdata = (logicalnot, logicaland, logicalor, logicaltrue,
               logicalfalse);
     treepointer = ↑treerecord ;
     treerecord = record
                    leftchild   : treepointer ;
                    data        : typesofdata;
                    value       : boolean;
                    rightchild  : treepointer ;
                  end;
```

Also we assume that for leaf nodes $t↑.data$ contains the current value of the variable represented at this node. With these preparations and assuming an expression with n variables pointed at by *tree* we can now write the first version of our algorithm for satisfiability:

```
for all 2ⁿ possible combinations do
begin
    generate the next combination;
    replace the variables by their values;
    evaluate tree by traversing it in postorder;
    if tree↑.value
        then output combination and stop
end
writeln ("no satisfiable combination")
```

Now let us concentrate on this modified version of postorder. Changing the original recursive version seems the simplest thing to do. We obtain the procedure of Program 7.6.

```
 1  procedure postordereval (tree : treepointer )
 2  begin
 3    if tree < > nil
 4    then
 5    begin
 6      postordereval (tree↑. leftchild);
 7      postordereval (tree↑. rightchild );
 8      case tree↑. data of
 9        logicalnot : tree↑. value := not tree↑. rightchild↑. value; .
10        logicaland: tree↑. value := tree↑. leftchild↑. value and
11                     tree↑. rightchild↑. value ;
12        logicalor  : tree↑. value := tree↑. leftchild↑. value or
13                     tree↑. rightchild↑. value ;
14        logicaltrue: tree↑. value := true;
15        logicalfalse tree↑. value := false;
16    end; {of case}
17    end; {of if}
18  end; {of postordereval}
```

Program 7.6 Algorithm *postordereval*

7.6 THREADED BINARY TREES

If we look carefully at the linked representation of any binary tree, we notice that there are more null links than actual pointers. As we saw before, there are $n+1$ null links and $2n$ total links. A clever way to make use of these null links has been devised by A. J. Perlis and C. Thornton. Their idea is to replace the null links by pointers, called threads, to other nodes in the tree. If $p↑.rchild$ is normally equal to **nil**, we will replace it *by a pointer to the node which would be printed after p when traversing the tree in inorder.* A null *leftchild* link at node p is replaced *by a pointer to the node which immediately precedes node p* in inorder. Figure 7.10 shows the binary tree of Figure 7.3(b) with its new threads drawn in as dotted lines.

The tree t has 9 nodes and 10 null links which have been replaced by threads. If we traverse t in inorder, the nodes will be visited in the order $H\ D\ I\ B\ E\ A\ F\ C\ G$. For example, node E has a predecessor thread which points to B and a successor thread which points to A.

In the memory representation we must be able to distinguish between threads and normal pointers. This is done by adding two boolean fields to the record, *leftthread* and *rightthread*.

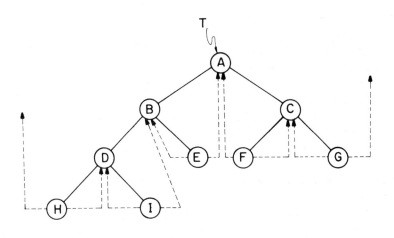

Figure 7.10 Threaded tree corresponding to Figure 7.3(b)

If *tree↑.leftthread* = true, the *tree↑.leftchild* contains a thread and otherwise it contains a pointer to the leftchild. Similarly if *tree↑.rightthread* = true, then *tree↑.rightchild* contains a thread and otherwise it contains a pointer to the rightchild.

This node structure is now given by the following Pascal type declaration:

type *threadedpointer* = ↑*threadedtree* ;
    threadedtree = **record**
                    leftthread   : **boolean**;
                    leftchild   : *threadedpointer* ;
                    data   : **char**;
                    rightchild : *threadedpointer* ;
                    rightthread: **boolean**;
          end;

In Figure 7.10 we see that two threads have been left dangling in *leftchild* of H and *rightchild* of G. In order that we leave no loose threads we will assume a head node for all threaded binary trees. Then the complete memory representation for the tree of Figure 7.10 is shown in Figure 7.11. The tree *t* is the left subtree of the head node. We assume that an empty binary tree is represented by its head node as

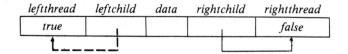

This assumption will permit easy algorithm design. Now that we have made use of the old null links we will see that the algorithm for inorder traversal is simplified. First, we observe that for any node x in a binary tree, if $x\uparrow.rightthread$ = true, then the inorder successor of x is $x\uparrow.rightchild$ by definition of threads. Otherwise the inorder successor of x is obtained by following a path of left child links from the right child of x until a node with *leftthread* = true is reached. The algorithm *insuc* (Program 7.7) finds the inorder successor of any node x in a threaded binary tree.

The interesting thing to note about procedure *insuc* is that it is now possible to find the inorder successor of any arbitrary node in a threaded binary tree without using an additional stack. If we wish to list in inorder all the nodes in a threaded binary tree, then we can make repeated calls to the procedure *insuc*. Since the tree is the left subtree of the head node and because of the choice of *rightthread* = false for the head node, the inorder sequence of nodes for tree t is obtained by the procedure *tinorder* (Program 7.8).

The computing time is still O(n) for a binary tree with n nodes. The constant here will be somewhat smaller than for procedure *inorder*3.

We have seen how to use the threads of a threaded binary tree for inorder traversal. These threads also simplify the algorithms for preorder and postorder traversal. Before closing this section let us see how to make insertions into a threaded tree. This will give us a procedure for growing threaded trees. We shall study only the case of inserting a node t as the right child of a node s. The case of insertion of a left child is given as an exercise. If s has an empty right subtree, then the insertion is simple and diagrammed in Figure 7.12(a). If the right subtree of s is nonempty, then this right subtree is made the right subtree of t after insertion. When this is done, t becomes the inorder predecessor of a node which has a *leftthread* = *true* field and consequently there is a thread which has to be updated to point to t. The node containing this thread was previously the inorder successor of s. Figure 7.12(b) illustrates the insertion for this case. In both cases s is the inorder predecessor of t. The details are spelled out in algorithm *insertright*, Program 7.9.

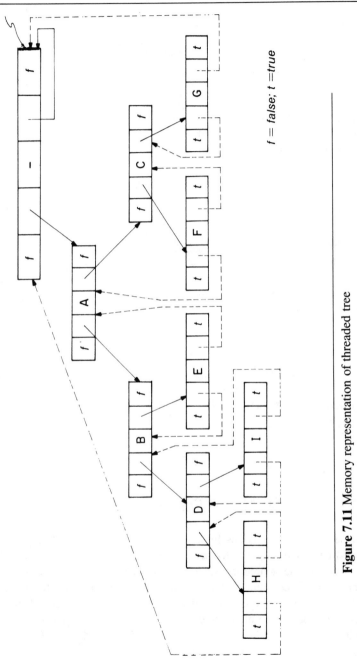

Figure 7.11 Memory representation of threaded tree

f = false; t =true

```
 1  function insuc (tree : threadedpointer ) : threadedpointer ;
 2  {find the inorder successor of tree in a threaded binary tree}
 3  var temp : threadedpointer ;
 4  begin
 5      temp := tree↑.rightchild ;
 6      if not tree↑.rightthread
 7      then while not temp↑.leftthread do
 8              temp := temp↑.leftchild;
 9      insuc := temp ;
10  end; {of insuc}
```

Program 7.7 Algorithm *insuc*

```
 1  procedure tinorder (tree : threadedpointer );
 2  {traverse the threaded binary tree in inorder}
 3  var temp : threadedpointer :
 4  begin
 5      temp := tree ;
 6      repeat
 7          temp := insuc (temp);
 8          if temp < > tree
 9          then write(temp↑.data);
10      until temp = tree ;
11  end; {of tinoder}
```

Program 7.8 Algorithm *tinorder*

7.7 BINARY TREE REPRESENTATION OF TREES

We have seen several representations for and uses of binary trees. In this section we will see that every tree can be represented as a binary tree. This is important because the methods for representing a tree as suggested in Section 7.1 had some undesirable features. One form of representation used variable size nodes. While the handling of nodes of variable size is not impossible, it is considerably more difficult than the handling of fixed size nodes. An alternative would be to use fixed size nodes, each node having k child fields, if k is the maximum degree of any node (see Figure 7.13). As Lemma 7.4 shows, this would be very wasteful in space.

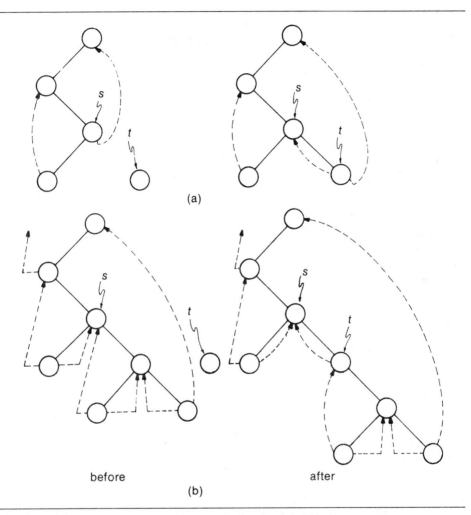

(a)

before   after

(b)

Figure 7.12 Insertion of *t* as a right child of *s* in a threaded binary tree

Lemma 7.4: If *T* is a *k*-ary tree (i.e., a tree of degree *k*) with *n* nodes, each having a fixed size as in Figure 7.13, then $n(k-1) + 1$ of the *nk* link fields are nil, $n \geq 1$.

Proof: Since each non-nil link points to a node and exactly one link points to each node other than the root, the number of non-nil links in an *n* node tree is exactly $n - 1$. The total number of link fields in a *k*-ary tree with *n* nodes is *nk*. Hence, the number of null links is $nk - (n - 1) = n(k-1) + 1$. □

```
 1 procedure insertright (s, t : threadedpointer);
 2 {insert node t as the right child of s in a threaded binary
 3 tree}
 4 var temp : threadedpointer ;
 5 begin
 6    t↑.rightchild := s↑.rightchild ;
 7    t↑.rightthread := s↑.rightthread ;
 8    t↑.leftchild := s ;
 9    t↑.leftthread := true; {leftchild is a thread}
10    s↑.rightchild := t; {attach t to s}
11    s↑.rightthread := false;
12    if not t↑.rightthread
13    then
14    begin
15       temp := insuc (t);
16       temp↑.leftchild := t ;
17    end;
18 end; {of insertright}
```

Program 7.9 Algorithm *insertright*

DATA			
CHILD 1	CHILD 2	....	CHILD k

Figure 7.13 Possible node structure for a k-ary tree

Lemma 7.4 implies that for a 3-ary tree more than 2/3 of the link fields are nil! The proportion of nil links approaches 1 as the degree of the tree increases. The importance of using binary trees to represent trees is that for binary trees only about 1/2 of the link fields are nil.

In arriving at the binary tree representation of a tree we shall implicitly make use of the fact that the order of the children of a node is not important. Suppose we have the tree of Figure 7.14.

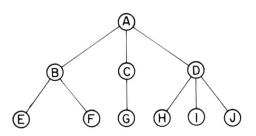

Figure 7.14 A sample tree

We observe that the reason we needed nodes with many link fields is that the prior representation was based on the parent-child relationship and a node can have any number of children. To obtain a binary tree representation, we need a relationship, between the nodes, that can be characterized by at most two quantities. One such relationship is the leftmost-child-next-right-sibling relationship. Every node has at most one leftmost child and at most one next right sibling. In the tree of Figure 7.14, the leftmost child of *B* is *E* and the next right sibling of *B* is *C*. Strictly speaking, since the order of children in a tree is not important, any of the children of a node could be its leftmost child and any of its siblings could be its next right sibling. For the sake of definiteness, we choose the nodes based upon how the tree is drawn. The binary tree corresponding to the tree of Figure 7.14 is thus obtained by connecting together all siblings of a node and deleting all links from a node to its children except for the link to its leftmost child. The node structure corresponds to that of

DATA	
CHILD	SIBLING

Using the transformation described above, we obtain the following representation for the tree of Figure 7.14.

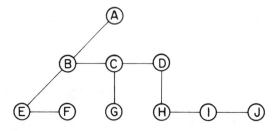

This does not look like a binary tree, but if we tilt it roughly 45° clockwise we get the tree of Figure 7.15. Some additional examples are given in Figure 7.16.

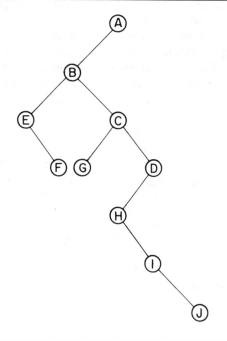

Figure 7.15 Associated binary tree for tree of Figure 7.14

One thing to notice is that the *rchild* of the root node of every resulting binary tree will be empty. This is because the root of the tree we are transforming has no siblings. On the other hand, if we have a forest then these can all be transformed into a single binary tree by first obtaining the binary tree representation of each of the trees in the

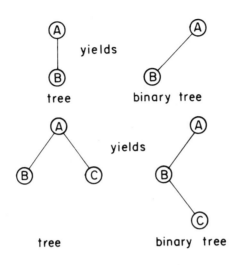

Figure 7.16 Binary tree transformations

forest and then linking all the binary trees together through the *sibling* field of the root nodes. For instance, the forest with three trees

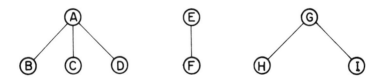

yields the binary tree

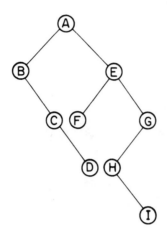

We can define this transformation in a formal way as follows:

If $T_1, \ldots, T_n$ is a forest of trees, then the binary tree corresponding to this forest, denoted by $B(T_1, \ldots, T_n)$

(1) is empty if $n=0$

(2) has root equal to root (T_1); has left subtree equal to $B(T_{11}, T_{12}, \ldots, T_{1m})$ where $T_{11}, \ldots, T_{1m}$ are the subtrees of root(T_1); and has right subtree $B(T_2, \ldots, T_n)$

Preorder and inorder traversals of the corresponding binary tree T of a forest F have a natural correspondence with traversals on F. Preorder traversal of T is equivalent to visiting the nodes of F in *tree preorder* which is defined by

(1) If F is empty then return

(2) Visit the root of the first tree of F

(3) Traverse the subtrees of the first tree in tree preorder

(4) Traverse the remaining trees of F in preorder

Inorder traversal of T is equivalent to visiting the nodes of F in *tree inorder* as defined by

(1) If F is empty then return

(2) Traverse the subtrees of the first tree in tree inorder

(3) Visit the root of the first tree

(4) Traverse the remaining trees in tree inorder

The above definitions for forest traversal will be referred to as preorder and inorder. The proofs that preorder and inorder on the corresponding binary tree are the same as preorder and inorder on the forest are left as exercises. There is no natural analog for postorder traversal of the corresponding binary tree of a forest. Nevertheless, we can define the *postorder traversal of a forest* as

(1)   If F is empty then return

(2)   Traverse the subtrees of the first tree of F in tree postorder

(3)   Traverse the remaining trees of F in tree postorder

(4)   Visit the root of the first tree of F

This traversal is used later on in Section 7.10 for describing the minimax procedure.

7.8 SET REPRESENTATION

In this section we study the use of trees in the representation of sets. We shall assume that the elements of the sets are the numbers $1, 2, 3, ..., n$. These numbers might, in practice, be indices into a symbol table where the actual names of the elements are stored. We shall assume that the sets being represented are pairwise disjoint; i.e., if S_i and S_j, $i \neq j$, are two sets then there is no element which is in both S_i and S_j. For example, if we have 10 elements numbered 1 through 10, they may be partitioned into three disjoint sets, $S_1 = \{1, 7, 8, 9\}$, $S_2 = \{2, 5, 10\}$, and $S_3 = \{3, 4, 6\}$. The operations we wish to perform on these sets are

(1)   Disjoint set union ... if S_i and S_j are two disjoint sets, then their union $S_i \cup S_j = \{$all elements x such that x is in S_i or $S_j\}$. Thus, $S_1 \cup S_2 = \{1, 7, 8, 9, 2, 5, 10\}$. Since we have assumed that all sets are disjoint, following the union of S_i and S_j we can assume that the sets S_i and S_j no longer exist independently, i.e., they are replaced by $S_i \cup S_j$ in the collection of sets.

(2)   Find (i) ... find the set containing element i. Thus, 4 is in set S_3 and 9 is in set S_1.

The sets will be represented by trees. One possible representation for the sets S_1, S_2, and S_3 is

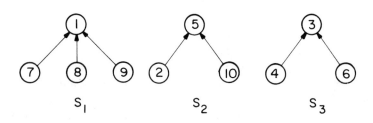

Note that the nodes are linked on the parent relationship, i.e., each node other than the root is linked to its parent. The advantage of this will become apparent when we present the *union* and *find* algorithms. First, to take the union of S_1 and S_2 we simply make one of the trees a subtree of the other. $S_1 \cup S_2$ could then have one of the following representations:

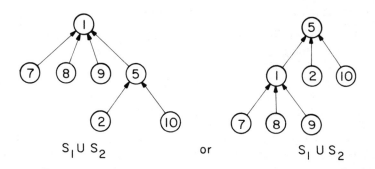

$$S_1 \cup S_2 \qquad \text{or} \qquad S_1 \cup S_2$$

In order to find the union of two sets, all that has to be done is to set the parent field of one of the roots to the other root. This can be accomplished easily if, with each set name, we keep a pointer to the root of the tree representing that set. If, in addition, each root has a pointer to the set name, then to determine which set an element is currently in, we follow parent links to the root of its tree and use the pointer to the set name. The data representation for S_1, S_2, and S_3 may then take the form:

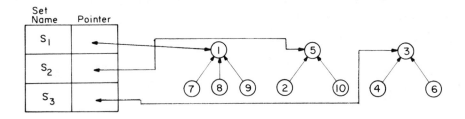

In presenting the *union* and *find* algorithms we shall ignore the actual set names and just identify sets by the roots of the trees representing them. This will simplify the discussion. The transition to set names is easy. If we determine that element i is in a tree with root j, and j has a pointer to entry k in the set name table, then the set name is just *name* [k]. If we wish to union sets S_i and S_j, then we wish to union the trees with roots $pointer(S_i)$ and $pointer(S_j)$. As we shall see, in many applications the set name is just the element at the root. The operation of *find(i)* now becomes: determine the root of the tree containing element i. $union(i,j)$ requires two trees with roots i and j to be joined. We shall assume that the nodes in the trees are numbered 1 through n so that the node index corresponds to the element index. Thus, element 6 is represented by the node with index 6. Consequently, each node needs only one field: the *parent* field to link to its parent. Root nodes have a *parent* field of zero. Based on the above discussion we see that the only data structure needed is an array, *parent* $[1 .. maxsets]$ of type integer. *maxsets* is an upper bound on the number of elements we might have. Our first attempt at arriving at *union, find* algorithms would result in the algorithms u and f given in Program 7.10.

```
1  procedure u (i,j : integer);
2  {replace the disjoint sets with roots i and j, i ≠ j with
3     their union}
4  begin
5     parent [i] := j;
6  end; {of u}

7  function f (i : integer) : integer;
8  {find the root of the tree containing element i}
9  var temp : integer;
10 begin
11    temp := i;
12    while parent [temp] > 0 do
13       temp := parent [temp];
14    f := temp;
15 end; {of f}
```

Program 7.10 Algorithm u and function f

While these two algorithms are very easy to state, their performance characteristics are not very good. For instance, if we start off with p elements each in a set of its own, i.e., $S_i = \{i\}$, $1 \le i \le p$, then the initial configuration consists of a forest with p nodes and *parent* $[i] = 0$, $1 \le i \le p$. Now let us process the following sequence of *union-find* operations:

$$u(1,2), f(1), u(2,3), f(1), u(3,4)$$
$$f(1), u(4,5), ..., f(1), u(n - 1,n)$$

This sequence results in the degenerate tree:

Since the time taken for a union is constant, all the $n - 1$ unions can be processed in time $O(n)$. However, each *find* requires following a chain of *parent* links from one to the root. The time required to process a *find* for an element at level i of a tree is $O(i)$. Hence, the total time needed to process the $n - 2$ finds is $O(\Sigma_{i=1}^{n-2} i) = O(n^2)$. We can do much better if care is taken to avoid the creation of degenerate trees. In order to accomplish this we shall make use of a *Weighting Rule for union (i,j). If the number of nodes in tree i is less than the number in tree j, then make j the parent of i, otherwise make i the parent of j.* Using this rule on the sequence of set unions given before we obtain the trees below:

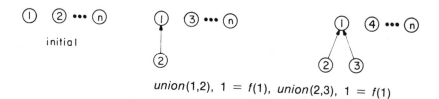

$union(1,2),\ 1 = f(1),\ union(2,3),\ 1 = f(1)$

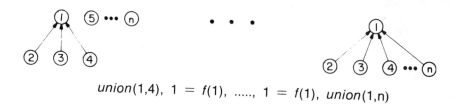

$union(1,4),\ 1 = f(1),\ .....,\ 1 = f(1),\ union(1,n)$

When the weighting rule is incorporated, the union procedure takes the form given in Program 7.11. Remember that the arguments of *union* must both be roots. The time required to process all the *n* finds is only O(*n*) since in this case the maximum level of any node is 2. This, however, is not the worst case. In Lemma 7.5 we show that using the weighting rule, the maximum level for any node is $\lfloor \log n \rfloor + 1$. First, let us see how easy it is to implement the weighting rule. We need to know how many nodes there are in every tree. To do this easily, we maintain a count field in the root of every tree. If *i* is a root node, then *count*[*i*] = number of nodes in that tree. The count can be maintained in the *parent* field as a negative number. This is equivalent to using one bit field to distinguish a count from a pointer. No confusion is created as for all other nodes the *parent* is positive.

```
 1  procedure union(i, j : integer);
 2  {union sets with roots i and j, i≠j, using the
 3    weighting rule. parent [i ] = − count [i ] and parent [j ]
 4    = −count [j ]}
 5  var temp : integer;
 6  begin
 7    temp := parent [i ] + parent [j ]
 8    if parent [i ] > parent [j ]
 9    then
10    begin       {i has fewer nodes}
11      parent [i ] := j ;
12      parent [j ] := temp ;
13    end
14    else
15    begin       {j has fewer nodes}
16      parent [j ] := i ;
17      parent [i ] := temp ;
18    end;
19  end; {of union}
```

Program 7.11 Algorithm *union*

The time required to perform a union has increased somewhat but is still bounded by a constant, i.e., it is O(1). The *find* algorithm remains unchanged. The maximum time to perform a find is determined by Lemma 7.5.

Lemma 7.5: Let *T* be a tree with *n* nodes created as a result of algorithm *union*. No node in *T* has level greater $\lfloor \log_2 n \rfloor + 1$.

Proof: The lemma is clearly true for $n = 1$. Assume it is true for all trees with i nodes, $i \leq n - 1$. We shall show that it is also true for $i = n$. Let T be a tree with n nodes created by the *union* algorithm. Consider the last union operation performed, $union(k, j)$. Let m be the number of nodes in tree j and $n - m$ the number in k. Without loss of generality we may assume $1 \leq m \leq n/2$. Then the maximum level of any node in T is either the same as that in k or is one more than that in j. If the former is the case, then the maximum level in T is $\leq \lfloor \log_2 (n - m) \rfloor + 1 \leq \lfloor \log_2 n \rfloor + 1$. If the latter is the case then the maximum level in T is $\leq \lfloor \log_2 m \rfloor + 2 \leq \lfloor \log_2 n/2 \rfloor + 2 \leq \lfloor \log_2 n \rfloor + 1$. $\square$

Example 7.1 shows that the bound of Lemma 7.5 is achievable for some sequence of unions.

Example 7.1: Consider the behavior of algorithm *union* on the following sequence of unions starting from the initial configuration $parent\,[i] = -count\,[i] = -1$, $1 \leq i \leq n = 2^3$:

$$union(1,2), \quad union(3,4), \quad union(5,6), \quad union(7,8),$$
$$union(1,3), \quad union(5,7), \quad union(1,5).$$

The following trees are obtained:

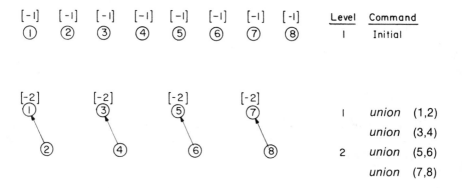

	Level	Command
	I	Initial
	I	*union* (1,2)
		union (3,4)
	2	*union* (5,6)
		union (7,8)

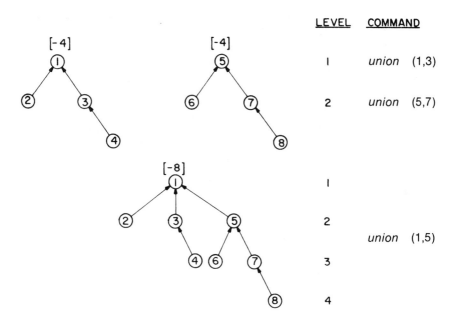

As is evident, the maximum level in any tree is $\lfloor \log_2 m \rfloor + 1$ if the tree has m nodes. □

As a result of Lemma 7.5, the maximum time to process a find is at most $O(\log n)$ if there are n elements in a tree. If an intermixed sequence of $n - 1$ *union* and m *find* operations is to be processed, then the worst case time becomes $O(n + m \log n)$. Surprisingly, further improvement is possible. This time the modification will be made in the find algorithm using the *Collapsing Rule: If j is a node on the path from i to its root and parent* $[i] \neq root(i)$ *then set parent* $[j]$ *to root* (i). The new algorithm then becomes Program 7.12. This modification roughly doubles the time for an individual find. However, it reduces the worst case time over a sequence of finds.

Example 7.2: Consider the tree created by algorithm *union* on the sequence of unions of Example 7.1. Now process the following 8 finds:

$$find(8), find(8), ..., find(8)$$

Using the old version f of algorithm *find, find*(8) requires going up three parent link fields for a total of 24 moves to process all eight finds. In algorithm *find*, the first *find*(8) requires going up three links and then resetting two links. Each of the remaining seven finds requires going up only one link field. The total cost is now only 12 moves.

```
 1 function find (i : integer) : integer;
 2 {find the root of the tree containing element i. Use
 3    the collapsing rule to collapse all nodes from i to
 4    the root temp.}
 5 var temp : integer;
 6      temp 1 : integer;
 7      temp 2 : integer;
 8 begin
 9    temp := i;
10    while parent [temp ] > 0 do {find root}
11      temp := parent[temp ];
12    temp 2 := i;
13    while temp 2 < > temp do
14    begin
15      temp 1 := parent [temp 2];
16      parent [temp 2] := temp;
17      temp 2 := temp 1;
18    end
19    find := temp;
20 end; {of find}
```

Program 7.12 Algorithm *find*

The worst case behavior of the *union-find* algorithms while processing a sequence of unions and finds is stated in Lemma 7.6. Before stating this lemma, let us introduce a very slow growing function $\alpha(m,n)$ which is related to a functional inverse of Ackermann's function $A(p,q)$. We have the following definition for $\alpha(m,n)$:

$$\alpha(m,n) = \min\{z \geq 1 \mid A(z,4\lceil m/n \rceil) > \log_2 n\}$$

The definition of Ackermann's function used here is

$$A(p,q) = \begin{cases} 2q & p = 0 \\ 0 & q = 0 \text{ and } p \geq 1 \\ 0 & p \geq 1 \text{ and } p = 1 \\ A(p-1, A(p,q-1)) & p \geq 1 \text{ and } q \geq 2 \end{cases}$$

The function $A(p,q)$ is a very rapidly growing function. You may prove the following three facts

$$A(3,4) = 2^{2^{2^{\cdot^{\cdot^{2}}}}} \left.\vphantom{\begin{matrix}2\\2\\2\\2\end{matrix}}\right\} \quad 65{,}536 \text{ two's} \qquad \cdots \text{ (a)}$$

$$A(p,q+1) > A(p,q) \qquad \cdots \text{(b)}$$

$$A(p+1,q) \geq A(p,q) \qquad \cdots \text{(c)}$$

If we assume $m \neq 0$ then (b) and (c) together with the definition of $\alpha(m,n)$ imply that $\alpha(m,n) \leq 3$ for $\log_2 n < A(3,4)$. But from (a), $A(3,4)$ is a very large number indeed! In Lemma 7.6 n will be the number of *unions* performed. For all practical purposes we may assume $\log_2 n < A(3,4)$ and hence $\alpha(m,n) \leq 3$.

Lemma 7.6: [Tarjan] Let $T(m,n)$ be the maximum time required to process any intermixed sequence of $m \geq n$ *finds* and $n-1$ *unions*. Then $k_1 m \alpha(m,n) \leq T(m,n) \leq k_2 m \alpha(m,n)$ for some positive constants k_1 and k_2. $\square$

Even though the function $\alpha(m,n)$ is a very slowly growing function, the complexity of *union-find* is not linear in m, the number of *finds*. As far as the space requirements are concerned, the space needed is one node for each element.

Let us look at an application of algorithms *union* and *find* to processing the equivalence pairs of Section 6.5. The equivalence classes to be generated may be regarded as sets. These sets are disjoint as no polygon can be in two equivalences classes. To begin with, all n polygons are in an equivalence class of their own; thus $parent[i] = -1, 1 \leq i \leq n$. If an equivalence pair, $i \equiv j$, is to be processed, we must first determine the sets containing i and j. If these are different, then the two sets are to be replaced by their union. If the two sets are the same, then nothing is to be done as the relation $i \equiv j$ is redundant; i and j are already in the same equivalence class. To process each equivalence pair we need to perform at most two finds and one union. Thus, if we have n polygons and $m \geq n$ equivalence pairs, the total processing time is at most $O(m \alpha(2m,m))$. While for very large n this is slightly worse than the algorithm of Section 6.5, it has the advantage of needing less space and also of being "on line."

In Chapter 8 we shall see another application of the *union-find* algorithms.

Example 7.3: We shall use the *union-find* algorithms to process the set of equivalence pairs of Section 6.5. Initially, there are 12 trees, one for each variable. $parent[i] = -1, 1 \leq i \leq 12$.

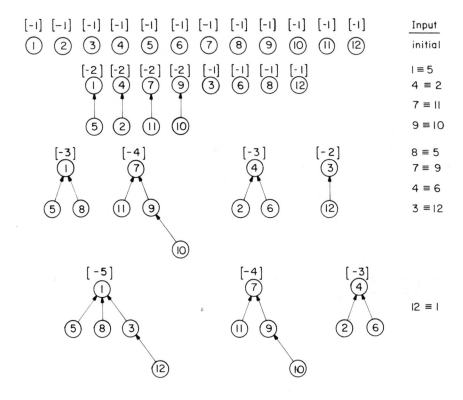

Each tree represents an equivalence class. It is possible to determine if two elements are currently in the same equivalence class at each stage of the processing by simply making two finds. □

7.9 DECISION TREES

Another very useful application of trees is in decision making. Consider the well-known *eight coins* problem. Given coins a, b, c, d, e, f, g, h, we are told that one is a counterfeit and has a different weight than the others. We want to determine which coin it is, making use of an equal arm balance. We want to do so using a minimum number of comparisons and at the same time determine whether the false coin is heavier or lighter than the rest. The tree below represents a set of decisions by which we can get the answer to our problem. This is why it is called a decision tree. The use of capital H or L means that the counterfeit coin is *h*eavier or *l*ighter. Let us trace through one possible sequence. If $a + b + c < d + e + f$, then we know that the false coin is present among the six and is neither g nor h. If on our next measurement we find that $a + d < b + e$, then by interchanging d and b we have no change in the inequality. This tells us two things: (1) that c or f is not the culprit, and (2) that b or d is also not the culprit. If $a + d$ was equal to $b + e$, then c or f would be the counterfeit coin. Knowing at this point that either a or e is the counterfeit, we compare a with a good coin, say b. If $a = b$, then e is heavy, otherwise a must be light.

By looking at this tree we see that all possibilities are covered, since there are eight coins which can be heavy or light and there are 16 terminal nodes. Every path requires exactly three comparisons. Though viewing this problem as a decision tree is very useful it does not immediately give us an algorithm. To solve the eight coins problem with a program, we must write a series of tests which mirror the structure of the tree. Moreover we must be sure that a single comparison yields one of three possibilities: $=$, $>$, or $<$. To perform the last comparison we will use the procedure *comp* (Program 7.13). To assure a three-way branch we assume the function *compare*(a, b : **integer**): **char** where the result is either '$<$,' '$=$,' or '$>$' with the obvious interpretations. The procedure *eightcoins* (Program 7.14) is now transparent and clearly mirrors the decision tree of Figure 7.17.

7.10 GAME TREES

Another interesting application of trees is in the playing of games such as tic-tac-toe, chess, nim, kalah, checkers, go, etc. As an example, let us consider the game of nim. This game is played by two players A and B. The game itself is described by a *board* which initially contains a pile of n toothpicks. The players A and B make moves alternately with A making the first move. A *legal move* consists of removing either 1, 2, or 3 of the toothpicks from the pile. However, a player cannot remove more toothpicks than there are on the pile. The player who removes the last toothpick loses the game and the other player wins. The *board configuration* at any time is completely specified by the number of toothpicks remaining in the pile. At any time the game status is determined by the board configuration together with the player whose turn it is to make the next move. A *terminal board configuration* is one which represents either a *win, lose,* or *draw* situation. All other configurations are *nonterminal*. In nim there is only one terminal configuration: there are no toothpicks in the pile. This configuration is a win for player A if B made the last move, otherwise it is a win for B. The game of nim cannot end in a draw.

A sequence $C_1, ..., C_m$ of board configurations is said to be *valid* if:

(1) C_1 is the starting configuration of the game;

(2) C_i, $0 < i < m$, are nonterminal configurations;

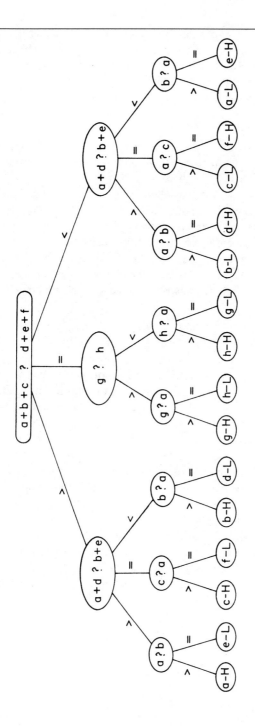

Figure 7.17 Eight coins decision tree

```
1 procedure comp (x,y,z : integer);
2 {x is compared against the standard coin z}
3 begin
4    if x > z then  writeln (x, 'heavy')
5              else writeln (y, 'light');
6 end; {of comp}
```

Program 7.13 Algorithm *comp*

```
1 procedure eightcoins ;
2 {eight weights of coins are input; the illegal one
3  is discovered using only three comparisons}
4 var a, b, c, d, e, f, g, h : integer;
5 begin
6    read(a,b,c,d,e,f,g,h);
7    case compare (a + b + c, d + e + f) of

8       '=' : if g > h then comp (g,h,a)
9                      else comp (h,g,a);
10      '=' : case compare (a + d, b + e) of
11                   '=' : comp (c,f,a);
12                   '>' : comp (a,e,b);
13                   '<' : comp (b,d,a);
14          end; {of case}
15      '<' : case compare (a + d, b + e) of
16                   '=' : comp (f,c,a);
17                   '>' : comp (d,b,a);
18                   '<' : comp (e,a,b);
19          end {of case}
20   end; {of case}
21 end; {of eightcoins}
```

Program 7.14 Algorithm *eightcoins*

(3) C_{i+1} is obtained from C_i by a legal move made by player A if i is odd and by player B if i is even. It is assumed that there are only finitely many legal moves.

A valid sequence $C_1 ..., C_m$ of board configurations with C_m a terminal configuration is an *instance* of the game. The *length* of the sequence $C_1, C_2, ..., C_m$ is m. A *finite game* is one in which there are no valid sequences of infinite length. All possible instances of a finite game may be represented by a *game tree*. The tree of Figure 7.18 is the game tree for nim with $n = 6$. Each node of the tree represents a board configuration.

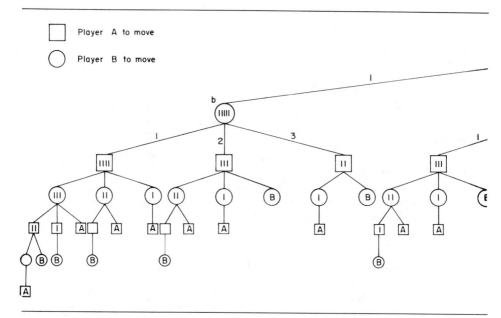

Figure 7.18 Complete game tree for Nim with $n = 6$

The root node represents the starting configuration C_1. Transitions from one level to the next are made via a move of A or B. Transitions from an odd level represent moves made by A. All other transitions are the result of moves made by B. Square nodes have been used in Figure 7.18 to represent board configurations when it was A's turn to move. Circular nodes have been used for other configurations. The edges from level 1 nodes to level 2 nodes and from level 2 nodes to level 3 nodes have been labeled with the move made by A and B, respectively (for example, an edge labeled 1 means 1 toothpick is to be removed). It is easy to figure out the labels for the remaining edges of the tree. Terminal configurations are represented by leaf nodes. Leaf nodes have been labeled by the name of the player who wins when that configuration is reached. By the nature of the game of nim, player A can win only at leaf nodes on odd levels while B can win only at leaf nodes on even levels. The degree of any node in a game tree is at most equal to the number of distinct legal moves. In nim there are at most three legal moves from any configuration. By definition, the number of legal moves from any configuration is finite. The *depth* of a game tree is the length of a longest instance of the game. The depth of the nim tree of Figure 7.18 is 7. Hence, from start to finish this game involves at most six moves. It is not difficult to see how similar game trees may be constructed for other finite games such as chess, tic-tac-toe, kalah, etc. (Strictly speaking, chess is not a finite game as it is possible to repeat board configurations in the game. We can view chess as a finite game by disallowing this possibility. We could, for instance, define the repetition of a board configuration as resulting in a draw.)

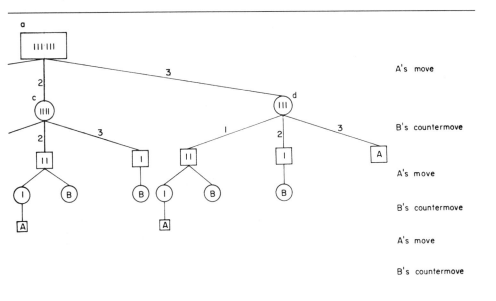

Now that we have seen what a game tree is, the next question is "of what use are they?" Game trees are useful in determining the next move a player should make. Starting at the initial configuration represented by the root of Figure 7.18 player A is faced with the choice of making any one of three possible moves. Which one should he or she make? Assuming that player A wants to win the game, the move that maximizes the chances of winning should be made. For the simple tree of Figure 7.18 this move is not too difficult to determine. We can use an evaluation function $E(X)$ which assigns a numeric value to the board configuration X. This function is a measure of the value or worth of configuration X to player A. So, $E(X)$ is high for a configuration from which A has a good chance of winning and low for a configuration from which A has a good chance of losing. $E(X)$ has its maximum value for configurations that are either winning terminal configurations for A or configurations from which A is guaranteed to win regardless of B's countermoves. $E(X)$ has its minimum value for configurations from which B is guaranteed to win.

For a game such as nim with $n = 6$ whose game tree has very few nodes, it is sufficient to define $E(X)$ only for terminal configurations. We could define $E(X)$ as

$$E(X) = \begin{cases} 1 & \text{if } X \text{ is a winning configuration for } A \\ -1 & \text{if } X \text{ is a losing configuration for } A \end{cases}$$

Using this evaluation function we wish to determine which of the configurations b, c, d player A should move the game into. Clearly, the choice is the one whose value is max $\{V(b), V(c), V(d)\}$ where $V(x)$ is the value of configuration x. For leaf nodes x, $V(x)$ is taken to be $E(x)$. For all other nodes x let $d \geq 1$ be the degree of x and let $c_1, c_2, ..., c_d$ be the configurations represented by the children of x. Then $V(x)$ is defined by

$$V(x) = \begin{cases} \max_{1 \leq i \leq d} \{V(c_i)\} & \text{if } x \text{ is a square node} \\ \min_{1 \leq i \leq d} \{V(c_i)\} & \text{if } x \text{ is a circular node} \end{cases} \qquad (7.3)$$

The justification for Eq. (7.3) is fairly simple. If x is a square node, then it is at an odd level and it will be A's turn to move from here if the game ever reaches this node. Since A wants to win he or she will move to that child node with maximum value. In case x is a circular node it must be on an even level and if the game ever reaches this node, then it will be B's turn to move. Since B is out to win the game, B will (barring mistakes) make a move that will minimize A's chances of winning. In this case the next configuration will be $\min_{1 \leq i \leq d} \{V(c_i)\}$. Equation (7.3) defines the *minimax* procedure to determine the value of a configuration x. This is illustrated on the hypothetical game of Figure 7.19. P_{11} represents an arbitrary board configuration from which A has to make a move. The values of the leaf nodes are obtained by evaluating the function $E(x)$. The value of P_{11} is obtained by starting at the nodes on level 4 and computing their values using Eq. (7.3). Since level 4 is a level with circular nodes, all unknown values on this level may be obtained by taking the minimum of the children values. Next, values on levels 3, 2, and 1 may be computed in that order. The resulting value for P_{11} is 3. This means that starting from P_{11} the best A can hope to do is reach a configuration of value 3. Even though some nodes have value greater than 3, these nodes will not be reached, as B's countermoves will prevent the game from reaching any such configuration (assuming B's countermoves are optimal for B with respect to A's evaluation function). For example, if A made a move to P_{21}, hoping to win the game at P_{31}, A would indeed be surprised by B's countermove to P_{32} resulting in a loss to A. Given A's evaluation function and the game tree of Figure 7.19, the best move for A to make is to configuration P_{22}. Having made this move, the game may still not reach configuration P_{52} as B would, in general, be using a different evaluation function, which might give different values to various board configurations. In any case, the *minimax* procedure can be used to determine the best move a player can make given his evaluation function. Using the minimax procedure on the game tree for nim (Figure 7.18) we see that the value of the root node is $V(a) = 1$. Since $E(X)$ for this game was defined to be 1 if A was guaranteed to win, this means that if A makes the optimal move from node a then no matter what B's countermoves, A will win. The optimal move is to node b. One may readily verify that from b A can win the game independent of B's countermove!

For games such as nim with $n = 6$, the game trees are sufficiently small that it is possible to generate the whole tree. Thus, it is a relatively simple matter to determine whether or not the game has a winning strategy. Moreover, for such games it is possible to make a decision on the next move by looking ahead all the way to terminal configurations. Games of this type are not very interesting since assuming no errors are made by either player, the outcome of the game is predetermined and both players should use similar evaluation functions, i.e., $E_A(X) = 1$ for X a winning configuration and $E_A(X) = -1$ for X a losing configuration for A; $E_B(X) = -E_A(X)$.

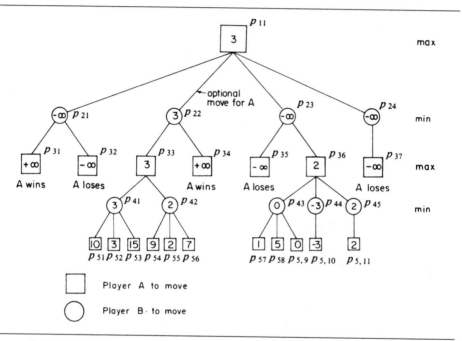

Figure 7.19 Portion of game tree for a hypothetical game. The value of terminal nodes is obtained from the evaluation function $E(x)$ for player A.

Of greater interest are games such as chess where the game tree is too large to be generated in its entirety. It is estimated that the game tree for chess $> 10^{100}$ nodes. Even using a computer which is capable of generating 10^{11} nodes a second, the complete generation of the game tree for chess would require more than 10^{80} years. In games with large game trees the decision as to which move to make next can be made only by looking at the game tree for the next few levels. The evaluation function $E(X)$ is used to get the values of the leaf nodes of the subtree generated and then Eq. (7.3) can be used to get the values of the remaining nodes and hence to determine the next move. In a game such as chess it may be possible to generate only the next few levels (say six) of the tree. In such situations both the quality of the resulting game and its outcome will depend upon the quality of the evaluating functions being used by the two players as well as of the algorithm being used to determine $V(X)$ by minimax for the current game configuration. The efficiency of this algorithm will limit the number of nodes of the search tree that can be generated and so will have an effect on the quality of the game.

Let us assume that player A is a computer and attempt to write an algorithm that A can use to compute $V(X)$. It is clear that the procedure to compute $V(X)$ can also be used to determine the next move that A should make. A fairly simple recursive procedure to evaluate $V(X)$ using minimax can be obtained if we recast the definition of minimax into the following form:

$$V'(X) = \begin{cases} e(X) & \text{if } X \text{ is a leaf of the subtree generated} \\ \max_{1 \le i \le d} \{-V'(c_i)\} & \text{if } X \text{ is not a leaf of the} \\ & \text{subtree generated and } c_i, \\ & 1 \le i \le d, \text{ are the children} \\ & \text{of } X \end{cases} \tag{7.4}$$

where $e(X) = E(X)$ if X is a position from which A is to move and $e(X) = -E(X)$ otherwise.

Starting at a configuration X from which A is to move, one can easily prove that Eq. (7.4) computes $V'(X) = V(X)$ as given by Eq. (7.3). In fact, values for all nodes on levels from which A is to move are the same as given by Eq. (7.3) while values on other levels are the negative of those given by Eq. (7.3).

The recursive procedure to evaluate $V'(X)$ based on Eq. (7.4) is then $ve(X,l)$ (Program 7.15). This algorithm evaluates $V'(X)$ by generating only l levels of the game tree beginning with X as root. You may verify that this algorithm traverses the desired subtree of the game tree in postorder.

An initial call to algorithm ve with $x = P_{11}$ and $l = 4$ for the hypothetical game of Figure 7.19 would result in the generation of the complete game tree. The values of various configurations would be determined in the order: $p_{31}, p_{32}, p_{21}, p_{51}, p_{52}, p_{53}, p_{41}, p_{54}, p_{55}, p_{56}, p_{42}, p_{33}, \ldots, p_{37}, p_{24}, p_{11}$. It is possible to introduce, with relative ease, some heuristics into algorithm ve that will result in the generation of only a portion of the possible configurations while still computing $V'(X)$ accurately.

Consider the game tree of Figure 7.19. After $V(p_{41})$ has been computed, it is known that $V(p_{33})$ is at least $V(p_{41}) = 3$. Next, when $V(p_{55})$ is determined to be 2, then we know then $V(p_{42})$ is at most 2. Since p_{33} is a max position, $V(p_{42})$ cannot affect $V(p_{33})$. Regardless of the values of the remaining children of p_{42}, the value of p_{33} is not

---

```
 1 function ve (x : node ; l : integer) : integer;
 2 {compute V´(n) by looking at most l moves ahead. e (x)
 3   is the evaluation function for player A. For convenience,
 4   it is assumed that starting from any board configuration x
 5   the legal moves of the game permit a transition only to the
 6   configurations c [1 .. d] if x is not a terminal
 7   configuration.}
 8 var ans : integer;
 9       temp, i : integer;
10 begin
11    if terminal (x) or (l = 0)
12    then ve := e (x)
13    else
14    begin
15      ans := −ve (c [1], l − 1);
16      for i := 2 to d do
17      begin
18        temp := −ve (c [i], l − 1)
19        if ans < temp then ans := temp
20      end;
21      ve := ans ;
22    end; {of if}
23 end; {of ve}
```

Program 7.15 Algorithm *ve*

determined by $V(p_{42})$ as $V(p_{42})$ cannot be more than $V(p_{41})$. This observation may be stated more formally as the following rule: The *alpha* value of a max position is defined to be the minimum possible value for that position. *If the value of a min position is determined to be less than or equal to the alpha value of its parent, then we may stop generation of the remaining children of this min position.* Termination of node generation under this rule is known as *alpha cutoff*. Once $V(p_{41})$ in Figure 7.19 is determined, the alpha value of p_{33} becomes 3. $V(p_{55}) \le$ alpha value of p_{33} implies that p_{56} need not be generated.

A corresponding rule may be defined for min positions. The *beta* value of a min position is the maximum possible value for that position. *If the value of a max position is determined to be greater than or equal to the beta value of its parent node, then we may stop generation of the remaining children of this max position.* Termination of node generation under this rule is called *beta cutoff*. In Figure 7.19, once $V(p_{35})$ is determined, the beta value of p_{23} is known to be at most $-\infty$. Generation of p_{57}, p_{58}, p_{59} gives $V(p_{43}) = 0$. Thus, $V(p_{43})$ is greater than or equal to the beta value of p_{23} and we may terminate the generation of the remaining children of p_{36}. The two rules stated above may be combined together to get what is known as *alpha-beta pruning*. When alpha-beta pruning is used on Figure 7.19, the subtree with root p_{36} is not generated at all! This is because when the value of p_{23} is being determined the alpha value of p_{11} is 3. $V(p_{35})$ is less than the alpha value of p_{11} and so an alpha cutoff takes place. It should be emphasized that the alpha or beta value of a node is a dynamic quantity. Its value at any time during the game tree generation depends upon which nodes have so far been generated and evaluated.

In actually introducing alpha-beta pruning into algorithm *ve* it is necessary to restate this rule in terms of the values defined by Eq. (7.4). Under Eq. (7.4) all positions are max positions since the values of the min positions of Eq. (7.3) have been multiplied by -1. The alpha-beta pruning rule now reduces to the following rule: let the *B*-value of a position be the minimum value that that position can have.

For any position X, let B be the B-value of its parent and let mb = -B. Then, if the value of X is determined to be greater than or equal to mb, we may terminate generation of the remaining children of X. Incorporating this rule into algorithm *ve* is fairly straightforward and results in algorithm *veb*. This algorithm has the additional parameter *mb* which is the negative of the *B*-value of the parent of *X*.

If *Y* is a position from which *A* is to move, then the initial call $veb(Y,l,maxinteger)$ correctly computes $V'(Y)$ with an *l* move look ahead. Further pruning of the game tree may be achieved by realizing that the *B*-value of a node *X* places a lower bound on the value grandchildren of *X* must have in order to affect *X*'s value. Consider the subtree of Figure 7.20(a). If $V'(GC(X)) \le B$ then $V'(C(X)) \ge -B$. Following the evaluation of $C(X)$, the *B*-value of *X* is max $\{B, -V'(C(X))\} = B$ as $V'(C(X)) \ge -B$. Hence unless $V'(GC(X)) > B$, it cannot affect $V'(X)$ and so *B* is a lower bound on the value $GC(X)$ should have. Incorporating this lower bound into algorithm *veb* yields algorithm *ab* (Program 7.17). The additional parameter *lb* is a lower bound on the value *X* should have.

We may easily verify that the initial call $ab(Y,l,mininteger,maxinteger)$ gives the same result as the call $ve(Y,l)$.

Figure 7.20(b) shows a hypothetical game tree in which the use of algorithm *ab* results in greater pruning than achieved by algorithm *veb*. Let us first trace the action of *veb* on the tree of Figure 7.20(b). We assume the initial call to be $veb(p_1,l,\textbf{maxint})$ where *l* is the depth of the tree. After examining the left subtree of P_1, the *B* value of P_1 is set to 10 and nodes P_3, P_4, P_5, and P_6 are generated. Following this, $V'(P_6)$ is determined to be 9 and then the *B*-value of P_5 becomes -9. Using this, we continue to evaluate the node P_7. In the case of *ab*, however, since the *B*-value of P_1 is 10, the lower bound for P_4 is 10 and so the effective *B*-value of P_4 becomes 10. As a result the node P_7 is not generated since no matter what its value $V'(P_5) \ge -9$ and this will not enable

```
 1 function veb (x : node ; l,mb : integer) : integer;
 2 {determine V'(x) as in Eq. (7.4) using the B-rule and looking
 3    only l moves ahead. Remaining assumptins and notations
 4    are the same as for algorithm ve. Configurations c [1..d ] are global}
 5 var ans : integer;
 6       temp, i : integer;
 7 begin
 8 if terminal (x) or (l = 0)
 9    then veb := e (x)
10    else
11    begin
12          ans := −maxint
13          i := 1;
14          while (i ≤ d) and (ans < mb) do
15          begin
16                temp := −veb (c [i ], l − 1, −ans);
17                if ans < temp then ans := temp ;
18                i := i + 1;
19          end; {of if}
20          veb := ans ;
21    end; {of if}
22 end; {of veb}
```

Program 7.16 Algorithm veb

$V'(P_4)$ to reach its lower bound.

7.11 HEAPS

In Section 7.3, we defined a complete binary tree. In this section, we present a special form of a complete binary tree that is useful in many applications.

Definition: A *max heap* is a complete binary tree such that if it is not empty, each element has a field called *key* and the *key* value in the root is the largest (ties are broken arbitrarily) *key* value in the binary tree. The left and right subtrees of the root are also max heaps.

Definition: A *min heap* is a complete binary tree such that if it is not empty, each element has a field called *key* and the *key* value in the root is the smallest (ties are broken arbitrarily) *key* value in the binary tree. The left and right subtrees of the root are also min heaps.

```
1  function ab (x : node ; l,lb,mb : integer) : integer;
2  {same as algorithm veb. lb is a lower bound on V´(x)}
3  var ans : integer;
4      temp,i : integer;
5  begin
6    if terminal (x) or (l = 0)
7    then ab := e (x)
8    else
9    begin
10     ans := lb ;
11     i := 1;
12     while (i ≤ d) and (ans < mb) do
13     begin
14       temp := −ab (c [i ], l − 1, −mb, −ans );
15       if ans < temp then ans := temp ;
16       i := i + 1;
17     end; {of while}
18     ab := ans ;
19   end; [of if}
20 end; {of ab}
```

Program 7.17 Algorithm *ab*

Some example max heaps are shown in Figure 7.21 and some min heaps are shown in Figure 7.22.

Heaps find application when a *priority queue* is to be maintained. In this kind of queue, the element to be deleted is the one with highest (or lowest) priority. At any time, an element with arbitrary priority can be inserted into the queue. In applications where an element with highest (lowest) priority is to be deleted each time, a max (min) heap may be used.

Example 7.4: Suppose that we are selling the services of a machine. Each user pays a fixed amount per use. However, the time needed by each user is different. We wish to maximize the returns from this machine under the assumption that the machine is not to be kept idle unless no user is available. This can be done by maintaining a priority queue of all persons waiting to use the machine. The value of the *key* field is the amount of time needed. Whenever the machine becomes available, the user with smallest time requirement is selected. Hence, a min heap is required. When a new user requests the machine, his/her request is put into the heap.

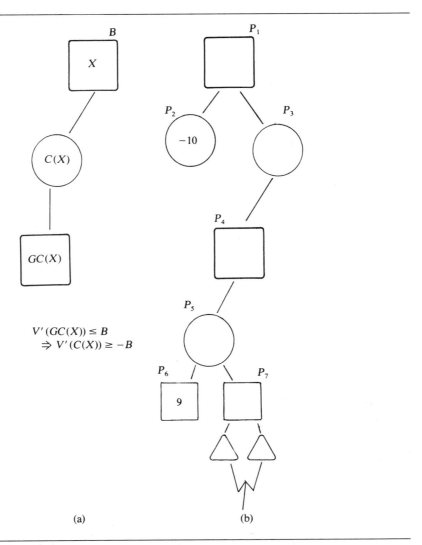

Figure 7.20 Games trees showing lower bounding

If each user needs the same amount of time on the machine but people are willing to pay different amounts for the service, then a priority queue on the amount of payment can be maintained. Whenever the machine becomes available, the user paying the most is selected. This requires a max heap. □

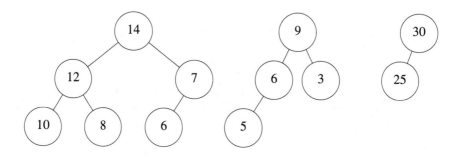

Figure 7.21 Max heaps

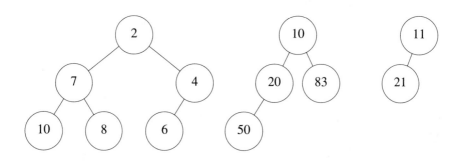

Figure 7.22 Min heaps

Example 7.5: Suppose that we are simulating a large factory. This factory has many machines and many jobs that require processing on some of these machines. An *event* is said to occur whenever a machine completes the processing of the job it is working on. When an event occurs, the job has to be moved to the queue for the next machine (if any) that it needs. If this queue is empty, the job can be assigned to the machine immediately. Also, a new job can be scheduled on the machine that has become idle (provided that its queue is not empty).

In order to determine the occurrence of events, a priority queue is used. This queue contains the finish time of all jobs that are presently being worked on. The next event occurs at the least time in the queue. So, a min heap can be used in this application. □

Before developing procedures to add to and delete from a heap, let us examine some other representations for a priority queue. We shall assume that each deletion removes the element with largest key value from the queue. The conclusions we draw are the same when the smallest element is to be deleted.

The simplest way to represent a priority queue is as an unordered linear list. Suppose that we have n elements each of size 1 in this queue. If the list is represented sequentially, additions are most easily performed at the end of this list. Hence, the insert time is $\Theta(1)$. A deletion requires a search for the element with largest key followed by its deletion. Since it takes $\Theta(n)$ time to find the largest element in an n element unordered list, the delete time is $\Theta(n)$. If a chain is used, additions can be performed at the front of the chain in $\Theta(1)$ time. Each deletion takes $\Theta(n)$ time. An alternative is to use an ordered linear list. The elements are in nondecreasing order in case a sequential representation is used and in nonincreasing order in case an ordered chain is used. The delete time for each representation is $\Theta(1)$ and the insert time $O(n)$. When a max heap is used, both additions and deletions can be performed in $O(\log n)$ time.

A max heap with five elements is shown in Figure 7.23(a). When an element is added to this heap, the resulting six element heap must have the structure shown in Figure 7.23(b). This is because a heap is a complete binary tree. If the element to be inserted has key value 1, it may be inserted as the left child of 2. If instead, the key value of the new element is 5, then this cannot be inserted as the left child of 2 (as otherwise, we will not have a max heap following the insertion). So, the 2 is moved down to its left child (Figure 7.23(c)) and we determine if placing the 5 at the old position of 2 results in a max heap. Since the parent element (20) is at least as large as the element (5) being inserted, it is all right to insert the new element at the position shown in the figure. Next, suppose that the new element has value 21 rather than 5. In this case, the 2 moves down to its left child as in Figure 7.23(c). The 21 cannot be inserted into the old position occupied by the 2 as the parent of this position is smaller than 21. Hence, the 20 is moved down to its right child and the 21 inserted in the root of the heap (Figure 7.23(d)).

To implement the insertion strategy described above, we need to go from an element to its parent. If a linked representation is used, an additional *parent* field is to be added to each node. However, since a heap is a complete binary tree, the formula based representation can be used. Lemma 7.3 enables us to locate the parent of any element easily. Program 7.18 performs an insertion into a max heap that contains n elements. This assumes that *heap* is an array with allowable indexes in the range 1..*MaxElements*. Further, it is assumed that the type *element* is a record with a *key* field in addition to other fields. As a complete binary tree with n elements has a height $\lceil \log_2(n+1) \rceil$, the

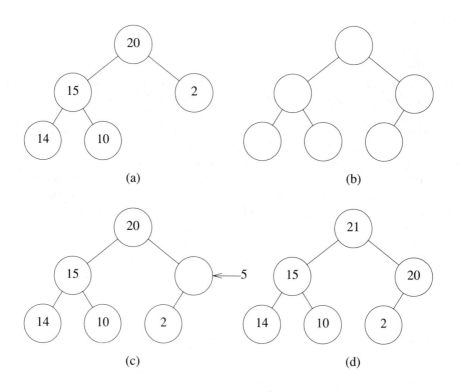

Figure 7.23 Insertion into a max heap

while loop of the insertion procedure is iterated O(log*n*) times.

When an element is to be deleted from a max heap, it is taken from the root of the heap. For instance, a deletion from the heap of Figure 7.23(d) results in the removal of the element 21. Since the resulting heap has only five elements in it, the binary tree of Figure 7.23(d) needs to be restructured to correspond to a complete binary tree with five elements. To do this, we remove the element in position 6. I.e., the element 2. Now, we have the right structure (Figure 7.24(a)) but the root is vacant and the element 2 is not in the heap. If the 2 is inserted into the root, the resulting binary tree is not a max heap. The element at the root should be the largest from among the 2 and the elements in the left and right children of the root. This element is 20. It is moved into the root thereby creating a vacancy in position 3. Since this position has no children, the 2 may be inserted here. The resulting heap is shown in Figure 7.23(a).

```
procedure InsertMaxHeap (x : element);
{Insert x into the global max heap heap [1..MaxElements ]}
{n is the present size of the heap}
var i : integer; NotDone : boolean;
begin
  if n = MaxElements then
  begin
    writeln('Heap full');
    halt;
  end;
  n := n +1; i := n; NotDone := true;
  while NotDone do
    if i := 1 then NotDone := false {at root}
    else if x.key <= heap [i div 2].key then NotDone := false
        else begin {move from parent to i}
                heap [i ] := heap [i div 2];
                i := i div 2;
             end;
  heap [i ] := x;
end; {of InsertMaxHeap}
```

Program 7.18 Insertion into a max heap

Now, suppose we wish to perform another deletion. The 20 is to be deleted. Following the deletion, the heap has the binary tree structure shown in Figure 7.24(b). To get this structure, the 10 is removed from position 5. It cannot be inserted into the root as it is not large enough. The 15 moves to the root and we attempt to insert the 10 into position 2. This is, however, smaller than the 14 below it. So, the 14 is moved up and the 10 inserted into position 4. The resulting heap is shown in Figure 7.24(c).

Program 7.19 implements this strategy to delete from a heap. Once again, since the height of a heap with n elements is $\lceil \log_2(n+1) \rceil$, the **while** loop of this procedure is iterated O(log$n$) times. Hence the complexity of a deletion is O(log n).

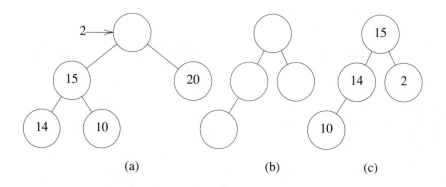

Figure 7.24 Deletion from a heap

7.12 BINARY SEARCH TREES

While a heap is well suited for applications that require priority queues, it is not suited for applications in which arbitrary elements are to be deleted from the element list. Deletion of an arbitrary element from an n element heap takes $O(n)$ time. This is no better than the time needed for arbitrary deletions from an unordered linear list.

A *binary search tree* has a better performance than any of the data structures studied so far when the functions to be performed are search, insert, and delete. In fact, with a binary search tree, these functions can be performed both by key value and by rank (i.e., find an element with key x; find the fifth smallest element; delete the element with key x; delete the fifth smallest element; insert an element and determine its rank).

Definition: A *binary search tree* is a binary tree. It may be empty. If it is not empty then it satisfies the following properties:

(1)   Every element has a key and no two elements have the same key. I.e., all keys are distinct.

(2)   The keys (if any) in the left subtree are smaller than the key in the root.

(3)   The keys (if any) in the right subtree are larger than the key in the root.

(4)   The left and right subtrees are also binary search trees.

---

procedure *DeleteMaxHeap* (**var** *x* : *element*);
{Delete from the max heap *heap* [1..*MaxElements*]}
{*n* is the current heap size}
var *i*, *r*, *j* : **integer**; *k* : *element*; *NotDone* : **boolean**;
begin
   if *n* = 0 **then begin** {heap empty}
                 writeln('Deletion from an empty heap');
                 halt;
              end;
   NotDone := **true**; *x* := *heap* [1]; *k* := *heap* [*n*]; *n* := *n* − 1;
   i := 1; *j* := 2; {*j* is left child of *i*}
   while (*j* <= *n*) **and** *NotDone* **do**
   begin
     if *j* < *n* **then if** *heap* [*j*].*key* < *heap* [*j* +1].*key* **then** *j* := *j* +1;
     {*j* points to larger child}
     if *k*.*key* >= *heap* [*j*].*key* **then** *NotDone* := **false**
                 else begin
                    heap [*i*] := *heap* [*j*]; {move child up}
                    {move *i* and *j* down}
                    i := *j*; *j* := 2∗*j*;
                 end;
   end;
   heap [*i*] := *k*;
end; {of *DeleteMaxHeap*}

Program 7.19 Deleting from a max heap

    There is some redundancy in the above definition. Properties (2), (3), and (4) together imply that the keys must be distinct. So, property (1) can be replaced by the property: The root has a key. The definition provided above is, however, clearer than the nonredundant version.

    Some example binary trees in which the elements have distinct keys are shown in Figure 7.25. The tree of Figure 7.25(a) is not a binary search tree. This is so despite the fact that it satisfies properties (1), (2), and (3). The right subtree fails to satisfy property (4). This subtree is not a binary search tree as its right subtree has a key value (22) that is smaller than that in the subtree's root (25). The binary trees of Figure 7.25(b) and (c) are binary search trees.

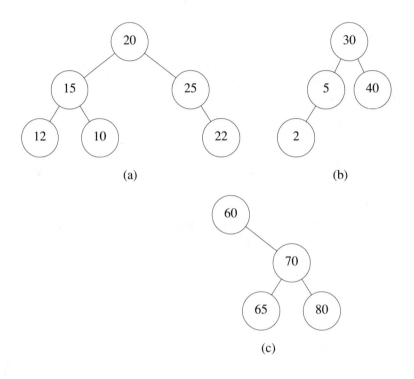

Figure 7.25 Binary trees

Searching A Binary Search Tree

Since the definition of a binary search tree is recursive, it is easiest to describe a recursive search method. Suppose we wish to search for an element with key x. We begin at the root. If the root is **nil**, then the search tree contains no elements and the search is unsuccessful. Otherwise, we compare x with the key in the root. If x equals this key, then the search terminates successfully. If x is less than the key in the root, then no element in the right subtree can have key value x and only the left subtree is to be searched. If x is larger than the key in the root, only the right subtree needs to be searched. The subtrees may be searched recursively as in Program 7.20. This function assumes a linked representation for the search tree. Each node has the three fields: *LeftChild*, *RightChild*, and *data*. *data* is of type *element* and has at least the field *key* which is of type **integer**.

---

function *search* (*t* : *TreePointer* ; *x* : **integer**): *TreePointer*;
{Search the binary search tree *t* for an element with key *x*}
{Return a pointer to the element if it is found. Return **nil** otherwise.}
begin
   if *t* = **nil then** *search* := **nil**
   else if *x* = *t*↑.*data.key* **then** *search* := *t*
      else if *x* < *t*↑.*data.key* **then** *search* := *search* (*t*↑.*LeftChild, x*)
         else *search* := *search* (*t*↑.*RightChild, x*);
end; {of *search*}

Program 7.20 Recursive search of a binary search tree

    The recursion of Program 7.20 is easily replaced by a **while** loop as in Program 7.21.

---

function *search* (*t* : *TreePointer* ; *x* : **integer**): *TreePointer*;
{Search the binary search tree *t* for an element with key *x*}
{Return a pointer to the element if it is found. Return **nil** otherwise.}
var *p* : *TreePointer*; *NotFound* : **boolean**;
begin
   p := *t*; *NotFound* := **true**;

   while (*p* < > **nil**) **and** *NotFound* **do**
     if *x* = *p*↑.*data.key* **then** *NotFound* := **false**
     else if *x* < *p*↑.*data.key* **then** *p* := *p*↑.*LeftChild*
          else *p* := *p*↑.*RightChild*;

   if *NotFound* **then** *search* := **nil**
        else *search* := *p*;
end; {of *search*}

Program 7.21 Iterative search of a binary search tree

    In case we wish to search by rank, each node should have an additional field *Left-Size* which is one plus the number of elements in the left subtree of the node. For the search tree of Figure 7.25(b), the nodes with keys 2, 5, 30, and 40, respectively, have *LeftSize* equal to 1, 2, 3, and 1. Program 7.22 searches for the *k*'th smallest element.

---

function *search* (*t* : *TreePointer* ; *k* : **integer**): *TreePointer*;
{Search the binary search tree *t* for the *k*th smallest element}
{Return a pointer to the element if it is found. Return **nil** otherwise.}
var *p* : *TreePointer*; *NotFound* : **boolean**; *i* : **integer**;
begin
    p := *t*; *NotFound* := **true**; *i* := *k*;

    while (*p* < > **nil**) **and** *NotFound* **do**
        if *i* = *p* ↑.*LeftSize* **then** *NotFound* := **false**
        else if *i* < *p* ↑.*LeftSize* **then** *p* := *p* ↑.*LeftChild*
            else begin
                i := *i* − *LeftSize*; {search for *i*th in right subtree}
                p := *p* ↑.*RightChild*;
            end;

    if *NotFound* **then** *search* := **nil**
            else *search* := *p*;
end; {of *search*}

Program 7.22 Searching a binary search tree by rank

As can be seen, a binary search tree of height *h* can be searched by key as well as by rank in O(*h*) time.

Insert

To insert a new element *x*, we must first verify that its key is different from those of existing elements. To do this a search is carried out. If the search is unsuccessful, then the element is inserted at the point the search terminated. For instance, to insert an element with key 80 into the tree of Figure 7.25(b), we first search for 80. This search terminates unsuccessfully and the last node examined is the one with key 40. The new element is inserted as the right child of this node. The resulting search tree is shown in Figure 7.26(a). Figure 7.26(b) shows the result of inserting the key 50 into the search tree of Figure 7.26(a).

Program 7.23 implements the insert strategy just described. In case nodes have a *LeftSize* field, then this is to be updated too. Regardless, the insertion can be performed in O(*h*) time where *h* is the height of the search tree.

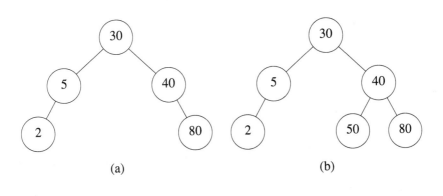

Figure 7.26 Inserting into a binary search tree

Delete

Deletion of a leaf element is quite easy. To delete 50 from the tree of Figure 7.26(b), the left child field of its parent is set to **nil** and the node disposed. This gives us the tree of Figure 7.26(a). To delete the 80, the right child field of 40 is set to **nil** obtaining the tree of Figure 7.25(b) and the node containing 80 disposed.

The deletion of a nonleaf element is accomplished by transforming it into the deletion of a leaf element. For instance, if we wish to delete the element with key 30 from the tree of Figure 7.26(b), then we find a suitable replacement for it. The 30 may be replaced by either the largest element in its left subtree or the smallest in its right subtree. Note that at least one of these subtrees contains an element as otherwise we are deleting a leaf element. Suppose we opt for the largest element in the left subtree. This has the key 5. It is moved into the root and the tree of Figure 7.27(a) obtained. Now we must delete the second 5. To do this, the 2 is moved up and the tree of Figure 7.27(b) obtained. The second 2 is in a leaf node and is easily deleted.

We leave the writing of the deletion procedure as an exercise. It should be evident that a deletion can be performed in O(h) time if the search tree has a height of h.

Height of a Binary Search Tree

Unless care is taken, the height of a binary search tree with n elements can become as large as n. This is the case, for instance, when Program 7.23 is used to insert the keys [1, 2, 3, ..., n], in this order, into an initially empty binary search tree. It can, however, be

```
procedure insert (var t : TreePointer ; x : element ; var success : boolean);
{Insert x into the binary search tree t}
var p, q : TreePointer; NotFound : boolean;
begin
    {Search for x.key.  q is parent of p}
    q := nil; p := t; NotDone := true;
    while (p < > nil) and NotFound do
        q := p;  {save p}
        if x.key = p↑.data.key then NotFound := false
        else if  x.key < p↑.data.key then p :=p↑.LeftChild
                                     else p := p↑.RightChild;

    {Perform insertion}
    if NotFound then success := false {x.key already in t}
    else begin {insert into t}
        new (p);
        with p↑ do
        begin
          LeftChild := nil; RightChild := nil; data := x;
        end;
        if q = nil
        then t := q
        else if x.key < q↑.data.key then q↑.LeftChild := p
                                    else q↑.RightChild := p;
        success := true;
    end;
end; {of insert}
```

Program 7.23 Insertion into a binary search tree

shown that when insertions and deletions are made at random using the procedures given above, the height of the binary search tree is O(log n) on the average.

Search trees with a worst case height of O(log$n$) are called *balanced search trees*. Balanced search trees that permit searches, inserts, and deletes to be performed in O(h) time exist. Most notable among these are AVL and B trees. You are referred to the books by Knuth, Horowitz, and Sahni that are cited in the readings section for a discussion of these balanced search trees.

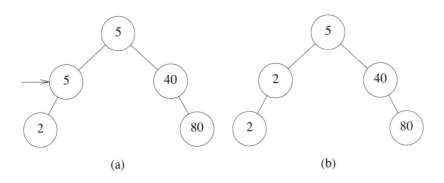

Figure 7.27 Deletion from a binary search tree

7.13 SELECTION TREES

Suppose we have k ordered sequences that are to be merged into a single ordered sequence. Each sequence consists of some number of records and is in nondecreasing order of a designated field called the *key*. An ordered sequence is called a *run*. Let n be the number of records in the k runs together. The merging task can be accomplished by repeatedly outputting the record with the smallest key. The smallest has to be found from k possibilities and it could be the leading record in any of the k-runs. The most direct way to merge k-runs would be to make $k - 1$ comparisons to determine the next record to output. For $k > 2$, we can achieve a reduction in the number of comparisons needed to find the next smallest element by using the idea of a selection tree. A *selection tree* is a binary tree where each node represents the smaller of its two children. Thus, the root node represents the smallest node in the tree. Figure 7.28 illustrates a selection tree for the case $k = 8$.

The construction of this selection tree may be compared to the playing of a tournament in which the winner is the record with the smaller key. Then, each nonleaf node in the tree represents the winner of a tournament and the root node represents the overall winner or the smallest key. A leaf node here represents the first record in the corresponding run. Since the records being merged are generally large, each node will contain only a pointer to the record it represents. Thus, the root node contains a pointer to the first record in run 4. The selection tree may be represented using the sequential allocation scheme for binary trees that results from Lemma 7.3. The number above each node in Figure 7.28 represents the address of the node in this sequential representation. The record pointed to by the root has the smallest key and so may be output. Now, the next record from run 4 enters the selection tree. It has a key value of 15. To restructure

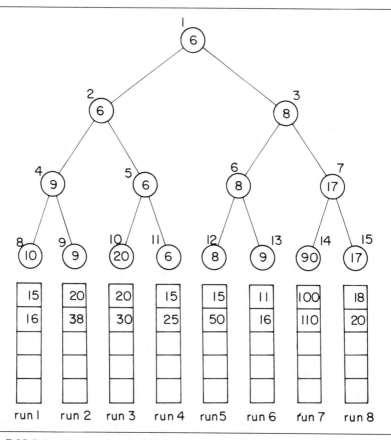

Figure 7.28 Selection tree for $k = 8$ showing the first three keys in each of the eight runs

the tree, the tournament has to be replayed only along the path from node 11 to the root. Thus, the winner from nodes 10 and 11 is again node 11 (15 < 20). The winner from nodes 4 and 5 is node 4 (9<15). The winner from 2 and 3 is node 3 (8 < 9). The new tree is shown in Figure 7.29. The tournament is played between sibling nodes and the result put in the parent node. Lemma 7.3 may be used to compute the address of sibling and parent nodes efficiently. After each comparison the next takes place at one higher level in the tree. The number of levels in the tree is $\lceil \log_2 k \rceil + 1$. So, the time to restructure the tree is $O(\log_2 k)$. The tree has to be restructured each time a record is merged into the output file. Hence, the time required to merge all n records is $O(n \log_2 k)$. The time required to set up the selection tree the first time is $O(k)$. Hence, the total time needed to merge the k runs is $O(n \log_2 k)$.

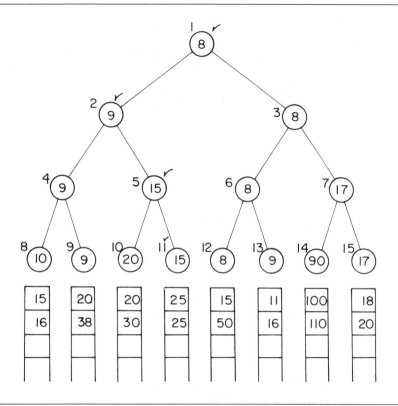

Figure 7.29 Selection tree of Figure 7.28 after one record has been output and the tree restructured. Nodes that were changed are ticked.

A slightly faster algorithm results if each node represents the loser of the tournament rather than the winner. After the record with smallest key is output, the selection tree of Figure 7.28 is to be restructured. Since the record with the smallest key value is in run 4, this restructuring involves inserting the next record from this run into the tree. The next record has key value 15. Tournaments are played between sibling nodes along the path from node 11 to the root. Since these sibling nodes represent the losers of tournaments played earlier, we would simplify the restructuring process by placing in each nonleaf node a pointer to the record that loses the tournament rather than to the winner of the tournament. A tournament tree in which each nonleaf node retains a pointer to the loser is called a *tree of losers*. Figure 7.30 shows the tree of losers corresponding to the selection tree of Figure 7.28. For convenience, each node contains the key value of a record rather than a pointer to the record represented. The leaf nodes represent the first record in each run. An additional node, node 0, has been added to represent the overall winner of the tournament. Following the output of the overall winner, the tree is restructured by playing tournaments along the path from node 11 to node 1. The records with which these tournaments are to be played are readily available from the parent nodes.

edge	cost	action
—	—	—
(2,3)	5	accept
(2,4)	6	accept
(4,3)	10	reject
(2,6)	11	accept
(4,6)	14	reject
(1,2)	16	accept
(4,5)	18	accept

Figure 7.30 Tree of losers corresponding to Figure 7.28

7.14 REFERENCES AND SELECTED READINGS

For other representations of trees see:

The Art of Computer Programming: Fundamental Algorithms, by D. Knuth, second edition, Addison-Wesley, Reading, 1973.

For the use of trees in generating optimal compiled code see:

Compilers: Principles, Techniques, and Tools, by A. Aho, R. Sethi, and J. Ullman, Addison Wesley, Massachusetts, 1986.

Tree traversal algorithms may be found in:

"Scanning list structures without stacks and tag bits," by G. Lindstrom, *Information Processing Letters*, vol. 2, no. 2, June 1973, pp. 47-51.

"Simple algorithms for traversing a tree without an auxiliary stack," by B. Dwyer, *Information Processing Letters*, vol. 2, no. 5, Dec. 1973, pp. 143-145.

For a further analysis of the set representation problem see:

Fundamentals of Computer Algorithms, E. Horowitz and S. Sahni, Computer Science Press, Maryland, 1978.

The computing time analysis of the UNION-FIND algorithms may be found in:

"Efficiency of a good but not linear set union algorithm," by R. Tarjan, *JACM*, vol. 22, no. 2, April 1975, pp. 215-225.

For more on game playing see:

Problem Solving Methods in Artificial Intelligence, by N. Nilsson, McGraw-Hill, New York, 1971.

Artificial Intelligence: The Heuristic Programming Approach, by J. Slagle, McGraw-Hill, New York, 1971.

Additional data structures that employ trees may be found in:

Data Structures and Network Algorithms, by R. Tarjan, Society for Industrial and Applied Mathematics, CBMS 44, 1983.

7.15 EXERCISES

1. For the following binary tree list the terminal nodes, the nonterminal nodes, and the level of each node.

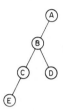

2. Draw the internal memory representation of the above binary tree using (a) sequential, (b) linked, and (c) threaded linked representations.

3. Write a procedure which reads in a tree represented as a list as in Section 7.1 and creates its internal representation using nodes with three fields, *tag, data, link.*

4. Write a procedure which reverses the above process and takes a pointer to a tree and prints out its list representation.

5. Write a nonrecursive version of procedure *preorder.*

6. Write a nonrecursive version of procedure *postorder* without using **goto**s.

Exercises 7-9 assume a linked representation for a binary tree.

7. Write an algorithm to list the *data* fields of the nodes of a binary tree T by level. Within levels nodes are to be listed left to right.

8. Give an algorithm to count the number of leaf nodes in a binary tree T. What is its computing time?

9. Write an algorithm *swaptree* (t) which takes a binary tree and swaps the left and right children of every node. For example, if t is the binary tree

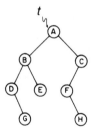

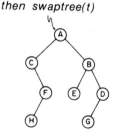

then swaptree(t)

10. Devise an external representation for formulas in the propositional calculus. Write a procedure which reads such a formula and creates a binary tree representation of it. How efficient is your procedure?

11. Procedure *postordereval* must be able to distinguish between the symbols ∧, ∨, ¬ and a pointer in the *data* field of a node. How should this be done?

12. What is the computing time for *postordereval*? First determine the logical parameters.

13. Write an algorithm which inserts a new node *t* as the left child of node *s* in a threaded binary tree. The left pointer of *s* becomes the left pointer of *t*.

14. Write a procedure which traverses a threaded binary tree in postorder. What are the time and space requirements of your method?

15. Define the inverse transformation of the one which creates the associated binary tree from a forest. Are these transformations unique?

16. Prove that preorder traversal on trees and preorder traversal on the associated binary tree gives the same result.

17. Prove that inorder traversal for trees and inorder traversal on the associated binary tree give the same result.

18. Using the result of Example 7.3, draw the trees after processing the instruction *union*(12,10).

19. Consider the hypothetical game tree:

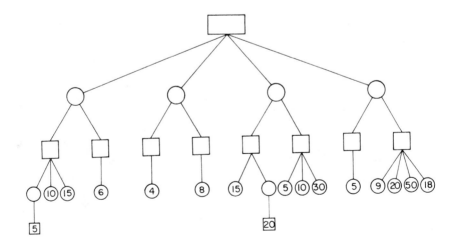

(a) Using the minimax technique (Eq. (7.3)) obtain the value of the root node.

(b) What move should player *A* make?

(c) List the nodes of this game tree in the order in which their value is computed by algorithm *ve*.

(d) Using Eq. (7.4) compute $V'(X)$ for every node X in the tree.

(e) Which nodes of this tree are not evaluated during the computation of the value of the root node using algorithm *ab* with x = root, l = **maxint**, lb = −**maxint**, and mb = **maxint**?

20. Show that $V'(X)$ computed by Eq. (7.4) is the same as $V(X)$ computed by Eq. (7.3) for all nodes on levels from which *A* is to move. For all other nodes show that $V(X)$ computed by Eq. (7.3) is the negative of $V'(X)$ computed by Eq. (7.4).

21. Show that algorithm *ab* when initially called with lb = −**maxint**, and mb = **maxint** yields the same results as *ve* does for the same X and l.

22. Prove that every binary tree is uniquely defined by its preorder and inorder sequences.

23. Do the inorder and postorder sequences of a binary tree uniquely define the binary tree? Prove you answer.

24. Answer Exercise 23 for preorder and postorder.

25. Write an algorithm to construct the binary tree with a given preorder and inorder sequence.

26. Do Exercise 23 for inorder and postorder.

27. Consider threading a binary tree using preorder threads rather than inorder threads as in the text. Is it possible to traverse a binary tree in preorder without a stack using these threads?

28. Write an algorithm for traversing an inorder threaded binary tree in preorder.

29. [Wilczynski] Following the conventions of LISP assume nodes with two fields: HEAD and TAIL. If $A = ((a\,(bc\,)))$ then HEAD(A) = $(a\,(bc\,))$, TAIL(A) = NIL, HEAD(HEAD(A)) = a, TAIL(HEAD(A)) = $((bc\,))$. CONS(A,B) gets a new node T, stores A in its HEAD, B in its TAIL, and returns T. B must always be a list. If $L = a$, $M = (bc\,)$ then CONS(L,M) = $(abc\,)$, CONS(M,M) = $((bc\,)bc\,)$. Three other useful functions are: ATOM(X) which is true if X is an atom else false, NULL(X) which is true if X is NIL else false, EQUAL(X,Y) which is true if X and Y are the same atoms or equivalent lists else false.

(a) Give a sequence of HEAD, TAIL operations for extracting a from the lists: $((cat\,)),((a\,)),((mart\,)),(((cb\,))a\,)$.

(b) Write recursive procedures for COPY, REVERSE, APPEND.

(c) Implement this "LISP" subsystem. Store atoms in an array, write procedures *makelist* and *listprint* for input and output of lists.

30. Write a Pascal procedure to delete an element X from a binary search tree T.

31. Write a Pascal procedure to merge k runs using a tree of winners.

32. Write a Pascal procedure to merge k runs using a tree of losers. Compare the run time of this procedure with that for the procedure of the previous exercise.

CHAPTER 8

GRAPHS

8.1 TERMINOLOGY AND REPRESENTATIONS

8.1.1 Introduction

The first recorded evidence of the use of graphs dates back to 1736 when Euler used them to solve the now classical Koenigsberg bridge problem. In the town of Koenigsberg (in Eastern Prussia) the river Pregal flows around the island Kneiphof and then divides into two. There are, therefore, four land areas bordering this river (Figure 8.1). These land areas are interconnected by means of seven bridges $a-g$. The land areas themselves are labeled $A-D$. The Koenigsberg bridge problem is to determine whether starting at some land area it is possible to walk across all the bridges exactly once returning to the starting land area. One possible walk would be to start from land area B; walk across bridge a to island A; take bridge e to area D; bridge g to C; bridge d to A; bridge b to B and bridge f to D. This walk does not go across all bridges exactly once, nor does it return to the starting land area B. Euler answered the Koenigsberg bridge problem in the negative: The people of Koenigsberg will not be able to walk across each bridge exactly once and return to the starting point. He solved the problem by representing the land areas as vertices and the bridges as edges in a graph (actually a multigraph) as in Figure 8.1(b). His solution is elegant and applies to all graphs. Defining the *degree* of a vertex to be the number of edges incident to it, Euler showed that there is a walk starting at any vertex, going through each edge exactly once and terminating at the start vertex iff the degree of each vertex is even. A walk which does this is called *Eulerian*. There is no Eulerian walk for the Koenigsberg bridge problem as all four vertices are of odd degree.

Since this first application of graphs, they have been used in a wide variety of applications. Some of these applications are: analysis of electrical circuits, finding shortest routes, project planning, identification of chemical compounds, statistical

358

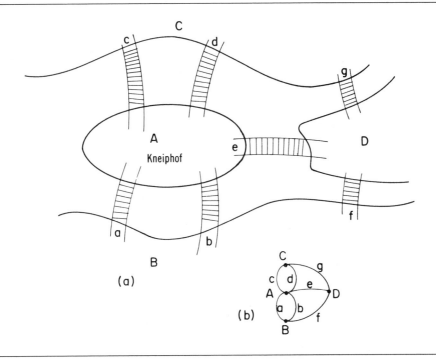

Figure 8.1 Section of the river Pregal in Koenigsberg and Euler´s graph

mechanics, genetics, cybernetics, linguistics, social sciences, etc. Indeed, it might well be said that of all mathematical structures, graphs are the most widely used.

8.1.2 Definitions and Terminology

A graph, G, consists of two sets V and E. V is a finite nonempty set of *vertices*. E is a set of pairs of vertices; these pairs are called *edges*. $V(G)$ and $E(G)$ will represent the sets of vertices and edges of graph G. We will also write $G = (V,E)$ to represent a graph. In an *undirected graph* the pair of vertices representing any edge is unordered. Thus, the pairs (v_1,v_2) and (v_2,v_1) represent the same edge. In a *directed graph* each edge is represented by a directed pair $<v_1,v_2>$. v_1 is the *tail* and v_2 the *head* of the edge. Therefore $<v_2,v_1>$ and $<v_1,v_2>$ represent two different edges. Figure 8.2 shows three graphs G_1, G_2, and G_3. The graphs G_1 and G_2 are undirected. G_3 is a directed graph.

$V(G_1) = \{1,2,3,4\};$ $E(G_1) = \{(1,2),(1,3),(1,4),(2,3),(2,4),(3,4)\}$
$V(G_{2)} = \{1,2,3,4,5,6,7\};$ $E(G_2) = \{(1,2),(1,3),(2,4),(2,5),(3,6),(3,7)\}$
$V(G_3) = \{1,2,3\};$ $E(G_3) = \{<1,2>,<2,1>,<2,3>\}.$

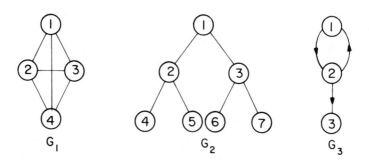

Figure 8.2 Three sample graphs

Note that the edges of a directed graph are drawn with an arrow from the tail to the head. The graph G_2 is also a tree while the graphs G_1 and G_3 are not. Trees can be defined as a special case of graphs, but we need more terminology for that. If (v_1,v_2) or $<v_1,v_2>$ is an edge in $E(G)$, then we require $v_1 \neq v_2$. In addition, since $E(G)$ is a set, a graph may not have multiple occurrences of the same edge. When this restriction is removed from a graph, the resulting data object is referred to as a multigraph. The data object of Figure 8.3 is a multigraph which is not a graph.

The number of distinct unordered pairs (v_i,v_j) with $v_i \neq v_j$ in a graph with n vertices is $n(n-1)/2$. This is the maximum number of edges in any n vertex undirected graph. An n vertex undirected graph with exactly $n(n-1)/2$ edges is said to be *complete*. G_1 is the complete graph on four vertices while G_2 and G_3 are not complete graphs. In the case of a directed graph on n vertices the maximum number of edges is $n(n-1)$.

If (v_1,v_2) is an edge in $E(G)$, then we shall say the vertices v_1 and v_2 are *adjacent* and that the edge (v_1,v_2) is *incident* on vertices v_1 and v_2. The vertices adjacent to vertex 2 in G_2 are 4, 5, and 1. The edges incident on vertex 3 in G_2 are (1,3), (3,6), and (3,7). If $<v_1,v_2>$ is a directed edge, then vertex v_1 will be said to be *adjacent to* v_2 while v_2 is *adjacent from* v_1. The edge $<v_1,v_2>$ is incident to v_1 and v_2. In G_3 the edges incident to vertex 2 are $<1,2>$, $<2,1>$, and $<2,3>$.

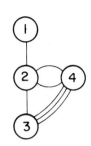

Figure 8.3 Example of a multigraph that is not a graph

A *subgraph* of G is a graph G' such that $V(G') \subseteq V(G)$ and $E(G') \subseteq E(G)$. Figure 8.4 shows some of the subgraphs of G_1 and G_3.

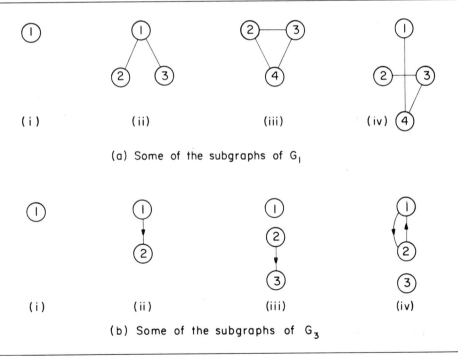

(a) Some of the subgraphs of G_1

(b) Some of the subgraphs of G_3

Figure 8.4 (a) Subgraphs of G_1 and (b) Subgraphs of G_3

A *path* from vertex v_p to vertex v_q in graph G is a sequence of vertices $v_p, v_{i_1}, v_{i_2},$ ..., v_{i_n}, v_q such that $(v_p, v_{i_1}), (v_{i_1}, v_{i_2}),$ ..., (v_{i_n}, v_q) are edges in $E(G)$. If G' is directed then the path consists of $<v_p, v_{i_1}>, <v_{i_1}, v_{i_2}>,$ ..., $<v_{i_n}, v_q>$, edges in $E(G')$. The *length* of a path is the number of edges on it. A *simple path* is a path in which all vertices except possibly the first and last are distinct. A path such as (1,2) (2,4) (4,3) we write as 1,2,4,3. Paths 1,2,4,3 and 1,2,4,2 are both of length 3 in G_1. The first is a simple path while the second is not. 1,2,3 is a simple directed path in G_3. 1,2,3,2 is not a path in G_3 as the edge $<3,2>$ is not in $E(G_3)$. A *cycle* is a simple path in which the first and last vertices are the same. 1,2,3,1 is a cycle in G_1. 1,2,1 is a cycle in G_3. For the case of directed graphs we normally add on the prefix ''directed'' to the terms cycle and path. In an undirected graph, G, two vertices v_1 and v_2 are said to be *connected* if there is a path in G from v_1 to v_2 (since G is undirected, this means there must also be a path from v_2 to v_1). An undirected graph is said to be connected if for every pair of distinct vertices v_i, v_j in $V(G)$ there is a path from v_i to v_j in G. Graphs G_1 and G_2 are connected while G_4 of Figure 8.5 is not. A *connected component* or simply a component of an undirected graph is a *maximal* connected subgraph. G_4 has two components H_1 and H_2 (see Figure 8.5). A *tree* is a connected acyclic (i.e., has no cycles) graph. A directed graph G is said to be *strongly connected* if for every pair of distinct vertices v_i, v_j in $V(G)$ there is a directed path from v_i to v_j and also from v_j to v_i. The graph G_3 is not strongly connected as there is no path from v_3 to v_2. A *strongly connected component* is a maximal subgraph that is strongly connected. G_3 has two strongly connected components (see Figure 8.6).

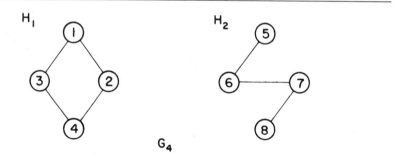

Figure 8.5 A graph with two connected components

The degree of a vertex is the number of edges incident to that vertex. The degree of vertex 1 in G_1 is 3. In case G is a directed graph, we define the *in-degree* of a vertex v to be the number of edges for which v is the head. The *out-degree* is defined to be the number of edges for which v is the tail. Vertex 2 of G_3 has in-degree 1, out-degree 2, and degree 3. If d_i is the degree of vertex i in a graph G with n vertices and e edges, then

Figure 8.6 Strongly connected components of G_3

it is easy to see that $e = (1/2)\Sigma_{i=1}^{n}d_i$.

In the remainder of this chapter we shall refer to a directed graph as a *digraph*. An undirected graph will sometimes be referred to simply as a graph.

8.1.3 Graph Representations

While several representations for graphs are possible, we shall study only the three most commonly used: adjacency matrices, adjacency lists, and adjacency multilists. Once again, the choice of a particular representation will depend upon the application one has in mind and the functions one expects to perform on the graph.

Adjacency Matrix

Let $G = (V,E)$ be a graph with n vertices, $n \geq 1$. The adjacency matrix of G is a two-dimensional $n \times n$ array, say A, with the property that $A[i,j] = 1$ iff the edge (v_i,v_j) ($<v_i,v_j>$ for a directed graph) is in $E(G)$. $A[i,j] = 0$ if there is no such edge in G. The adjacency matrices for the graphs G_1, G_3, and G_4 are shown in Figure 8.7. The adjacency matrix for an undirected graph is symmetric as the edge (v_i,v_j) is in $E(G)$ iff the edge (v_j,v_i) is also in $E(G)$. The adjacency matrix for a directed graph need not be symmetric (as is the case for G_3). The space needed to represent a graph using its adjacency matrix is n^2 bits. About half this space can be saved in the case of undirected graphs by storing only the upper or lower triangle of the matrix.

From the adjacency matrix, one may readily determine if there is an edge connecting any two vertices i and j. For an undirected graph the degree of any vertex i is its row sum $\Sigma_{j=1}^{n} A[i,j]$. For a directed graph the row sum is the out-degree while the column sum is the in-degree. Suppose we want to answer a nontrivial question about graphs

	1	2	3	4
1	0	1	1	1
2	1	0	1	1
3	1	1	0	1
4	1	1	1	0

(i)

	1	2	3
1	0	1	0
2	1	0	1
3	0	0	0

(ii)

	1	2	3	4	5	6	7	8
1	0	1	1	0	0	0	0	0
2	1	0	0	1	0	0	0	0
3	1	0	0	1	0	0	0	0
4	0	1	1	0	0	0	0	0
5	0	0	0	0	0	1	0	0
6	0	0	0	0	1	0	1	0
7	0	0	0	0	0	1	0	1
8	0	0	0	0	0	0	1	0

(iii)

Figure 8.7 Adjacency matrices for (i)G_1, (ii)G_3, and (iii)G_4

such as how many edges are there in G or is G connected. Using adjacency matrices all algorithms will require at least $O(n^2)$ time as $n^2 - n$ entries of the matrix (diagonal entries are zero) have to be examined. When graphs are sparse, i.e., most of the terms in the adjacency matrix are zero, one would expect that the former question would be answerable in significantly less time, say $O(e + n)$ where e is the number of edges in G and $e << n^2/2$. Such a speed-up can be made possible through the use of linked lists in which only the edges that are in G are represented. This leads to the next representation for graphs.

Adjacency Lists

In this representation the n rows of the adjacency matrix are represented as n linked lists. There is one list for each vertex in G. The nodes in list i represent the vertices that are adjacent from vertex i. Each node has at least two fields: *vertex* and *link*. The *vertex* fields contain the indices of the vertices adjacent to vertex i. The adjacency lists for G_1, G_3, and G_4 are shown in Figure 8.8. Each list has a headnode. The headnodes are sequential providing easy random access to the adjacency list for any particular vertex. The declarations in Pascal for the adjacency list representation would be

type *nextnode* = ↑*node* ;
    node = **record**
            vertex : **integer**;
            link : *nextnode* ;
        end;
    headnodes : **array**[1..n] **of** *nextnode*;

In the case of an undirected graph with n vertices and e edges, this representation requires n headnodes and $2e$ list nodes. Each list node has two fields. In terms of the number of bits of storage needed, this count should be multiplied by log n for the headnodes and log n + log e for the list nodes as it takes O(log m) bits to represent a number of value m. Often you can sequentially pack the nodes on the adjacency lists, thereby eliminating the use of records. In this case, an array *node* [1..n + 2e + 1] may be used. *node* [i] gives the starting point of the list for vertex i, $1 \le i \le n$ and *node* [n+1] is set to n + 2e +2. The vertices from vertex i are stored in *node* [i], ..., *node* [i + 1] − 1, $1 \le i \le n$. Figure 8.9 gives such a sequential representation for the graph G_4 of Figure 8.5.

The degree of any vertex in an undirected graph may be determined by just counting the number of nodes in its adjacency list. The total number of edges in G may, therefore, be determined in time O($n + e$). In the case of a digraph the number of list nodes is only e. The out-degree of any vertex may be determined by counting the number of nodes on its adjacency list. The total number of edges in G can, therefore, be determined in O($n + e$). Determining the in-degree of a vertex is a little more complex. In case there is a need to access repeatedly all vertices adjacent to another vertex then it may be worth the effort to keep another set of lists in addition to the adjacency lists. This set of lists, called *inverse adjacency lists*, will contain one list for each vertex. Each list will contain a node for each vertex adjacent to the vertex it represents (see Figure 8.10).

Alternatively, one could adopt a simplified version of the list structure used for sparse matrix representation in Section 6.6. Each node would now have four fields and would represent one edge. The node structure would be

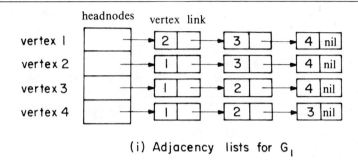

(i) Adjacency lists for G_1

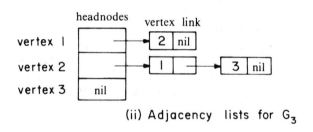

(ii) Adjacency lists for G_3

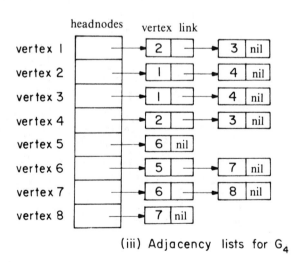

(iii) Adjacency lists for G_4

Figure 8.8 Adjacency Lists

[1] 10	[9] 24	[17] 3
[2] 12	[10] 2	[18] 6
[3] 14	[11] 3	[19] 5
[4] 16	[12] 1	[20] 7
[5] 18	[13] 4	[21] 6
[6] 19	[14] 1	[22] 8
[7] 21	[15] 4	[23] 7
[8] 23	[16] 2	

Figure 8.9 Sequential representation of graph G_4

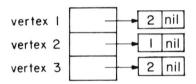

Figure 8.10 Inverse adjacency lists for G_3

tail	head	column link for head	row link for tail

Figure 8.11 shows the resulting structure for the graph G_3. The headnodes are stored sequentially.

The nodes in the adjacency lists of Figure 8.8 were ordered by the indices of the vertices they represented. It is not necessary that lists be ordered in this way and, in general, the vertices may appear in any order. Thus, the adjacency lists of Figure 8.12 would be just as valid a representation of G_1.

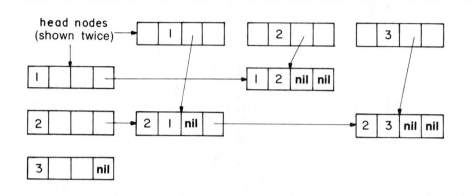

Figure 8.11 Orthogonal list representation for G_3

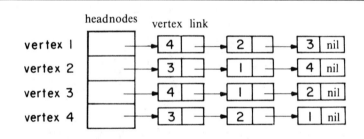

Figure 8.12 Alternate order adjacency list for G_1

Sometimes the edges of a graph have weights assigned to them. These weights may represent the distance from one vertex to another or the cost of going from one vertex to an adjacent vertex. In this case the adjacency matrix entries $A[i,j]$ would keep this information too. In the case of adjacency lists this weight information may be kept in the list nodes by including an additional field. A graph with weighted edges is called a *network*.

8.2 TRAVERSALS, CONNECTED COMPONENTS, AND SPANNING TREES

Given the root nodes of a binary tree, one of the most common things one wishes to do is to traverse the tree and visit the nodes in some order. In the chapter on trees, we defined three ways (preorder, inorder, and postorder) for doing this. An analogous problem arises in the case of graphs. Given an undirected graph $G = (V, E)$ and a vertex v in $V(G)$ we are interested in visiting all vertices in G that are reachable from v (i.e., all vertices connected to v). We shall look at two ways of doing this: depth first search and breadth first search.

Depth First Search

Depth first search of an undirected graph proceeds as follows. The start vertex v is visited. Next an unvisited vertex w adjacent to v is selected and a depth first search from w initiated. When a vertex u is reached such that all its adjacent vertices have been visited, we back up to the last vertex visited which has an unvisited vertex w adjacent to it and initiate a depth first search from w. The search terminates when no unvisited vertex can be reached from any of the visited ones. This procedure is best described recursively as in Program 8.1. This procedure assumes a global array $visited[1..n]$ of type boolean that is initialized to **false**.

```
1  procedure dfs(v : integer);
2  {Given an undirected graph G = (V,E) with n vertices and an
3   array visited[n] initially set to false, this algorithm visits
4   all vertices reachable from v. visited is global.}
5  var w : integer ;
6  begin
7      visited [v ] := true;
8      for each vertex w adjacent to v do
9          if not visited [w ] then dfs(w );
10 end; {of dfs}
```

Program 8.1 Algorithm *dfs*

In case G is represented by its adjacency lists then the vertices w adjacent to v can be determined by following a chain of links. Since the algorithm *dfs* would examine each node in the adjacency lists at most once and there are $2e$ list nodes, the time to complete the search is $O(e)$. If G is represented by its adjacency matrix, then the time to determine all vertices adjacent to v is $O(n)$. Since at most n vertices are visited, the total time is $O(n^2)$.

The graph G of Figure 8.13(a) is represented by its adjacency lists as in Figure 8.13(b). If a depth first search is initiated from vertex v_1, then the vertices of G are visited in the order: $v_1, v_2, v_4, v_8, v_5, v_6, v_3, v_7$. We can verify that $dfs(v_1)$ visits all vertices connected to v_1. So, all the vertices visited, together with all edges in G incident to these vertices, form a connected component of G.

Breadth First Search

Starting at vertex v and marking it as visited, breadth first search differs from depth first search in that all unvisited vertices adjacent to v are visited next. Then unvisited vertices adjacent to these vertices are visited and so on. A breadth first search beginning at vertex v_1 of the graph in Figure 8.13(a) would first visit v_1 and then v_2 and v_3. Next vertices v_4, v_5, v_6, and v_7 will be visited and finally v_8. Algorithm *bfs* (Program 8.2) gives the details.

Each vertex visited gets into the queue exactly once, so the **while** loop is iterated at most n times. If an adjacency matrix is used, then the loop takes $O(n)$ time for each vertex visited. The total time is, therefore, $O(n^2)$. In case adjacency lists are used the loop has a total cost of $d_1 + \cdots + d_n = O(e)$ where d_i = degree (v_i). Again, all vertices visited, together with all edges incident to them, form a connected component of G.

We now look at two simple applications of graph traversal: (1) finding the components of a graph, and (2) finding a spanning tree of a connected graph.

Connected Components

If G is an undirected graph, then one can determine whether or not it is connected by simply making a call to either *dfs* or *bfs* and then determining if there is any unvisited vertex. The time to do this is $O(n^2)$ if adjacency matrices are used and $O(e)$ if adjacency lists are used. A more interesting problem is to determine all the connected components of a graph. These may be obtained by making repeated calls to either $dfs(v)$ or $bfs(v)$, with v a vertex not yet visited. This leads to algorithm *comp* (Program 8.3) which determines all the connected components of G. The algorithm uses *dfs*. *bfs* may be used instead if desired. The computing time is not affected.

If G is represented by its adjacency lists, then the total time taken by *dfs* is $O(e)$. The output can be completed in time $O(e)$ if *dfs* keeps a list of all newly visited vertices. Since the **for** loops take $O(n)$ time, the total time to generate all the connected components is $O(n + e)$.

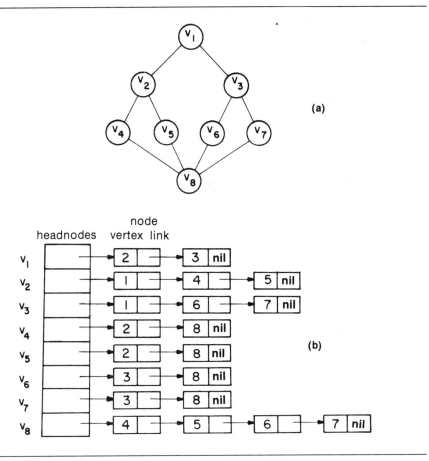

node
vertex link
headnodes

Figure 8.13 Graph G and its adjacency lists

By the definition of a connected component, there is a path between every pair of vertices in the component and there is no path in G from vertex v to w if v and w are in two different components. Hence, if A is the adjacency matrix of an undirected graph (i.e., A is symmetric) then its transitive closure A^+ may be determined in $O(n^2)$ time by first determining the connected components. $A^+[i,j] = 1$ iff there is a path from vertex i to j. For every pair of distinct vertices in the same component $A^+[i,j] = 1$. On the diagonal $A^+[i,i] = 1$ iff the component containing i has at least two vertices. We shall take a closer look at transitive closure in Section 8.3.

```
1  procedure bfs (v : integer);
2  {A breadth first search of G is carried out beginning at vertex
3  v. All vertices visited are marked as visited [i ] := true. The
4  graph G and array visited are global and visited is initialized
5  to false. initializequeue, addqueue, emptyqueue, and deletequeue
6  are procedures/functions to handle queue operations}
7  var w : integer,
8      q : queue;
9  begin
10     visited [v ] := true;
11     initializequeue (q);        {q is a queue}
12     addqueue (q,v);             {add vertex to queue}
13     while not emptyqueue (q) do
14     begin
15       deletequeue (q,v):         {remove from queue vertex v}
16       for all vertices w adjacent to v do
17         if not visited [w ]
18         then
19         begin
20           addqueue (q,w);
21           visited [w ] := true;
22         end; {of if and for}
23     end; {of while}
24  end; {of bfs}
```

Program 8.2 Algorithm *bfs*

Spanning Trees and Minimum Cost Spanning Trees

When the graph G is connected, a depth first or breadth first search starting at any vertex visits all the vertices in G. In this case the edges of G are partitioned into two sets T (for tree edges) and B (for back edges), where T is the set of edges used or traversed during the search and B the set of remaining edges. The set T may be determined by inserting the statement $T := T \cup \{(v,w)\}$ in the **then** clauses of *dfs* and *bfs*. The edges in T form a tree which includes all the vertices of G. Any tree consisting solely of edges in G and including all vertices in G is called a *spanning tree*. Figure 8.14 shows a graph and some of its spanning trees. When either *dfs* or *bfs* is used, the edges of T form a spanning tree. The spanning tree resulting from a call to *dfs* is known as a *depth first spanning tree*. When *bfs* is used, the resulting spanning tree is called a *breadth first spanning tree*.

```
1  procedure comp (g : undirectedgraph );
2  {determine the connected components of g. g has n ≥ 1 vertices.
3   visited is now a local array.}
4  var visited : array [1..n] of boolean;
5      i : integer;
6  begin
7    for i := 1 to n do
8      visited [i] := false; {initialize all vertices as unvisted}
9    for i := 1 to n do
10     if not visited [i]
11     then
12     begin
13       dfs(i); {find a component}
14       outputnewvertices : {output all newly visited vertices
15                            together with all edges incident to them}
16     end; {of if and for}
17 end; {of comp}
```

Program 8.3 Algorithm *comp*

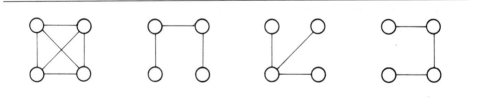

Figure 8.14 A complete graph and three of its spanning trees

Figure 8.15 shows the spanning trees resulting from a depth first and breadth first search starting at vertex v_1 in the graph of Figure 8.13. If any of the edges (v,w) in B (the set of back edges) is introduced into the spanning tree T, then a cycle is formed. This cycle consists of the edge (v,w) and all the edges on the path from w to v in T. If the edge (8,7) is introduced into the *dfs* spanning tree of Figure 8.15(a), then the resulting cycle is 8,7,3,6,8.

Spanning trees find application in obtaining an independent set of circuit equations for an electrical network. First, a spanning tree for the network is obtained. Then the edges in B (i.e., edges not in the spanning tree) are introduced one at a time. The

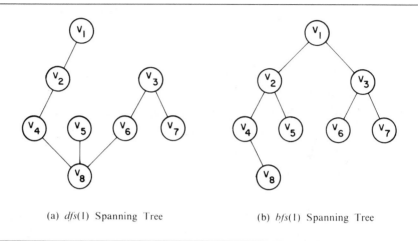

Figure 8.15 *dfs* and *bfs* spanning trees for graph of Figure 8.13

introduction of each such edge results in a cycle. Kirchoff's second law is used on this cycle to obtain a circuit equation. The cycles obtained in this way are independent (i.e., none of these cycles can be obtained by taking a linear combination of the remaining cycles) as each contains an edge from B which is not contained in any other cycle. Hence, the circuit equations so obtained are also independent. In fact, it may be shown that the cycles obtained by introducing the edges of B one at a time into the resulting spanning tree form a cycle basis and so all other cycles in the graph can be constructed by taking a linear combination of the cycles in the basis (see Harary in the references for further details).

It is not difficult to imagine other applications for spanning trees. One that is of interest arises from the property that a spanning tree is a minimal subgraph G' of G such that $V(G') = V(G)$ and G' is connected (by a minimal subgraph, we mean one with the fewest number of edges). Any connected graph with n vertices must have at least $n - 1$ edges and all connected graphs with $n - 1$ edges are trees. If the nodes of G represent cities and the edges represent possible communication links connecting two cities, then the minimum number of links needed to connect the n cities is $n - 1$. The spanning trees of G will represent all feasible choices. In any practical situation, however, the edges will have weights assigned to them. These weights might represent the cost of construction, the length of the link, etc. Given such a weighted graph one would then wish to select for construction a set of communication links that would connect all the cities and have minimum total cost or be of minimum total length. In either case the links selected will have to form a tree (assuming all weights are positive). In case this is not so, then the selection of links contains a cycle. Removal of any one of the links on this cycle will result in a link selection of less cost connecting all cities. We are, therefore, interested in finding a spanning tree of G with minimum cost. The cost of a spanning tree is the sum of the costs of the edges in that tree.

One approach to determining a minimum cost spanning tree of a graph has been given by Kruskal. In this approach a minimum cost spanning tree, T, is built edge by edge. Edges are considered for inclusion in T in nondecreasing order of their costs. An edge is included in T if it does not form a cycle with the edges already in T. Since G is connected and has n > 0 vertices, exactly $n - 1$ edges will be selected for inclusion in T.

As an example, consider the graph of Figure 8.16(a). The edges of this graph are considered for inclusion in the minimum cost spanning tree in the order (2,3), (2,4), (4,3), (2,6), (4,6), (1,2), (4,5), (1,5), and (5,6). This corresponds to the cost sequence 5, 6, 10, 11, 14, 16, 18, 19, and 33. The stages in Kruskal's algorithm are shown in Figure 8.17. The first two edges (2,3) and (2,4) are included in T. The next edge to be considered is (4,3). This edge, however, connects two vertices already connected in T and so it is rejected. The edge (2,6) is selected while (4,6) is rejected as the vertices 4 and 6 are already connected in T and the inclusion of (4,6) would result in a cycle. Finally, edges (1,2) and (4,5) are included. At this point, T has $n - 1$ edges and is a tree spanning n vertices. The spanning tree obtained (Figure 8.16(b)) has cost 56.

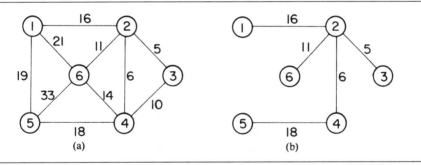

Figure 8.16 Graph and a spanning tree of minimum cost

It is somewhat surprising that this straightforward approach should always result in a minimum spanning tree. We shall soon prove that this is indeed the case. First, let us look into the details of the algorithm. For clarity, the Kruskal algorithm is written out more formally in Figure 8.18. Initially, E is the set of all edges in G. The only functions we wish to perform on this set are (1) determining an edge with minimum cost (line 3), and (2) deleting that edge (line 4). Both these functions can be performed efficiently if the edges in E are maintained as a sorted sequential list. In Chapter 7 we shall see how to sort these edges into nondecreasing order in time $O(e \log e)$, where e is the number of

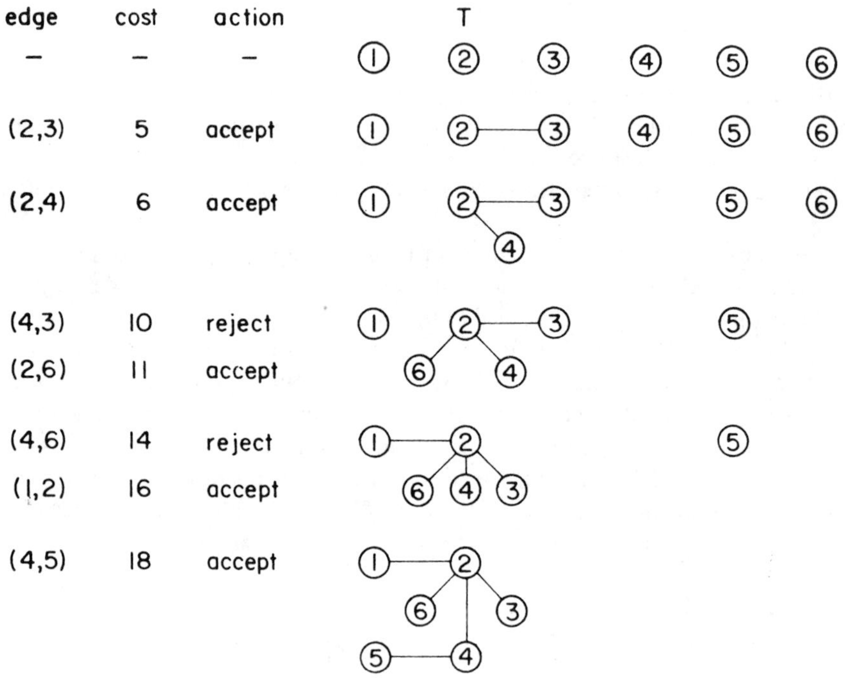

edge	cost	action	T

Figure 8.17 Stages in Kruskal's algorithm leading to a minimum cost spanning tree

edges in E. Actually, it is not essential to sort all the edges so long as the next edges for line 3 can be determined easily. This is an instance where the heap of Heapsort (Section 7.6) is ideal as it permits the next edge to be determined and deleted in $O(\log e)$ time. The construction of the heap itself takes $O(e)$ time.

In order to be able to perform steps 5 and 6 efficiently, the vertices in G should be grouped together in such a way that one may easily determine if the vertices v and w are already connected by the earlier selection of edges. In case they are, then the edge (v,w) is to be discarded. If they are not, then (v,w) is to be added to T. One possible grouping is to place all vertices in the same connected component of T into a set (all connected components of T will also be trees). Then, two vertices v,w are connected in T iff they are in the same set. For example, when the edge $(4,3)$ is to be considered, the sets would be $\{1\}$, $\{2,3,4\}$, $\{5\}$, $\{6\}$. Vertices 4 and 3 are already in the same set and so the edge $(4,3)$ is rejected. The next edge to be considered is $(2,6)$. Since vertices 2 and 6 are in different sets, the edge is accepted. This edge connects the two components $\{2,3,4\}$ and

```
1  T := ∅
2  while T contains less than n − 1 edges and E not empty do begin
3      choose an edge (v,w) from E of lowest cost;
4      delete (v,w) from E;
5      if (v,w) does not create a cycle in T
6          then add (v,w) to T
7          else discard (v,w)
8  end
9  if T contains fewer than n − 1 edges then writeln ('no spanning tree')
```

Figure 8.18 Early form of minimum spanning tree algorithm-Kruskal

{6} together and so these two sets should be unioned to obtain the set representing the new component. Using the set representation of Section 5.8 and the *find* and *union* algorithms of that section we can obtain an efficient implementation of lines 5 and 6. The computing time is, therefore, determined by the time for lines 3 and 4 which in the worst case is $O(e \log e)$. We leave the writing of the resulting algorithm as an exercise. Theorem 8.1 proves that the algorithm resulting from Figure 8.18 does yield a minimum spanning tree of G. First, we shall obtain a result that will be useful in the proof of this theorem.

Definition: A *spanning forest* of a graph $G = (V,E)$ is a collection of vertex disjoint trees $T_i = (V_i,E_i), 1 \le i \le k$ such that $V = \bigcup_{1 \le i \le k} V_i$ and $E_i \subseteq E(G), 1 \le i \le k$.

Lemma 8.1: Let $T_i = (V_i,E_i), 1 \le i \le k, k > 1$, be a spanning forest for the connected undirected graph $G = (V,E)$. Let w be a weighting function for $E(G)$ and let $e = (u,v)$ be an edge of minimum weight such that if $u \in V_i$ then $v \notin V_i$. Let $i = 1$ and $E' = \bigcup_{1 \le j \le k} E_j$. There is a spanning tree for G which includes $E' \cup \{e\}$ and has minimum weight among all spanning trees for G that include E'.

Proof: If the lemma is false, then there must be a spanning tree $T = (V,A)$ for G such that A includes E' but not e and T has a weight less than the weight of the minimum spanning tree for G including $E' \cup \{e\}$. Since T is a spanning tree, it has a path from u to v. Consequently, the addition of e to A creates a unique cycle (Exercise 22). Since $u \in V_1$ and $v \notin V_1$, it follows that there is another edge, $e' = (u',v')$ on this cycle such that $u' \in V_1$ and $v' \notin V_1$ (v' may be v). By assumption, $w(e) \le w(e')$. Deletion of the edge e' from $A \cup \{e\}$ breaks this cycle and leaves behind a spanning tree T' that includes $E' \cup \{e\}$. But since $w(e) \le w(e')$, it follows that the weight of T' is no more than the weight of T. This contradicts the assumption on T. Hence, there is no such T and the lemma is proved. □

Theorem 8.1: The algorithm described in Figure 8.18 generates a minimum spanning tree.

Proof: The proof follows from Lemma 8.1 and the fact that the algorithm begins with a spanning forest with no edges and then examines the edges of G in nondecreasing order of weight. □

8.3 SHORTEST PATHS AND TRANSITIVE CLOSURE

Graphs may be used to represent the highway structure of a state or country with vertices representing cities and edges representing sections of highway. The edges may then be assigned weights which might be either the distance between the two cities connected by the edge or the average time to drive along that section of highway. A motorist wishing to drive from city A to city B would be interested in answers to the following questions:

(1)   Is there a path from A to B ?

(2)   If there is more than one path from A to B, which is the shortest path?

The problems defined by (1) and (2) above are special cases of the path problems we shall be studying in this section. The length of a path is now defined to be the sum of the weights of the edges on that path rather than the number of edges. The starting vertex of the path will be referred to as the *source* and the last vertex the *destination*. The graphs will be digraphs to allow for one-way streets. Unless otherwise stated, we shall assume that all weights are positive.

Single Source All Destinations

In this problem we are given a directed graph $G = (V,E)$, a weighting function $w(e), w(e) \geq 0$, for the edges of G and a source vertex v_0. The problem is to determine the shortest paths from v_0 to all the remaining vertices of G. It is assumed that all the weights are positive. As an example, consider the directed graph of Figure 8.19(a). The numbers on the edges are the weights. If v_0 is the source vertex, then the shortest path from v_0 to v_1 is $v_0\ v_2\ v_3\ v_1$. The length of this path is $10 + 15 + 20 = 45$. Even though there are three edges on this path, it is shorter than the path $v_0\ v_1$ which is of length 50. There is no path from v_0 to v_5. Figure 8.19(b) lists the shortest paths from v_0 to $v_1,\ v_2,\ v_3$ and v_4. The paths have been listed in nondecreasing order of path length. If we attempt to devise an algorithm which generates the shortest paths in this order, then we can make several observations. Let S denote the set of vertices (including v_0) to which the shortest paths have already been found. For w not in S, let $dist[w]$ be the length of the shortest path starting from v_0 going through only those vertices which are in S and ending at w. We observe that:

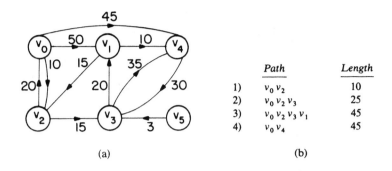

Figure 8.19 Graph and shortest paths from v_0 to all destinations

(1) If the next shortest path is to vertex u, then the path begins at v_0, ends at u, and goes through only those vertices which are in S. To prove this we must show that all of the intermediate vertices on the shortest path to u must be in S. Assume there is a vertex w on this path that is not in S. Then, the v_0 to u path also contains a path from v_0 to w which is of length less than the v_0 to u path. By assumption the shortest paths are being generated in nondecreasing order of path length, and so the shorter path v_0 to w must already have been generated. Hence, there can be no intermediate vertex which is not in S.

(2) The destination of the next path generated must be that vertex u which has the minimum distance, $dist[u]$, among all vertices not in S. This follows from the definition of $dist$ and observation (1). In case there are several vertices not in S with the same $dist$, then any of these may be selected.

(3) Having selected a vertex u as in (2) and generated the shortest v_0 to u path, vertex u becomes a member of S. At this point the length of the shortest paths starting at v_0, going through vertices only in S and ending at a vertex w not in S may decrease; i.e., the value of $dist[w]$ may change. If it does change, then it must be due to a shorter path starting at v_0 going to u and then to w. The intermediate vertices on the v_0 to u path and the u to w path must all be in S. Further, the v_0 to u path must be the shortest such path, otherwise $dist[w]$ is not defined properly. Also, the u to w path can be chosen so as to not contain any intermediate vertices. Therefore, we may conclude that if $dist[w]$ is to change (i.e., decrease), then it is because of the path from v_0 to u to w where the path from v_0 to u is the shortest such path and the path from u to w is the edge $<u,w>$. The length of this path is $dist[u] = $ length $(<u,w>)$.

The algorithm *shortestpath* as first given by Dijkstra makes use of these observations to determine the cost of the shortest paths from v_0 to all other vertices in G. The actual generation of the paths is a minor extension of the algorithm and is left as an exercise. It is assumed that the n vertices of G are numbered 1 through n. The set s is maintained as a boolean array with $s[i]$ = **false** if vertex i is not in S and $s[i]$ = **true** if it is. It is assumed that the graph itself is represented by its cost adjacency matrix with $cost[i,j]$ being the weight of the edge $<i,j>$. $cost[i,j]$ will be set to some large number, **maxint**, in case the edge $<i,j>$ is not in $E(G)$. For $i = j$, $cost[i,j]$ may be set to any nonnegative number without affecting the outcome of the algorithm. Program 8.4 describes the algorithm completely. The data types *adjacencymatrix* and *distance* are as below.

type *adjacencymatrix* = **array** [1..*maxn*, 1..*maxn*] **of integer**;
    distance = **array** [1..*maxn*] **of integer**;

Analysis of Algorithm *shortestpath*

From our earlier discussion, it is easy to see that the algorithm works. The time taken by the algorithm on a graph with n vertices is $O(n^2)$. To see this, note that the **for** loop of line 12 takes $O(n)$ time. The **for** loop of line 19 is executed $n-2$ times. Each execution of this loop requires $O(n)$ time at line 21 to select the next vertex and again at lines 24-27 to update *dist*. So the total time for this loop is $O(n^2)$. In case a list of T vertices currently not in S is maintained, then the number of nodes on this list would at any time be $n-i$. This would speed up lines 21 and 24-27, but the asympototic time would remain $O(n^2)$. This and other variations of the algorithm are explored in the exercsies.

Any shortest path algorithm must examine each edge in the graph at least once since any of the edges could be in a shortest path. Hence, the minimum possible time for such an algorithm would be $O(e)$. Since cost adjacency matrices were used to represent the graph, it takes $O(n^2)$ time just to determine which edges are in G and so any shortest path algorithm using this representation must take $O(n^2)$. For this representation, then, algorithm *shortestpath* is optimal to within a constant factor. Even if a change to adjacency lists is made, only the overall time for the **for** loop of lines 24-27 can be brought down to $O(e)$ (since the *dist* can change only for those vertices adjacent from u). The total time for line 21 remains $O(n^2)$.

Example 8.1: Consider the eight vertex digraph of Figure 8.20(a) with cost adjacency matrix as in 8.20(b). The values of *dist* and the vertices selected at each iteration of the **while** loop of line 21 for finding all the shortest paths from Boston are shown in Figure 8.21. Note that the algorithm terminates when only seven of the eight vertices are in S. By the definition of *dist*, the distance of the last vertex, in this case Los Angeles, is correct as the shortest path from Boston to Los Angeles can go through only the remaining six vertices. □

```
1  procedure shortestpath (v : integer; cost : adjacencymatrix ;
2                              var dist : distance ; n : integer);
3  {dist [j ], 1 ≤ j ≤n is set to the length of the shortest path
4    from vertex v to vertex j in a digraph g with n vertices.
5    dist [v ] is set to zero. g is represented by its cost adjacency
6    matrix, cost [1 .. n, 1 .. n ]}
7  var s : array [1 .. maxn] of boolean;
8      i : integer;
9      u : integer;
10     w : integer;
11 begin
12    for i := 1 to  n do {initialize set S to empty}
13    begin
14      s [i ] := false;
15      dist [i ] := cost [v,i ];
16    end;
17    s [v ] := true;
18    dist [v ] := 0;
19    for i := 1 to n - 2 do {determine n - 1 paths from vertex v}
20    begin
21      u := choose (dist, n); {choose returns a value u:
22              dist [u ] = minimum [dist [w ]] where s [w ] = false}
23      s [u ] := true;
24      for w := 1 to n do
25        if not s [w ] then
26          if dist [u ] + cost [u,w ] < dist [w ]
27                then dist [w ] := dist [u ] + cost [u,w ];
28    end; {of for i}
29 end; {of shortestpath}
```

Program 8.4 Algorithm *shortestpath*

All Pairs Shortest Paths

The *all pairs shortest path problem* calls for finding the shortest paths between all
pairs of vertices $v_i, v_j, i \neq j$. One possible solution to this is to apply the algorithm *shortestpath* n times, once with each vertex in $V(G)$ as the source. The total time taken
would be $O(n^3)$. For the all pairs problem, we can obtain a conceptually simpler algorithm which will work even when some edges in G have negative weights so long as G
has no cycles with negative length. The computing time of this algorithm will still be
$O(n^3)$ though the constant factor will be smaller.

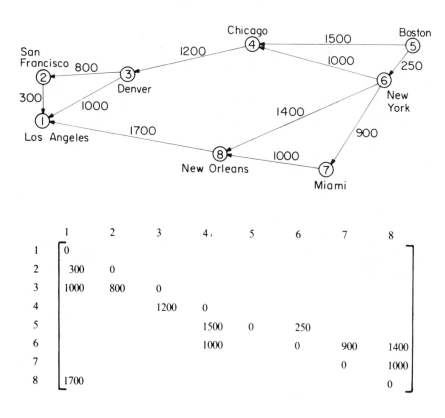

Figure 8.20 Digraph for Example 8.1

The graph G is represented by its cost adjacency matrix with $cost\,[i,i] = 0$ and $cost\,[i,j] = \textbf{maxint}$ in case edge $<i,j>, i \neq j$ is not in G. Define $A^k[i,j]$ to be the cost of the shortest path from i to j going through no intermediate vertex of index greater than k. Then, $A^n[i,j]$ will be the cost of the shortest i to j path in G since G contains no vertex with index greater than n. $A^0[i,j]$ is just $cost\,[i,j]$ since the only i to j paths allowed can have no intermediate vertices on them. The basic idea in the all pairs algorithm is to successively generate the matrices $A^0, A^1, A^2, \dots, A^n$. If we have already generated A^{k-1}, then we may generate A^k by realizing that for any pair of vertices i,j either (1) the shortest path from i to j going through no vertex with index greater than k does not go through the vertex with index k and so its cost is $A^{k-1}[i,j]$; or (2) the shortest such path does go through vertex k. Such a path consists of a path from i to k and another one from

Iteration	S	Vertex Selected	dist	LA [1]	SF [2]	D [3]	C [4]	B [5]	NY [6]	M [7]	NO [8]
Initial		—		$+\infty$	$+\infty$	$+\infty$	1500	0	250	$+\infty$	$+\infty$
1	5	6		$+\infty$	$+\infty$	$+\infty$	1250	0	250	1150	1650
2	5,6	7		$+\infty$	$+\infty$	$+\infty$	1250	0	250	1150	1650
3	5,6,7	4		$+\infty$	$+\infty$	2450	1250	0	250	1150	1650
4	5,6,7,4	8		3350	$+\infty$	2450	1250	0	250	1150	1650
5	5,6,7,4,8	3		3350	3250	2450	1250	0	250	1150	1650
6	5,6,7,4,8,3	2		3350	3250	2450	1250	0	250	1150	1650
	5,6,7,4,8,3,2										

Figure 8.21 Action of *Shortestpath*

k to j. These paths must be the shortest paths from i to k and from k to j going through no vertex with index greater than $k-1$, and so their costs are $A^{k-1}[i,k]$ and $A^{k-1}[k,j]$. Note that this is true only if G has no cycle with negative length containing vertex k. If this is not true, then the shortest i to j path going through no vertices of index greater than k may make several cycles from k to k and thus have a length substantially less than $A^{k-1}[i,k] + A^{k-1}[k,j]$ (see Example 8.2). Thus, we obtain the following formulas for $A^k[i,j]$:

$$A^k[i,j] = \min\{A^{k-1}[i,j], A^{k-1}[i,k] + A^{k-1}[k,j]\}, k\geq1$$

and

$$A^0[i,j] = COST[i,j].$$

Example 8.2: Figure 8.22 shows a digraph together with its matrix A^0. For this graph $A^2[1,3]\neq\min\{A^1[1,3], A^1[1,2] + A^1[2,3]\} = 2$. Instead we see that $A^2[1,3] = -\infty$ as the length of the path

$$1, 2, 1, 2, 1, 2, ..., 1, 2, 3$$

can be made arbitrarily small. This is so because of the presence of the cycle 1, 2, 1 which has a length of -1. □

The algorithm *allcosts* (Program 8.5) computes $A^n[i,j]$. The computation is done in place using the array a. The reason this computation can be carried out in place is that $A^k[i,k] = A^{k-1}[i,k]$ and $A^k[k,j] = A^{k-1}[k,j]$ and so the in place computation does not alter the outcome.

Figure 8.22 Graph with negative cycle

```
1 procedure allcosts (cost, var a : adjacencymatrix; n : integer);
2 {cost [1 ..n, 1 .. n] is the cost adjacency matrix of a graph with n
3   vertices; a [i,j] is the cost of the shortest path between vertices
4   vᵢ,vⱼ cost [i,i] = 0, 1 ≤ i ≤ n}
5 var i : integer;
6     j : integer;
7     k : integer;
8 begin
9   for i := 1 to n do
10    for j := 1 to n do
11      a [i,j] := cost [i,j]; {copy cost into a}
12    for k := 1 to n do {for a path with highest vertex index k}
13      for i := 1 to n do {for all possible pairs of vertices}
14        for j := 1 to n do
15          if (a [i,k] + a [k,j]) < a [i,j]
16            then a [i,j] := a [i,k] + a [k,j];
17 end; {of allcosts}
```

Program 8.5 Algorithm *allcosts*

This algorithm is especially easy to analyze because the looping is independent of the data in the matrix a.

The total time for procedure *allcosts* is $O(n^3)$. An exercise examines the extensions needed to actually obtain the (i,j) paths with these lengths. Some speed up can be obtained by noticing that the innermost **for** loop needs be executed only when $a[i,k]$ and $a[k,j]$ are not equal to **maxint**.

Example 8.3: Using the graph of Figure 8.23(a) we obtain the cost matrix of Figure 8.23(b). The initial a matrix, A^0, plus its value after three iterations A^1, A^2, A^3 is given in Figure 8.24. □

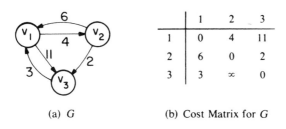

(a) *G*   (b) Cost Matrix for *G*

Figure 8.23 Directed graph and its cost matrix

A^0	1	2	3
1	0	4	11
2	6	0	2
3	3	∞	0

A^1	1	2	3
1	0	4	11
2	6	0	2
3	3	7	0

A^2	1	2	3
1	0	4	6
2	6	0	2
3	3	7	0

A^3	1	2	3
1	0	4	6
2	5	0	2
3	3	7	0

Figure 8.24 Matrices A^k produced by *allcosts* for the digraph of Figure 8.23

Transitive Closure

A problem related to the all pairs shortest path problem is that of determining for every
pair of vertices i,j in G the existence of a path from i to j. Two cases are of interest, one
when all path lengths (i.e, the number of edges on the path) are required to be positive
and the other when path lengths are to be nonnegative. If A is the adjacency matrix of G,
then the Matrix A^+ having the property $A^+[i,j] = 1$ if there is a path of length > 0 from i
to j and 0 otherwise is called the *transitive closure* matrix of G. The matrix A^* with the
property $A^*[i,j]=1$ if there is a path of length ≥ 0 from i to j and 0 otherwise is the
reflexive transitive closure matrix of G.

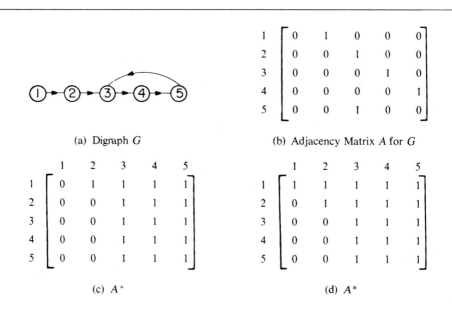

(a) Digraph G

(b) Adjacency Matrix A for G

(c) A⁺

(d) A*

Figure 8.25 Graph G and its adjacency matrix A, A⁺ and A*

Figure 8.25 shows A^+ and A^* for a digraph. Clearly, the only difference between A^* and A^+ is in the terms on the diagonal. $A^+[i,i]=1$ iff there is a cycle of length >1 containing vertex i while $A^*[i,i]$ is always one as there is a path of length 0 from i to i. If we use algorithm *allcosts* with $cost[i,j]=1$ if $<i,j>$ is an edge in G and $cost[i,j]=+\infty$ if $<i,j>$ is not if G, then we can easily obtain A^+ from the final matrix A by letting $A^+[i,j]=1$ iff $A[i,j]<+\infty$. A^* can be obtained from A^+ by setting all diagonal elements equal to 1. The total time is $O(n^3)$. Some simplification is achieved by slightly modifying the algorithm. In this modification the computation of lines 15 and 16 of *allcosts* becomes $a[i,j]:=a[i,j]$ **or** $(a[i,k]$ **and** $a[k,j])$ and $cost[i,j]$ is just the adjacency matrix of G. With this modification, a need only be a **boolean** matrix and then the final matrix A will be A^+.

8.4 ACTIVITY NETWORKS, TOPOLOGICAL SORT, AND CRITICAL PATHS

Topological Sort

All but the simplest of projects can be subdivided into several subprojects called activities. The successful completion of these activities will result in the completion of the entire project. A student working towards a degree in Computer Science will have to complete several courses successfully. The project in this case is to complete the major, and the activities are the individual courses that have to be taken. Figure 8.26 lists the courses needed for a computer science major at a hypothetical university. Some of these courses may be taken independently of others while other courses have prerequisites and can be taken only if all their prerequisites have already been taken. The data structures course cannot be started until certain programming and math courses have been completed. Thus, prerequisites define precedence relations between courses. The relationships defined may be more clearly represented using a directed graph in which the vertices represent courses and the directed edges represent prerequisites. This graph has an edge $<i,j>$ iff course i is a prerequisite for course j.

Definition: A directed graph G in which the vertices represent tasks or activities and the edges represent precedence relations between tasks is an *activity on vertex network* or AOV network.

Definition: Vertex i in an AOV network G is a *predecessor* of vertex j iff there is a directed path from vertex i to vertex j. i is an *immediate predecessor* of j iff $<i,j>$ is an edge in G. If i is a predecessor of j, then j is a *successor* of i. If i is an immediate predecessor of j, then j is an *immediate successor* of i.

Figure 8.26(b) is the AOV network corresponding to the courses of Figure 8.26(a). C3, C4, and C10 are the immediate predecessors of C7. C2, C3, and C4 are the immediate successors of C1. C12 is a successor of C4 but not an immediate successor. The precedence relation defined by the set of edges on the set of vertices is readily seen to be transitive. (Recall that a relation $\cdot$ is transitive iff it is the case that for all triples i,j,k, $i \cdot j$ and $j \cdot k \Rightarrow i \cdot k$.) In order for an AOV network to represent a feasible project, the precedence relation should also be irreflexive.

Definition: A relation $\cdot$ is *irreflexive* on a set S if for no element x in S it is the case that $x \cdot x$. A precedence relation which is both transitive and irreflexive is a *partial order*.

If the precedence relation is not irreflexive, then there is an activity which is a predecessor of itself and so must be completed before it can be started. This is clearly impossible. When there are no inconsistencies of this type, the project is feasible. Given an AOV network one of our concerns would be to determine whether or not the

Course Number	Course Name	Prerequisites
C1	Introduction to Programming	None
C2	Numerical Analysis	C1, C14
C3	Data Structures	C1, C14
C4	Assembly Language	C1, C13
C5	Automata Theory	C15
C6	Artificial Intelligence	C3
C7	Computer Graphics	C3, C4, C10
C8	Machine Arithmetic	C4
C9	Analysis of Algorithms	C3
C10	Higher Level Languages	C3, C4
C11	Compiler Writing	C10
C12	Operating Systems	C11
C13	Analytic Geometry and Calculus I	None
C14	Analytic Geometry and Calculus II	C13
C15	Linear Algebra	C14

(a) Courses Needed for a Computer Science Degree at Some Hypothetical University

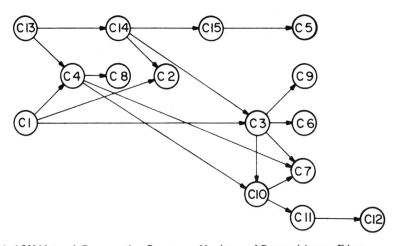

(b) AOV-Network Representing Courses as Vertices and Prerequisites as Edges

Figure 8.26 An activity on vertex network

precedence relation defined by its edges is irreflexive. This is identical to determining whether or not the network contains any directed cycles. A directed graph with no directed cycles is an *acyclic* graph. Our algorithm to test an AOV network for feasiblility will also generate a linear ordering, $v_{i_1}, v_{i_2}, ..., v_{i_n}$, of the vertices (activities). This linear ordering will have the property that if i is a predecessor of j in the network then i precedes j in the linear ordering. A linear ordering with this property is called a *topological order.* For the network of Figure 8.26(b) two of the possible topological orders are: C1, C13, C4, C8, C14, C15, C5, C2, C3, C10, C7, C11, C12, C6, C9 and C13, C14, C15, C5, C1, C4, C8, C2, C3, C10, C7, C6, C9, C11, C12. If a student were taking just one course per term, then he would have to take them in topological order. If the AOV network represented the different tasks involved in assembling an automobile, then these tasks would be carried out in topological order on an assembly line. The algorithm to sort the tasks into topological order is straightforward and proceeds by listing out a vertex in the network that has no predecessor. Then, this vertex together with all edges leading out from it is deleted from the network. These two steps are repeated until either all vertices have been listed or all remaining vertices in the network have predecessors and so none can be removed. In this case there is a cycle in the network and the project is infeasible. Figure 8.27 is a crude form of the algorithm.

---

1   input the AOV network. Let n be the number of vertices.
2   **for** $i := 1$ **to** n **do** {output the vertices}
3   **begin**
4   **if** every vertex has a predecessor
5   **then** [the network has a cycle and is infeasible. **stop**];
6   pick a vertex v which has no predecessors;
7   output v;
8   delete v and all edges leading out of v from the network;
9   **end**;

Figure 8.27 Design of a topological sorting algorithm

Trying this out on the network of Figure 8.28 we see that the first vertex to be picked in line 4 is v_1, as it is the only one with no predecessors. v_1 and the edges $<v_1,v_2>$, $<v_1,v_3>$, and $<v_1,v_4>$ are deleted. In the resulting network (Figure 8.28(b)), v_2, v_3, and v_4 have no predecessor. Any of these can be the next vertex in the topological order. Assume that v_4 is picked. Deletion of v_4 and the edges $<v_4,v_6>$ and $<v_4,v_5>$ results in the network of Figure 8.28(c). Either v_2 or v_3 may next be picked. Figure 8.28 shows the progress of the algorithm on the network. In order to obtain a complete algorithm that can be easily translated into a computer program, it is necessary to specify the data representation for the AOV network. The choice of a data representation, as always, depends on the functions you wish to perform. In this problem, the functions are: (1) decide whether a vertex has any predecessors (line 4), and (2) delete a vertex together with all its incident edges. (1) is efficiently done if for each vertex a count of the number of its immediate predecessors is kept. (2) is easily implemented if the network is represented by its adjacency lists. Then the deletion of all edges leading out of vertex v can be carried out by decreasing the predecessor count of all vertices on its adjacency list. Whenever the count of a vertex drops to zero, that vertex can be placed onto a list of vertices with a zero count. Then the selection in line 6 just requires removal of a vertex from this list. Filling in these details into the algorithm of Figure 8.27, we obtain the Pascal program *topologicalorder* (Program 8.6).

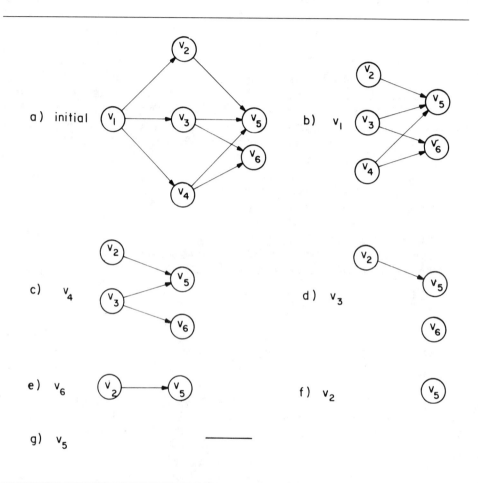

Figure 8.28 Action of algorithm of Figure 8.27 on an AOV network

The algorithm assumes that the network is represented by adjacency lists. But now the headnodes of these lists contain two fields: *count* and *link*. The data types needed are

type *nextnode* = ↑*node*;
    node = **record**
            vertex : **integer**;

             link : *nextnode*;
        end;
  headnodes = **record**
                  count : **integer**;
                  link : *nextnode*;
            end;
  adjacencylists = **array** [1 .. *n*] **of** *headnodes*;

The *count* field contains the in-degree of that vertex and *link* is a pointer to the first node on the adjacency list. Each list node has two fields: *vertex* and *link*. *count* fields can be easily set up at the time of input. When edge $<i,j>$ is input, the count of vertex j is incremented by 1. The list of vertices with zero count is maintained as a stack. A queue could have been used but a stack is slightly simpler. The stack is linked through the *count* field of the headnodes since this field is of no use after the *count* has become zero. Figure 8.29(a) shows the input to the algorithm in the case of the network of Figure 8.28(a).

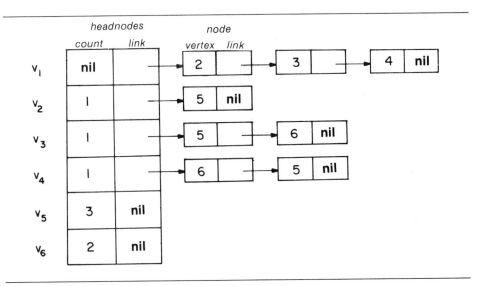

Figure 8.29 Input for procedure *topologicalorder*

```
 1  procedure topologicalorder (var adlist : adjacencylists ; n : integer);
 2  {The n vertices of an AOV network are listed in topological order.
 3    The network is represented as a set of adjacency lists with
 4    adlist [i ].count = the in-degree of vertex i.}
 5  var i : integer;
 6      j : integer;
 7      k : integer;
 8      top : integer;
 9      ptr : nextnode;
10      done : boolean;
11  begin
12    top := 0; {initialize stack}
13    for  :=  1 to n do {create a linked stack of vertices with}
14      if adlist [i ].count = 0 {no predecessors}
15      then
16      begin
17        adlist [i ].count := top;
18        top := i;
19      end;
20    i := 1;
21    done := false;
22    while ((i <= n) and not done) do
23    begin {print the vertices in topological order}
24      if top = 0
25      then
26      begin
27        writln('network has a cycle');
28        done := true;
29      end
30      else
31      j := top;
32      top := adlist [top ].count ; {unstack a vertex}
33      writeln (j);
34      ptr := adlist [j ].link;
35      while ptr < > nil do
36      begin {decrease the count of the successor vertices of j}
37        k := ptr ↑. vertex ; {k is a successor of j}
38        adlist [k ].count := adlist [k ].count − 1; {decrease count}
39        if adlist [k ].count = 0 {add vertex k to stack}
40        then
41        begin
42          adlist [k ].count := top;
43          top := k;
```

```
44          end; {of if};
45          ptr := ptr↑.link;
46          end; {of while ptr < > nil}
47       i := i + 1;
48       end; {of while (i ≤ n) and not done}
49   end; {of topologicalorder}
```

Program 8.6 Procedure *topologicalorder*

As a result of a judicious choice of data structures the algorithm is very efficient. For a network with n vertices and e edges, the loop of lines 13-19 takes $O(n)$ time; lines 24-34 take $O(n)$ time over the entire algorithm; the **while** loop takes time $O(d_i)$ for each vertex i, where d_i is the out-degree of vertex i. Since this loop is encountered once for each vertex output, the total time for this part of the algorithm is $O((\sum_{i=1}^{n} d_i)+n) = O(e + n)$. Hence, the asymptotic computing time of the algorithm is $O(e+n)$. It is linear in the size of the problem!

Critical Paths

An activity network closely related to the AOV network is the activity on edge or AOE network. The tasks to be performed on a project are represented by directed edges. Vertices in the network represent events. Events signal the completion of certain activities. Activities represented by edges leaving a vertex cannot be started until the event at that vertex has occurred. An event occurs only when all activities entering it have been completed. Figure 8.30(a) is an AOE network for a hypothetical project with 11 tasks or activities $a_1, ..., a_{11}$. There are nine events $v_1, v_2, ..., v_9$. The events v_1 and v_9 may be interpreted as "start project" and "finish project," respectively. Figure 8.30(b) gives interpretations for some of the nine events. The number associated with each activity is the time needed to perform that activity. Thus, activity a_1 requires 6 days while a_{11} requires 4 days. Usually, these times are only estimates. Activities a_1, a_2, and a_3 may be carried out concurrently after the start of the project. a_4, a_5, and a_6 cannot be started until events v_2, v_3, and v_4, respectively, occur. a_7 and a_8 can be carried out concurrently after the occurrence of event v_5 (i.e., after a_4 and a_5 have been completed). In case additional ordering constraints are to be put on the activities, dummy activities whose time is zero may be introduced. Thus, if we desire that activities a_7 and a_8 not start until both events v_5 and v_6 have occurred, a dummy activity a_{12} represented by an edge $<v_6, v_5>$ may be introduced. Activity networks of the AOE type have proved very useful in the performance evaluation of several types of projects. This evaluation includes determining such facts about the project as what is the least amount of time in which the project may be completed (assuming there are no cycles in the network); which activities should be speeded up in order to reduce completion time; etc.

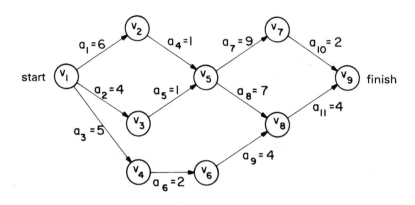

event	interpretation
v_1	start of project
v_2	completion of activity a_1
v_5	completion of activities a_4 and a_5
v_8	completion of activities a_8 and a_9
v_9	completion of project

Figure 8.30 An AOE network

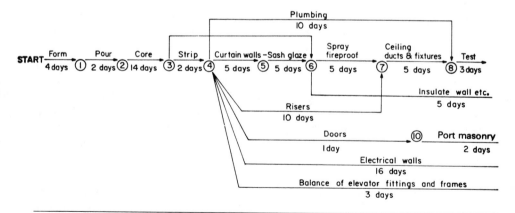

Figure 8.31 AOE network for the construction of a typical floor in a multistory building [Engineering News-Record (McGraw-Hill Book Company, Inc., Jan. 26, 1961).]

Several sophisticated techniques such as PERT (performance evaluation and review technique), CPM (critical path method), and RAMPS (resource allocation and multiproject scheduling) have been developed to evaluate network models of projects. CPM was originally developed in connection with maintenance and construction projects. Figure 8.31 shows a network used by the Perinia Corporation of Boston in 1961 to model the construction of a floor in a multistory building. PERT was originally designed for use in the development of the Polaris missile system.

Since the activities in an AOE network can be carried out in parallel the minimum time to complete the project is the length of the longest path from the start vertex to the finish vertex (the length of a path is the sum of the times of activities on this path). A path of longest length is a *critical path*. The path v_1, v_2, v_5, v_7, v_9 is a critical path in the network of Figure 8.30(a). The length of this critical path is 18. A network may have more than one critical path (the path v_1, v_2, v_5, v_8, v_9 is also critical). The *earliest time* an event v_i can occur is the length of the longest path from the start vertex v_1 to the vertex v_i. The earliest time event v_5 can occur is 7. The earliest time an event can occur determines the *earliest start time* for all activities represented by edges leaving that vertex. Denote this time by $e(i)$ for activity a_i. For example, $e(7) = e(8) = 7$. For every

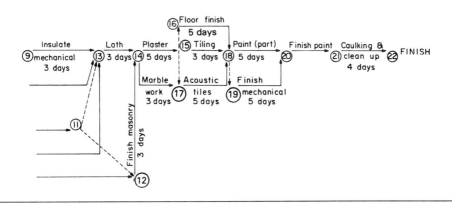

activity a_i we may also define the *latest time*, $l(i)$, an activity may start without increasing the project duration (i.e., length of the longest path from start to finish). In Figure 8.30(a) we have $e(6)=5$ and $l(6)=8$, $e(8)=7$ and $l(8)=7$. All activities for which $e(i)=l(i)$ are called *critical activities*. The difference $l(i)-e(i)$ is a measure of the criticality of an activity. It gives the time by which an activity may be delayed or slowed without increasing the total time needed to finish the project. If activity a_6 is slowed down to take 2 extra days, this will not affect the project finish time. Clearly, all activities on a critical path are critical and speeding noncritical activities will not reduce the project duration.

The purpose of critical path analysis is to identify critical activities so that resources may be concentrated on these activities in an attempt to reduce project finish time. Speeding a critical activity will not result in a reduced project length unless that activity is on all critical paths. In Figure 8.30(a) the activity a_{11} is critical but speeding it up so that it takes only 3 days instead of 4 does not reduce the finish time to 17 days. This is so because there is another critical path v_1, v_2, v_5, v_7, v_9 that does not contain this activity. The activities a_1 and a_4 are on all critical paths. Speeding a_1 by 2 days reduces the critical path length to 16 days. Critical path methods have proved very valuable in evaluating project performance and identifying bottlenecks.

Critical path analysis can also be carried out with AOV networks. The length of a path would now be the sum of the activity times of the vertices on that path. For each activity or vertex, we could analogously define the quantities $e(i)$ and $l(i)$. Since the activity times are only estimates, it is necessary to re-evaluate the project during several stages of its completion as more accurate estimates of activity times become available. These changes in activity times could make previously noncritical activities critical and vice versa. Before ending our discussion on activity networks, let us design an algorithm to evaluate $e(i)$ and $l(i)$ for all activities in an AOE network. Once these quantities are known, then the critical activities may be easily identified. Deleting all noncritical activities from the AOE network, all critical paths may be found by just generating all paths from the start to finish vertex (all such paths will include only critical activities and so must be critical, and since no noncritical activity can be on a critical path, the network with noncritical activities removed contains all critical paths present in the original network).

In obtaining the $e(i)$ and $l(i)$ for the activities of an AOE network, it is easier to first obtain the earliest event occurrence time, $ee[j]$, and latest event occurrence time, $le[j]$, for all events, j, in the network. Then if activity a_i is represented by edge $<k,l>$, we can compute $e(i)$ and $l(i)$ from the formulas

$$e(i)=ee[k]$$

and (8.1)

$$l(i)=le[l]-\text{duration of activity} a_i$$

The times $ee[j]$ and $le[j]$ are computed in two stages: a forward stage and a backward stage. During the forward stage we start with $ee[1]=0$ and compute the remaining early start times, using the formula

$$ee[j] = \max_{i \varepsilon P(j)} \{ee[i] + \text{duration of} <i,j> \} \qquad (8.2)$$

where $P(j)$ is the set of all vertices adjacent to vertex j. In case this computation is carried out in topological order, the early start times of all predecessors of j would have been computed prior to the computation of $ee[j]$. The algorithm to do this is obtained easily from algorithm *topologicalorder* by inserting the step

> **if** $ee[k] < ee[j] + ptr\uparrow.dur$
> **then** $ee[k] := ee[j] + ptr\uparrow.dur;$

between lines 38 and 39. It is assumed that the array ee is initialized to zero and that dur is another field in the adjacency list nodes which contains the activity duration. This modification results in the evaluation of Eq. (8.2) in parallel with the generation of a topological order. $ee(j)$ is updated each time the $ee(i)$ of one of its predecessors is known (i.e., when i is ready for output). The step **writeln(j)** of line 33 may be omitted.

To illustrate the working of the modified *topologicalorder* algorithm let us try it out on the network of Figure 8.30(a). The adjacency lists for the network are shown in Figure 8.32(a). The order of nodes on these lists determines the order in which vertices will be considered by the algorithm. At the outset the early start time for all vertices is 0, and the start vertex is the only one in the stack. When the adjacency list for this vertex is processed, the early start time of all vertices adjacent from v_1 is updated. Since vertices 2, 3 and 4 are now in the stack, all their predecessors have been processed and Eq. (8.2) evaluated for these three vertices. $ee[6]$ is the next one determined. When vertex v_6 is being processed, $ee[8]$ is updated to 11. This, however, is not the true value for $ee[8]$ since Eq. (8.2) has not evaluated over all predecessors of v_8 (v_5 has not yet been considered). This does not matter since v_8 cannot get stacked until all its predecessors have been processed. $ee[5]$ is next updated to 5 and finally to 7. At this point $ee[5]$ has been determined as all the predecessors of v_5 have been examined. The values of $ee[7]$ and $ee[8]$ are next obtained. $ee[9]$ is ultimately determined to be 18, the length of a critical path. You may readily verify that when a vertex is put into the stack its early time has been correctly computed. The insertion of the new statement does not change the asymptotic computing time; it remains $O(e+n)$.

In the backward stage the values of $le[i]$ are computed using a procedure analogous to that used in the forward stage. We start with $le[n]=ee[n]$ and use the equation

$$le[j] = \min_{i \varepsilon S(j)} \{le[i] - \text{duration of} <j,i> \} \qquad (8.3)$$

where $S(j)$ is the set of vertices adjacent from vertex j. The initial values for $le[i]$ may

Line	Queue	Run 1	Run 2	Run 3	Output	Next Block Being Read From
1		20 25	23 29	24 28	no output	run 1
2	25	26 28	29	24 28	20 23	run 1
3		26 28	29	28	24 25	run 3
4		29 30	29	28	26 28	run 2
5		30	29	31 33	28 29	run 1
6		33 +∞	34 36	31 33	29 30	run 3
7		+∞	34 36	33	31 33	run 2
8		+∞	36	40 43	33 34	run 3
9		+∞	60	40 43	36 38	run 2
10		+∞	60	+∞	40 43	no next
11	+∞		70 +∞	+∞	50 60	no next
12			+∞	+∞	70 +∞	

Figure 8.32 Action of Modified Topological Order

be set to $ee[n]$. Basically, Eq. (8.3) says that if $<j,i>$ is an activity and the latest start time for event i is $le[i]$, then event j must occur no later than $le[i]$ – duration of $<j,i>$. Before $le[j]$ can be computed for some event j, the latest event time for all successor events (i.e., events adjacent from j) must be computed. These times can be obtained in a manner identical to the computation of the early times by using inverse adjacency lists and inserting the step $le[k]:=\min\{le[k],le[j]-ptr\uparrow.dur\}$ at the same place as before in algorithm *topologicalorder*. The *count* field of a headnode will initially be the out-degree of the vertex.

Figure 8.33 describes the process on the network of Figure 8.30(a). In case the forward stage has already been carried out and a topological ordering of the vertices obtained, then the values of $le[i]$ can be computed directly, using equation (8.3), by performing the computations in the reverse topological order. The topological order generated in Figure 8.32(b) is $v_1, v_4, v_6, v_3, v_2, v_5, v_8, v_7, v_9$. We may compute the values of $le[i]$ in the order 9, 7, 8, 5, 2, 3, 6, 4, 1 as all successors of an event precede that event in this order. In practice, one would usually compute both ee and le. The procedure would then be to compute ee first using algorithm *topologicalorder* modified as discussed for the forward stage and to then compute le directly from Eq. (8.3) in reverse topological order.

Using the values of ee (Figure 8.32) and of le (Figure 8.33 and Eq. 8.1) we may compute the early and late times $e(i)$ and $l(i)$ and the degree of criticality of each task. Figure 8.34 gives the values. The critical activities are a_1, a_4, a_7, a_8, a_{10}, and a_{11}. Deleting all noncritical activities from the network we get the directed graph of Figure 8.35. All paths from v_1 to v_9 in this graph are critical paths and there are no critical paths in the original network that are not paths in the graph of Figure 8.35.

As a final remark on activity networks we note that the algorithm *topologicalorder* detects only directed cycles in the network. There may be other flaws, such as vertices not reachable from the start vertex (Figure 8.36). When a critical path analysis is carried out on such networks, there will be several vertices with $ee[i]=0$. Since all activity times are assumed >0 only the start vertex can have $ee[i]=0$. Hence, critical path analysis can also be used to detect this kind of fault in project planning.

8.5 REFERENCES AND SELECTED READINGS

Euler's original paper on the Koenigsberg bridge problem makes interesting reading. This paper has been reprinted in:

"Leonhard Euler and the Koenigsberg Bridges," *Scientific American*, vol. 189, no. 1, July 1953, pp. 66-70.

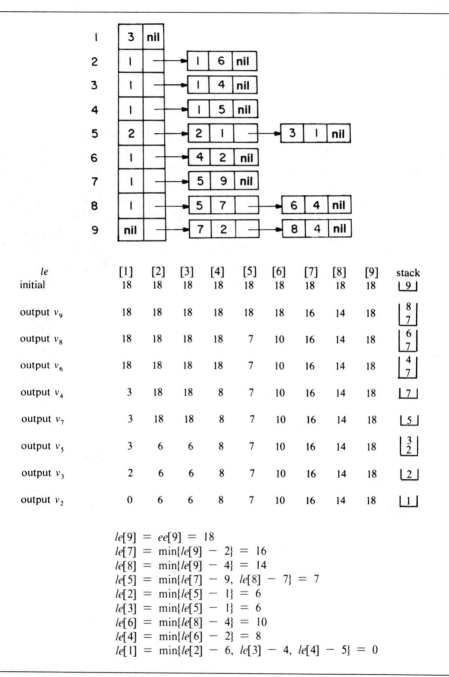

Figure 8.33 Inverted Adjacency Lists for AOE Network of Figure 8.30(a)

activity	e	l	$l - e$
a_1	0	0	0
a_2	0	2	2
a_3	0	3	3
a_4	6	6	0
a_5	4	6	2
a_6	5	8	3
a_7	7	7	0
a_8	7	7	0
a_9	7	10	3
a_{10}	16	16	0
a_{11}	14	14	0

Figure 8.34 Early, late, and criticality values

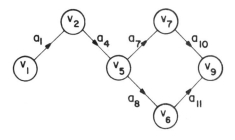

Figure 8.35 Graph obtained after deleting all noncritical activities

Good general references for this chapter are:

Graph Theory, by F. Harary, Addison-Wesley, Reading, Massachusetts, 1972.

The Theory of Graphs and its Applications, by C. Berge, John Wiley, 1962.

Further algorithms on graphs may be found in:

The Design and Analysis of Computer Algorithms, by A. Aho, J. Hopcroft and J. Ullman, Addison-Wesley, Reading, Massachusetts, 1974.

Graph Theory with Applications to Engineering and Computer Science, by N. Deo, Prentice-Hall, Englewood Cliffs, New Jersey, 1974.

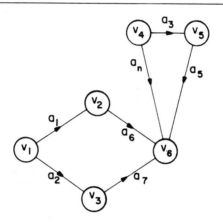

Figure 8.36 AOE network with some nonreachable activities

Combinatorial Optimization, by E. Lawler, Holt, Reinhart and Winston, 1976.

"Depth-first search and linear graph algorithms," by R. Tarjan, *SIAM Journal on Computing*, vol. 1, no. 2, 1972, pp. 146-159.

Flows in Networks, by L. Ford and D. Fulkerson, Princeton University Press, 1962.

Integer Programming and Network Flows, by T.C. Hu, Addison-Wesley, Reading, Massachusetts, 1970.

For more on activity networks and critical path analysis see:

Project Management with CPM and PERT, by Moder and C. Phillips, Van Nostrand Reinhold Co., 1970.

8.6 EXERCISES

1. Does the multigraph below have an Eulerian walk? If so, find one.

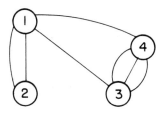

2. For the following digraph obtain:
    - (a)   the in degree and out degree of each vertex
    - (b)   its adjacency matrix
    - (c)   its adjacency list representation
    - (d)   its adjacency multilist representation
    - (e)   its strongly connected components

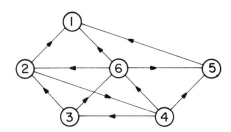

3. Devise a suitable representation for graphs so they can be stored on disk. Write an algorithm which reads in such a graph and creates its adjacency matrix. Write another algorithm which creates the adjacency lists from the disk input.

4. Draw the complete undirected graphs on one, two, three, four, and five vertices. Prove that the number of edges in an n vertex complete graph is $n(n-1)/2$.

5. Is the directed graph below strongly connected? List all the simple paths.

6. Show how the graph above would look if represented by its adjacency matrix, adjacency lists, adjacency multilist.

7. For an undirected graph G with n vertices and e edges show that $\sum_1^n d_i = 2e$ where d_i = degree of vertex i.

8. (a) Let G be a connected undirected graph on n vertices. Show that G must have at least $n - 1$ edges and that all connected undirected graphs with $n - 1$ edges are trees.

    (b) What is the minimum number of edges in a strongly connected digraph on n vertices? What shape do such digraphs have?

9. For an undirected graph G with n vertices prove that the following are equivalent:

    (a) G is a tree

    (b) G is connected, but if any edge is removed the resulting graph is not connected

    (c) For any distinct vertices $u \; \varepsilon \; V(G)$ and $v \; \varepsilon \; V(G)$ there is exactly one simple path from u to v

    (d) G contains no cycles and has $n - 1$ edges

10. A *bipartite graph* $G = (V,E)$ is an undirected graph whose vertices can be partitioned into two disjoint sets V_1 and $V_2 = V - V_1$ with the properties (a) no two vertices in V_1 are adjacent in G and (b) no two vertices in V_2 are adjacent in G. The graph G_4 of Figure 8.5 is bipartite. A possible partitioning of V is $V_1 = \{1,4,5,7\}$ and $V_2 = \{2,3,6,8\}$. Write an algorithm to determine whether a graph G is bipartite. In case G is bipartite your algorithm should obtain a partitioning of the vertices into two disjoint sets V_1 and V_2 satisfying properties (a) and (b) above. Show that if G is represented by its adjacency lists, then this algorithm can be made to work in time $O(n + e)$ where $n = |V|$ and $e = |E|$.

11. Show that every tree is a bipartite graph.

12. Prove that a graph G is bipartite iff it contains no cycles of odd length.

13. Program 8.7 was obtained by Stephen Barnard to find an Eulerian circuit in an undirected graph in case there was such a circuit.

---

function *euler* (*v* : *vertex*): *path*;
1 **begin**
2 *path* := {∅};
3 **for** all *vertices w* adjacent to *v* **and** edge (*v*,*w*) not yet used **do begin**
4   mark edge (*v*,*w*) as used;
5   *path* := {(*v*,*w*)} ∪ *euler* (*w*) ∪ *path*;
6 **end**;
7   *euler* := *path*;
8 **end** {*euler*}

Program 8.7

(a) Show that if *G* is represented by its adjacency multilists and *path* by a linked list, then algorithm *euler* works in time O(*n* + *e*).

(b) Prove by induction on the number of edges in *G* that the above algorithm does obtain an Euler circuit for all graphs *G* having such a circuit. The initial call to Euler can be made with any vertex *v*.

(c) At termination, what has to be done to determine whether or not *G* has an Euler circuit?

14. Apply depth first and breadth first search to the complete graph on four vertices. List the vertices in the order they would be visited.

15. Show how to modify algorithms *dfs* as it is used in *comp* to produce a list of all newly visited vertices.

16. Prove that when algorithm *dfs* is applied to a connected graph the edges of *T* form a tree.

17. Prove that when algorithm *bfs* is applied to a connected graph the edges of *T* form a tree.

18. Show that $A^+ = A^* \times A$ where matrix multiplication of the two matrices is defined as $a_{ij}^+ = \vee_{k=1}^n a_{ik}^* \wedge a_{kj}$. $\vee$ is the logical *or* operation and $\wedge$ is the logical *and* operation.

19. Obtain the matrices A^+ and A^* for the digraph of Exercise 5.

20. Another way to represent a graph is by its incidence matrix, INC. There is one row for each vertex and one column for each edge. Then INC[*i*,*j*] = 1 if edge *j* is incident to vertex *i*. The incidence matrix for the graph of Figure 8.13(a) is:

$$
\begin{array}{c}
\;\;1\;2\;3\;4\;5\;6\;7\;8\;9\;10 \\
\begin{array}{c}1\\2\\3\\4\\5\\6\\7\\8\end{array}
\left[
\begin{array}{cccccccccc}
1 & 1 & 0 & 0 & 0 & 0 & 0 & 0 & 0 & 0 \\
1 & 0 & 1 & 1 & 0 & 0 & 0 & 0 & 0 & 0 \\
0 & 1 & 0 & 0 & 1 & 1 & 0 & 0 & 0 & 0 \\
0 & 0 & 1 & 0 & 0 & 0 & 1 & 0 & 0 & 0 \\
0 & 0 & 0 & 1 & 0 & 0 & 0 & 1 & 0 & 0 \\
0 & 0 & 0 & 0 & 1 & 0 & 0 & 0 & 1 & 0 \\
0 & 0 & 0 & 0 & 0 & 1 & 0 & 0 & 0 & 1 \\
0 & 0 & 0 & 0 & 0 & 0 & 1 & 1 & 1 & 1 \\
\end{array}
\right]
\end{array}
$$

The edges of Figure 8.13(a) have been numbered from left to right, top to bottom. Rewrite algorithm *dfs* so it works on a graph represented by its incidence matrix.

21. If ADJ is the adjacency matrix of a graph $G = (V,E)$ and INC is the incidence matrix, under what conditions will $ADJ = INC \times INC^T - I$ where INC^T is the transpose of matrix INC? Matrix multiplication is defined as in Exercise 18. I is the identity matrix.

22. Show that if T is a spanning tree for the undirected graph G, then the addition of an edge e, $e \notin E(T)$ and $e \in E(G)$, to T creates a unique cycle.

23. By considering the complete graph with n vertices, show that the number of spanning trees is at least $2^{n-1} - 1$.

24. The *radius* of a tree is the maximum distance from the root to a leaf. Given a connected, undirected graph write an algorithm for finding a spanning tree of minimum radius. (Hint: use breadth first search.) Prove that your algorithm is correct.

25. The *diameter* of a tree is the maximum distance between any two vertices. Given a connected, undirected graph write an algorithm for finding a spanning tree of minimum diameter. Prove the correctness of your algorithm.

26. Write out Kruskal's minimum spanning tree algorithm (Figure 8.18) as a complete program. You may use as procedures the algorithms *union* and *find* of Chapter 7. Use algorithm *sort* to sort the edges into nondecreasing order by weight.

27. Using the idea of algorithm *shortestpath*, give an algorithm to find a minimum spanning tree whose worst case time is $O(n^2)$.

28. Use algorithm *shortestpath* to obtain in nondecreasing order the lengths of the shortest paths from vertex 1 to all remaining vertices in the digraph:

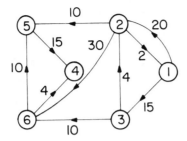

29. Rewrite algorithm *shortestpath* under the following assumptions:

    (a) G is represented by its adjacency lists, where each node has three fields: *vertex*, *cost*, and *link*. *cost* is the length of the corresponding edge and n the number of vertices in G.

    (b)   Instead of representing S, the set of vertices to which the shortest paths have already been found, the set $T = V(G) - S$ is represented using a linked list.

    What can you say about the computing time of your new algorithm relative to that of *shortestpath*?

30. Modify algorithm *shortestpath* so that it obtains the shortest paths in addition to the lengths of these paths. What is the computing time of your algorithm?

31. Using the directed graph below, explain why *shortestpath* will not work properly. What is the shortest path between vertices v_1 and v_7?

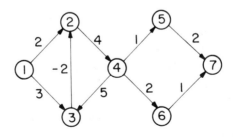

32. Modify algorithm *allcosts* so that it obtains a shortest path for all pairs of vertices i, j. What is the computing time of your new algorithm?

33. By considering the complete graph with n vertices show that the maximum number of simple paths between two vertices is $O((n - 1)!)$.

34. Use algorithm *allcosts* to obtain the lengths of the shortest paths between all pairs of vertices in the graph of Exercise 31. Does *allcosts* give the right answers? Why?

35. Does the following set of precedence relations (<) define a partial order on the elements 1 thru 5? Why?

$1 < 2; 2 < 4; 2 < 3; 3 < 4; 3 < 5; 5 < 1$

36. (a) For the AOE network below obtain the early, $e(\ )$, and late, $l(\ )$, start times for each activity. Use the forward-backward approach.

(b) What is the earliest time the project can finish?

(c) Which activities are critical?

(d) Is there any single activity whose speed up would result in a reduction of the project length?

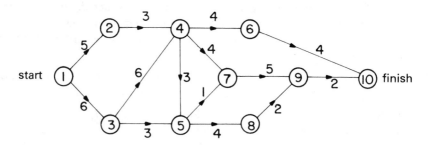

37. Define a critical AOE network to be an AOE network in which all activities are critical. Let G be the undirected graph obtained by removing the directions and weights from the edges of the network.

(a) Show that the project length can be decreased by speeding exactly one activity if there is an edge in G which lies on every path from the start vertex to the finish vertex. Such an edge is called a bridge. Deletion of a bridge from a connected graph disconnects the graph into two connected components.

(b) Write an $O(n + e)$ algorithm using adjacency lists to determine whether the connected graph G has a bridge. In case G has a bridge, your algorithm should output one such bridge.

38. Write a set of computer programs for manipulating graphs. Such a collection should allow input and output of arbitrary graphs, determining connected components and spanning trees. The capabililty of attaching weights to the edges should also be provided.

39.   Make sure you can define the following terms:

adjacent(v)   connected (v_p, v_q)
adjacent-to(v)   connected(G)
adjacent-from(v)   connected component
degree(v)   strongly connected
in-degree(v)   tree
out-degree(v)   network
path   spanning tree
simple path
cycle
subgraph

CHAPTER 9
INTERNAL SORTING

9.1 SEARCHING

In this chapter, we use the term *file* to mean a collection of records, each record having one or more fields. This is to be distinguished from the use of this term in the Pascal language. The fields used to distinguish among the records are known as *keys*. Since the same file may be used for several different applications, the key fields for record identification will depend on the particular application. For instance, we may regard a telephone directory as a file, each record having three fields: name, address, and phone number. The key is usually the person's name. However, we may wish to locate the record corresponding to a given number, in which case the phone number field would be the key. In yet another application we may desire the phone number at a particular address, so this field too could be the key.

Once we have a collection of records there are at least two ways in which to store them: sequentially or nonsequentially. For the time being let us assume we have a sequential file f and we wish to retrieve a record with a certain key value k. If f has n records with $f[i].key$ the key value for record i, then we may carry out the retrieval by examining the key values $f[n].key, ..., f[1].key$ in that order, until the correct record is located. Such a search is known as sequential search since the records are examined sequentially. Program 9.1 gives a sequential search procedure that uses the following data types:

```
type records = record
                    key : integer;
                    other : fields;
               end;
     afile = array [0..n] of records;
```

```
1 procedure seqsrch (f: afile; var i : integer; n,k : integer);
2 {search a file f with key values f[1].key, ...,f[n].key for a record
3   such that f[i].key = k. If there is no such record, i is set to 0.}
4 begin
5   f[0].key := k;
6   i := n;
7   while f[i].key <> k do
8     i := i − 1;
9 end; {of seqsrch}
```

Program 9.1 Sequential search

This procedure is quite similar to Program 3.11. Only the datatypes have been changed. Note that the introduction of the dummy record 0 with $key f[0].key = k$ in f simplifies the search by eliminating the need for an end of file test ($i < 1$) in the **while** loop. While this might appear to be a minor improvement, it actually reduces the running time by 50% for large n. If no record in the file has key value k, then $i = 0$, and the above procedure requires $n + 1$ comparisons. The number of key comparisons made in case of a successful search depends on the position of the key in the file. If all keys are distinct and key $f[i].key$ is being searched for, then $n − i + 1$ key comparisons are made. The average number of comparisons for a successful search is, therefore,

$$\sum_{1 \le i \le n} (n − i + 1)/n = (n + 1)/2.$$

For large n this many comparisons is very inefficient. However, we all know that it is possible to do much better when looking up phone numbers. What enables us to make an efficient search? The fact that the entries in the file (i.e., the telephone directory) are in lexicographic order (on the name key) is what enables one to look up a number while examining only a very few entries in the file. So, if the file is ordered one should be able to search for specific records quickly. One of the better known methods for searching an ordered sequential file is called binary search. The procedure for this was developed in Chapter 2. In Chapter 3, we showed that using binary search, an ordered file could be searched in $O(\log n)$ time.

Getting back to our example of the telephone directory, we notice that neither of the two ordered search methods suggested above corresponds to the one actually employed by humans in searching the directory. If we are looking for a name beginning with W, we start the search towards the end of the directory rather than at the middle. A search method based on this interpolation search would then begin by comparing key $f[i].key$ with $i = \dfrac{k − f[l].key}{f[u].key − f[l].key} n$ ($f[l].key$ and $f[u].key$ are the values of the smallest and largest keys in the file). The behavior of such an algorithm will clearly depend on the distribution of the keys in the file.

We have seen that as far as the searching problem is concerned, something is to be gained by maintaining the file in an ordered manner if the file is to be searched repeatedly. Let us now look at another example where the use of ordered files greatly reduces the computational effort. The problem we are now concerned with is that of comparing two files of records containing data which is essentially the same data but has been obtained from two different sources. We are concerned with verifying that the two files contain the same data. Such a problem could arise, for instance, in the case of the U.S. Internal Revenue Service which might receive millions of forms from various employers stating how much they paid their employees and then another set of forms from individual employees stating how much they received. So we have two files of records, and we wish to verify that there is no discrepancy between the information in the files. Since the forms arrive at the IRS in essentially a random order, we may assume a random arrangement of the records in the files. The key here would probably be the social security numbers. Let the two files be $F1$ and $F2$ with keys $F1[i].key$ and $F2[i].key$. Let us make the following assumptions about the required verification: (1) if corresponding to a key $F1[i].key$ in the employer file there is no record in the employee file, a message is to be sent to the employee; and (2) if the reverse is true, then a message is to be sent to the employer; and (3) if there is a discrepancy between two records with the same key a message to that effect is to be output.

If one proceeded to carry out the verification directly, one would probably end up with an algorithm similar to $verify1$ (Program 9.2). One may readily verify that the worst case asymptotic computing time of the Program 9.2 is $O(mn)$.

On the other hand if we first ordered the two files and then made the comparison it would be possible to carry out the verification task in time $O(t_{sort}(n)+t_{sort}(m) + n + m)$ where $t_{sort}(n)$ is the time needed to sort a file of n records. As we shall see, it is possible to sort n records in $O(n\log n)$ time, so the computing time becomes $O(\max\{n\log n, m\log m\})$. The algorithm $verify2$, Program 9.3, achieves this.

We have seen two important uses of sorting: (1) as an aid in searching, and (2) as a means for matching entries in files. Sorting also finds application in the solution of many other more complex problems, e.g., from operations research and job scheduling. In fact, it is estimated that over 25 percent of all computing time is spent on sorting with some installations spending more than 50 percent of their computing time sorting files. Consequently, the problem of sorting has great relevance in the study of computing. Unfortunately, no one method is the "best" for all initial orderings of the file being sorted. We shall therefore study several methods, indicating when one is superior to the others.

```
 1 procedure verify1(F1, F2 : afile; l,n,m : integer);
 2 {Compare two unordered files F1 and F2 of size n and m, respectively.
 3 l is the maximum of m and n. The output is
 4   (a) all records found in F1 but not in F2
 5   (b) all records found in F2 but not in F1
 6   (c) all records that are in F1 and F2 with the same key
 7       but have different values for other fields}
 8 var i,j :integer;
 9   marked : array[1..n] of boolean;
10 begin
11   for i := 1 to l do marked[i] := false;
12   for i := 1 to n do
13   begin
14     seqsrch (F2,j,m,F1[i].key);
15     if j = 0 then writeln(F1[i].key, 'not in F2.') {satisfies (a)}
16     else
17     begin
18       if F1[i].other <> F2[j].other
19       then {satisifies (c)}
20         writeln('discrepancy in ', F1[i].key,F1[i].other,F2[j].other);
21       marked[j] :=true; {mark the record as being seen}
22     end;
23   end
24   for i := 1 to m do
25     if not marked[i] then writeln (F2[i].key, 'not in F1.'); {satisfies (b)}
26 end; {of verify1}
```

Program 9.2 Verifying using a sequential search

First let us formally state the problem we are about to consider. We are given a file of records $(R_1, R_2, ..., R_n)$. Each record, R_i, has key value K_i. In addition we assume an ordering relation $(<)$ on the keys so that for any two key values x and y either $x=y$ or $x<y$ or $y<x$. The ordering relation $(<)$ is assumed to be transitive, i.e., for any three values x, y, and z, $x<y$ and $y<z$ implies $x<z$. The sorting problem then is that of finding a permutation, σ, such that $K_{\sigma(i)} \leq K_{\sigma(i+1)}$, $1 \leq i \leq n-1$. The desired ordering is then $(R_{\sigma(1)}, R_{\sigma(2)},$

Note that in the case when the file has several key values that are identical, the permutation, σ, defined above is not unique. We shall distinguish one permutation, σ_s, from all the others that also order the file. Let σ_s be the permutation with the following properties:

```
1  procedure verify2(var F1, F2 : afile; n,m : integer);
2  {Same task as verify1. However this time sort F1 and F2 so that
3   the keys are in increasing order in each file. We assume that the
4   keys in each file are distinct}
5  var i,j : integer
6  begin
7    sort(F1, n); {sort the file by key}
8    sort(F2, m);
9    i := 1; j := 1;
10   while ((i <= n) and (j <= m)) do
11     case compare (F1[i].key, F2[j].key) of
12     '<' : begin
13         writeln(F1[i].key, 'not in F2.');
14         i := i + 1;
15         end
16     '=' : begin
17           if not (F1[i].other = F2[j].other)
18             then
19             writeln ('discrepancy in ', F1[i].other,F2[j].other);
20           i := i + 1; j := j + 1;
21         end;
22     '>' : begin
23           writeln (F2[j].key,'not in F1.');
24           j := j + 1;
25         end;
26     end; {of case and while}
27     if i <= n then printrest (F1, i, n, 1)
28     {printrest prints the records of the file that are missing}
29     else if j <= m then printrest (F2, j, m, 2);
30  end; {of verify2}
```

Program 9.3 Fast verification of two files

(1) $K_{\sigma_s(i)} \le K_{\sigma_s(i+1)}, 1 \le i \le n - 1$

(2)   If $i < j$ and $K_i = K_j$ in the input file, then R_i precedes R_j in the sorted file

A sorting method generating the permutation σ_s will be said to be *stable*.

   To begin with we characterize sorting methods into two broad categories: (1) internal methods, i.e., methods to be used when the file to be sorted is small enough so that the entire sort can be carried out in main memory; and (2) external methods, i.e., methods to be used on larger files. In this text we shall study internal sorting methods only. The following internal sorting methods will be developed:

(1)   Insertion sort

(2)   Quick sort

(3)   Merge sort

(4)   Heap sort

(5)   Radix sort

9.2 INSERTION SORT

The basic step in this method is to insert a record R into a sequence of ordered records, $R_1, R_2, ..., R_i, (K_1 \leq K_2, ..., \leq K_i)$ in such a way that the resulting sequence of size $i + 1$ is also ordered. Program 9.4 accomplishes this insertion. It assumes the existence of an artificial record R_0 with key $K_0 = -\textbf{maxint}$ (i.e, all keys are $\geq K_0$). Also the type *afile* is defined as

type *afile* = **array** [0 .. *maxn*] **of** *records*;

```
 1  procedure insert (r : records ; var list : afile; i : integer);
 2  {Insert record r with key r . key into the ordered
 3     sequence list [0], ..., list [i ]
 4     in such a way that the resulting sequence is
 5     also ordered on the field key.
 6     We assume that list contains a dummy record at index zero
 7     such that r . key ≥ list [0] . key for all i}
 8  var j : integer;
 9  begin
10     j := i;
11     while r . key < list [j ] . key do
12     begin
13        list [j + 1] := list [j ];
14        j := j − 1;
15     end;
16     list [j + 1] := r;
17  end; {of insert}
```

Program 9.4 Insertion into a sorted file

Again, note that the use of R_0 enables us to simplify the **while** loop, avoiding a test for end of file, i.e., $j < 1$.

Insertion sort is carried out by beginning with the ordered sequence R_0, R_1 and then successively inserting the records $R_2, R_3, ..., R_n$ into the sequence. Since each insertion leaves the resultant sequence ordered, the file with n records can be ordered making $n - 1$ insertions. The details are given in algorithm *InsertionSort* (Program 9.5).

```
1 procedure InsertionSort(var list : afile; n : integer);
2 {sort list in nondecreasing value of the file key. Assume n > 0.}
3 var j : integer;
4 begin
5     list [0] . key := −maxint;
6     for j := 2 to n do
7         insert (list [j ],list,j − 1);
8 end; {of InsertionSort}
```

Program 9.5 Insertion sort

Analysis of Insertion Sort

In the worst case algorithm *insert* $(r, list, i)$ makes $i + 1$ comparisons before making the insertion. Hence the computing time for the insertion is $O(i)$. Procedure *InsertionSort* invokes procedure *insert* for $j = 1, 2, ..., n - 1$ resulting in an overall worst case time of $O(\sum_{j=1}^{n-1} j + 1) = O(n^2)$.

One may also obtain an estimate of the computing time of this method based upon the relative disorder in the input file. We shall say that the record R_i is *left out of order* (LOO) iff $R_i < \max_{1 \le j < i}\{R_j\}$. Clearly, the insertion step has to be carried out only for those records that are LOO. If k is the number of records LOO, then the computing time is $O((k + 1)n)$. The worst case time is still $O(n^2)$. One can also show that the average time is also $O(n^2)$.

Example 9.1: Assume $n = 5$ and the input sequence is (5, 4, 3, 2, 1) [note we assume for convenience that the records have only one field which also happens to be the key]. Then, after each insertion we have the following:

$-\infty, 5, 4, 3, 2, 1$ [initial sequence]
$-\infty, 4, 5, 3, 2, 1$ $i = 2$
$-\infty, 3, 4, 5, 2, 1$ $i = 3$
$-\infty, 2, 3, 4, 5, 1$ $i = 4$
$-\infty, 1, 2, 3, 4, 5$ $i = 5$

Note that $-\infty$ denotes $-$**maxint** and this is an example of the worst case behavior. $\square$

Example 9.2: $n = 5$ and the input sequence is $(2, 3, 4, 5, 1)$. After each execution of *insert* we have:

$-\infty, 2, 3, 4, 5, 1$ [initial]
$-\infty, 2, 3, 4, 5, 1$ $i = 2$
$-\infty, 2, 3, 4, 5, 1$ $i = 3$
$-\infty, 2, 3, 4, 5, 1$ $i = 4$
$-\infty, 1, 2, 3, 4, 5$ $i = 5$

In this example only R_5 is LOO and the time for each $i = 2$, 3, and 4 is $O(1)$ while for $i = 5$ it is $O(n)$. $\square$

It should be fairly obvious that this method is stable. The fact that the computing time is $O(kn)$ makes this method very desirable in sorting sequences where only a very few records are LOO (i.e., $k<<n$). The simplicity of this scheme makes it about the fastest sorting method for $n \leq 20 - 25$ elements, depending upon the implementation and machine properties. For variations on this method see Exercises 2 and 3.

9.3 QUICK SORT

We now turn our attention to a sorting scheme with a very good average behavior. The quick sort scheme developed by C. A. R. Hoare has the best average behavior among all the sorting methods we shall be studying. In Insertion Sort the key K_i currently controlling the insertion is placed into the right spot with respect to the sorted subfile $(R_1, ..., R_{i-1})$. Quick sort differs from insertion sort in that the key K_i controlling the process is placed at the right spot with respect to the whole file. Thus, if key K_i is placed in position $s(i)$, then $K_j \leq K_{s(i)}$ for $j < s(i)$ and $K_j \geq K_{s(i)}$ for $j > s(i)$. Hence after this positioning has been made, the original file is partitioned into two subfiles, one consisting of records $R_1, ..., R_{s(i)-1}$ and the other of records $R_{s(i)}+1, ..., R_n$. Since in the sorted sequence all records in the first subfile may appear to the left of $s(i)$ and all in the second subfile to the right of $s(i)$, these two subfiles may be sorted independently. The method is best stated recursively as Program 9.6. Procedure *interchange* (x, y) performs $t := x$; $x := y$; $y := t$.

```
1  procedure QuickSort(var list : afile; m,n : integer);
2  {sort records list [m ], ..., list [n ] into nondecreasing
3   order on field key.
4   Key k = list [m ] . key is arbitrarily chosen as the control key.
5   Pointers i and j are used to partition the subfile so
6   that at any time list [l ] . key ≤ k,l < i and
7   list [l ] . key ≥ k, l > j. It is assumed that
8   list [m ] . key ≤ list [n + 1] . key}
9  var i,j,k : integer;
10 begin
11    if m < n
12    then
13    begin
14      i := m; j := n + 1; k := list [m ] . key;
15      repeat
16        repeat
17          i := i + 1;
18        until list [i ] . key >= k;
19        repeat
20          j := j − 1;
21        until list [j ] . key <= k;
22        if i < j
23        then interchange (list [i ],list [j ]);
24      until i >= j;
25      interchange (list [m ],list [j ]);
26      QuickSort (list,m,j − 1);
27      QuickSort (list,j + 1,n);
28    end; {of if}
29 end; {of QuickSort}
```

Program 9.6 Quick sort

Example 9.3: The input file has 10 records with keys (26, 5, 37, 1, 61, 11, 59, 15, 48, 19). The table below gives the status of the file at each call of *QuickSort*. Square brackets are used to demarcate subfiles yet to be sorted.

R_1	R_2	R_3	R_4	R_5	R_6	R_7	R_8	R_9	R_{10}	m	n
[26	5	37	1	61	11	59	15	48	19]	1	10

[11	5	19	1	15]	26	[59	61	48	37]	1	5
[1	5]	11	[19	15]	26	[59	61	48	37	1	2
1	5	11	[19	15]	26	[59	61	48	37]	4	5
1	5	11	15	19	26	[59	61	48	37]	7	10
1	5	11	15	19	26	[48	37]	59	[61]	7	8
1	5	11	15	19	26	37	48	59	[61]	10	10
1	5	11	15	19	26	37	48	59	61		

□

Analysis of Quick Sort

The worst case behavior of this algorithm is examined in Exercise 4 and shown to be $O(n^2)$. However, if we are lucky then each time a record is correctly positioned, the subfile to its left will be of the same size as that to its right. This would leave us with the sorting of two subfiles each of size roughly $n/2$. The time required to position a record in a file of size n is $O(n)$. If $T(n)$ is the time taken to sort a file of n records, then when the file splits roughly into two equal parts each time a record is positioned correctly we have

$$T(n) \leq cn + 2T(n/2), \text{ for some constant } c$$

$$\leq cn + 2(cn/2 + 2T(n/4))$$

$$\leq 2cn + 4T(n/4)$$

.

.

.

$$\leq cn \log_2 n + nT(1) = O(n \log_2 n)$$

In our presentation of quick sort, the record whose position was being fixed with respect to the subfile currently being sorted was always chosen to be the first record in that subfile. Exercise 5 examines a better choice for this control record. Lemma 9.1 shows that the average computing time for quick sort is $O(n \log_2 n)$. Moreover, experimental results show that as far as average computing time is concerned, it is the best of the internal sorting methods we shall be studying.

Unlike insertion sort where the only additional space needed was for one record, quick sort needs stack space to implement the recursion. In case the files split evenly as in the above analysis, the maximum recursion depth would be $\log n$ requiring a stack space of $O(\log n)$. The worst case occurs when the file is split into a left subfile of size $n - 1$ and a right subfile of size 0 at each level of recursion. In this case, the depth of recursion becomes n requiring stack space of $O(n)$. The worst case stack space can be reduced by a factor of 4 by realizing that right subfiles of size less than 2 need not be stacked. An asymptotic reduction in stack space can be achieved by *sorting smaller subfiles first*. In this case the additional stack space is at most $O(\log n)$.

Lemma 9.1: Let $T_{avg}(n)$ be the expected time for procedure *QuickSort* to sort a file with n records. Then there exists a constant k such that $T_{avg}(n) \le kn\log_e n$ for $n \ge 2$.

Proof: In the call to *QuickSort* $(1, n)$, k_1 gets placed at position j. This leaves us with the problem of sorting two subfiles of size $j - 1$ and $n - j$. The expected time for this is $T_{avg}(j - 1) + T_{avg}(n - j)$. The remainder of the algorithm clearly takes at most cn time for some constant c. Since j may take on any of the values 1 to n with equal probability we have

$$T_{avg}(n) \le cn + \frac{1}{n}\sum_{j=1}^{n}(T_{avg}(j - 1) + T_{avg}(n - j)), \quad n \le 2 \tag{9.1}$$

$$= cn + \frac{2}{n}\sum_{j=0}^{n-1}T_{avg}(j)$$

We may assume $T_{avg}(0) \le b$ and $T_{avg}(1) \le b$ for some constant b. We shall now show $T_{avg}(n) \le kn\log_e n$ for $n \ge 2$ and $k = 2(b + c)$. The proof is by induction on n.

Induction Base: For $n = 2$ we have from Eq. (9.1)

$$T_{avg}(2) \le 2c + 2b \le kn\log_e 2$$

Induction Hypothesis: Assume $T_{avg}(n) \le kn\log_e n$ for $1 \le n < m$

Induction Step: From Eq. (9.1) and the induction hypothesis we have

$$T_{avg}(m) \le cm + \frac{4b}{m} + \frac{2}{m}\sum_{j=2}^{m-1}T_{avg}(j) \tag{9.2}$$

$$\le cm + \frac{4b}{m} + \frac{2k}{m}\sum_{j=2}^{m-1}j\log_2 j$$

Since $j\log_e j$ is an increasing function of j, Eq. (9.2) yields

$$T_{avg}(m) \le cm + \frac{4b}{m} + \frac{2k}{m}\int_{2}^{m}x\log_e x\ dx$$

$$= cm + \frac{4b}{m} + \frac{2k}{m}\left[\frac{m^2\log_e m}{2} - \frac{m^2}{4}\right]$$

$$= cm + \frac{4b}{m} + km\log_e m - \frac{km}{2}$$

$\leq km\log_e m, \text{ for } m \geq 2.$ □

9.4 HOW FAST CAN WE SORT?

Both of the sorting methods we have seen have a worst case behavior of $O(n^2)$. It is natural at this point to ask the question: '' What is the best computing time for sorting that we can hope for?'' The theorem we shall prove shows that if we restrict our question to algorithms for which the only operations permitted on keys are comparisons and interchanges then $O(n \log_2 n)$ is the best possible time.

The method we use is to consider a tree which describes the sorting process by having a vertex represent a key comparison and the branches indicate the result. Such a tree is called a *decision tree*. A path through a decision tree represents a possible sequence of computations that an algorithm could produce.

As an example of such a tree, let us look at the tree obtained for insertion sort working on a file with tree records in it. The input sequence is three records R_1, R_2, and R_3 so the root of the tree is labeled (1,2,3). Depending on the outcome of the comparison between keys K_1 and K_2, this sequence may or may not change. If $K_2 < K_1$, then the sequence becomes (2,1,3), otherwise it stays (1,2,3). The full tree resulting from these comparisons is shown below. The left nodes are number I-VI and are the only points at which the algorithm may terminate. Hence only six permutations of the input sequence are obtainable from this algorithm. Since all six of these are different and 3! = 6, it follows that this algorithm has enough leaves to constitute a valid sorting algorithm for three records. The maximum depth of this tree is 3. The table below gives six different orderings of key values 7, 9, 10 which show that all six permutations are possible. The tree is not a full binary tree of depth 3 and so it has fewer than $2^3 = 8$ leaves. The possible output permutations are

LEAF	PERMUTATION	SAMPLE INPUT KEY VALUES WHICH GIVE THE PERMUTATION
I	1 2 3	(7,9,10)
II	1 3 2	(7,10,9)
III	3 1 2	(9,10,7)
IV	2 1 3	(9,7,10)
V	2 3 1	(10,7,9)
VI	3 2 1	(10,9,7)

The decision tree is

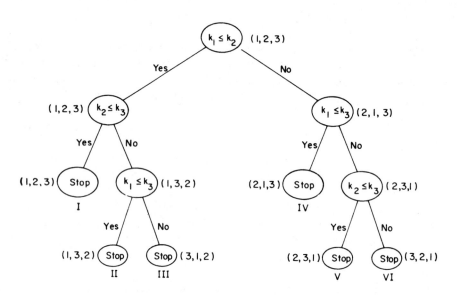

Theorem 9.1: Any decision tree that sorts n distinct elements has a height of at least $\log_2(n!) + 1$.

Proof: When sorting n elements there are $n!$ different possible results. Thus, any decision tree must have $n!$ leaves. But a decision tree is also a binary tree which can have at most 2^{k-1} leaves if its height is k. Therefore, the height must be at least $\log_2 n! + 1$. $\square$

Corollary: Any algorithm which sorts by comparisons only must have a worst case computing time of $\Omega(n \log_2 n)$.

Proof: We must show that for every decision tree with $n!$ leaves there is a path of length $cn\log_2 n$, c a constant. By the theorem, there is a path of length $\log_2 n!$. Now

$$n! = n(n-1)(n-2) \cdots (3)(2)(1)$$
$$\leq (n/2)^{n/2},$$

so $\log_2 n! \geq (n/2)\log_2(n/2) = O(n\log_2 n)$. $\square$

9.5 MERGE SORT

Before looking at the merge sort algorithm to sort n records let us see how one may merge two files $(x_1, ..., x_m)$ and $(x_{m+1}, ..., x_n)$ that are already sorted to get a third file $(z_1, ..., z_n)$ that is also sorted. Since this merging scheme is very simple, we directly present the algorithm as Program 9.7.

Analysis of Merge Sort

At each iteration of the while loop, k increases by 1. The total increment in k is $n - l + 1$. Hence the **while** loop is iterated at most $n - l + 1$ times. The **if** statement moves at most one record per iteration. The total time is therefore $O(n - l + 1)$. If records are of length M then the time is really $O(M(n - l + 1))$. When M is greater than 1 we could use linked lists for $(x_1, ..., x_m)$ and $(x_{m+1}, ..., x_n)$ and obtain a new sorted linked list containing these $n - l + 1$ records. Now, we won't need the additional space for $n - l + 1$ records as needed above for Z. Instead only space for $n - l + 1$ links is needed. The merge time becomes independent of M and $O(n - l + 1)$. Note that $n - l + 1$ is the number of records being merged. $\square$

Merge sort begins by interpreting the input as n sorted files each of length 1. These are merged pairwise to obtain $n/2$ files of size 2 (if n is odd, then one file is of size 1). These $n/2$ files are then merged pairwise and so on until we are left with only one file. The example below illustrates the process.

Example 9.4: The input file is $(26, 5, 77, 1, 61, 11, 59, 15, 48, 19)$. The tree below illustrates the subfiles being merged at each pass:

```
 1  procedure merge(var x,z : afile;l,m,n : integer);
 2  {(x [l ], · · · ,x [m ]) and (x [m + 1], ..., x [n ]) are
 3  two sorted lists with keys
 4  such that x [l ]. key ≤ · · · ≤ x [m ]. key, and
 5  x [m + 1]. key ≤ · · · ≤ x [n ]. key. These records are merged to
 6  obtain the sorted list (z [l ], ..., z [n ]) such that
 7  z [l ]. key ≤ · · · ≤ z [n ]. key}
 8  var i,j,k,t : integer:
 9  begin
10     i := l;
11     k := l;
12     j := m + 1; {i, j, and k are positions in the three files}
13     while ((i <= m) and (j <= n)) do
14     begin
15        if x [i ]. key <= x [j ]. key
16        then
17        begin
18           z [k ] := x [i ];
19           i := i + 1;
20        end
21        else
22        begin
23           z [k ] := x [j ];
24           j := j + 1;
25        end;
26        k := k + 1;
27     end; {of while}
28     if i > m
29     then        {(z_k, ..., z_n) := (x_j, ..., x_n)}
30        for t := j to n do
31           z [k + t − j ] :=x [t ]
32     else        {(z_k, ..., z_m) := (x_j, ..., x_m)}
33        for t := i to m do
34           z [k + t − i ] := x [t ];
35  end; {of merge}
```

Program 9.7 Merging two sorted files

As is apparent from the example above, merge sort consists of several passes over the records being sorted. In the first pass, files of size 1 are merged. In the second, the size of the files being merged is 2. On the i'th pass the files being merged are of size 2^{i-1}. Consequently, a total of $\lceil \log_2 n \rceil$ passes are made over the data. Since two files can be merged in linear time (algorithm *merge*), each pass of merge sort takes $O(n)$time. As there are $\lceil \log_2 n \rceil$ passes, the total computing time is $O(n \log n)$.

In formally writing the algorithm for a merge, it is convenient to first present an algorithm (Program 9.8) to perform one merge pass of the merge sort.

```
 1  procedure MergePass(var x,y : afile; n,l : integer);
 2  {This algorithm performs one pass of the merge sort. It merges
 3   adjacent pairs of subfiles of length l from the list x to list
 4   y. n is the number of records in x.}
 5  var i, t : integer;
 6  begin
 7    i := 1;
 8    while i <= (n − 2*l + 1) do
 9    begin
10      merge (x,y,i,i + l − 1, i + 2*l − 1);
11      i := i + 2*l;
12    end;
13    {merge remaining file of length < 2*l}
14    if (i + l − 1) < n then merge (x,y,i,i + l − 1, n)
15    else
16      for t := i to n do
17        y [t] := x [t];
18  end; {of MergePass}
```

Program 9.8 Merge pass

It is easy to verify that the above algorithm results in a stable sorting procedure. Exercise 8 discusses a variation of the merge sort discussed above. In this variation the prevailing order within the input file is taken into account to obtain initially sorted subfiles of length ≥ 1.

```
 1 procedure MergeSort(var x : afile; n : integer);
 2 {Sort the file x = (x [1], ..., x [n]) into nondecreasing order on the
 3  keys x [1] . key, ..., x [n] . key}
 4 var l : integer;
 5     y : afile;
 6 begin
 7  {l is the size of the subfile currently being merged}
 8  l := 1;
 9  while l < n do
10  begin
11    MergePass (x,y,n,l);
12    l := 2 * l;
13    MergePass (y,x,n,l); {interchange role of x and y}
14    l := 2 * l;
15  end
16 end; {of MergeSort}
```

Program 9.9 Merge sort

Recursive Formulation of Merge Sort

Merge sort may also be arrived at recursively. In the recursive formulation we divide the file to be sorted into two roughly equal parts called the left and the right subfiles. These subfiles are sorted using the algorithm recursively and then the two subfiles are merged together to obtain the sorted file. First, let us see how this would work on our earlier example.

Example 9.5: The input file (26, 5, 77, 1, 61, 11, 59, 15, 49, 19) is to be sorted using the recursive formulation of merge sort. If the subfile from l to u is currently to be sorted then its two subfiles are indexed from l to $\lfloor (l + u)/2 \rfloor$ and from $\lfloor (l + u)/2 \rfloor + 1$ to u. The subfile partitioning that takes place is described by the following binary tree. Note that the subfiles being merged are different from those being merged in algorithm *MergeSort*.

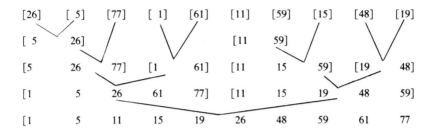

From the preceding example we may draw the following conclusion. If algorithm *merge* is used to merge sorted subfiles from one array into another, then it is necessary to copy subfiles. For example to merge [5, 26] and [77] we would have to copy [77] into the same array as [5, 26]. To avoid this unnecessary copying of subfiles using sequential allocation, we look to a linked list representation for subfiles. This method of representation will permit the recursive version of merge sort to work efficiently.

Each record is assumed to have three fields: *link*, *key*, and *other*. The record structure is defined as

type *records* = **record**
           key : **integer**;
           other : *fields*;
           link : **integer**;
      end;
    afile = **array** [0 .. *n*] **of** *records*;

$r[i].link$ and $r[i].key$ are the link and key value fields in record i, $1 \le i \le n$. Note that for this application, the *link* fields are of type **integer** and not of type **pointer**. We assume that initially $afile[i].link = 0$, $1 \le i \le n$. Thus each record is initially in a chain containing only itself. Let q and r be pointers to two chains of records. The records on each chain are assumed linked in nondecreasing order of the key field. Let *ListMerge(q,r,p)* be an algorithm to merge the two chains q and r to obtain p which is also linked in nondecreasing order of key values. Then the recursive version of merge sort is given by algorithm *rMergeSort* (Program 9.10). To sort the file $x_1, ..., x_n$ this algorithm is invoked as *rMergeSort* (x,l,n,p). p is returned as the start of a chain ordered as described earlier. In case the file is to be physically rearranged into this order then one of the schemes discussed in Section 9.8 may be used. *ListMerge* is given in Program 9.11.

One may readily verify that this linked version of merge sort results in a stable sorting procedure and that the computing time is O(n log n).

```
1  procedure rMergeSort(var x : afile; l,u : integer; var p:integer);
2  {The list x = (x[l], ..., x[u]) is to be sorted on the field key.
3   link is a link field in each record and is initially set to 0.
4   The sorted list is a chain beginning at p.
5   x[0] is a record for intermediate results used only in ListMerge}
6  var mid,q,r : integer;
7  begin
8    if l >= uthen p := l
9    else begin
10     mid := (l + u) div 2;
11     rMergeSort (x,l,mid,q);
12     rMergeSort (x,mid +1,u,r);
13     ListMerge (x,q,r,p);
14   end; {of if}
15 end; {of rMergeSort}
```

Program 9.10 Recursive merge sort

9.6 HEAP SORT

While the merge sort scheme discussed in the previous section has a computing time of $O(n \log n)$ both in the worst case and as average behavior, it requires additional storage proportional to the number of records in the file being sorted. The sorting method we are about to study will require only a fixed amount of additional storage and at the same time will have as its worst case and average computing time $O(n \log n)$. In this method, we utilize a max-heap (see Section 7.11). The deletion and insertion algorithms associated with max-heaps directly yield an $O(n\log n)$ sorting method. The n records are first inserted into an initially empty heap. Next, the records are extracted from the heap one at a time. It is possible to create the heap of n records faster by using the procedure *adjust* (Program 9.12). This procedure takes a binary tree T whose left and right subtrees satisfy the heap property but whose root may not and adjusts T so that the entire binary tree satisfies the heap property.

Analysis of Procedure Adjust

If the depth of the tree with root i is k, then the **while** loop is executed at most k times. Hence the computing time of the algortihm is $O(k)$. □

The heap sort algorithm now takes the form given in Program 9.13.

Example 9.6: The input file is (26, 5, 77, 1, 61, 11, 59, 15, 48, 19). Interpreting this as a binary tree we have the following transformations:

```
 1  procedure ListMerge (x : afile; u,y : integer; var z : integer);
 2  {The linked lists u and y are merged to obtain z. In u, y,
 3    and z the records are linked in order of nondecreasing key
 4    values. The file of records is named x of type afile.}
 5  var i,j : integer;
 6  begin
 7    i := u ; j := y ; z := 0;
 8    while ((i < > 0) and (j < > 0)) do
 9      if x [i] . key <= x [j] . key
10      then
11      begin
12        x [z ].link := i;
13        z := i ; i := x [i ].link;
14      end
15      else
16      begin
17        x [z ].link := j;
18        z := j ; j := x [j ].link;
19      end;
20    {move remainder}
21    if i = 0 then x [z ].link := j
22             else x [z ].link := i;
23    z := x [0].link;
24  end; {of ListMerge}
```

Program 9.11 Merging linked lists

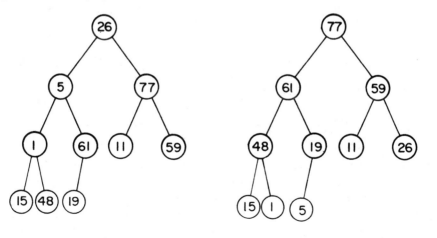

| Input File | Initial Heap |

The figures on pages 433 and 434 depict the heap after restructuring and the sorted part of the file.

Analysis of Heap Sort

Suppose $2^{k-1} \leq n < 2^k$ so that the tree has k levels and the number of nodes on level i is 2^{i-1}. In the first **for** loop, *adjust* is called once for each node that has a child. Hence the time required for this loop is the sum, over each level, of the number of nodes on a level times the maximum distance the node can move. This is no more than

$$\sum_{1 \leq i \leq k} 2^{i-1}(k-i) = \sum_{1 \leq i \leq i-1} 2^{k-i-1} i \leq n \sum_{1 \leq i \leq k-1} i/2^i < 2n = O(n)$$

In the next **for** loop, $n-1$ applications of *adjust* are made with maximum depth $k = \lceil \log_2(n+1) \rceil$. Hence the computing time for this loop is $O(n \log n)$. Consequently, the total computing time is $O(n \log n)$. Note that apart from variables, the only additional space needed is space for one record to carry out the interchange in the second **for** loop.

9.7 SORTING ON SEVERAL KEYS

Let us now look at the problem of sorting records on several keys, $K^1, K^2, ..., K^r$ (K^1 is the most significant key and K^r the least). A file of records $R_1, ..., R_n$ will be said to be sorted with respect to the keys K^1, K^2, *to the r-tuple* $(y_1, ..., y_r)$ *iff either* $x_i = y_i$, $1 \leq i \leq j$ *and* $x_{j+1} < y_{j+1}$ *for some* $j < r$ *or* $x_i = y_i$, $1 \leq i \leq r$.

For example, the problem of sorting a deck of cards may be regarded as a sort on two keys, the suit and face values, with the following ordering relations

Suits: $\clubsuit < \diamondsuit < \heartsuit < \spadesuit$

Face values: $2 < 3 < 4 \cdots < 10 < J < Q < K < A$

There appear to be two popular ways to accomplish the sort. The first is to sort on the most significant key K^1 obtaining several "piles" of records each having the same value for K^1. Then each of these piles is independently sorted on the key K^2 into "subpiles" such that all the records in the same subpile have the same values for K^1 and K^2. The subpiles are then sorted on K^3, etc., and the piles put together. In the example above this would mean first sorting the 52 cards into four piles, one for each of the suit values. Then sort each pile on the face value. Now place the piles on top of each other to obtain the ordering

```
1  procedure adjust(var tree :afile; i,n : integer);
2  {Adjust the binary tree with root i to satisfy the heap property.
3    The left and right subtrees of i, i.e., with root 2i and 2i + 1,
4    already satisfy the heap property.  No node has index greater
5    than n.}
6  var j : integer;
7      k : integer;
8      r : records;
9      done : boolean;
10 begin
11   done := false;
12   r := tree [i ];
13   k := tree [i ] . key;
14   j := 2 * i;
15   while ((j <= n) and not done) do
16   begin {first find max of left and right child}
17     if j < n then if  tree [j ] . key < tree [j + 1] . key then j := j + 1;
18     {compare max. child with k. If k is max, then done.}
19     if k >= tree [j ] . key
20     then
21       done := true
22     else
23     begin
24       tree [j div 2] := tree [j ]; {move j'th record up the tree}
25       j := 2*j;
26     end;
27   end;
28   tree [j div 2] := r;
29 end; { of adjust}
```

Program 9.12 Adjusting a max-heap

$$2\clubsuit, ..., A\clubsuit, ..., 2\spadesuit, ..., A\spadesuit$$

A sort proceeding in this fashion will be referred to as a most significant digit first (MSD) sort. The second way, quite naturally, is to sort on the least significant digit first (LSD). This would mean sorting the cards first into 13 piles corresponding to their face values (key K^2). Then, place the 3's on top of the 2's ..., the kings on top of the queens, the aces on top of the kings; turn the deck upside down and sort on the suit (K^1) using some stable sorting method obtaining four piles, each of which is orderd on K^2; combine the piles to obtain the required ordering on the cards.

```
1  procedure HeapSort(var r : afile ; n : integer);
2  {the file r = (r[1],...,r[n]) is sorted into nondecreasing order on
3    the field key}
4  var i : integer;
5      t : records;
6  begin
7    for i := (n div 2) downto 1 do {convert r into a heap}
8      adjust (r,i,n);
9    for i := (n − 1) downto 1 do {sort r}
10   begin
11     t := r[i + 1]; {interchange r_1 and r_{j+1}}
12     r[i + 1] := r[1];
13     r[1] := t;
14     adjust (r, 1,i); {recreate heap}
15   end;
16 end; {of HeapSort}
```

Program 9.13 Heap sort

Comparing the two procedures outlined about (MSD and LSD) you notice that LSD is simpler as the piles and subpiles obtained do not have to be sorted independently (provided the sorting scheme used for sorting on key K^i, $1 \le i \le r$ is stable). This in turn implies less overhead.

LSD and MSD only specify the order in which the different keys are to be sorted on and not the sorting method to be used within each key. The technique generally used to sort cards is a MSD sort in which the sorting on suit is done by a bin sort (i.e., four "bins" are set up, one for each suit value and the cards are placed into their corresponding "bins"). Next, the cards in each bin are sorted using an algorithm similar to Insertion Sort. However, there is another way to do this. First use a bin sort on the face value. To do this we need 13 bins, one for each distinct face value. Then collect all the cards together as described above and perform bin sort on the suits using four bins. Note that a bin sort requires only $O(n)$ time if the spread in key values is $O(n)$.

LSD or MSD sorting can be used to sort records on only one logical key by interpreting this key as being composed of several keys. For example, if the keys are numeric, then each decimal digit may be regarded as a key. So if all the keys are in the range $0 \le K \le 999$, then we can use either the LSD or MSD sorts for three keys (K^1, K^2, K^3), where K^1 is the digit in the hundredths place, K^2 the digit in the tens place, and K^3 the digit in the units place. Since all the keys lie in the range $0 \le K^i \le 9$, the sort within the keys can be carried out using a bin sort with 10 bins. This, in fact, is essentially the process used to sort records punched on cards using a card sorter. In this

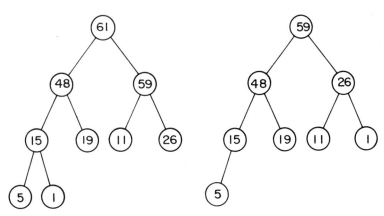

Sorted: 77   61, 77

Heap size: i = 9   i = 8

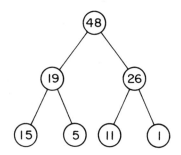

Sorted: 59, 61, 77

Heap size: i = 7

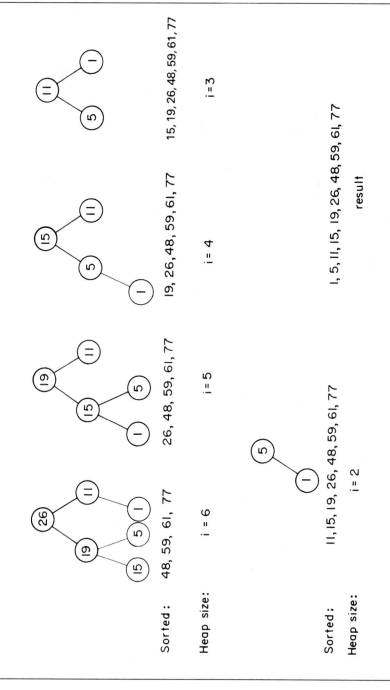

Sorted: 48, 59, 61, 77   26, 48, 59, 61, 77   19, 26, 48, 59, 61, 77   15, 19, 26, 48, 59, 61, 77

Heap size: i = 6   i = 5   i = 4   i = 3

Sorted: 11, 15, 19, 26, 48, 59, 61, 77   1, 5, 11, 15, 19, 26, 48, 59, 61, 77

Heap size: i = 2   result

case using the LSD process would be more convenient as it eliminates maintaining several independent subpiles. If the key is interpreted as above the resulting sort is called a radix 10 sort. If the key decomposition is carried out using the binary representation of the keys, then we obtain a radix 2 sort. In general, we could choose any radix r obtaining a radix r sort. The number of bins required is r.

Let us look in greater detail at the implementation of an LSD radix r sort. We assume that the records $R_1, ..., R_n$ have keys that are d-tuples $(x_1, x_2, ..., x_d)$ and $0 \leq x_i < r$. Thus, we shall need r bins. The records are assumed to have a *link* field. The records in each bin will be linked together into a linear linked list with $f[i]$, $0 \leq i \leq r$, a pointer to the first record in bin i and $e[i]$ a pointer to the last record in bin i. These lists will essentially be operated as queues. Procedure *RadixSort* formally presents the LSD radix r method in Program 9.14. This procedure assumes that *rminus1* is defined as a constant with value $r - 1$. Also it is assumed that the key field of each record is an array $key[1 .. d]$ with $0 \leq key[i] \leq kr = r - 1$.

Analysis of Radix Sort

The algorithm makes d passes over the data, each pass taking $O(n + r)$ time. Hence the total computing time is $O(d(n + r))$. In the sorting of numeric data, the value of d will depend on the choice of the radix r and also on the largest key. Different choices of r will yield different computing times.

Example 9.7: We shall illustrate the operation of algorithm *RadixSort* while sorting a file of 10 numbers in the range [0,999]. Each decimal digit in the key will be regarded as a subkey. So, the value of d is 3 and that of r is 10. The input file is linked and has the form given on page 437. The nodes are labeled $R_1, ..., R_{10}$. The figures on pages 437-439 illustrate the $r = 10$ case and the list after the queues have been collected from the 10 bins at the end of each phase. By using essentially the method above but by varying the radix, we can obtain (see Exercises 11 and 12) linear time algorithms to sort n record files when the keys are in the range $0 \leq K_i < n^k$ for some constant k. □

9.8 PRACTICAL CONSIDERATIONS FOR SORTING

Apart from radix sort, all the sorting methods we have looked at require excessive data movement; i.e., as the result of a comparison, records may be physically moved. This tends to slow down the sorting process when records are large. In sorting files in which the records are large it is necessary to modify the sorting methods so as to minimize data movement. Methods such as insertion sort and merge sort can be easily modified to work with a linked file rather than a sequential file. In this case each record will require an additional link field. Instead of physically moving the record, its link field will be changed to reflect the change in the position of that record in the file. At the end of the

```
1   procedure RadixSort(var r : afile;d,n : integer);
2   {records r = (r[1], ..., r[n]) are sorted on the keys key[1], ..., key[d].
3    The range of each key is 0≤key[i]≤rminus1. rminus1 is a constant.
4    Sorting within a key is done using a bin sort.}
5   var e,f :array [0 .. rminus1] of integer; {queue pointers}
6       i,j,p,t : integer;
7       k : 0 .. kr;
8   begin
9   for i := 1 to n do {link into a chain starting at p}
10       r[i].link := i+1;
11   r[n].link := 0;p := 1;
12   for i := d downto 1 do {sort on key[i]}
13   begin
14       for j := 0 to rminus1 do {initialize bins to be empty queues}
15       f[j] := 0;
16       while p < > 0 do {put records into queues}
17       begin
18       k := r[p]↑. key[i];
19       if f[k] = 0 then f[k] := p
20                    else r[e[k]]↑. link := p;
21       e[k] := p;
22       p := r[p]↑. link; {get next record}
23       end; {of while}
24       j := 0;
25       while f[j] = 0 do
26           j := j + 1; {find first nonempty queue}
27       p := f[j]; t := e[j];
28       for k := j+1 to rminus1 do {concatenate remaining queues}
29           if f[k]< >0
30           then
31           begin
32               r[t]↑. link := f[k];
33               t := e[k];
34           end; {of if and for}
35       r[t]↑. link := 0;
36   end ; {of for of line 12}
37   end; {of RadixSort}
```

Program 9.14 LSD radix sort

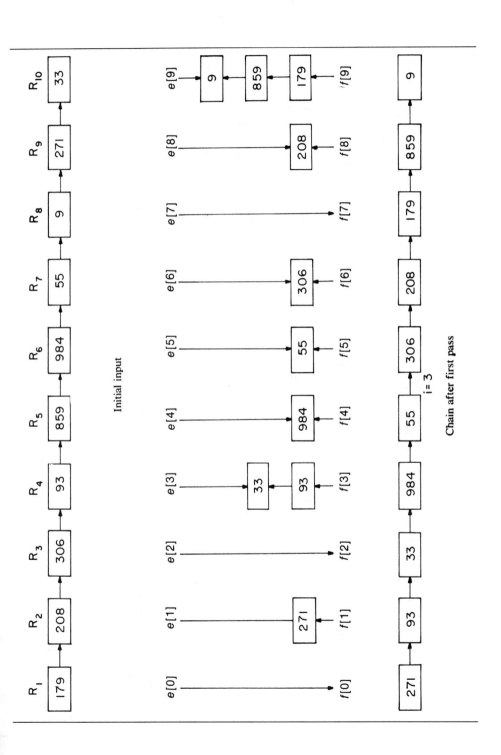

Initial input

Chain after first pass

i = 3

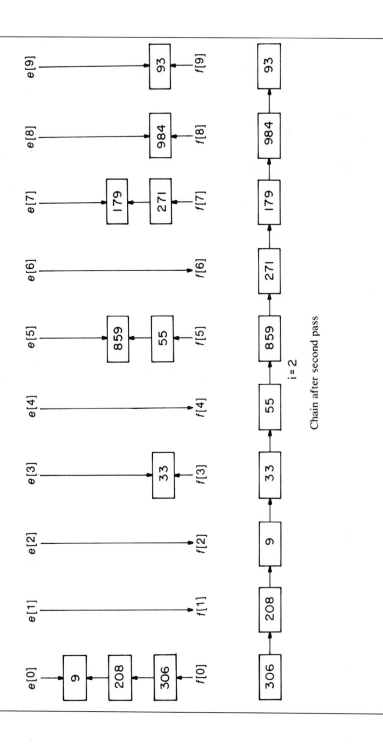

Chain after second pass

i = 2

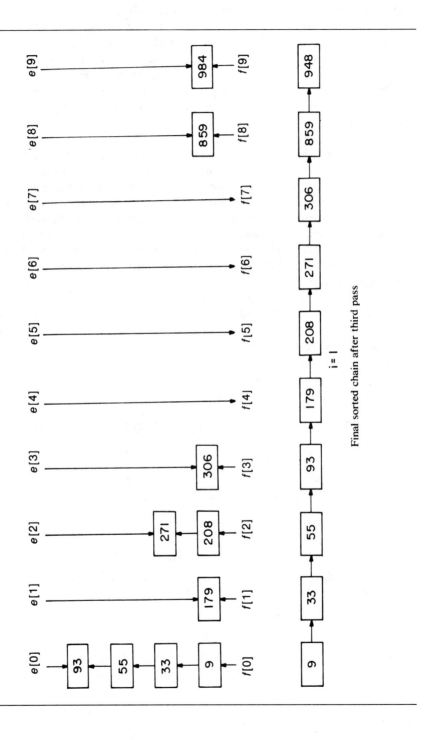

sorting process, the records are linked together in the required order. In many applications (e.g., when we just want to sort files and then output them record by record on some external media in the sorted order) this is sufficient. However, in some applications it is necessary to physically rearrange the records *in place* so that they are in the required order. Even in such cases considerable savings can be achieved by first performing a linked list sort and then physically rearranging the records according to the order specified in the list. This rearranging can be accomplished in linear time using some additional space.

If the file, F, has been sorted so that at the end of the sort p is a pointer to the first record in a linked list of records then each record in this list will have a key which is greater than or equal to the key of the previous record (if there is a previous record), see Figure 9.1. To physically rearrange these records into the order specified by the list, we begin by interchanging records R_1 and R_p. Now, the record in the position R_1 has the smallest key. If $p \neq 1$ then there is some record in the list with link field $=1$. If we could change this link field to indicate the new position of the record previously as position 1 then we would be left with records R_2, ..., R_n linked together in nondecreasing order. Repeating the above process will, after $n - 1$ iterations, result in the desired rearrangement. The snag, however, is that in a singly linked list we do not know the predecessor of a node. To overcome this difficulty, our first rearrangement algorithm *list*1 (Program 9.15), begins by converting the singly linked list p into a doubly linked list and then proceeds to move records into their correct places.

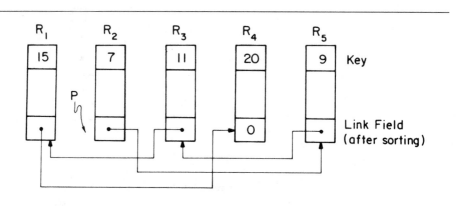

Figure 9.1 List sort

Example 9.8: After a list sort on the input file (35,18,12,42,26,14) has been made the file is linked as below (only three fields of each record are shown):

```
 1  procedure list1(var r : afile; n : integer; p : integer);
 2  {p is a pointer to list of n sorted records linked together
 3   by the field link. linkb is assumed to be present in each
 4   record. The records are rearranged so that the resulting
 5   records r [1], ..., r [n] are consecutive and sorted.
 6   Type definitions are as for merge except for an extra link field}
 7  var i,u,s : integer;
 8      a : records;
 9  begin
10      u := 0; x := p;
11      while s < > 0 do {convert p into a doubly linked list using linkb}
12      begin
13        r [s ].linkb := u;
14        u := s;
15        s := r [s ].link;
16      end;
17      for i := 1 to n − 1 do {move r_p to position i while}
18      begin                 {maintaining the list}
19        if p < > i
20        then
21        begin
22          if r [i ].link < > 0 then r [r [i ].link ].linkb := p;
23          r [r [i ].linkb ].link := p;
24          a := r [p ]; r [p ] := r [i ]; r [i ] := a;
25        end;
26        p := r [i ].link;
27      end;
28  end; {of list1}
```

Program 9.15 List1

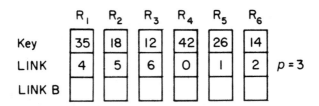

Following the links starting at R_p we obtain the logical sequence of records $R_3, R_6, R_2,$

R_5, R_1 and R_4 corresponding to the key sequence 12, 14, 18, 26, 35, and 42. Filling in the backward links, we have

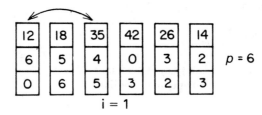

The configuration at the end of each execution of the **for** loop is

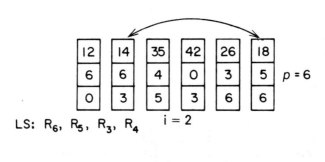

The logical sequence of the remaining list (LS) is: $R_6, R_2 R_5, R_3, R_4$. The remaining execution yields

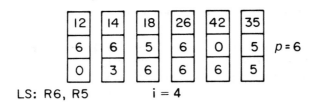

LS: R6, R5   i = 4

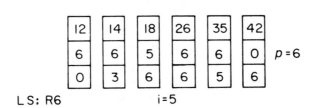

L S: R6   i = 5

Analysis of Procedure *list*1

If there are n records in the file then the time required to convert the chain P into a doubly linked list is $O(n)$. The **for** loop is iterated $n - 1$ times. In each iteration at most two records are interchanged. This requires three records to move. If each record is m words long, then the cost per interchange is $3m$. The total time is therefore $O(nm)$. The worst case of $3(n - 1)$ record moves is achievable. For example, consider the input key sequence $R_1, R_2, \cdots, R_n$, with $R_2 < R_3 < \ldots < R_n$ and $R_1 > R_n$. For $n = 4$ and keys 4,1,2,3 the file after each iteration has the following form: $i = 1$: 1,4,2,3; $i = 2$: 1,2,4,3; $i = 3$: 1,2,3,4. A total of nine record moves is made.

Several modifications to algorithm *list*1 are possible. One that is of interest was given by M. D. MacLaren. This results in a rearrangement algorithm in which no additional link fields are necessary. In this algorithm (Program 9.16), after the record R_p is exchanged with R_i the link field of the new R_i is set to p to indicate that the original record was moved. This, together with the observation that p must always be $\geq i$, permits a correct reordering of the records. The computing time remains O(nm).

```
 1 procedure list2(var r :afile; n : integer; p : integer);
 2 {same function as list1 except that a second link field, linkb,
 3   is not required}
 4 var i,q : integer;
 5     t : records;
 6 begin
 7   for i := 1 to n − 1 do
 8   begin
 9     {find correct record to place into i-th position.  The index
10      of this record must be ≥ i as records in positions
11      1, 2, ..., i − 1 are already correctly positioned}
12     while p < i do
13       p := r [p ].link;
14     q := r [p ].link;        {r_q is next record with largest key}
15     if p < > i {interchange r_i and r_p moving r_p to its}
16     then          {correct spot as r_p has i-th smallest key.}
17     begin         {Also set link from old position of r_j to}
18       t := r [i ];                          {new one}
19       r [i ] := r [p ]; r [p ] := t ; r [i ].link := p;
20     end; {of if}
21     p := q;
22   end; {of for}
23 end; {of list2}
```

Program 9.16 List2

Example 9.9: The data is the same as in Example 9.8. After the list sort we have

	R_1	R_2	R_3	R_4	R_5	R_6	
key	35	18	12	42	26	14	
link	4	5	6	0	1	2	$p = 3$

After each iteration of the **for** loop, we have

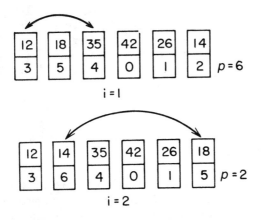

12	18	35	42	26	14	
3	5	4	0	1	2	$p = 6$

$i = 1$

12	14	35	42	26	18	
3	6	4	0	1	5	$p = 2$

$i = 2$

Now $p < 3$ and so it is advanced to $r[p].link = 6$.

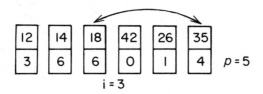

12	14	18	42	26	35	
3	6	6	0	1	4	$p = 5$

$i = 3$

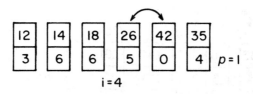

i = 4

Again $p < 5$ and following links from $r[p]$ we find $r[6]$ to be the record with fifth smallest key.

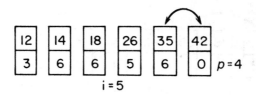

i = 5

Analysis of Procedure *list2*

The sequence of record moves for *list2* is identical to that for *list1*. Hence, in the worst case $3(n-1)$ record moves for a total cost of $O(nm)$ are made. No node is examined more than once in the **while** loop. So the total time for the **while** loop is $O(n)$. While the asymptotic computing time for both *list1* and *list2* is the same and the same number of record moves is made in either case, we would expect *list2* to be slightly faster than *list1* because each time two records are interchanged *list1* does more work than *list2* does. *list1* is inferior to *list2* on both space and time considerations.

The list sort technique discussed above does not appear to be well suited for use with sort methods such as quick sort and heap sort. The sequential representation of the heap is essential to heap sort. In such cases as well as in the methods suited to list sort, one can maintain an auxiliary table with one entry per record. The entries in this table serve as an indirect reference to the records. Let this table be type *tablelist* which is defined as *tablelist* = **array** [1 .. *maxn*] **of integer**. At the start of the sort $t[i] = i$, $1 \le i \le n$. If the sorting algorithm requires an interchange of R_i and R_j, then only the table entries need to be interchanged, i.e., $t[i]$ and $t[j]$. At the end of the sort, the record with the smallest key is $R_{t[1]}$ and that with the largest $R_{t[n]}$. In general, following a table sort $R_{t[i]}$ is the record with the i'th smallest key. The required permutation on the records is therefore $R_{t[1]}, R_{r[2]}, ..., R_{t[n]}$ (see Figure 9.2). This table is adequate even in situations such as binary search, where a sequentially ordered file is needed. In other situations, it may be necessary to physically rearrange the records according to the permutation specified by t.

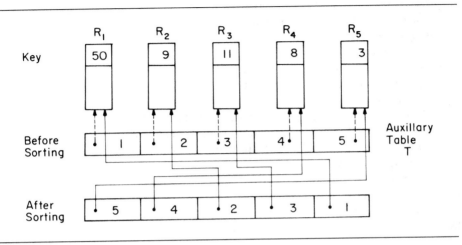

Figure 9.2 Table sort

The algorithm to rearrange records corresponding to the permutation $t[1], t[2], ..., t[n]$ is a rather interesting application of a theorem from mathematics: every permutation is made up of disjoint cycles. The cycle for any element i is made up of $i, t[i], t^2[i], \cdots t^k[i]$ (where $t^j[i] = t[t^{j-1}[i]]$) and $t^0[i] = i$ such that $t^k[i] = i$. Thus, the permutation t of Figure 9.2 has two cycles, the first involving R_1 and R_5 and the second involving R_4, R_3, and R_2. Procedure *table* (Program 9.17) utilizes this cyclic decomposition of a permutation. First, the cycle containing R_1 is followed and all records moved to their correct positions. The cycle containing R_2 is the next one examined unless this cycle has already been examined. The cycles for $R_3, R_4, ..., R_{n-1}$ are followed in that order, achieving a reordering of all the records. While processing a trivial cycle for R_1 (i.e., $t[i] = i$), no rearrangement involving records R_i is required since the condition $t[i] = i$ means that the records with the i'th smallest key is R_i. In processing a nontrivial cycle for record R_i (i.e., $t[i] \neq i$), R_i is moved to a temporary position p, then the record at $t[i]$ is moved to i; next the records at $t[t[i]]$ is moved to $t[i]$, and so on until the end of the cycle $t^k[i]$ is reached and the record at p is moved to $t^{k-1}[i]$.

Example 9.10: Following a table sort on the file f we have the following values for t (only the key values for the eight records of f are shown):

```
1 procedure table(var r : afile; n : integer; var t : tablelist);
2 {The records r [1], ..., r [n ] are rearranged to correspond to the
3  sequence r [t [1]], ⋯ r [t [n ]], n ≥ 1}
4 var i,j,k : integer;
5     p : records;
6 begin
7   for i := 1 to n − 1 do
8   if t [i ] < > i
9   then                {there is a nontrivial cycle starting at i}
10  begin               {move r [i ] to a temporary spot p and follow}
11    p := r [i ];      {cycle i,t [i ], t [t [i ]], ..., until the correct spot}
12    j := i;
13    repeat
14      k := t [j ];
15      r [j ] := r [k ];
16      t [j ] := j;
17      j := k;
18    until t [j ] = i;
19    r [j ] := p; {j is position for record p}
20    t [j ] := j;
21  end;
22 end; {of table}
```

Program 9.17 Table sort

	R_1	R_2	R_3	R_4	R_5	R_6	R_7	R_8
f	35	14	12	42	26	50	31	18
t	3	2	8	5	7	1	4	6

There are two nontrivial cycles in the permutation specified by t. The first is R_1, R_3, R_8, R_6, and R_1. The second is R_4, R_5, R_7, R_4. During the first iteration ($i = 1$) of the **for** loop of algorithm *table*, the cycle $R_1, R_{t[1]}, R_{t^2[1]}, R_{t^3[1]}, R_1$ is followed. Record R_1 is moved to a temporary spot P. $R_{t[1]}$ (i.e., R_3) is moved to the position R_1; $R_{t^2[1]}$ (i.e., R_8) is moved to R_3; R_6 to R_8 and finally P to R_6. Thus, at the end of the first iteration we have

f	12	14	18	42	26	35	31	50
t	1	2	3	5	7	6	4	8

For i = 2, 3, $t[i]$ = i, indicating that these records are already in their correct positions. When i = 4, the next nontrivial cycle is discovered and the records on this cycle R_4, R_5, R_7, R_4 are moved to their correct positions. Following this we have

f	12	14	18	26	31	35	42	50
t	1	2	3	4	5	6	7	8

For the remaining values of $i(i$ = 5, 6, and 7), $t[i]$ = i, and no more nontrivial cycles are found. □

Analysis of Procedure *table*

If each record uses m words of storage then the additional space needed is m words for p plus a few more for variables such as i, j, and k. To obtain an estimate of the computing time we observe that the **for** loop is executed $n-1$ times. If for some value of i, $t[i] \neq i$ then there is a nontrivial cycle including $k > 1$ distinct records $R_i, R_{t[i]}, ..., R_{t^{k-1}[i]}$. Rearranging these records requires $k+1$ record moves. Following this, the records involved in this cycle are not moved again at any time in the algorithm since $t[j]=j$ for all such records R_j. Hence no record can be in two different nontrivial cycles. Let k_l be the number of records on a nontrivial cycle starting at R_l when $i=l$ in the algorithm. Let $k_l=0$ for a trivial cycle. Then, the total number of record moves is $\sum_{\substack{l=0 \\ k_l \neq 0}}^{n-1} (k_l+1)$. Since the records on nontrivial cycles must be different, $\sum k_l \leq n$. The total record moves is thus maximum when $\sum k_l = n$ and there are $\lfloor n/2 \rfloor$ cycles. When n is even, each cycle contains two records. Otherwise one contains three and the others two. In either case the number of record moves is $\lfloor 3n/2 \rfloor$. One record move costs $O(m)$ time. The total computing time is therefore $O(mn)$. □

In comparing the algorithms *list2* and *table* for rearranging records we see that in the worst case *list2* makes $3(n-1)$ record moves while *table* makes only $\lfloor 3n/2 \rfloor$ record moves. For larger values of m it would therefore be worthwhile to make one pass over the sorted list of records creating a table t corresponding to a table sort. This would take $O(n)$ time. Then algorithm *table* could be used to rearrange the records in the order specified by t.

Of the several sorting methods we have studied there is no one method that is best. Some methods are good for small n, others for large n. Insertion sort is good when the file is already partially ordered. Because of the low overhead of the method it is also the best sorting method for "small" n. Merge sort has the best worst case behavior but requires more storage than heap sort and has slightly more overhead than merge sort. Quick sort has the best average behavior but its worst case behavior is $O(n^2)$. The behavior of radix sort depends on the size of the keys and the choice of r.

Figure 9.3 gives the average running times for *InsertionSort*, *QuickSort*, *MergeSort*, and *HeapSort*. Figure 9.4 is a plot of these times. As can be seen for *n* up to about 20, *InsertionSort* is the fastest. *QuickSort* is the fastest for values of *n* from about 20 to about 45. For larger values of *n*, *MergeSort* is the fastest. In practice, therefore, it would be worthwhile to combine *InsertionSort*, *QuickSort*, and *MergeSort* so that *MergeSort* uses *QuickSort* for subfiles of size less than about 45 and *QuickSort* uses *InsertionSort* when the subfile size is below about 20.

n	quick	merge	heap	insert
0	0.041	0.027	0.034	0.032
10	1.064	1.524	1.482	0.775
20	2.343	3.700	3.680	2.253
30	3.700	5.587	6.153	4.430
40	5.085	7.800	8.815	7.275
50	6.542	9.892	11.583	10.892
60	7.987	11.947	14.427	15.013
70	9.587	15.893	17.427	20.000
80	11.167	18.217	20.517	25.450
90	12.633	20.417	23.717	31.767
100	14.275	22.950	26.775	38.325
200	30.775	48.475	60.550	148.300
300	48.171	81.600	96.657	319.657
400	65.914	109.829	134.971	567.629
500	84.400	138.033	174.100	874.600
600	102.900	171.167	214.400	
700	122.400	199.240	255.760	
800	142.160	230.480	297.480	
900	160.400	260.100	340.000	
1000	181.000	289.450	382.250	

Times are in hundredths of a second

Figure 9.3 Average times for sort methods

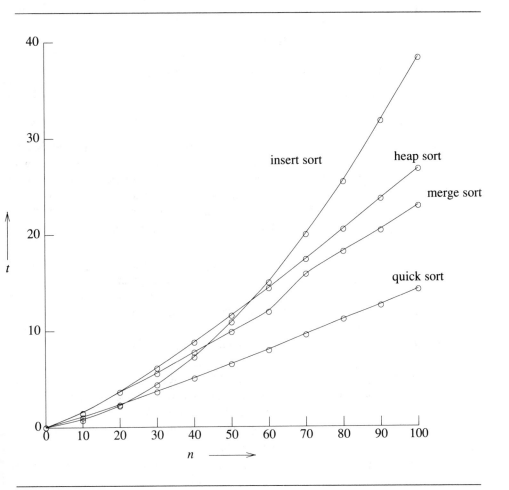

Figure 9.4 Plot of average times

9.9 REFERENCES AND SELECTED READINGS

A comprehensive discussion of sorting and searching may be found in:

The Art of Computer Programming: Sorting and Searching, by D. Knuth, vol. 3, Addison-Wesley, Reading, Massachusetts, 1973.

Two other useful references on sorting are

Sorting and Sort Systems, by H. Lorin, Addison-Wesley, Reading, Massachusetts, 1975.

Internal Sorting Methods Illustrated with PL/1 Programs, by R. Rich, Prentice-Hall, Englewood Cliffs, 1972.

Figures 9.3 and 9.4 are taken from

Software Development in Pascal, by S. Sahni, Camelot Publishing Co., 1985.

9.10 EXERCISES

1. [Count sort] About the simplest known sorting method arises from the observation that the position of a record in a sorted file depends on the number of records with smaller keys. Associated with each record there is a *count* field used to determine the number of records which must precede this one in the sorted file. Write an algorithm to determine the *count* of each record in an unordered file. Show that if the file has n records then all the *counts* can be determined by making at most $n(n-1)/2$ key comparisons.

2. The insertion of algorithm *insert* was carried out by (a) searching for the spot at which the insertion is to be made and (b) making the insertion. If as a result of the search it was decided that the insertion had to be made between R_i and R_{i+1}, then records $R_{i+1}, ..., R_n$ were moved one space to locations $R_{i+2}, ..., R_{n+1}$. This was carried out in parallel with the search of (a). (a) can be sped up using the idea of *BinarySearch*. Write an *insert* algorithm incorporating this.

3. Phase (b) (see Exercise 2) can be sped up by maintaining the sorted file as a linked list. In this case the insertion can be made without any accompanying movement of the other records. However, now (a) must be carried out sequentially as before. Such an insertion scheme is known as list insertion. Write an algorithm for list insertion. Note that the insertion algorithms of Exercises 3 and 4 can be used for a sort without making any changes in *InsertionSort*.

4. (a) Show that algorithm *QuickSort* takes $O(n^2)$ time when the input file is already in sorted order.
   (b) Why is $K_m \leq K_{n+1}$ required in *QuickSort*?

5. (a) The quick sort algorithm *QuickSort* presented in Section 9.3 always fixes the position of the first record in the subfile currently being sorted. A better choice for this record is to choose the record with key value which is the median of the keys of the first, middle, and last record in the subfile. Thus, using this median of three rule we correctly fix the position of the record R_i with $K_i =$ median $\{K_m, K_{(m+n)/2}, K_n\}$; i.e., K_i is the second largest key, e.g., median $\{10,5,7\}=7=$ median $\{10,7,7\}$. Write a nonrecursive version of *QuickSort* incorporating this median of three rule to determine the record whose position is to be fixed. Also, adopt the suggestion of Section 9.8 and use insertion sort to sort subfiles of size less than 21. Show that this algorithm takes $O(n \log n)$ time on an already sorted file.

(b) Show that if smaller subfiles are sorted first then the recursion in algorithm *QuickSort* can be simulated by a stack of depth O(*log n*).

6. Quick sort is an unstable sorting method. Give an example of an input file in which the order of records with equal keys is not preserved.

7. (a) Prove that algorithm *MergeSort* is stable.

(b) Heap sort is unstable. Give an example of an input file in which the order of records with equal keys is not preserved.

8. In the merge sort scheme discussed in Section 9.5 the sort was started with *n* sorted files each of size 1. Another approach would be to first make one pass over the data determining sequences of records that are in order and then using these as the initially sorted files. In this case, a left-to-right pass over the data of Example 9.4 would result in the above partitioning of the data file into sorted subfiles. This would be followed by pairwise merging of the files until only one file remains.

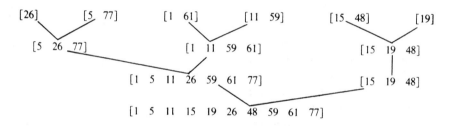

Rewrite the merge sort algorithm to take into account the existing order in the records. How much time does this algorithm take on an initially sorted file? Note that the original algorithm took O(*n* log *n*) on such an input file. What is the worst case computing time of the new algorithm? How much additional space is needed? Use linked lists.

9. Does algorithm *RadixSort* result in a stable sort when used to sort numbers as in Example 9.7?

10. Write a sort algorithm to sort records $R_1, ..., R_n$ lexically on keys $(K^1, ..., K^r)$ for the case when the range of each key is much larger than *n*. In this case the bin sort scheme used in *RadixSort* to sort within each key becomes inefficient (why?). What scheme would you use to sort within a key if we desired an algorithm with
(a) good worst case behavior
(b) good average behavior
(c) *n* is small, say <15

11. If we have n records with integer keys in the range $[0,n^2)$, then they may be sorted in $O(n \log n)$ time using heap or merge sort. Radix sort on a single key, i.e., $d=1$ and $r=n^2$ takes $O(n^2)$ time. Show how to interpret the keys as two subkeys so that radix sort will take only $O(n)$ time to sort n records. (Hint: each key, K_i, may be written as $K_i = K_i^1 n + K_i^2$ with K_i^1 and K_i^2 integers in the range $[0,n)$.)

12. Generalize the method of the previous exercise to the case of integer keys in the range $(0,n^p)$ obtaining an $O(pn)$ sorting method.

13. Write the status of the following file F at the end of each phase of the following algorithms:

    (a) *InsertionSort*

    (b) *QuickSort*

    (c) *MergeSort*

    (d) *HeapSort*

    (e) *RadixSort* – radix 10

$$F = (12,2,16,30,8,28,4,10,20,6,18)$$

14. Write a table sort version of quick sort. Now during the sort, records are not physically moved. Instead, $t[i]$ is the index of the record that would have been in position i if records were physically moved around as in algorithm *QuickSort*. To begin with $t[i]=i$, $1 \le i \le n$. At the end of the sort $t[i]$ is the index of the record that should be in the i'th position in the sorted file. So now algorithm *table* of Section 9.8 may be used to rearrange the records into the sorted order specified by t. Note that this reduces the amount of data movement taking place when compared to *QuickSort* for the case of large records.

15. Write an algorithm similar to algorithm *table* to rearrange the records of a file if with each record we have a *count* of the number of records preceding it in the sorted file (see Exercise 1).

16. Under what conditions would an MSD radix sort be more efficient than an LSD radix sort?

17. Assume you are given a list of five-letter English words and are faced with the problem of listing out these words in sequences such that the words in each sequence are anagrams, i.e., if x and y are in the same sequence, then word x is a permutation of word y. You are required to list out the fewest such sequences. With this restriction show that no word can appear in more than one sequence. How would you go about solving this problem?

18. Assume you are working in the census department of a small town where the number of records, about 3,000, is small enough to fit into the internal memory of a computer. All the people currently living in this town were born in the United States. There is one record for each person in this town. Each record contains

(a) the state in which the person was born

(b) county of birth

(c) name of person

How would you produce a list of all persons living in this town? The list is to be ordered by state. Within each state the persons are to be listed by their counties, the counties being arranged in alphabetical order. Within each county, the names are also listed in alphabetical order. Justify any assumptions you may make.

19. Use the composing strategy outlined at the end of Section 9.8 to combine *InsertionSort*, *QuickSort*, and *MergeSort* into a single sorting scheme. Compare the average run time of this with that of the individual sorting methods.

20. Experiment with *RadixSort* to see how it performs relative to the sorting procedures compared in Figure 9.3.

21. Obtain Figures 9.3 and 9.4 for the case of worst case run time.

CHAPTER 10

HASHING

10.1 HASH TABLES

In Section 7.13, we introduced the binary search tree as a data structure that can be used when we have a collection of distinct values or identifiers and the operations to be performed are search, insert, and delete. When a binary search tree is used, the search for an identifier is carried out via a sequence of comparisons. In this chapter we shall study an alternate to this strategy. In *hashing*, the identifiers are stored in a table called the *hash table*. The address or location of an identifier, X, is obtained by computing some arithmetic function, f, of X. $f(X)$ gives the address of X in the table. This address will be referred to as the hash or home address of X. The memory available to maintain the symbol table is assumed to be sequential. This memory is referred to as the hash table, ht. The hash table is partitioned into b buckets, $ht[0]$, ..., $ht[b-1]$. Each bucket is capable of holding s records. Thus, a bucket is said to consist of s slots, each slot being large enough to hold one record. Usually $s=1$ and each bucket can hold exactly one record. A hashing function, $f(X)$, is used to perform an identifier transformation on X. $f(X)$ maps the set of possible identifiers onto the integers 0 through $b-1$. If the identifiers were restricted to be at most six characters long with the first one being a letter and the remaining either letters or decimal digits, then there would be $T = \sum_{0 \le i \le 5} 26 \times 36^i > 1.6 \times 10^9$ distinct possible values for X. Any reasonable application, however, would use far less than all of these identifiers.

The ratio n/T is the *identifier density*, while $\alpha = n/(sb)$ is the *loading density* or *loading factor*. Since the number of identifiers, n, in use is usually several orders of magnitude less than the total number of possible identifiers, T, the number of buckets, b, in the hash table is also much less than T. Therefore, the hash function f must map several different identifiers into the same bucket. Two identifiers I_1, I_2 are said to be *synonyms* with respect to f if $f(I_1) = f(I_2)$. Distinct synonyms are entered into the same

456

bucket so long as all the *s* slots in that bucket have not been used. An *overflow* is said to occur when a new identifier *I* is mapped or hashed by *f* into a full bucket. A *collision* occurs when two nonidentical identifiers are hashed into the same bucket. When the bucket size *s* is 1, collisions and overflows occur simultaneously.

As an example, let us consider the hash table *ht* with $b=26$ buckets, each bucket having exactly two slots, i.e., $s=2$. Assume that there are $n=10$ distinct identifiers in the program and that each identifier begins with a letter. The loading factor, α, for this table is $10/52 = 0.19$. The hash function *f* must map each of the possible identifiers into one of the numbers 1-26. If the internal binary representation for the letters A-Z corresponds to the numbers 1-26, respectively, then the function *f* defined by $f(X)=$ the first character of *X* will hash all identifiers *X* into the hash table. The identifiers *GA*, *D*, *A*, *G*, *L*, *A*2, *A*1, *A*3, *A*4, and *E* will be hashed into buckets 7, 4, 1, 7, 12, 1, 1, 1, 1, and 5, respectively, by this function. The identifiers *A*, *A*1, *A*2, *A*3, and *A*4 are synonyms. So also are *G* and *GA*. Figure 10.1 shows the identifiers *GA*, *D*, *A*, *G*, and *A*2 entered into the hash table.

	SLOT 1	SLOT 2
1	A	A2
2	0	0
3	0	0
4	D	0
5	0	0
6	0	0
7	GA	G
⋮	⋮	⋮
26	0	0

Zeros indicate empty slots

Figure 10.1 Hash table with 26 buckets and two slots per bucket

Note that *GA* and *G* are in the same bucket and each bucket has two slots. Similarly, the synonyms *A* and *A2* are in the same bucket. The next identifier, *A*1, hashes into the bucket *ht* [1]. This bucket is full and a search of the bucket indicates that *A*1 is not in the bucket. An overflow has now occurred. Where in the table should *A*1 be entered so that it may be retrieved when needed? We will look into overflow handling strategies in Section 10.3. In the case where no overflows occur, the time required to enter or search for identifiers using hashing depends only on the time required to compute the hash function *f* and the time to search one bucket. Since the bucket size *s* is usually small (for internal tables *s* is usually 1) the search for an identifier within a bucket is carried out using sequential search. The time, then, is independent of n, the number of identifiers in use. For tree tables, this time was, on the average, $\log n$. The hash function in the above example is not very well suited for the use we have in mind because of the very large number of collisions and resulting overflows that occur. This is so because it is not unusual to find programs in which many of the variables begin with the same letter. Ideally, we would like to choose a function f which is both easy to compute and results in very few collisions. Since the ratio b/T is usually very small, it is impossible to avoid collisions altogether.

In summary, hashing schemes perform an identifier transformation through the use of a hash function f. It is desirable to choose a function f which is easily computed and also minimizes the number of collisions. Since the size of the identifier space, T, is usually several orders of magnitude larger than the number of buckets b, and s is small, overflows necessarily occur. Hence a mechanism to handle overflows is also needed.

10.2 HASHING FUNCTIONS

A hashing function, f, transforms an identifier X into a bucket address in the hash table. As mentioned earlier the desired properties of such a function are that it be easily computable and that it minimize the number of collisions. A function such as the one discussed earlier is not a very good choice for a hash function for symbol tables even though it is fairly easy to compute. The reason for this is that it depends only on the first character in the identifier. Since many programs use several identifiers with the same first letter, we expect several collisions to occur. In general, then, we would like the function to depend upon all the characters in the identifiers. In addition, we would like the hash function to be such that it does not result in a biased use of the hash table for random inputs; i.e., if X is an identifier chosen at random from the identifier space, then we want the probability that $f(X)=i$ to be $1/b$ for all buckets i. Then a random X has an equal chance of hashing into any of the b buckets. A hash function satisfying this property will be termed a *uniform hash function*.

Several kinds of uniform hash functions are in use. We shall describe four of these.

(1) Mid-Square

One hash function that has found much use in symbol table applications is the "middle of square" function. This function, f_m, is computed by squaring the identifier and then using an appropriate number of bits from the middle of the square to obtain the bucket address; the identifier is assumed to fit into one computer word. Since the middle bits of the square will usually depend upon all of the characters in the identifier, it is expected that different identifiers would result in different hash addresses with high probability even when some of the characters are the same. Figure 10.2 shows the bit configurations resulting from squaring some sample identifiers. The number of bits to be used to obtain the bucket address depends on the table size. If r bits are used, the range of values is 2^r, so the size of hash tables is chosen to be a power of 2 when this kind of scheme is used.

IDENTIFIER	INTERNAL REPRESENTATION	
X	X	X^2
A	1	1
A1	134	20420
A2	135	20711
A3	136	21204
A4	137	21501
A9	144	23420
B	2	4
C	3	11
G	7	61
DMAX	4150130	21526443617100
DMAX1	415013034	5264473522151420
AMAX	1150130	1345423617100
AMAX1	115013034	3454246522151420

Figure 10.2 Internal representations of X and X^2 in octal notation. X is input right justified, zero filled, six bits or two octal digits per character

(2) Division

Another simple choice for a hash function is obtained by using the modulo (**mod**) operator. The identifier X is divided by some number M and the remainder is used as the hash address for X.

$$f_D(X)=X \bmod M$$

This gives bucket addresses in the range $0-(M-1)$ and so the hash table is at least of size $b=M$. The choice of M is critical. If M is a power of 2, then $f_D(X)$ depends only on the least significant bits of X. For instance, if each character is represented by six bits and identifiers are stored right justified in a 60-bit word with leading bits filled with zeros (Figure 10.3) then with $M=2^i$, $i\leq6$ the identifiers $A1$, $B1$, $C1$, $X41$, $DNTXY1$, etc. all have the same bucket address. With $M=2^i$, $i\leq12$ the identifiers AXY, BXY, $WTXY$, etc. have the same bucket address.

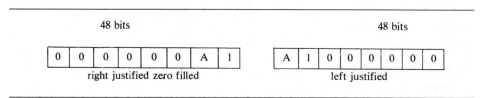

Figure 10.3 Identifier $A1$ right and left justified and zero filled (six bits per character)

Since programmers have a tendency to use many variables with the same suffix, the choice of M as a power of 2 would result in many collisions. This choice of M would have even more disastrous results if the identifier X is stored left justified zero filled. Then, all one character identifiers would map to the same bucket, 0, for $M=2^i$, $i\leq54$; all two character identifiers would map to the bucket 0 for $M=2^i$, $i\leq48$, etc. As a result of this observation, we see that when the division function f_D is used as a hash function, the table size should not be a power of 2 while when the "middle of square" function f_m is used the table size is a power of 2. If M is divisible by 2 then odd keys are mapped to odd buckets (as the remainder is odd) and even keys are mapped to even buckets. The use of the hash table is thus biased.

Let us try some other values for M and see what kind of identifiers get mapped to the same bucket, the goal being that we wish to avoid a choice of M that will lead to many collisions. This kind of analysis is possible as we have some idea as to the relationships between different variable names programmers tend to use. For instance, the knowledge that a program tends to have variables with the same suffix led us to reject $M=2^i$. For similar reasons even values of M prove undesirable. Let $X=x_1x_2$ and $Y=x_2x_1$ be two identifiers each consisting of the characters x_1 and x_2. If the internal binary representation of x_1 has value $C(x_1)$ and that for x_2 has value $C(x_2)$ then if each character is represented by six bits, the numeric value of X is $2^6C(x_1)+C(x_2)$ while that for Y is $2^6C(x_2)+C(x_1)$. If p is a prime number dividing M then

$$(f_D(X)-f_D(Y))\bmod p$$

$$= (2^6C(x_1)\bmod p + C(x_2)\bmod p - 2^6C(x_2)\bmod p - C(x_1)\bmod p)\bmod p$$

If $p = 3$, then

$$(f_D(X)-f_D(Y))\text{mod}p$$

$$= (64 \text{ mod } 3\ C(x_1)\text{mod } 3 + C(x_2)\text{mod } 3$$

$$- 64 \text{ mod } 3\ C(x_2)\text{mod } 3 - C(x_1)\text{mod } 3) \text{ mod } 3$$

$$= C(x_1)\text{mod } 3 + C(x_2)\text{mod } 3 - C(x_2)\text{mod } 3 - C(x_1)\text{mod } 3$$

$$= 0 \text{ mod } 3$$

i.e., permutations of the same set of characters are hashed at a distance a factor of 3 apart. Programs in which many variables are permutations of each other would again result in a biased use of the table and hence result in many collisions. This happens because 64 mod 3 = 1. The same behavior can be expected when 7 divides M as 64 mod 7 = 1. These difficulties can be avoided by choosing M as a prime number. Then, the only factors of M are M and 1. Knuth has shown that when M divides $r^k \pm a$ where k and a are small numbers and r is the radix of the character set (in the above example $r=64$), then X mod M tends to be a simple superposition of the characters in X. Thus, a good choice for M would be: M *a prime number such that M does not divide* $r^k \pm a$ *for small k and a*. In Section 10.3 we shall see other reasons for choosing M as a prime number. In practice it has been observed that it is sufficient to choose M such that it has no prime divisors less than 20.

(3) Folding

In this method the identifier X is partitioned into several parts, all but the last being of the same length. These parts are then added together to obtain the hash address for X. There are two ways of carrying out this addition. In the first, all but the last part are shifted so that the least significant bit of each part lines up with the corresponding bit of the last part (Figure 10.4(a)). The different parts are now added together to get $f(X)$. This method is known as *shift folding*. The other method of adding the parts is *folding at the boundaries*. In this method, the identifier is folded at the part boundaries and digits falling into the same position are added together (Figure 10.4(b)) to obtain $f(X)$.

(4) Digit Analysis

This method is particularly useful in the case of a static file where all the identifiers in the table are known in advance. Each identifier X is interpreted as a number using some radix r. The same radix is used for all the identifiers in the table. Using this radix, the digits of each identifier are examined. Digits having the most skewed distributions are deleted. Enough digits are deleted so that the number of digits left is small enough to give an address in the range of the hash table. The criterion used to find the digits to be used as addresses, based on the measure of uniformity in the distribution of values in each digit, is to keep those digits having no abnormally high peaks

| P_1 | P_2 | P_3 | P_4 | P_5 |

$P_1 = 123 \quad P_2 = 203 \quad P_3 = 241 \quad P_4 = 112 \quad P_5 = 20$

P_1	123
P_2	203
P_3	241
P_4	112
P_5	20
	699

P_1	123
P_2^r	302
P_3	241
P_4^r	211
P_5	20
	897

(a) shift folding

(b) folding at the boundaries $P_i^r =$ reverse of P_i

Figure 10.4 Two methods of folding

or valleys and those having small standard deviation. The same digits are used for all identifiers.

Experimental results presented in Section 10.3 suggest the use of the division method with a divisor M that has no prime factors less than 20 for general purpose applications.

10.3 OVERFLOW HANDLING

In order to be able to detect collisions and overflows, it is necessary to initialize the hash table, ht, to represent the situation when all slots are empty. Assuming that no record has identifier zero, then all slots may be initialized to zero.† When a new identifier gets hashed into a full bucket, it is necessary to find another bucket for this identifier. The simplest solution would probably be to find the closest unfilled bucket. Let us illustrate this on a 26-bucket table with one slot per bucket. Assume the identifiers to be $GA, D, A, G, L, A\,2, A\,1, A\,3, A\,4, Z, ZA, E$. For simplicity we choose the hash function $f(X) =$ first character of X. Initially, all entries in the table are zero. $f(GA)=7$, this bucket is empty, so GA and any other information making up the record are entered into $ht\,[7]$. D and A get entered into the buckets $ht\,[4]$ and $ht\,[1]$, respectively. The next identifier G has $f(G)=7$. This slot is already used by GA. The next vacant slot is $ht\,[8]$ and so G is

† A clever way to avoid initializing the hash table has been discovered by T. Gonzalez (see Exercise 6).

entered there. *L* enters *ht* [12]. *A2* collides with *A* at *ht* [1], the bucket overflows and *A2* is entered at the next vacant slot *ht* [2]. *A* 1, *A* 3, and *A4* are entered at *ht* [3], *ht* [5], and *ht* [6], respectively. *Z* is entered at *ht* [26], *ZA* at *ht* [9] (the hash table is used circularly), and *E* collides with *A3* at *ht* [5] and is eventually entered at *ht* [10]. Figure 10.5 shows the resulting table. This method of resolving overflows is known as *linear probing* or *linear open addressing*.

1	A
2	A2
3	A1
4	D
5	A3
6	A4
7	GA
8	G
9	ZA
10	E
11	0
12	L
13	0
	0
≈	⋮ ≈
	0
26	Z

Figure 10.5 Hash table with linear probing (26 buckets, 1 slot per bucket)

In order to search the table for an identifier, x, it is necessary to first compute $f(x)$ and then examine keys at positions $ht[f(x)]$, $ht[f(x)+1]$, ..., $ht[f(x)+j]$ such that $ht[f(x)+j]$ either equals x (x is in the table) or *blankident* (x is not in the table) or we eventually return to $ht[f(x)]$ (the table is full). The resulting algorithm is Program 10.1. The data types used are

type *identifier* = **packed array** [1..*maxchar*] **of char**
          hashtable = **array**[1..*maxsize*] **of** *identifer*;

```
 1 procedure LinearSearch (x : identifier; ht : hashtable; var j : integer;
                                                    b : integer);
 2 {Search the hash table ht [0..b − 1] (each bucket has exactly one
 3   slot) using linear probing. If ht [ j ] = blankident then the j'th bucket
 4   is empty and x can be entered into the table. Otherwise ht [ j ] = x
 5   which is already in the table. f is the hash function.}
 6 var i : integer
 7 begin
 8   i := f (x); j := i;
 9   while (ht [ j ] < > x) and (ht [ j ] < > blankident ) do
10   begin
11     j := ( j + 1) mod b; {treat the table as circular}
12     if j = i then {no empty slots}
13             tablefull;
14   end;
15 end; {of LinearSearch}
```

Program 10.1 Linear search

Our earlier example shows that when linear probing is used to resolve overflows, identifiers tend to cluster together, and moreover, adjacent clusters tend to coalesce, thus increasing the search time. To locate the identifier, ZA, in the table of Figure 10.5, it is necessary to examine $ht\,[26], ht\,[1], ..., ht\,[9]$, a total of 10 comparisons. This is far worse than the worst case behavior for tree tables. If each of the identifiers in the table of Figure 10.1 was retrieved exactly once, then the number of buckets examined would be 1 for A, 2 for $A2$, 3 for $A1$, 1 for D, 5 for $A3$, 6 for $A4$, 1 for GA, 2 for G, 10 for ZA, 6 for E, 1 for L, and 1 for Z for a total of 39 buckets examined. The average number examined is 3.25 buckets per identifier. An analysis of the method shows that the expected average number of identifier comparisons, P, to look up an identifier is approximately $(2-\alpha)/(2-2\alpha)$ where α is the loading density. This is the average over all possible sets of identifiers yielding the given loading density and using a uniform function f. In the above example $\alpha = 12/26 = .47$ and $P = 1.5$. Even though the average number of probes is small, the worst case can be quite large.

One of the problems with linear open addressing is that it tends to create clusters of identifiers. Moreover, these clusters tend to merge as more identifiers are entered, leading to bigger clusters. Some improvement in the growth of clusters and hence in the average number of probes needed for searching can be obtained by *quadratic probing*. Linear probing was characterized by searching the buckets $(f\,(x)+i)\bmod\ b$, $0 \le i \le b-1$ where b is the number of buckets in the table. In quadratic probing, a quadratic function of i is used as the increment. In particular, the search is carried out by examining buckets $f\,(x)$, $(f\,(x)+i^2)\bmod\ b$, and $(f\,(x)-i^2)\bmod\ b$ for $1 \le i \le (b-1)/2$. When b is a prime number of the form $4j+3$, for j an integer, the quadratic search described above examines every bucket in the table. The proof that when b is of the form $4j+3$, quadratic probing examines all the buckets 0 to $b-1$, relies on some results from number theory. We shall not go into the proof here. The interested reader should see Radke [1970] for a proof. Figure 10.6 lists some primes of the form $4j+3$. Another possibility is to use a series of hash functions $f_1, f_2, ..., f_m$. This method is known as *rehashing*. Buckets $f_i(x)$, $1 \leq i \leq m$ are examined in that order. An alternate method for handling bucket overflow, random probing, is discussed in Exercise 10.3.

Prime	j	Prime	j
3	0	43	10
7	1	59	14
11	2	127	31
19	4	251	62
23	5	503	125
31	7	1019	254

Figure 10.6 Some primes of the form $4j+3$

One of the reasons linear probing and its variations perform poorly is that searching for an identifier involves comparison of identifiers with different hash values. In the hash table of Figure 10.5, for instance, searching for the identifier ZA involved comparisons with the buckets $ht[1]$ to $ht[8]$, even though none of the identifiers in these buckets had a collision with $ht[26]$ and so could not possibly be ZA. Many of the comparisons being made could be saved if we maintained lists of identifiers, one list per bucket, each list containing all the synonyms for that bucket. If this were done, a search would then involve computing the hash address $f(x)$ and examining only those identifiers in the list for $f(x)$. Since the sizes of these lists is not known in advance, the best way to maintain them is as linked chains. Additional space for a link is required in each slot. Each chain will have a head-node. The head-node, however, will usually be much smaller than the other nodes since it has to retain only a link. Since the lists are to be accessed at random, the head-nodes should be sequential. We assume they are numbered 1 to M if the hash function f has range 1 to M.

Using chaining to resolve collisions and the hash function used to obtain Figure 10.5, the hash chains of Figure 10.7 are obtained. When a new identifier, x, is being inserted into a chain, the insertion can be made at either end. This is so because the address of the last node in the chain is known as a result of the search that determined x was not in the list for $f(x)$. In the example of Figure 10.7 new identifiers were inserted at the front of the chains. The number of probes needed to search for any of the identifiers is now one for each of $A4$, D, E, G, L, and ZA; two for each of $A3$, GA and Z;

three for A1; four for A2 and five for A for a total of 24. The average is now two which is considerably less than for linear probing. Additional storage, however, is needed for links. The algorithm that results when chaining is used is given in Program 10.2. The data types are

type *identifier* = **packed array**[1..*maxchar*] **of char**;
  listpointer = ↑*listnode*;
  listnode = **record**
        ident = *identifier*;
        link = *listpointer*;
      end;
  hashtable = **array**[1..*maxsize*] **of** *listpointer*;

The expected number of identifier comparisons can be shown to be + $\alpha/2$ where α is the loading density n/b (b = number of head-nodes). For $\alpha=0.5$ this figure is 1.25 and for $\alpha=1$ it is about 1.5. This scheme has the additional advantage that only the b head-nodes must be sequential and reserved at the beginning. Each head-node, however, will be at most one half to one word long. The other nodes will be much bigger and need be allocated only as needed. This could represent an overall reduction in space required for certain loading densities despite the links. If each record in the table is five words long, $n=100$ and $\alpha=0.5$, then the hash table will be of size $200\times 5= 1000$ words. Only 500 of these are used as $\alpha=0.5$. On the other hand, if chaining is used with one full word per link, then 200 words are needed for the head nodes ($b=200$). Each head node is one word long. One hundred nodes of six words each are needed for the records. The total space needed is thus 800 words, or 20 percent less than when no chaining was being used. Of course, when α is close to 1, the average number of probes using linear probing or its variations becomes quite large and the additional space used for chaining can be justified by the reduction in the expected number of probes needed for retrieval. If you wish to delete an entry from the table, then this can be done by just removing that node from its chain. The problem of deleting entries while using open addressing to resolve collisions is tackled in Exercise 1.

The results of this section tend to imply that the performance of a hash table depends only on the method used to handle overflows and is independent of the hash function so long as a uniform hash function is being used. While this is true when the identifiers are selected at random from the identifier space, it is not true in practice. In practice, there is a tendency to make a biased use of identifiers. Many identifiers in use have a common suffix or prefix or are simple permutations of other identifiers. Hence, in practice we would expect different hash functions to result in different hash table performance. The table of Figure 10.8 presents the results of an empirical study conducted by Lum, Yuen, and Dodd. The values in each column give the average number of bucket accesses made in searching eight different tables with 33,575, 24,050, 4909, 3072, 2241, 930, 762, and 500 identifiers each. As expected, chaining outperforms linear open addressing as a method for overflow handling. In looking over the figures for the various

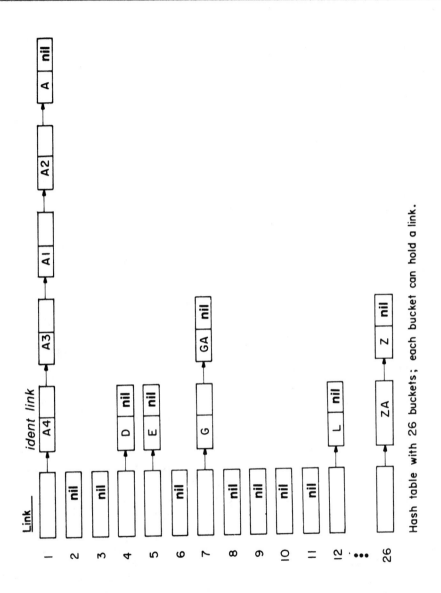

Figure 10.7 Hash chains corresponding to Figure 10.5

```
 1 procedure ChainSearch (x : identifier; var ht : hashtable;
 2                         b : integer; var i : listpointer);
 3   {Search the hash table ht [0..b − 1] for x. Either ht [i ] = nil or
 4   it is a pointer to the list of identifiers x :f (x) = i. List
 5   nodes have field ident and link. Either j points to the node
 6   already containing x or j = nil.}
 7 var found : boolean;
 8   begin
 9   j := ht [f (x)]; {compute head-node address}
10     {search the chain starting at j}
11     found := false;
12     while (j < > nil) and not found do
13       if j↑. ident = x then found := true
14                        else j := j↑. link;
15 end; {of ChainSearch}
```

Program 10.2 Chain search

hash functions, we see that division is generally superior to the other types of hash functions. For a general application, it is therefore recommended that the division method be used. The divisor should be a prime number, though it is sufficient to choose a divisor that has no prime factors less than 20. The table also gives the theoretical expected number of bucket accesses based on random keys.

10.4 THEORETICAL EVALUATION OF OVERFLOW TECHNIQUES

The experimental evaluation of hashing techniques indicates a very good performance over conventional techniques such as balanced trees. The worst case performance for hashing can, however, be very bad. In the worst case an insertion or a search in a hash table with n identifiers may take $O(n)$ time. In this section we present a probabilistic analysis for the expected performance of the chaining method and state without proof the results of similar analyses for the other overflow handling methods. First, we formalize what we mean by expected performance.

Let $HT[0: b-1]$ be a hash table with b buckets, each bucket having one slot. Let f be a uniform hash function with range $[0, b-1]$. If n identifiers $X_1, X_2, ..., X_n$ are entered into the hash table then there are b^n distinct hash sequences $f(X_1), f(X_2), ..., f(X_n)$. Assume that each of these is equally likely to occur. Let S_n denote the expected number of identifier comparisons needed to locate a randomly chosen X_i, $1 \leq i \leq n$. Then, S_n is the average number of comparisons needed to find the j'th key X_j; averaged over $1 \leq j \leq n$ with

hash function type	$\alpha = n/b$ .5		.75		.9		.95	
	C	L	C	L	C	L	C	L
MIDSQ	1.26	1.73	1.40	9.75	1.45	27.14	1.47	37.53
DIV	1.19	4.52	1.31	7.20	1.38	22.42	1.41	25.79
FOLD S	1.33	21.75	1.48	65.10	1.40	77.01	1.51	118.57
FOLD B	1.39	22.97	1.57	48.70	1.55	69.63	1.51	97.56
DA	1.35	4.55	1.49	30.62	1.52	89.20	1.52	125.59
THEO	1.25	1.50	1.37	2.50	1.45	5.50	1.48	10.50

Number of slots per bucket = 1

C = chaining
L = linear open addressing
α = loading density
MIDSQ = middle of square
DIV = division
FOLD S = shift folding
FOLD B = folding at boundaries
DA = digit analysis
THEO = theoretical expectation
    based on random keys

Figure 10.8 Average number of bucket accesses per identifier retrieved (condensed from Lum, Yuen and Dodd, CACM, April 1971, Vol. 14, No. 4

each j equally likely and averaged over all b^n hash sequences assuming each of these to also be equally likely. Let U_n be the expected number of identifier comparisons when a search is made for an identifier not in the hash table. This hash table contains n identifiers. The quantity U_n may be defined in a manner analogous to that used for S_n.

Theorem 10.1 Let $\alpha = n/b$ be the loading density of a hash table using a uniform hashing function f. Then

    (1) for linear open addressing

$$U_n \approx \frac{1}{2}\left[1 + \frac{1}{(1-\alpha)^2}\right]$$

$$S_n \approx \frac{1}{2}\left[1 + \frac{1}{1-\alpha}\right]$$

    (2) for rehashing, random probing, and quadratic probing

$$U_n \approx 1/(1-\alpha)$$

$$S_n \approx -\left[\frac{1}{\alpha}\right]\log_e(1-\alpha)$$

    (3) for chaining

$$U_n \approx \alpha$$

$$S_n \approx 1 + \alpha/2$$

Proof: Exact derivations of U_n and S_n are fairly involved and can be found in Knuth's book *The Art of Computer Programming: Sorting and Searching*. Here, we present a derivation of the approximate formulas for chaining. First, we must make clear our count for U_n and S_n. In case the identifier X being searched for has $f(X)=i$ and chain i has k nodes on it (not including the head-node) then k comparisons are needed if X is not on the chain. If X is j nodes away from the head node, $1 \le j \le k$, then j comparisons are needed.

When the n identifiers distribute uniformly over the b possible chains, the expected number in each chain is $n/b = \alpha$. Since $U_n =$ expected number of identifiers on a chain, we get $U_n = \alpha$.

When the i'th identifier, X_i, is being entered into the table, the expected number of identifiers on any chain is $(i-1)/b$. Hence, the expected number of comparisons needed to search for X_i after all n identifiers have been entered is $1+(i-1)/b$ (this assumes that new entries will be made at the end of the chain). We therefore get

$$S_n = \frac{1}{n}\sum_{i=1}^{n}\{1+(i-1)/b\} = 1 + \frac{n-1}{2b} \approx 1 + \frac{\alpha}{2} \quad \square$$

10.5 REFERENCES AND SELECTED READINGS

Several interesting and enlightening works on hash tables exist. Some of these are

"Scatter storage techniques," by R. Morris, *CACM*, vol. 11, no. 1, January 1968, pp. 38-44.

"Key to address transform techniques: A fundamental performance study on large existing formatted files," by V. Lum, P. Yuen, and M. Dodd, *CACM*, vol. 14, no. 4, April 1971, pp. 228-239.

"The quadratic quotient method: A hash code eliminating secondary clustering," by J. Bell, *CACM*, vol. 13, no. 2, February 1970, pp. 107-109.

"Full table quadratic searching for scatter storage," by A. Day, *CACM*, vol. 13, no. 8, August 1970, pp. 481-482.

"Identifier search mechanisms: A survey and generalized model," by D. Severence, *ACM Computing Surveys*, vol. 6, no. 3, September 1974, pp. 175-194.

"Hash table methods," by W. Mauer and T. Lewis, *ACM Computing Surveys*, vol. 7, no. 1, March 1975, pp. 5-20.

The Art of Computer Programming: Sorting and Searching, by D. Knuth, Addison-Wesley, Reading, Massachusetts, 1973.

"Reducing the retrieval time of scatter storage techniques," by R. Brent, *CACM*, vol. 16, no. 2, February 1973, pp. 105-109.

"General performance analysis of key-to-address transformation methods using an abstract file concept," by V. Lum, *CACM*, vol. 16, no. 10, October 1973, pp. 603-612.

"The use of quadratic residue research," by C. E. Radke, *CACM*, vol. 13, no. 2, Feb. 1970, pp. 103-105.

10.6 EXERCISES

1. Write an algorithm to delete identifier x from a hash table which uses hash function f and linear open addressing to resolve collisions. Show that simply setting the slot previously occupied by x to *blankident* does not solve the problem. How must algorithm *LinearSearch* be modified so that a correct search is made in the situation when deletions are permitted? Where can a new identifier be inserted?

2. (a) Show that if quadratic searching is carried out in the sequence $(f(x) + q^2)$, $(f(x) + (q - 1)^2)$, ..., $(f(x) + 1)$, $f(x)$, $(f(x) - 1)$, ..., $(f(x) - q^2)$ with $q = (b - 1)/2$ then the address difference mod b between successive buckets being examined is

    $$b - 2, b - 4, b - 6, ..., 5, 3, 1, 1, 3, 5, ..., b - 6, b - 4, b - 2$$

    (b) Write an algorithm to search a hash table $ht[0:b - 1]$ of size b for the identifier x. User f as the hash function and the quadratic probe scheme discussed in the text to resolve. In case x is not in the table, it is to be entered. Use the results of part (a) to reduce the computations.

3. [Morris 1968] In random probing, the search for an identifier, X, in a hash table with b buckets is carried out by examining buckets $f(x)$, $f(x)+S(i)$, $1 \le i \le b-1$ where $S(i)$ is a pseudo random number. The random number generator must satisfy the property that every number from 1 to $b - 1$ must be generated exactly once.

    (a) Show that for a table of size 2^r, the following sequence of computations generates numbers with this property:

    Initialize R to 1 each time the search routine is called.
    On successive calls for a random number do the following:
    $R := R * 5$
    $R := \log$ order $r + 2$ bits of R
    $S(i) := R/4$

    (b) Write an algorithm, incorporating the above random number generator, to search and insert into a hash table using random probing and the middle of square hash function, f_m.

    It can be shown that for this method, the expected value for the average number of comparisons needed to search for X is $-(1/\alpha)\log(1 - \alpha)$ for large table sizes. α is the loading factor.

4. Write an algorithm to list all the identifiers in a hash table in lexicographic order. Assume the hash function f is $f(x) = $ first character of X and linear probing is used. How much time does your algorithm take?

5. Let the binary representation of identifier X be $x_1 x_2$. Let $|x|$ denote the number of bits in x and let the first bit of x_1 be 1. Let $|x_1| = \lceil |x|/2 \rceil$ and $|x_2| = \lfloor |x|/2 \rfloor$. Consider the following hash function

$$F(x) = \text{middle } k \text{ bits of } (x_1 \text{ XOR } x_2)$$

where XOR is exclusive or. Is this a uniform hash function if identifiers are drawn at random from the space of allowable Pascal identifiers? What can you say about the behavior of this hash function in a real symbol table usage?

6. [T. Gonzalez] Design a symbol table representation which allows you to search, insert, and delete an identifier x in $O(1)$ time. Assume that $1 \le X \le m$ and that $m+n$ units of space are available where n is the number of insertions to be made. (Hint: use two arrays $a[1..n]$ and $b[1..m]$ where $a[i]$ will be the i'th identifier inserted into the table. If x is the i'th identifier inserted then $b[x]=i$.) Write algorithms to search, insert and delete identifiers. Note that you cannot initialize either a or b to zero as this would take $O(n + m)$ time. Note that x is an integer.

7. [T. Gonzalez] Let $S = \{x_1, x_2, \ldots, x_n\}$ and $T = \{y_1, y_2, \ldots, y_r\}$ be two sets. Assume $1 \le x_i \le m$, $1 \le i \le n$ and $1 \le y_i \le m$, $1 \le i \le r$. Using the idea of Exercise 6 write an algorithm to determine if $S \subseteq T$. Your algorithm should work in $O(r + n)$ time. Since $S \equiv T$ iff $S \subseteq T$ and $T \subseteq S$, this implies that one can determine in linear time if two sets are equivalent. How much space is needed by your algorithm?

8. [T. Gonzalez] Using the idea of Exercise 6 write an $O(n + m)$ time algorithm to carry out the function of algorithm *verify2* of Section 9.1. How much space does your algorithm need?

9. Using the notation of Section 10.4 show that when linear open addressing is used

$$S_n = \frac{1}{n} \sum_{i=0}^{n-1} U_i$$

Using this equation and the approximate equality

$$U_n \approx \frac{1}{2} \left[1 + \frac{1}{(1 - \alpha)^2} \right] \text{ where } \alpha = \frac{n}{b}$$

show that $S_n \approx \dfrac{1}{2} \left[1 + \dfrac{1}{(1 - \alpha)} \right]$

INDEX